MANAGING DISASTERS

M.K. Hariharan
Management Consultant

R. Rajeswari
Professor, Management

FIRST EDITION: 2014

Himalaya Publishing House

MUMBAI • NEW DELHI • NAGPUR • BENGALURU • HYDERABAD • CHENNAI • PUNE • LUCKNOW • AHMEDABAD • ERNAKULAM • BHUBANESWAR • INDORE • KOLKATA • GUWAHATI

First Edition : 2014

Published by : Mrs. Meena Pandey for **Himalaya Publishing House Pvt. Ltd.,**
"Ramdoot", Dr. Bhalerao Marg, Girgaon, **Mumbai - 400 004.**
Phone: 022-23860170/23863863, Fax: 022-23877178
E-mail: himpub@vsnl.com; Website: www.himpub.com

Branch Offices :

New Delhi : "Pooja Apartments", 4-B, Murari Lal Street, Ansari Road, Darya Ganj, New Delhi - 110 002. Phone: 011-23270392, 23278631; Fax: 011-23256286

Nagpur : Kundanlal Chandak Industrial Estate, Ghat Road, Nagpur - 440 018. Phone: 0712-2738731, 3296733; Telefax: 0712-2721215

Bengaluru : No. 16/1 (Old 12/1), 1st Floor, Next to Hotel Highlands, Madhava Nagar, Race Course Road, Bengaluru - 560 001. Phone: 080-32919385; Telefax: 080-22286611

Hyderabad : No. 3-4-184, Lingampally, Besides Raghavendra Swamy Matham, Kachiguda, Hyderabad - 500 027. Phone: 040-27560041, 27550139; Mobile: 09390905282

Chennai : No. 8/2, 2nd Madley Street, Ground Floor, T. Nagar, Chennai - 600 017. Mobile: 09345345055

Pune : First Floor, "Laksha" Apartment, No. 527, Mehunpura, Shaniwarpeth (Near Prabhat Theatre), Pune - 411 030. Phone: 020-24496323/24496333; Mobile: 09370579333

Lucknow : House No 731, Shekhupura Colony, Near B.D. Convent School, Aliganj, Lucknow - 226 022. Mobile: 09307501549

Ahmedabad : 114, "SHAIL", 1st Floor, Opp. Madhu Sudan House, C.G. Road, Navrang Pura, Ahmedabad - 380 009. Phone: 079-26560126; Mobile: 09377088847

Ernakulam : 39/176 (New No: 60/251) 1st Floor, Karikkamuri Road, Ernakulam, Kochi - 682011, Phone: 0484-2378012, 2378016; Mobile: 09344199799

Bhubaneswar : 5 Station Square, Bhubaneswar - 751 001 (Odisha). Phone: 0674-2532129, Mobile: 09338746007

Indore : Kesardeep Avenue Extension, 73, Narayan Bagh, Flat No. 302, IIIrd Floor, Near Humpty Dumpty School, Indore - 452 007 (M.P.). Mobile: 09301386468

Kolkata : 108/4, Beliaghata Main Road, Near ID Hospital, Opp. SBI Bank, Kolkata - 700 010, Phone: 033-32449649, Mobile: 09883055590, 07439040301

Guwahati : House No. 15, Behind Pragjyotish College, Near Sharma Printing Press, P.O. Bharalumukh, Guwahati - 781009, (Assam). Mobile: 09883055590, 09883055536

DTP by : Asmita Pankar

Printed at : M/s. Charita Impressions, Hyderabad on behalf of HPH.

Preface

Disaster management is actually a management of resources and informations relating to disastrous events and is measured by how one coordinates these resources, effectively and efficiently, to the common benefit. The managerial ability to effectively deal with a disaster, is an issue to reckon with.

Disasters, both natural and man-made, have been an inevitable part of human life. It is evident that the disaster problems cannot be singled out. They are cut across various disciplines and as such addressing a single area of concern does not mean a solution to the disaster management problems. The issue of addressing the disaster management problems has been taken up by many organizations, nationally and internationally.

We believe, a book on disaster management, should be able to give the multi-dimensions and characteristics of disaster, so as the role of various agencies, like United Nations, Government of India, in preventing an effective control of disasters. This also pictures the roles of various non-government organizations, volunteers, relief organizations, etc., in assisting counter disaster.

Disaster management deals with issues relating to planning, risk assessing, organizing, coordinating, communicating, etc., both at individual and organizational levels. This book gives insight into the above areas of a disaster, by giving very valuable information and analysis. This book involves studies in the issues of disaster and development, national policies on disaster management across the world and the problems of disaster management in depth. Certain case studies are provided with an idea to give practical examples, however, their results and remedies cannot be copied for all, as disasters are different and different in nature and treatment. This is particularly so, as the case studies and their out come, can neither pre-empt nor avert eventualities.

This book contains three sections: Disaster and Development, Prevention and Management of Disaster. Some relevant case studies are appended to each sections of the book. Some photographs to show the aftermath of disaster is also given to get an eye sight. This volume contains well researched materials on the aspects of various disasters.

While dealing with the subjects, care has been taken to include the syllabi of various Universities in India in general and few in particular.

It is always the practice to express a disaster in terms of loss of life, loss of property, loss of resources, etc., and quantify the total loss. However, this signifies a need to go beyond a certain disaster and evolve suitable strategies in future to counter these phenomena. The very purpose and aim of the disaster management is to minimize the loss of life and resources.

We are grateful to M/s. Himalaya Publishing House Pvt. Ltd. for publishing this manuscript for public reading.

— M.K. Hariharan
— R. Rajeswari

Acknowledgements

Many Universities in India and abroad have included Disaster Management in the syllabi for postgraduate studies. The inclusion of Disaster as a subject recently, attains vital importance, as modern world faces disaster very frequently. Being a recent introduction, number of books on this topic is less. M/s. Himalaya Publishing House Pvt. Limited has taken initiative and pain to publish a book on this topic, to narrow the gap. We take this opportunity to express our profound gratitude to them. We appreciate their efforts in bringing out this book, which is intended to benefit large section of professionals, students, Organizations, Governments, etc.

We have referred various articles, newspaper articles, books, internet literature, and personal discussions to gather information and data for this textbook. We have listed some such references and many are not mentioned here. We are indebted to all the eminent persons who have contributed their best and researched in this area. We express our heartfelt gratitude to them.

Our first initiative, on writing this book, came from the aftermath and suffering of people in India and other countries from the Tsunami. We had experienced the difficulties faced by the organizations in managing the Tsunami havoc. The absence of a sound disaster management system was evident. The Government could not salvage the situation, people suffered, many lost relatives and resources. The very site of the failure of the various systems, prompted us to focus on this area and come out with a work, which could be of value to the public.

We sincerely thank our relatives, family, friends, and advisors for encouraging us to work on this topic and also adjust our absence with them in many occasions. We also thank them for reminding us every time about the necessity of such a book, about the target audience who are mostly students, and the success this book gives to them.

We believe, this work will be of substance to the readers.

— M.K. Hariharan
— R. Rajeswari

Contents

1 Introduction to Disaster Management

Learning Objectives

- Concept of Disaster and Disaster Management
- Evolution of Disaster
- Dimensions of Disaster
- Principles of Disaster
- Components of Disaster
- Organizational Structure for Disaster Management
- Standard Operating Procedures
- Concept of Mitigation

Structure

1.1 INTRODUCTION TO DISASTER MANAGEMENT

A serious disruption of the functioning of a society, causing widespread human, material, or environmental losses which exceed the ability of the affected society (or community) to cope with using only its own resources.

Most of the days, our media carry reports of disaster striking several parts of the world. Since primitive times, the relationship with the nature has gone through several stages and moving into gaining mastery over the nature, more so after the leap of industrialization. Our vulnerability to disaster is no longer weak as we were before. However, the rapid growth of the twentieth century has affected the environment very badly, causing certain segments of the population (the poor and downtrodden) more vulnerable to disaster.

Disasters were around since history and they appear to be increasing year-after-year, both in terms of intensity, and frequency. Disasters leave unforgettable impressions on the public, although they are most unwanted guests. If one looks at the past couple of years, countless lives have been swallowed by the cyclones, Tsunamis, earthquakes, landslides, floods, storms, volcanic eruptions, and many more. A large segment of the society has lost their homes, near ones, properties, suffered injuries, and material losses.

The increase in disaster are mounting year-by-year and widening as well. Table 1 shows four-fold increase in the incidents of disaster during the period 1981 to 2006. There have been more than five-fold increase in the economic loss to the nations. One must also appreciate that these losses could be more but for the improved medical treatments, advanced information of disasters and better management.

Table 1: Incidents of Disaster

1981	1986	1991	1996	2001	2006
197	440	837	1270	1688	1838
Source: EM-DAT:OFDA/CRED (http://www.cred.be/					

The risk of disaster can be expected to be more in the future, particularly for developing countries, due to increase in extreme natural events such as climate change, etc., added with the vulnerability of the population to these natural events. This factor restricts and impairs the development and in many cases this underdevelopment paves the way for recurrence of disaster. Many countries depend upon bilateral and multilateral donors for development work and are stepping up their efforts to prevent disaster. Many countries work with the idea that prevention and precautions will avert future disasters or at least mitigate them. As disasters make a country suffer economically, precautions always help stabilize their growth and development.

Vulnerability and hazards are the two factors which are to be contained to reduce the risk of disaster. The general socio-economic conditions of a country are the determinants of the above factor. Therefore the need of the hour is for employing a normal institutional, regional, and sectoral developmental strategy in vulnerable areas.

All these leads to the point of how to predict, prevent, and mitigate major disasters? We have advanced in the technological and scientific systems of predicting possible cyclones, earthquakes, floods, droughts, fires, seasonal climatic conditions and even suggesting remedial. It goes without doubt that through proper planning and management, we can reduce the effects and hazards of disasters, such as earthquakes. One would see that, in an earthquake, buildings collapse more because of defective construction rather than the earthquake tremours.

However the history says that, numbers of disasters are increasing day-by-day. Small local disasters even go unreported. Natural disasters are caused by extreme occurrence in nature for which the society is unprepared. The natural disasters destroy the basic conditions of life for the victims, who lack the resources to recover in the short period.

Disaster management is a management of crisis of unusual situations, explicitly demanding the commitment of officials at all levels with clearly defined authorities to discharge assigned roles with perfection. Disaster management is a continuous process which relies on feedbacks, informations, resources, manpower, etc., for trouble-free, hassle-free, weakness-free, and foolproof system.

1.2 EVOLUTION OF DISASTER MANAGEMENT

Natural disasters always have occurred. Earthquakes, floods, wildfires, tornadoes, and hurricanes happened before human activity and likely will happen long afterward. But what really makes a disaster is how humans react to the occurrence of a natural hazard, and disaster management has gone through many changes.

Ancient History

Long before there was an America, Red Cross, or FEMA (Federal Emergency Management Agency), people were learning to deal with disasters. The Japanese have been keeping accurate records of earthquakes and tsunamis long before contact with Europeans. Some of these records even have been used to help estimate the recurrence interval of known seismic events such as the massive earthquakes on the West Coast, which caused tsunamis across the Pacific Ocean in Japan.

Early America

For a long time in America, disasters were thought of as acts of God, events that mankind had no power to prevent. Moreover, political manipulation prevented many from understanding the true nature of hazards.

FEMA and Legislative Acts

The idea that disasters are punishment for human sin or simply acts of God that we have no influence over have been replaced by management, policy and practices based on geological and meteorological science.

The word 'disaster' originated from the middle French, word 'disastre' meaning 'bad or evil star', in Greek finds its root in astrology, which implies that when the stars pose in bad positions, bad or evil events will occur.

Disasters take place when the hazards strike at vulnerable areas. A disaster can be natural or man-made hazards that inflict the society and the environment. The hazards occur in the non-vulnerable areas do not form disasters, as in the case of an earthquake in the unpopulated area.

It is always the practice to define all the disasters as man-made, as it is felt that human actions can prevent hazards which can result in disaster. There are complex disasters, which are the results of complex reasons and there is no single root cause. Similarly, a disaster can pave the way for another disaster, for example, an earthquake followed by a tsunami, resulting in flash floods, loss of life, devastation, etc.

1.3 DEFINITION OF DISASTER

Disasters can be defined in many ways:

"Any situation in which there is a sudden disruption of normalcy within society causing wide-spread damage to life and property"

A serious disruption is the functioning of a society, causing widespread human, material or environmental losses which exceed the ability of the affected society (or community) to cope with using only its own resources.

According to FEMA,

'It is an event or a series of events which seriously disrupts normal life.'

Disaster may be defined as "a break in the smooth-going life". A disaster may be personal, family, office-related, or social. Though temporary, it disturbs us to a great extent.

The Word Disaster is Closely Related with the Following Words to a Larger Extent:

1. **Hazard:** Dangerous conditions or events with potential for injury, loss of life and/or damage to property, agriculture, and environment.

   Hazards can be classified in many ways. One such method of classification is their nature of origin.

   (a) Natural hazards with meteorological, biological, or geological origin.

   (b) Unnatural hazards with man-made or technological origin.

   A hazard is a rare or extreme event in the natural or man-made environment that adversely affects human life and property.

2. **Emergency:** Intense time period or a level of urgency.

3. **Vulnerability:** Certain community or groups are settled in areas susceptible to loss resulting from a particular phenomenon, or set of hazards and disasters.

1.4 WHAT IS DISASTER MANAGEMENT?

It is a discipline that involves preparing for disaster before it occurs, disaster response (e.g., emergency evacuation, quarantine, mass decontamination, etc.), and supporting, and rebuilding society after natural disaster.

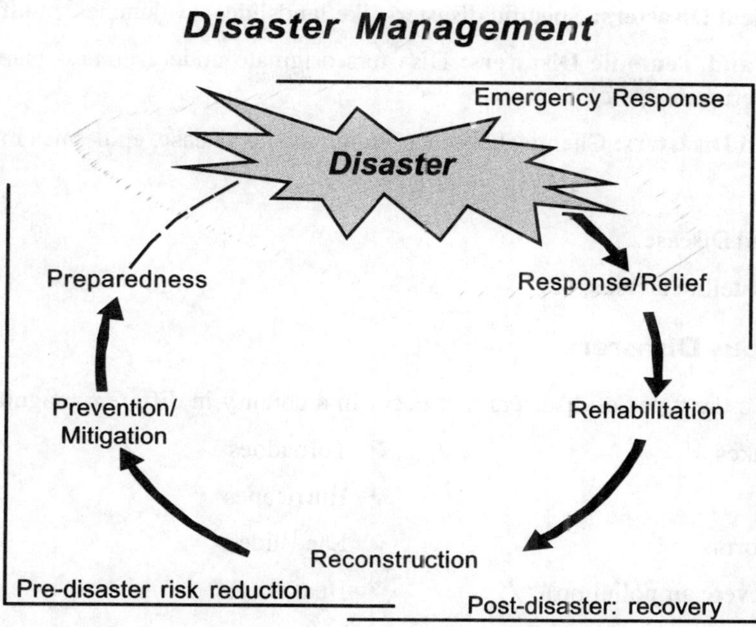

Aims of Disaster Management

The main aim of disaster management is to minimize the loss of life and property and is based on the following three factors:

- ❖ Reduce (avoid, if possible) the potential losses from hazards.
- ❖ Assure prompt and appropriate assistance to victims when necessary.
- ❖ Achieve rapid and durable recovery.

Classification of Disasters

Disasters are classified according to their speed of occurrence (slow or sudden) or according to their cause (natural or man-made).

Accordingly, the disasters can be classified as Natural and Anthropogenic disasters.

Natural Disasters

A natural disaster is the effect of a natural hazard that affects the environment, and leads to financial, environmental, and human losses. The resulting loss depends on the capacity of the population to support or resist the disaster, and their resilience.

These are extreme climatological, geological, or hydrological processes leading to a disaster.

The natural disasters can be classified on the basis of the following:

- ❖ **Meteorological Disasters:** Material related, Geography based – storms, cyclones, cold spells, heat waves, drought, etc.

- **Typological Disasters:** Specific disasters like landslides, avalanches, mudflows, and floods.
- **Telluric and Tectonic Disasters:** Disasters originate underground – tsunami, earthquake, volcanic eruptions, etc.
- **Biological Disasters:** Chemical based, communicable disease, epidemics insects and swarms
- Fire
- Health and Disease
- **Space:** Satellite attacks, etc.

Types of Various Disasters

Following are the types of disasters that occur in a country in different magnitudes.

- Earthquakes
- Fires
- Snow storms
- Smog (severe air pollution)
- Epidemics
- Droughts
- Toxicological accidents
- Lahars
- Floods
- Tsunami
- Food shortage
- Civil disturbances
- Tornadoes
- Hurricanes
- Landslides
- Heat waves
- Cyclonic storms
- Building collapse
- Nuclear accidents
- Volcanic eruptions
- Limnic eruptions
- Blizzards
- Water contamination

Effects of Major Disasters

Disasters have brought insignificant impact on the numbers, health status, and population life-styles. They inflict severe damages in the following areas:

- Deaths.
- Increase in transmitted disease.
- Critical injuries requiring long-term treatments.
- Polluting water resources.
- Damaging systems.
- Inflicting severe food shortage and famine.
- Retarding population movements.

All these damages also cause health problems which is common to all disasters such as transmitted diseases, population displacement, socio-economic reactions, climate changes, shortage of water, and food, mental imbalances, and damage to infrastructure.

Causes

Man happens to be the rootcause for the outburst of disasters. The act of man often disrupts the nature resulting in disasters.

These types of natural disasters are caused by reasons like:

- Nuclear test.
- Excess exploitation of groundwater.
- Terrorism.
- Excess usage of artificial manure/pesticides.

Anthropogenic Disasters

Anthropogenic disasters are man-made disasters. It is caused by an element of human negligence, intent or error, or caused by the failure of a man-made system. The following are the few examples of anthropogenic disasters:

- Civil Disturbances – riots and demonstrations – babri masjid case.
- Conventional Warfare – direct fights/wars.
- Non-conventional Warfare – war from a different places, remote operations.
- Refugees.
- Accidents.
- Technological Accidents – mishap at a nuclear power station, leak at chemical plant, etc.

Dimensions of Disaster

Disasters have various dimensions as given below:

1. **Frequency:** Most of the disasters are rare and they appear more only in certain highly prone geographical locations. This frequent happening of disaster may weaken people in that area on adhering to the warnings and they often tend to ignore such warnings.
2. **Predictability:** Some of the disasters can be easily predicted than others. For example, weather-related disasters such as tornados, floods, and hurricanes can be easily predicted, whereas others like – earthquakes, landslides, and man-made disasters are less predictable.
3. **Time:** The time factor in respect of a disaster is on the speed at which the disaster occurs, the time available with the authorities to warn and evacuate people and the extent of duration of the disaster. For example, a situation arising out of flash floods are less controllable than slow floods where there is time to take action. The disaster impact might last for minutes, hours, or

even days and worst damage is generally caused by the longest time factor, a rapid onset, no opportunity for public warning, and long duration of the impact phase.

4. **Controllability:** Some disasters allow for effective warning and control measures for reducing the impact. Whereas others do not provide time to control the situation. The authorities do have emergency plans to control some of the effects of the disaster. For example, sand bagging river banks to reduce water damage and by blasting dikes and dams to divert flood waters.

5. **Intensity and Scope:** Intensity refers to the extent of impact or distraction caused by a disaster. A disaster can be very intense and highly destructive, causing death, injury and poverty and property damage or less intense with relatively less damage to the property and individuals. Scope refers to the geographic area impacted by the disaster.

1.5 PRINCIPLES OF DISASTER MANAGEMENT

Disaster management fundamentally deals with a response to human misery and losses of people's livelihoods and assets, whereas the disaster risk management is concerned with mitigating or preventing such losses; both processes tend to be rather anthropocentric. People and societies engage in such humanitarian actions because they believe it is the 'right thing to do', and therefore this field is closely tied to ethics and morality. Ethics is not about what is; rather, it is about what should be. Ethical theories use principles tied to the norms of society in order to assess and justify actions and behaviours. In this sense, they are prescriptive and normative (describing what ought to be) as opposed to descriptive, which describes what is (though one hopes the two are closely linked!).

The basis for a set of disaster management principles could lie within the context of a social contract between the government and its citizens, or upon moral theory. A social contract is based upon the idea that the purpose of the government is to make life better for its citizens, and for that purpose they consent to be governed.

Why are Principles Needed for Disaster Management?

The Oxford dictionary defines a principle as a *'fundamental truth as: (a) basis of reasoning. Principles guide people's decisions and actions, policies and procedures developed by organizations, and laws and doctrines of political entities'*. The Collins English Language Dictionary further defines a principle as *'A general rule that you try to obey in the way that you try to achieve something. Principled actions or behaviour, based on clear guidance concerning the way to act.'* These definitions place emphasis on the implicit authority contained in a principle as a 'fundamental truth' or 'general rule'. Their purpose concerns practical action, thus principles exist to 'guide actions', 'achieve something', or define the 'way to act'.

If there is not a clear understanding and statement of principles, then there cannot be a consistent, cohesive and embracing disaster management strategy, or effective communication between different organizations.

The Principles of Disaster Management are:

1. **Disaster Management is the Responsibility of all Spheres of Government:** No single service or department in itself has the capability to achieve comprehensive disaster management. Each affected service or department must have a disaster management plan which is coordinated through the Disaster Management Advisory Forum.
2. **Disaster Management should use Resources that Exist for a Day-to-day Purpose:** There are limited resources available specifically for disasters, and it would be neither cost-effective nor practical to have large holdings of dedicated disaster resources. However, municipalities must ensure that there is a minimum budget allocation to enable appropriate response to incidents as they arise, and to prepare for and reduce the risk of disasters occurring.
3. **Organizations should Function as an Extension of their Core Business:** Disaster management is about the use of resources in the most effective manner. To achieve this during disasters, organizations should be employed in a manner to reflect their day-to-day roles. But it should be done in a coordinated manner across all relevant organizations, so that it is multi-disciplinary and multi-agency.
4. **Individuals are Responsible for their Own Safety:** Individuals need to be aware of the hazards that could affect their community and the counter measures, which include the Municipal Disaster Management Plan, that are in place to deal with them.
5. **Disaster Management Planning should Focus on Large-scale Events:** It is easier to scale down a response than it is to scale up if arrangements have been based on incident scale events. If you are well prepared for a major disaster you will be able to respond very well to smaller incidents and emergencies, nevertheless, good multi-agency responses to incidents do help in the event of a major disaster.
6. **Disaster Management Planning should Recognize the Difference between Incidents and Disasters:** Incidents – e.g., fires that occur in informal settlements, floods that occur regularly, still require multi-agency and multi-jurisdictional coordination. The scale of the disaster will indicate when it is beyond the capacity of the municipality to respond, and when it needs the involvement of other agencies.
7. **Disaster Management Operational Arrangements are Additional to and do not Replace Incident Management Operational Arrangements:** Single service incident management operational arrangements will need to continue, whenever practical, during disaster operations.
8. **Disaster Management Planning must Take Account of the Type of Physical Environment and the Structure of Population:** The physical shape and size of the municipality and the spread of population must be considered when developing counter disaster plans to ensure that appropriate prevention, preparation, response, and recovery mechanisms can be put in place in a timely manner.
9. **Disaster Management Arrangements must Recognize the Involvement and Potential Role of Non-government Agencies:** Significant skills and resources needed during disaster operations are controlled by non-government agencies. These agencies must be consulted and included in the planning process.

A key factor worth remembering is that a Disaster Management Plan should be part of the day-to-day planning, establishment, and management of local facilities and resources and therefore should be developed to link with other land use and disaster plans for the municipality and province.

1.6 COMPONENTS OF DISASTER MANAGEMENT

The following nine components, form the basic framework of disaster preparedness upon which the National Disaster Management strategy can be developed.

Components of Disaster Management

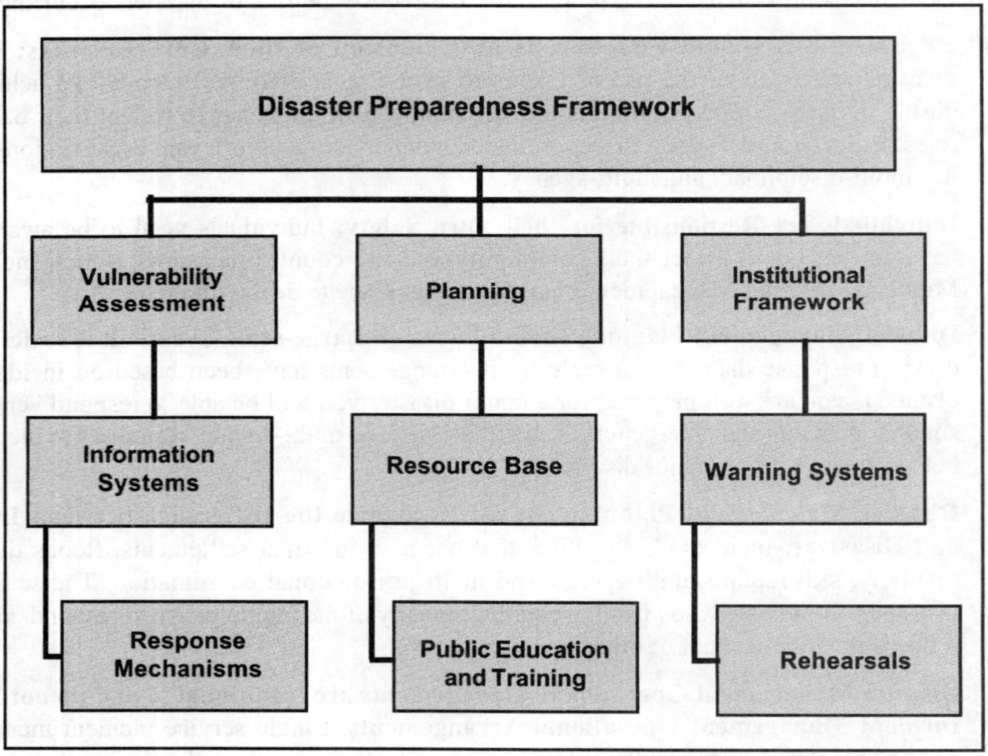

Vulnerability Assessment

A sound disaster management system requires proper and valid information system for developing and compiling vulnerability assessments.

The term vulnerability stems from the fact that certain communities or groups are settled in areas susceptible to loss resulting from a particular phenomenon, or a set of disasters and hazards.

Information about the vulnerability is fundamental, more often overlooked, but proved important to assess dangers. A manager even though he is aware of the geographic region and the possible hazards, may not be able to act on this, in the absence of an approved system to assess vulnerabilities. In such a situation he will be working in darkness.

Planning

Planning is nothing but a decision taken in advance – what to do, when to do, how to do, and for whom to do. The main objective of disaster preparedness is to have proper plans designed and agreed upon in place. All these plans must be implementable and properly committed with agreed resources.

Institutional Framework

A full proof disaster preparedness plan requires a well-coordinated disaster preparedness and response system. There is no standard way to ensure effective coordination. Each design will depend upon the traditions and governmental structure of the nation under review. There is a need to ensure horizontal coordination at Central Government and subnational levels among various ministries and specialized agencies and a vertical coordination between the Central and local authorities. It is preferable to avoid creating new agencies, instead strategy should be to strengthen the existing institutions and work strongly with the established systems and structures.

The sanctions for disaster responses are generally made at senior levels of the government. In fact, most of the countries make their Prime Ministers or Presidents to approve the plans and trigger the mechanism for implementing the plans.

An effective disaster preparedness plan involves inter-ministerial responses to disaster warnings and occurrences. In India, most of the committees are inter-ministerial in nature and are headed by permanent secretaries of the government. These committees include, in addition to the senior executives, representative from the focal point. Normally, the focal point should be designated properly to ensure effective disaster preparedness and also to act as a coordination mechanism.

Information Systems

Information is wealth and is precious. For any disaster preparedness plan to be successful, it should have sound information system. A disaster preparedness plan should have information system to ensure the coordination of different groups. The information system should start from primary collection of data, early warning systems, and monitoring systems for slow onset. Similarly, for sudden onset disasters, a system must be in place for prediction, warning, safe evacuation, etc.

Resource Base

The requirements to meet the various needs of disaster will rely upon the types of disasters, the plan anticipates. Those needs must be identified and must cover all aspects of disaster relief and recovery implementation. Specific arrangements must be made whereby the requisite funds, services, and materials, can be acquired and dispersed on time and at will. The range of relief materials and requirements are too expensive and too difficult to handle. Some of the major relief requirements include, warning systems, food, medicine, shelter, communication systems, manpower, equipment for mass clearance, and technical experts, etc.

Response Mechanism

For any disaster management plan to be effective, the response to warnings and directions must be sound. The success of any disaster plan would depend upon the responsiveness of the public to follow and act upon warnings. The success also depends on the collection of responses at various stages of the warning process and the staging of responses for designing a disaster preparedness plan.

Public Education and Training

The success of the disaster preparedness plan depends on the capacity to anticipate the various requirements for a disaster relief operation and the requisite capability of mobilizing those requirements on time. The success of the planning process will again depend on the extent of awareness the beneficiaries derive out of it and know what to except and how to go. This envisages the requirement of an education process for those threatened by disaster.

The different forms of education can be through: (a) public education in schools for children and young adults detailing on information and actions, which should be taken in the event of a disaster threat or occurrence; (b) special training courses for adult population through workshops or part of ongoing programmes or through training; (c) extension programmes designed for the community of village-based population for providing relevant information and acting in a way they are trained during an event; and (d) public information, through television, radio, and print media gives wide publicity and awareness for such programmes, even though they cannot replace direct instructions. However, sensitively crafted messages can be a supplement to the education process.

Rehearsals

A disaster preparedness rehearsal portrays the full dynamics of a disaster relief operation. The need to rehearse a disaster preparedness plan cannot be avoided. The rehearsals will focus on points made in separate training programmes and will test the system as a whole and help plug gaps and loop-holes.

1.7 ORGANIZATIONAL STRUCTURE

The organizational structure designed for a disaster management system must be effective and devoid of bureaucracy. If too much approvals and sanctions are designed, the system will get affected and will become ineffective. Example of a typical organization is given below:

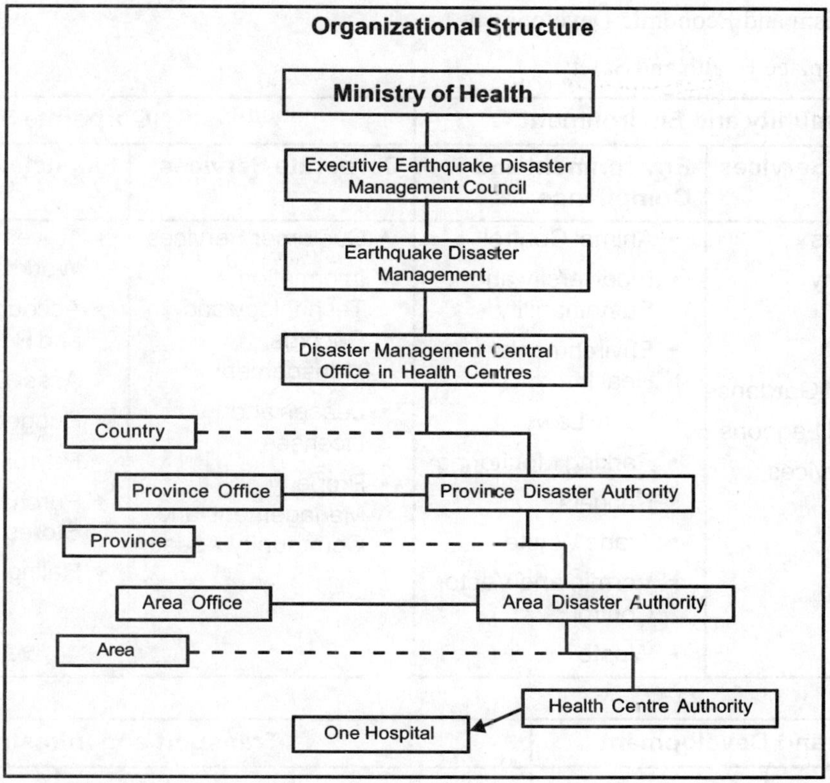

The Organizational Structure

Council is comprised of the Chief Executive Office and four departments:

- ❖ Community and Environment
- ❖ Corporate Services
- ❖ Planning and Development
- ❖ Transport and Infrastructure with various subsections to manage the wide range of services the council provide.

Chief Executive Office (Executive Services) Department

- ❖ Communications
- ❖ Emergency Management – Disaster Management
- ❖ Human Resources Management
- ❖ Inter-government and Regional Relationships
- ❖ Organizational Development
- ❖ Quality

- Tourism and Economic Development
- Workplace Health and Safety

Community and Environment		Corporate Services	
Community Services	**Environment and Compliance**	**Corporate Services**	**Financial Services**
• Cemeteries • Community Services • Libraries • Parks and Gardens • Pools and Lagoons • Youth Services	• Animal Control • Biodiversity and Sustainability • Environmental Health • Local Laws • Parking Monitoring • Rangers • Trade Waste • Vermin and Vector Control • Waste	• Customer Services • Information Technology and Records Management • Leases and Licenses • Property Management and Community Assets	• 10-year Capital Works Plan • Accounts Payable and Receivable • Asset Coordination • Budgeting • Payroll • Purchasing and Stores • Rating

Planning and Development		Transport and Infrastructure		
Development	**Strategic Planning**	**Infrastructure**	**Transport**	**Water and Sewerage**
• Building Applications • Building and Plumbing Inspections • Development Applications • Development Compliance	• Social Planning • Priority Infrastructure • Strategic Planning • Town Plan (IPA)	• Airports • Strategic Asset Management Plans • Design Services • Development • Quarry • Shute Harbour	• Bridges • Drainage • Fleet Operations and Management • Footpaths • Lighting – Street and Footpaths • Roads	• Sewer • Water

1.8 DISASTER MANAGEMENT SCHEMES AND SOPs

Natural Disaster Management Programmes

A central sector plan scheme on natural disaster management programme is being implemented from 1993 to 1994. The objectives of the scheme is to focus on disaster preparedness with an emphasis on mitigation and preparedness measures and to enhance the capability of the country to reduce the adverse impact of natural disasters. The programme is also expected to increase the level of awareness of community about disasters. The activities undertaken under the scheme include:

(a) Human resource development – organizing/sponsoring programmes to enhance the awareness/ skill of Government functionaries at Central, State, and District levels as well as NGOs, CBOs, Panchayath Leaders for successful implementations of disaster reduction programmes.

(b) Research and consultancy services.

(c) Documentation of major events of natural calamities.

(d) Vulnerability assessment projects.

(e) Establishment of National Centre of Disaster Management.

(f) Creation of natural disaster management faculties in the state-level training institutes.

(g) Public education and community awareness programmes.

(h) Regional cooperation.

1.9 STANDARD OPERATING PROCEDURES

The worldover it has been experienced that a prompt, well-coordinated and effective response mounted in the aftermath of disasters not only minimizes loss of life and property but also facilitates early recovery. The important ingredients of an effective response system are integrated institutional arrangements, state-of-the-art forecasting and early warning systems, fail-safe communication system, rapid evacuation of threatened communities, quick deployment of specialized response forces, and coordination and synergy among various agencies at various levels in dealing with any disaster. Most importantly, all the agencies and their functionaries must clearly understand their roles and responsibilities and the specific actions they have to take for responding to disaster or threatening disaster situations.

All natural disasters except drought, pest attacks, and hailstorm will be handled by the Ministry of Home Affairs. Drought, pest attacks, and hailstorm are dealt by the Ministry of Agriculture and Cooperation. This standard operating procedure (SOP) will deal with natural disasters such as flood, cyclone, earthquake, landslides, avalanche, etc., which fall under the nodal responsibility of Ministry of Home Affairs.

This SOP lays down, in a comprehensive manner, the specific actions required to be taken by various Ministries and Departments of Government of India and Organizations under the control of Government of India at the National level and concerned State Governments and the district administration for responding to natural disasters of any magnitude and dimension.

Objectives of SOP

The objectives of the SOP are:

(a) It lays down guidelines, in a comprehensive manner, to provide a standard method for receiving reports/information about disaster situations from the concerned Ministries/Departments/ Agencies and State Governments and thereafter issuing Alert messages to all concerned.

(b) It also standardizes the information requirements for various event categories. SOP also cover sending of information updates for unfolding events.

(c) The SOP establishes protocols to be put in place for alerting the PMO and the Cabinet Secretariat. It also lays down the procedures to be followed for receiving reports, analyzing them and thereafter issuing alerts through various modes to the concerned authorities.

(d) The SOP is designed to specify actions that are required to be taken by the Integrated Operation Centre in the Ministry of Home Affairs for reporting on disaster events.

(e) The SOP specifies duties and responsibilities for the personnel working in the Integrated Operation Centre for issuing messages related to disaster events.

(f) The instructions contained in the SOP are not to be regarded as exhaustive. All other actions that might be considered necessary by the Ministry of Home Affairs would require to be taken on the instructions of Home Secretary/Secretary (Border Management)/Joint Secretary (DM).

(g) To provide, in a concise and convenient form, a list of major executive actions involved in responding to natural disasters and necessary measures for preparedness, response, and relief required to be taken,

(h) To ensure that all concerned Ministries, Departments, and Organizations of the Government of India, State Governments and District Administrations know the precise measures required to be done at each stage of the process and also to ensure that all actions are closely and continuously coordinated.

(i) To indicate various actions which would be required by the State Governments/UT Administrations within their sphere of responsibilities so that they may prepare and review the Contingency Action Plans accordingly.

The instructions contained in this SOP should not be regarded as exhaustive of all the actions that might be considered necessary. It will also be necessary for each Ministry, Department and Organization which are required to provide Emergency Support Functions (ESF) and the State Governments/UTs which face one or the other natural disasters to prepare detailed SOPs so as to translate each action point in a number of steps required to be taken by each of them.

All Central Ministries concerned, State Governments, District Authorities and other stakeholders will prepare detailed SOPs in consonance with the SOP, National Policy, and various Guidelines issued by NDMA. These SOPs shall prescribe the manner in which various response and relief activities like evacuation, search and rescue, casualty and emergency health management, food, drinking water, sanitation and hygiene, clothing, shelter, management of relief camps, and restoration of essential services, etc., have to be undertaken.

The SOP encompasses the following five phases of disaster management for effective and efficient response to natural disasters:

1. **Preparedness Phase:** This phase will include taking all necessary measures for planning, capacity building and other preparedness so as to be in a state of readiness to respond, in the event of a natural disaster. This stage will also include development of search and rescue teams, mobilization of resources and taking measures in terms of equipping, providing training, conducting mock drills/exercises, etc.

2. **Early Warning Phase:** This phase will include all necessary measures to provide timely, qualitative and quantitative warnings to the disaster managers to enable them to take pre-emptive measures for preventing loss of life and reducing loss/damage to the property. On the

occurrence of a natural disaster or imminent threat thereof, all the concerned agencies will be informed/notified for initiating immediate necessary follow-up action.

3. **Response Phase:** This phase will include all necessary measures to provide immediate succour to the affected people by undertaking search, rescue, and evacuation measures.
4. **Relief Phase:** This phase will include all necessary measures to provide immediate relief and succour to the affected people in terms of their essential needs of food, drinking water, health and hygiene, clothing, and shelter.
5. **Restoration Stage:** This phase will include all necessary measures to stabilize the situation and restore the utilities.

The following factors are to be reckoned while considering and preparing a Standard Operating Procedure.

Components of the Standard Operation Procedure

1. Activity
   (a) Preparedness
   (b) Response
2. Name of the Procedure
3. Number and Revision of the Procedure
4. Objective of the Procedure
5. Responsibility for the Procedure
6. Steps of the Procedure
7. Description and Sequence of the Steps of the Procedure
8. Special Situations
9. Attachments to the Procedure
10. Updating the Procedure

SOP Teams

1. Survey and assessment team
2. Main disaster relief column/group
3. Supplies, canteen services, mass cooking, and feeding team
4. Radio communication team
5. Relief teams
6. Search, rescue, and evacuation team
7. Public relations and information
8. Psychological support
9. Medical team

1.10 CONCEPT OF MITIGATION

Mitigation provides a link between the disaster and development. Communities, agencies, and individuals can use their resources to reduce the risk of hazards through mitigation projects. They can also ensure future mitigation through their efforts.

The term mitigation is widely used in measures, which reduce and minimize the impacts of a disaster on life, property, and the economy of a country. Mitigation includes both at the planning and implementation of measures to reduce the risks associated with known natural and human disasters and the process of planning for effective response to disasters. They can also ensure that their other development initiatives contain components that mitigate against future disasters. This also includes long-term risk reduction and preparedness measures. Mitigation measures can be classified as structural and non-structural. Structural mitigation includes measures to reduce the socio-economic hazard, whereas the non-structural mitigation includes policies and practices. Example of structural mitigation include construction of dams, hazard resistant buildings, etc., whereas the non-structural measures include land use policies, education, awareness, crop diversification, etc.

In the broadest form, mitigation has become a collective term used to describe pre-disaster measures and include long-term risk reduction and preparedness plans.

Definition

The most common definition for mitigation is 'actions taken to reduce both human suffering and property loss resulting from extreme natural phenomena'.

Concept of Mitigation

The concept of mitigation stems from the fact that disasters can always happen and mitigation process tries to lessen the impact of the hazard by improving the ability of the communities to deal with its destructive impact. It simply means that mitigation is a risk reduction process.

The scope of mitigation extends to a wide range of activities and protection measures that include constructions, agricultural diversification, land use planning, etc.

Saving life and reducing economic disruption has been a vital part of mitigation strategies. Rising population levels across the globe have resulted in making people more vulnerable to risks. This is relevant as the incidents of natural hazards are on the increase. However, the histories of disasters have shown that disasters are largely preventable. There are a number of ways to reduce the impact of a disaster and to mitigate the effects of a possible hazard, conflict or accident. The fight against the disasters has to be fought by everyone together, just as we fight against disease. Involvement of public and private sector investment, changes in social attitudes of communities and improvements in overall practices of the individuals are the need of the hour.

While the governments can use public funds to improve and create their countries infrastructure and promote physical environment in disaster prone areas, private individual must learn to how to protect themselves. Just as public health relies on personal hygiene, public protection relies on personal safety as well.

The type of cooking stove public use and their awareness that a sudden earthquake could tip it over is more important in reducing a risk of fire than having a community to maintain a large fire brigade. The location of a house and the type of construction are factors which play an important role than large engineering projects conceived with all precautions.

The dangerous effect of any disasters is the deaths and injuries caused to the population and the loss of property. The justification for mitigation starts from the scale of disasters and the number of people they are capable of killing. Understanding the disaster and understanding the manner in which people are killed and injured is a prerequisite for reducing casualties.

Impact-based Targeting

Understanding how the occurrence of a natural hazard or an accident becomes a disaster enables us to alert people of an impending disaster. For example, some buildings are more vulnerable to earthquakes than others and identifying those vulnerable buildings most at risk, can indicate better mitigation measures. Identifying locations and situations, where risks coincide, helps indicate the elements most at risk. These elements would largely comprised of buildings, networks, and social groups that are most likely sufferers of a disaster. These elements may also be least able to recover after the disaster. It is possible to identify the buildings most likely to be damaged in a disaster and mitigation focused on to those elements may reduce risk.

Risk Reduction Measures

Reducing Hazard Vulnerability

Protection against hazards can be achieved by modifying or removing the causes of the threat or by reducing the impact of the threat if it occurs. It is impossible to prevent the geological or meteorological process from occurring, like earthquake occur, volcanoes erupt, and hurricanes rage. Therefore the focus of mitigation strategies against these hazards is on reducing the vulnerability to the disaster. It is also possible to reduce certain natural hazards, for example chances of flooding is reduced by construction of levees along the banks of the river. Similarly, the destructive agents of some natural hazards can be contained by engineering excellences. In certain cases, to avoid mudflow and landslides, planting trees help.

Tools, Powers, and Budgets

From the hazard profiles, it is known that protection is complex and needs to be built-up through range of diverse activities carried out at the same time. It is not possible for a single authority, even the government, to provide full protection. For example, it is impossible for the government to provide wind-resistant housing for every citizen, in the cyclone-prone areas. However, the governments can influence the citizens towards protecting themselves and the rest of the community. Governments can probably enact certain rules and regulations and force people to adhere to the norms. The government can use legislative powers, project initiation, administrative functions, and spending as tools to bring about changes. It is possible to create safety standards, construction codes, and building regulations to help the community. Nearly 40 earth-prone countries adopt construction standards conducive to these areas.

The powers and budgets available to the decision makers in mitigating the disaster risks are very important. There is no standard solution to mitigating a disaster risk.

Mitigation Actions

The different techniques and the authorities might consider to offer an appropriate package for disaster mitigation are as follows:

1. Engineering
2. Spatial planning
3. Management
4. Economic development
5. Societal measures
6. Conflict reduction

Engineering

Engineering measures are those that result in stronger hazard-resistant individual structures which can withstand the hazards. Design standards, building codes, and performance specifications are important from the point of designers. Engineering designs against the various hazards my include designs for countering vibration, load surcharges, wind loads, impacts, combustibility, flood resistance, safety, etc. Building codes are highly useful defense for achieving stronger engineered structures, including large private properties, public buildings, infrastructure, transportation networks, and industrial facilities. Training techniques to teach builders the practicalities of disaster resistant construction are now better understood and form part of the action available to the mitigation planner.

Spatial Planning

It can be seen that many hazards are highly localized with their likely effects confined to specific known areas, like landslides affecting steep soft plains, floods affecting flood plains, etc., the adverse impact of the disasters can be minimized if it is possible to avoid hazardous areas for settlements or sites for important structures. Therefore, the urban planning needs to integrate awareness of risk mitigation into a normal planning procedure. Location of public sector facilities are easier to control than private locations or land use. An important principle is deconcentration of elements at risk: services provided by one central facility are always more at risk than those provided by several smaller facilities. For example, the Gujarat earthquake damaged the central telephone exchange in that area, collapsing the entire communication system. The reconstruction took place establishing many small exchanges in place, whereby the possibility of total failure through a single exchange is averted and the telephone system made less vulnerable.

The deconcentration is applicable to population densities in a city and a denser concentration of population is always at risk and more vulnerable to disaster potential than if they are more dispersed.

However, it is to be clearly understood, unless and until the local community recognizes the true extent of the hazard and accepts the fact that the risks outweigh the benefits to them of being in that location. It is always desirable to relocate to safer places and protect themselves.

Management

There are certain organizational and procedural measures attached to disaster mitigation process. It is always time-consuming process for achieving significant reduction in the potential for disaster. Changes in physical planning, upgrading structures, and building characteristics are processes that take years together. The objectives and policies of mitigation processes have to be sustained over a period of time and have to necessarily survive changes in the political system, budgetary priority, etc.

It is important to note that a consensus approach is needed for institutionalizing the disaster mitigation strategies as the risks are of continual importance. Training, education, professional competence, and political will are the need of the hour for the success of institutionalizing the disaster mitigation. The involvement of professionals in the field of engineering, planning, social science, etc., has become a practice. Increasing the exposure of these people to international expertise and transfer of technology in disaster mitigation is an important part of capability building in the affected country. Information is a very critical part of disaster mitigation planning and it is seen that many countries do not even have the basic observatories to neither monitor hazards nor have the resources to carry-out their jobs.

The mitigation management include administrative and organizational powers, checking procedures and planning powers to realize mitigation plans, consultation procedures, and representation of the community in mitigation decisions and management of the implementation of activities.

Economic Development

Economic development is the key to disaster mitigation and it is said that a strong economy is the best protection against a disaster. Strong economy is one which has sufficient reserves to invest in stronger buildings and infrastructure and also to invest for rebuilding. Mitigation measures can help a community reduce economic losses, withstand the losses and recover fast and solid.

It is always the poor who are affected the most in a disaster and it is those segment which takes time to recover. If they lose their house, animals or other belongings, they have no means of recovering them. They are the ones without insurance and credit access and can become destitute.

Economic development is to be the main objective of any regional planner or national government agency, regardless of mitigation objectives. The process of economic development is complex and disaster mitigation must be seen as a part of the process of economic development. Some elements of development planning are directly relevant to reducing disaster risks. Diversification of the economy is an important aspect of growth. A single industry economy is more vulnerable than a diversified economy.

Societal Measures

The mitigation of disasters will only happen where is a consensus that it is desirable, affordable, and feasible. In many places the threat of the disaster is not known and not recognized and the steps taken by the people to protect themselves are often not forthcoming. It is therefore important for disaster mitigation planning to develop a disaster safety culture in which the awareness about the disasters are made known to the public and the people protect themselves as much as they can and support efforts made to protect them. There are many methods of creating public awareness, through broadcasts, literature, posters, and general education.

It is always desirable to know about the hazards in the prone-area and to understand the hazards as a fact of life. Information about the hazards should be made a part of curriculum and their understanding should include being aware of what to do in the event, and a sense construction to effect their safety. The aim of the mitigation strategy is to reduce the losses in the event of a hazard and primarily to reduce the death and injury. The secondary role is to minimize the economic losses to public and private sectors. The main objective, however, remains to encourage the people to protect themselves as far as possible. A mitigation programme should concentrate on all aspects of engineering, spatial planning, societal inputs, economic and managerial inputs to achieve best results. A mitigation programme that concentrates solely on any one factor may result in unbalanced condition and may fail.

Conflict Reduction

Conflict reduction should be part of mitigation and the reduction measures must start by identifying the rootcause of conflict. Issues relating to land tenure, employment, access to resources, religious or ethnic intolerance are the various sources of conflict. It is important to anticipate and address these issues, before they erupt.

1.11 DISASTER MANAGEMENT CYCLE

Every activity just does not appear; all of them have a life cycle, so does disasters. Disasters have life cycles of occurrence and hence the management strategy should match the phases of an emergency. There are four phases in disaster management and they are:

(a) Mitigation
(b) Preparedness
(c) Response
(d) Recovery

Mitigation

Mitigation refers to measures planned to eliminate or reduce vulnerability, the possibility of occurrence of a disaster and the impact of its occurrence. The mitigation phase begins with the identification of hazard and vulnerability analysis. The hazard is first identified and its dangerous impacts on the society and property is analysed. Then mitigation strategies are worked out in detail to reduce the loss. Mitigation is explained in detail in the preceding chapter.

Preparedness

Preparedness is a state of being ready and prepared to face an emergency situation and to react promptly and effectively. Preparedness really means evolving and developing a complete action plan for meeting the emergency situation. The early warning system gives several hours for planning and acting in the case hurricanes, floods, etc., however in the case of natural hazards like earthquake, little or no time is available for action. Preparing for an emergency, especially those strikes without time and notice, needs a concrete plan. It is also important to take stock of the resources available and the best manner in which they can be put to best use. An important feature of an emergency plan is that it should work in an emergency situation.

The very purpose of an emergency plan is to evolve a systematic way of responding to an emergency situation. The plan should consider the following elements to make a proper disaster preparedness action plan:

(a) Identifying the vulnerable areas and situations.

(b) Developing a suitable strategy for course of action.

(c) Best use of the resources for optimal benefit.

(d) Identifying and using the government bodies responsible to emergency situations.

(e) Deploying an officer responsible and accountable for actions.

(f) Establishing control room or emergency operation Centre (EOC) for quick actions.

Response

The plans ultimate test is the effectiveness of response to warnings and hazard impacts. Various responses will have to be mobilized at different stages of the warning process. The staging of the responses becomes essential for developing a preparedness plan. Response activities occur during and immediately following a disaster. They are indented to provide emergency assistance to the victims of a disaster event and reduce the possibility of a secondary damage. Responses include:

(a) Warning and notification.

(b) Immediate safety of communities.

(c) Public welfare.

(d) Property security.

(e) Restoration.

Warning

Warning is the first and foremost stage of response. The specific groups which need to be warned of a disaster are the general public, departments, agencies, and individuals, who would respond to the emergency. The general public are normally informed through media, radio, and television and those in immediate dangers are either informed directly or through public address system. The people who are likely to be affected must be alerted and told what to do, how to do, and what not to do, in an emergency situation.

Immediate Safety

Immediate public safety involves providing spot emergency medical services, search and rescue operations and evacuation of the mass from the affected area. Therefore, the primary objective should be the safety of people and aid to the injured.

Public Welfare

Public welfare covers the caring for the people after the disaster and assessing the damage. It is mandatory for all agencies to work closely and effectively to get optimum results. Providing shelter, food, clothing, and medical aid are the prime concerns in public welfare.

Property Security

This stage deals with the necessary protection to properties and this is the job of the local police. It is the responsibility of the police to see that the property is safe and looting and vandalism does not occur. The fire department, public works department, roads department, rural and urban bodies also play a significant role in protecting the property.

Restoration

Restoration involves repairing and restoring the utility services and further involves removing the debris from the disaster area. In the restoration phase, reconstruction of the infrastructure facilities are taken up.

Recovery

This is the final phase of the disaster management cycle and the process continues till normalcy is restored. The recovery phase is classified into two types namely, short-term and long-term. Short-term recoveries would be immediate reconnection of electrical lines, telephone lines, repairs to buildings, etc., whereas the long-term recovery involves construction process for years together. Long-term recovery extends over a number of years, for complete revamp of the area. A key element in the recovery phase is to develop and implement means and ways to reduce the vulnerability to repeated occurrences of disaster and to build an understanding between States and Central Government for assistance.

1.12 TYPES OF MITIGATION MEASURES

It is necessary to have a decision making structure to facilitate decision making. The following questions suggest such a structure:

(a) What risk is being reduced?

(b) To what level should the risk be reduced?

(c) What are the criterias used for risk reduction?

(d) Who decides the criteria?

(e) What is the political system and process for implementations?

Based on the above questions, suitable mitigations measures are suggested and following are the classifications:

Active and Passive

Certain incentives are offered by authorities to promote certain measures and certain activities are prohibited by the authorities which are punitive.

Long-term and Short-term

The mitigation actions can be short-term and long-term, depending upon their duration. The short-term actions are shorter in duration and are temporary, like sand bag reinforcements of a Dyke. Long-term actions are long duration jobs which aim at permanent solutions.

Structural and Non-structural

Structural measures include physical improvements such as construction of dams, buildings, etc. and non-structural measures include policies, procedures and practices, which help reduce risk.

Restrictive and Incentive

Restrictive measures seek to promote safety by declaring certain action punitive and restrictive through legal recourse.

Sectoral-based Activities

Sectoral-based activities start from the vantage point of a sector, such as agriculture and tries to build risk reduction and mitigation efforts in those sectors.

The strategy should be done to introduce hazard resistant crops or encourage diverse crops.

Mitigation as a Development Process

After a major disaster, some areas would be completely levelled and new buildings planned. Re-development refers to the complete replacement of structures and provides an opportunity to reduce the likelihood of a similar structural collapse. It is important for the engineers to see whether the building standards respond to a hazard. The planners need to find out the possibility of rezoning and using the affected area for a lower density uses. It is also desirable to get the preferences of the affected people for their resettlement.

Hazards are part of natural and man-made situations and exposure to hazards must be a part of planning process. The loss of human life and property can be drastically reduced by a timely warning and in the same way, timely response, after a disaster, can substantially than the rich nations, basically because the former cannot withstand the losses. This also forces the developing nations to divert funds meant for other activities for disaster relief, whereby hindering the phase of economic development. As the disaster hinders the business people, they suffer on livelihood prospects. Part dealing of the problems is highly inadequate for economic development. The economic development can be badly affected, if the disasters frequently affect them, so as the loss of human development. Disaster mitigation seeks to reduce vulnerability of societies and communities to disasters and should look beyond disaster containment to creating hazard resilient situations. The hazard resilient situation consists of the following:

(a) Sustainable livelihoods, as to how people use their resources, assets, and activities to make a living.

(b) Sustainable phase that incorporates conflict transformations into social values and culture.

Mitigation as Investment

In any planning process, there are certain factors influencing the decision making process. These include the costs, benefits, effects, models, and tools, which are used to derive analytical results, to narrow down on specific issues. The same process happens in the case of mitigation plans. The governments decide on how much they should spend on vulnerability reduction and also on single investments whereby the mitigation process reduce the recurrent loss of capital goods and production. Normally in any development programme, there is a surge for capital resources and priorities needs to be set for spending. This is where the decision makers compare development alternatives and select the best alternative. Politicians rarely go for long-term investments in mitigation plans, as short-term actions help them on electoral terms. They are bothered about immediate day-to-day survival, the most inevitable for them.

Normally the governments take decisions whether to spend or not on mitigation programmes, based on timeframe, with immediate effect or staggered situation of disaster recovery.

Government decisions are influenced by opportunity cost, present value situations, etc., and spending on mitigation should be less than the present value of the expected loss. It is difficult to make an accurate estimation of the loss, as monetary values are not possible for all. The losses could be monetary (damage and destruction of buildings and installations), indirect monetary (clean up costs, production loss, etc.), direct non-monetary effects (death, injuries, loss of articles, loss of schooling, health, stress), and ecological loss. There are also secondary benefits which are difficult to quantify.

Private Sector Participation

A very close interaction between the private business and the government is essential to ensure appropriate risk reduction strategies, implementation of plans, security, and insurance to properties. Like the government, the private sector also holds vast human resources in the form of technical manpower. Also the donation from the private sector is large in the form of goods and services.

The private sector contributions to disaster mitigation can be in defining, assigning, and implementing institutional roles, training and achieving high response, assessing institutional needs, developing programmes, improving disaster consciousness, and improving access to accurate data and information.

Community Involvement

The need of the hour for disaster preparedness is money, technology, skills, and an understanding community. The most important is the human resource.

Most disaster development programmes are top-down approaches, with community involvement for implementation of programmes. The victims of a disaster and beneficiaries of the development programmes are individuals in the locality and the failure to involve them in the pre- and post-disaster planning and programmes, will prove fatal and result in inadequately conceptualized programmes. The best result is always when people are involved in preparedness, vulnerability reduction, and development.

Therefore, it is required to train and educate the community on pre- and post-disaster situations. Community is required to be better informed through well-defined awareness and educational programmes. It is also expected that the community works closely with local authorities, NGOs, etc., all sections of people, opinion makers, local leaders, all must represent the rehabilitation process, re-settlement, etc., the people involvement also elicit government commitment to a higher level.

Mitigation Packages Effectiveness

The effectiveness of a mitigation option depends on it's forcefulness and efficacy. Cost-effectiveness depends on the kind of disaster under purview. Generally, natural disasters are worth high investment and require long-term programmes.

Mitigation is effective, when it is a medium- to long-term development programme which incorporates hazard reduction measures into regular investment projects.

A science dip-SENDROM is a novel sensor network architecture, based on state-of-the-art technologies, developed to manage the rescue operations after large-scale disasters. This architecture mainly consists of sensor nodes deployed prior to a disaster and central nodes – stored nearby emergency operations centres and airports and linked to the SENDROM databases – that query the sensor nodes following a disaster.

1.13 QUESTIONS

1. Define Disaster.
2. What are the components of disaster management?
3. Elucidate the principles of disaster management.
4. Explain the concept of mitigation.
5. Prepare a standard operating procedure by forecasting a natural disaster in your area.

2

Natural Disasters – Mitigation Efforts

Learning Objectives

- To understand the various types of natural disasters and their mitigation efforts.
- To equip the reader with the knowledge of various types of disasters.
- To facilitate the preparation of precautionary measures to mitigate various disasters
- To understand how the natural disasters happen
- To give a detailed knowledge on mitigation strategies

Structure

2.1 Meteorological or Climatic

2.2 Hydrological Disasters

2.3 Geological Disasters

2.4 Human Epidemics and Pandemics

2.5 Technological Hazards

2.6 Questions

The National Disaster Management Act, 2005 defines disaster as:

Disaster means catastrophe, mishap, calamity, or grave occurrence affecting any area, arising from natural or man-made causes, or by accident or negligence, which result in substantial loss of life or human suffering, or damage to, and destruction of property, or damage to, or degradation of environment, and is of such a nature or magnitude as to be beyond the coping capacity of the community of the affected area.

Disaster can be natural or man-made or complex and slow or sudden. The natural disasters are caused when hazards occur in vulnerable areas, resulting in substantial damage, disruption, and possible casualties and leaving the affected communities unable to function normally.

The natural disasters can be classified according to their nature of occurrence and are largely divided into the following

1. Meteorological or Climatic Disasters
2. Hydrological Disasters
3. Geological Disasters

2.1 METEOROLOGICAL OR CLIMATIC DISASTERS

These are caused by extreme conditions in the climate prompted by the nature and include drought, hailstorm, hurricanes and cyclones, heat wave, glacial effect, tornado, and ice storm, etc.

Drought

Drought is an abnormally dry period, with no or less water to support urban people's environmental or agricultural needs. This is the result of inadequacy of rainfall or lack of irrigation facilities or deficient availability of water. It can also be situation resulting from the demand supply gap between the demand people put forth against the supply the nature provides. Droughts extended beyond a point can result in starvation deaths, peculiar diseases, or wild fire. One example is the severe drought in Western Australia, continuously for ten years, beginning to affect urban populations also.

Drought is a normal, recurrent feature of climate. It occurs almost everywhere, although its features vary from region-to-region. Defining drought is therefore difficult; it depends on differences in regions, needs, and disciplinary perspectives. Based on the many definitions that have appeared in the literature, for example, we might define drought in Libya as occurring when annual rainfall is less than 180 mm, but in Bali, drought might be considered to occur after a period of only six days without rain! In the most general sense, drought originates from a deficiency of precipitation over an extended period of time, resulting in a water shortage for some activity, group, or environmental sector.

- ❖ Drought originates from a deficiency of precipitation over an extended period of time, resulting in a water shortage for some activity, group, or environmental sector.
- ❖ Precipitation – Atmospheric water vapour that is pulled down by gravity and deposited on the earth's surface.

Causes of Drought

The essential features of drought are: (a) It is a slow onset category disaster and unable to predict its beginning at end. (b) It's as unusually dry period resulting in water scarcity. (c) Drought is a recurrent feature of the nature and part of climate, which shows variations and drought is part of it.

The types of droughts are: *(a) Hydrological Drought,* resulting from the reduction of natural stream flows and groundwater levels *(b) Meteorological Drought* occurs on deficient rainfall from the normal rainfall levels and is the most severest form of drought with hot weather and hot waves. When there is a prolonged period of below average precipitation, there occurs a natural water shortage, and *(c) Agricultural drought,* a very dangerous situation caused by absence of moisture on the soil, leading to shortage of foodgrains.

The basic cause of drought is the deficient rainfall added with other vulnerable factors such as over farming, excessive irrigation, deforestation, and soil erosion, most of them are human induced. Drought basically is a natural disaster and its effects are endangered further by the over population, deforestation, soil erosion, exploitation of groundwater, loss of biodiversity and pollution.

The Impact and Consequences of Drought are

- Diminished crop growth or yield productions.
- Dust storms.
- Famine.
- Habitat damage.
- Malnutrition, dehydration.
- Mass migration.
- Reduced electricity production.
- Shortages of water for industrial users.
- Wild fires.
- Land degradation.
- Nonavailability of quality seeds.
- Deficient investment capability of farmers.
- Damage to natural ecosystem.

Drought Management and Mitigation

The impacts of the drought slowly spread to the society as the availability of drinking water diminishes, reduction in energy generation, shortfall in production of foodgrains, groundwater depletion famine, loss of life, and social problems, etc., all leading to mitigation of disaster.

The mitigation strategies for drought monitoring is by continuous monitoring of rainfalls, availability of water in reservoirs, lakes and rivers, and comparing them with the current and future needs of the various sectors of the society. This includes water supply augmentation, rain water harvesting in houses and fields, and conservation of water at all levels.

There are various mitigation strategies which are used to reduce the impact of drought and they are:

(a) **Drought planning,** the basic principle of which is to improve the effectiveness of drought preparedness and response system by enhancing monitoring, mitigation, and response measures. Planning helps effective coordination between the State and Central agencies in dealing with drought. This further helps establishing relationships, authority, and coordination among the various officials.

(b) **Drought monitoring,** is the process involving continuous monitoring of rainfall, water levels at reservoirs, wells, natural lakes, rivers, etc., and comparing with the current needs of the public and society.

(c) **Public awareness and education system,** is the process of educating the masses on the various effects of drought and the various strategies to be adopted for combating drought. Includes organizing meetings for the public and the media, implementing mass water conservation awareness programmes, publishing and distributing water conservation techniques, agricultural drought management techniques, and rain water harvesting techniques, etc., through leaflets and other published documents. This is an awareness generating situation.

(d) **Water supply augmentation and conservation** is through rain water harvesting at houses and agricultural places increases water availability. Pooling the available water in one location or allowing the water to infiltrate at the place of waterfall are examples of rain water harvesting. Expansion of irrigation could be another strategy.

(e) **Livelihood planning** is by identifying jobs which are of less usage of water or alternate employment other than agriculture.

(f) **Other general measures of mitigation** include the following:

- ***Cloud Seeding:*** an artificial technique to induce rainfall.
- Desalination of sea water for irrigation or consumption.
- ***Land Use:*** Carefully planned crop rotation can help to minimize erosion and allow farmers to plant less water-dependent crops in drier years.
- ***Recycled Water:*** Former waste water (sewage) that has been treated and purified for reuse.
- ***Transvasement:*** Building canals or redirecting rivers as massive attempts at irrigation drought-prone areas.
- ***Outdoor Water-use Restriction:*** Regulating the use of sprinklers, hoses or buckets on outdoor plants, the washing of motor vehicles or other outdoor hard surfaces (including roofs and paths), topping up of swimming pools.

Hailstorm

Hailstorm is a natural disaster caused by thunderstorm carrying numerous hailstones which destroy the area in which they hit. The impact of the hailstorms are highly damaging and devastating. They destroy paddy fields, ruining crops, and damaging equipment. The typical case can be the hailstorm which hit the Volkswagen car factory, damaging approximately 30,000 brand new cars kept ready for dispatch. Such will be the power of hailstorms.

Creating early warning system, educating the public, and timely evacuation are the best strategies used for mitigation of hailstorm.

Hurricanes and Cyclones

A cyclone is a storm accompanied by high speed whistling and howling winds. It brings torrential rains. A cyclonic storm develops over tropical oceans like the Indian Ocean and Bay of Bengal and the Arabian Sea. Its strong winds blow at great speed, which can be more than 118 kilometres per hour.

Hurricanes, cyclones, and typhoons are different forms of the same phenomenon. The term cyclones refer to all classes of storms with low atmospheric pressure at the centre. They form because of clock-wise revolving of winds in the Southern hemisphere and anti-clock-wise revolving of wind in the Northern hemisphere, respectively, over the deep waters. The classification of the cyclones is based on their average wind speed near the centre. Storms up to 61 km/hrs are called Tropical Depression, from 61 to 115 km/hrs are called Tropical storm, and winds above 115 km/hrs are called hurricanes.

Hurricane is a low pressure, big scale weather system which generates its energy from the latent heat of condensation of water vapour over warm deep seas. A sound hurricane may have a range of 200 to 1,000 kms., with sustained wind speed exceeding 180 km/hrs.

A unique feature of hurricane is the eye, which is the point of monitoring and can be tracked and measured with the help of radars, aircrafts, and satellites. Hurricanes are categorized into five according to their speed and damage potential and are minimal, moderate, extensive, extreme, and catastrophic. The destructive potential of the hurricane is devastating due to high speed of the wind accompanied by torrential rains, floods, and water rise.

One example of devastating hurricane is Katrina, which devastated the Gulf Coast of the United States in 2005 and cyclone Nargis which hit the land in 2008 killing 150 thousands of people.

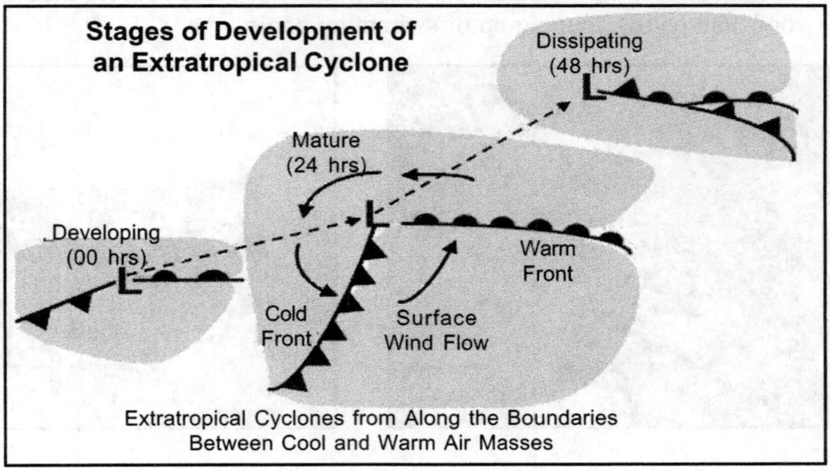

Extratropical Cyclones from Along the Boundaries Between Cool and Warm Air Masses

Effects of cyclone are:

- ❖ A cyclone causes heavy floods.
- ❖ It uproots electricity supply and telecommunication lines. Power supply shuts down and telephones stop functioning.
- ❖ The floodwaters can take time to recede.
- ❖ The floodwaters can turn the fields salty.
- ❖ Bridges, dams, and embankments suffer serious damages.

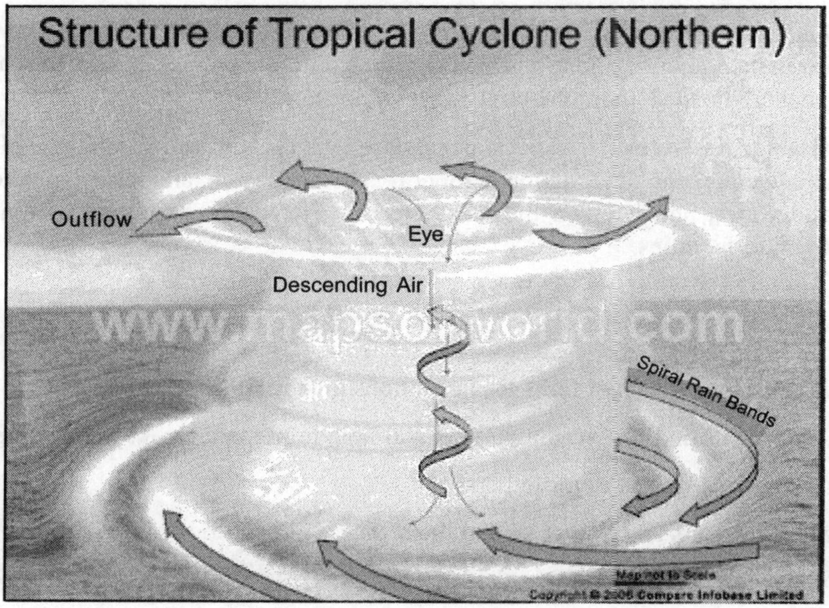

The mitigation measures for cyclone and hurricane can be:

1. **Risk Assessment:** The assessment of risk for a tropical cyclone is relatively as easy process. The following factors could be used to estimate the probability of storms and their intensities and probable strike at locations. Analysis of climatic records to determine the occurrences of earlier cyclones and their intensities and locations. Further analysis of the history of wind frequencies, strength, location, and frequencies of floods. An analysis of the previous hundred years about the occurrences of cyclone, their intensities, and nature.

2. **Warning and Response System:** The preparedness measures to counter the impact of cyclone are long-term as well as short-term. Long-term measures needs to be planned implemented and coordinated after long thought-out process involving the various agencies. These strategies will have to be implemented well ahead of seasonal threats. Short-term strategies will be temporary in nature.

3. **Public Warning System:** It is an important part of cyclone mitigation strategy to alert people of the danger and the existence of threat. It will also identify and declare the areas under threat and also alert communities to monitor further announcements. The different stages of alert are as follows:

   - ***Alert Stage:***

     This warning is given 48 hours prior to the time when a cyclone is expected to hit the land.

   - ***Warning Stage:***

     This is the stage when a cyclone gets formed. The warning is given 24 hours before the anticipated time of arrival of a cyclone.

   - ***Cyclone Arrival:***

     This warning is issued 12 hours before a cyclone is due to hit the land. The warning gives information about cyclone and will continue until the winds subside. In sea ports, danger signal are hoisted about the impending cyclone.

4. **Post-disaster Assistance:** The normal response by local authorities comprise of the following and include emergency evacuation, temporary shelter, search, and rescue, medical assistance, food and water, and later on the mass clearance of debris, relaying of roads, and other infrastructure facilities.

5. **Tips:**

   Listen to early warnings

   - Listen to the radio (All India Radio stations give weather warnings).
   - Keep monitoring the warnings. This will help to prepare for a cyclone emergency.
   - Pass on the information to others.
   - Ignore rumours and do not spread them; this will help to avoid panic situations.
   - Believe in the official information.

❖ When a cyclone alert is on for an area continue normal working but stay alert to the radio warnings.

❖ Remember that a cyclone alert means that the danger is within 24 hours. Stay alert.

❖ When the area is under cyclone warning get away from low-lying beaches or other low-lying areas close to the coast.

6. Do's and Dont's

Do's	Dont's
◆ Talk to children and explain about cyclones without scaring them. ◆ Have your dwellings checked before a cyclone season starts and carry-out whatever repairs that are needed.	◆ Fishermen are advised not to venture out into the sea. They should keep boats and rafts tied up in a safe place. ◆ Avoid taking shelters near old and damaged buildings or near trees.
◆ Create storm awareness by discussing effects of a cyclonic storm with family members so that everyone knows what one can and should do in an emergency. This helps to remove fear and anxiety and prepares everyone to respond to emergencies quickly. ◆ Keep your valuables and documents in containers, which cannot be damaged by water.	◆ Do not touch during the storm do not venture out unless advised to evacuate. ◆ If you have a vehicle and wish to move out of your house, leave early before the onset of a cyclone. It is often best to stay at home. ◆ Avoid remaining on the top floor of dwellings. Stay close to the ground. ◆ Power lines. One may get electrocuted.

Heat Wave

Heat wave is a very typical disaster and is characterized by the extreme heat it produces in a particular area accompanied by high humidity. Heat waves are actually a rare occurrence and happen on account of a combination of weather events in the atmosphere. The temperature felt by people living in hotter climate may be felt as a heat wave for people living in cooler areas. Severe heat waves have caused catastrophic crop failures, thousands of deaths from hyperthermia and widespread power shortages due to increased use of air-conditioning.

The following are few occurrence of heat waves worldover

European heat wave which occurred in 2003, was the worst hit. There is a potential for long-term events causing global warming.

During the 2007 Asian heat wave, the Indian city of Datia experienced temperatures of 48°C (118°F).

The UK declared a heat wave, on July 9th, 2010 for South East England and East Anglia. This was after temperatures reached 31.0^{0}C in London and night time temperatures levelled around 21^{0}C.

Japan experienced heat wave during July 2010, with high rising temperature for a longer period. The temperature rose above 35.0°C continuously for 33 days.

The mitigation process could be to alert people to stay within their house and not to venture around to avoid heat burns, conserve precious water for optimum usage, divert maximum electricity to the affected areas to augment usage of air-conditioners, provision of nutritious food, strengthening the medical assistance, etc.

Glacial Event (Ice Age)

A "glacial age" is a generic geological period of long-term reduction in the temperature on the Earth's surface and atmosphere, resulting in the presence or expansion of continental ice sheets, polar ice sheets, and alpine glaciers. An ice age is a geological period where climate condition would change the worldover, which was considered habitable earlier, would then be too cold to reside.

Ice Storm

An ice storm is a type of winter storm characterized by freezing rain. Ice storms occur when a layer of warm air in between two layers of cold air. Frozen precipitation melts while falling into the warm air layer, and then proceeds to refreeze in the cold layer above the ground. If the precipitate is partially melted, it will land on the ground as sleet. Normally, meteorologists can predict the ice storm precisely with when and where it will fall. However, there are ice storms which suddenly emerge as well. An ice storm in February 1994 resulted in huge accumulation of ice at Mississippi and caused exponential damages across many states.

Effect

The effect of ice storms are often devastating, they damage the electrical lines and create sagging wires throughout, they disrupt transportation, damage roads, destroy poles and pipelines, felling trees, and make human life miserable.

The ice storms cover everything with heavy layer of ice, and makes roads slippery and hazardous, often endangering vehicular traffic, and pedestrian traffic on slippery roads.

According to meteorologists, one quarter of an inch of ice accumulation can add about 500 pounds of weight per line span. Damage from ice storms is highly capable of shutting down entire metropolitan areas.

Tornado

It is a result of thunder storm and are violent, circular, rotating, and blows at a speed of 50-300 miles/hr. and even higher. Tornados normally occur one at a time cr a combination of few outbreaks and spread across large areas.

A tornado strikes in different shapes and sizes. They are typically in the form of visible condensation funnel with their narrow end touches the earth and is encircled by a cloud of dust and debris. The tornado strike with the speed of not less than 177 kms/hr. and spread across a minimum 250 ft. and travel several kilometres before weakening. There are occasions where tornados have taken a speed of more than 480 kms and travelled across 100 kms.

Life Cycle

The above images show the birth of a tornado, first the rotating cloud base lowers. This lowering becomes a funnel, which continues descending while winds build near the surface, kicking up dust and other debris. Finally, the visible funnel extends to the ground, and the tornado begins causing major damage. This tornado, near Dimmitt Texas, was one of the best – observed violent tornadoes in history.

2.2 HYDROLOGICAL DISASTERS

Flood

The word 'Flood' originated from the old English word 'Flod', or a word common to Germanic languages and is defined as "flood is a temporary inundation of large regions as a result of an increase in the levels of water in the reservoir, or of rivers flooding their banks because of heavy rains, cyclones, high winds, tsunami, and ice melting or dam bursts".

It is also defined as "an overflow or accumulation of an expanse of water that submerges land".

Causes of Flood

Floods can occur due to several causes and can differ from region-to-region. The causes of flood may vary from place-to-place and the sum of the causes are as follows:

(a) Torrential rains.

(b) Cyclone and hurricanes.

(c) Tsunami.

(d) Inundation of river beds.

(e) Landslides blocking the flow of streams.

(f) Dams and reservoir construction.

Types of Floods

Floods can be of the following types and nature:

Riverine

Slow Kinds: Runoff from sustained rainfall or rapid snowmelt exceeding the capacity of a river's channel. Causes include heavy rains from monsoon, hurricanes and tropical depressions, foreign winds, and warm rain affecting snow pack. Unexpected drainage obstructions such as landslide, ice, or debris can cause slow flooding upstream of the obstruction.

Fast Kinds: Include flash floods resulting from convective precipitation (intense thunderstorms) or sudden release from an upstream impoundment created behind a dam, landslide, or glacier.

Estuarine

Commonly caused by a combination of sea tidal surges caused by storm-force winds. A storm surge, from either a tropical cyclone or an extra tropical cyclone, falls within this category.

Coastal

Caused by severe sea storms, or as a result of another hazard (e.g., tsunami or hurricane). A storm surge, from either a tropical cyclone or an extra tropical cyclone, falls within this category.

Catastrophic

Caused by a significant and unexpected event, e.g., dam breakage, or as a result of another hazard.

Muddy

A muddy flood is produced by an accumulation of runoff generated on cropland. Sediments are then detached by runoff and carried as suspended matter or bed load. Muddy runoff is more likely detected when it reaches inhabited areas. Muddy floods are therefore a hill slope process, and confusion with mudflows produced by mass movements should be avoided.

Impact of Floods

(a) Loss of Life and Property: Important consequence of floods is the loss of life and damage to property. Infrastructural facilities such as bridges, roads, etc., and houses are damaged by the gushing water are important factors of flood damage. In addition there is extensive damage of livestock, lack of drinking water, contamination of water storages, etc., leads to the outbreak of epidemics and other infectious diseases.

(b) Deterioration of Soil: Floods affect soil characteristics in a big way. The land may be rendered uncultivable due to the erosion of top layer or even become saline on account of sea water flooding.

(c) Agricultural Land Inundation: The floods leave large areas of agricultural land inundated resulting in huge loss of crop leading to shortage of food famine.

Flood Control and Mitigation

Flood control aims to reduce flood damages. This can be done by reduction of flood by decreasing the amount of runoff by treatments like reforestations, vegetation, clearing of debris from the rivers, and conservation of ponds and lakes.

The basic approach to the problem of flood control should be to prevent flood waters from reaching potential damage centres. The various measures adopted for flood control are as follows:

(i) Construction of dams and reservoirs.

(ii) Diversion of flood waters.

(iii) Flood walls and sea walls and dikes.

(iv) Improvement of water channels.

(v) Drainage development and maintenance.

(vi) Flood disaster preparedness and response plan.

(vii) Flood forecasting and warning.

(viii) Flood relief and flood fighting including public health measures.

The success of the flood control depends upon the physical measures taken and their pre- and post-monsoon validation and repairs carried out.

Flood management comprises of the process of assessing the risks from flood and implement appropriate management measures on the basis of that information. These measures could be construction of flood protections and defenses, flood warning system and development of policies which reduce flood risks. The management of floods can be done by adopting the following measures.

1. **Preparedness Against Flood:** This is based on a overall master-plan followed by mini-plans at district level involving steps to be taken before and after the floods. And includes pre-monsoon inspection, regular maintenance and removal of drains, regular maintenance of river banks and canals, clearing of sewage drains and finally constitution of committees and authorities to act on crisis.

2. **Response Mechanism:** As safety lies in evacuating people to safer areas along with their belongings during the calamity, responses to the warnings are important. The response mechanism includes the early warning of the impending disaster, monitoring the latest situation, warning people to act and follow directions.
3. **Post-flood Management:** The essential requirements of post-disaster management are:
   (a) Speedy restoration of roads, rails tracks, and communication services.
   (b) Effecting water supply in the affected areas through tankers.
   (c) Supply of food, shelter, and clothing to the affected people.
   (d) Establishment of power, telephone, and sewerage lines.
   (e) Restoration of normalcy.
   (f) Adequacy of kerosene, gas, etc., for cooking.
   (g) Constitution of proper authority of surveying the loss, and compensation.
   (h) Assistance to the public for repair, and building.
   (i) Helping the agriculture sector with contingency plan.

It is to be noted that the damages caused by floods can only be minimized, and cannot be totally avoided.

Floods in India

Floods occur in almost all river basins of the country. Torrential rains, inadequate capacity of rivers to carry high flood discharge, inadequate drainages are the main causes of floods. Typhoons and hurricanes are also cause floods. Torrential rainfall compiled with inadequate carrying capacity of rivers resulting in inundation of banks is the main cause for flood in majority of the areas in India. Andhra Pradesh, Assam, Bihar, Odisha, Uttar Pradesh, West Bengal, Punjab, Rajasthan, Gujarat, Haryana, and Maharashtra are coastal areas vulnerable to floods.

Limnic Eruptions

A limnic eruption, also known as lake overturn, is a unique natural disaster, wherein sudden eruption of carbon dioxide from the deep lake water, suffocating wildlife, humans, and livestock. Such eruption could also result in tsunami in the lake because of the rising carbon dioxide displacing water.

The features of limnically active lakes are:

1. CO_2-saturated incoming water.
2. A cool lake bottom indicating an absence of direct volcanic interaction with lake waters.
3. An upper and lower thermal layer with differing CO_2 saturations.
4. Proximity to areas with volcanic activity.

The worst hit limnic eruptions are in 1984 in Cameroon, and in 1986 near lake Nyos, killing 1,800 people by asphyxiation and suffocation.

Maelstrom

A maelstrom is a powerful tidal whirlpool, a large swirling body of water with considerable downdraft.

Notable maelstroms

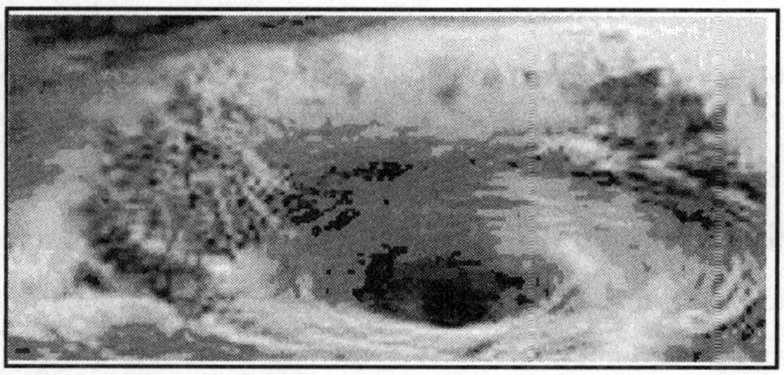

The largest known maelstrom is that of Norway, where the powerful whirlpool killed unlucky seafarers, fishermen, etc., the maelstrom can be devastating with exaggerated power and can reach speeds of 40 km/hr.

Sciche

A sciche is a standing wave in an enclosed or partially enclosed body of water. These are observed on reservoirs, lakes, and seas. One of the requirement for the formation of sciche is a partially bound water body, allowing natural phenomena to form a standing wave.

Tsunami

The term tsunami originated from Japanese term, 'Tsu' meaning harbour, and 'nami' meaning waves. Tsunamis are sometimes called tidal waves but actually they are different and nothing to do with tides.

Earthquakes, volcanic eruptions, underwater explosions including detonations of underwater nuclear devices, landslides, other mass movements, meteorite ocean impacts, and other disturbances above or below water, all have the potential to generate a tsunami. These factors are capable of displacing the sea water with a violent motion and swells up, ultimately surging over the land with devastating power.

Tsunamis are long-wavelength, long-period sea waves produced by the sudden or abrupt movement of large volumes of water. In the open ocean the distance between wave crests can surpass 100 kms (62 miles), and the wave periods can vary from five minutes to one hour. Such tsunamis travel 600-800 kms/hr., depending on water depth. Large waves produced by an earthquake or a submarine landslide can overrun nearby coastal areas in a matter of minutes. Tsunamis can also travel thousands of kilometres across open ocean and wreak destruction on far shores hours after the earthquake that generated them.

Ordinarily, subduction earthquakes under magnitude of 7.5 on the Richter scale do not cause tsunamis, although some instances of this have been recorded. Most destructive tsunamis are caused by earthquakes of magnitude of 7.5 or more.

A tsunami is usually composed of a series of waves, called a wave train, so its destructive force may be compounded as successive waves reach shore. People experiencing a tsunami should remember that the danger may not have passed with the first wave and should await official word that it is safe to return to vulnerable locations.

Some tsunamis do not appear on shore as massive breaking waves but instead resemble a quickly surging tide that inundates coastal areas.

Features of Tsunami

(a) Tsunamis differ from ordinary waves which are produced by the blowing wind over the water.

(b) Tsunamis picks up heights.

(c) Tsunamis can travel much faster than normal waves with speeds of over 800 kms/hr.

(d) Tsunamis often attack with multiple strikes and consist of more than 10 waves and they strike within 5-90 minutes gap.

(e) Tsunamis often flood heavily as huge water blocks enter the land.

Generation Mechanisms

The principal generation mechanism (or cause) of a tsunami is the displacement of a substantial volume of water or perturbation of the sea. This displacement of water is usually attributed to either earthquakes, landslides, volcanic eruptions, or more rarely by meteorites and nuclear tests. The waves formed in this way are then sustained by gravity.

Seismicity Generated Tsunamis

Tsunamis can be generated when the sea floor abruptly deforms and vertically displaces the overlying water. Tectonic earthquakes are a particular kind of earthquake that are associated with the earth's crustal deformation; when these earthquakes occur beneath the sea, the water above the deformed area is displaced from its equilibrium position.

More specifically, a tsunami can be generated when thrust faults associated with convergent or destructive plate boundaries move abruptly, resulting in water displacement, due to the vertical component of movement involved. Movement on normal faults will also cause displacement of the sea bed, but the size of the largest of such events is normally too small to give rise to a significant tsunami.

One of the deep water buoys used in the DART tsunami warning system

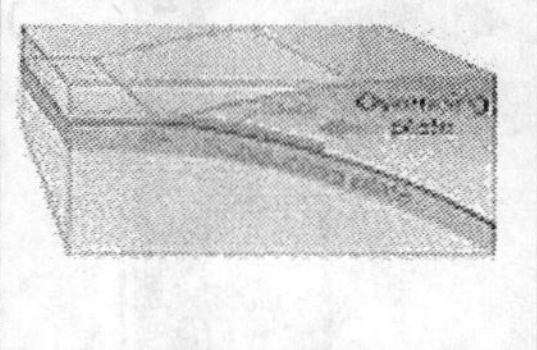	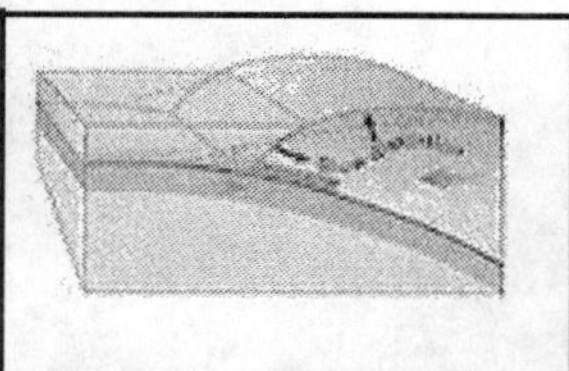	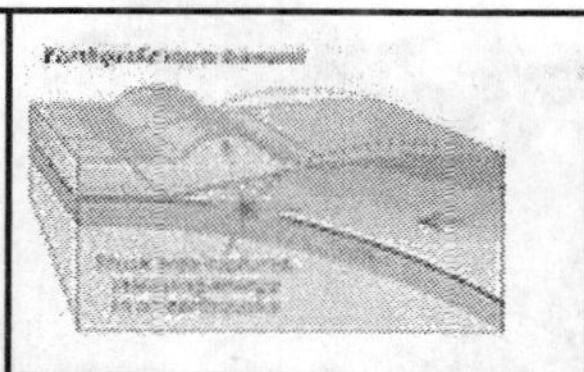	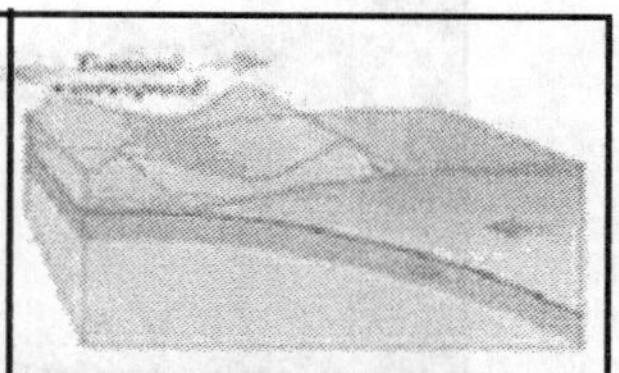
Drawing of tectonic plate boundary before earthquake.	Overriding plate bulges under strain, causing tectonic uplift.	Plate slips, causing subsidence and releasing energy into water.	The energy released produces tsunami waves.

The typical effects of tsunami are: (a) Physical damage, by inflicting water damage to homes, buildings, roads, bridges, and other infrastructure, (b) Environmental damage, by generation of tonnes of debris, weak buildings, and structures, leak of toxic chemicals, and negative impact on the fragile ecosystem, (c) Causalities, by the huge amount of lives which are carried away by the waves and buried, (d) Contamination of water, by the seas waters, (e) Destroying crops and food supplies, by flooding the standing crops gets destroyed so as food stored and further the land gets infertile on account of sea water and top layer washout.

Mitigation Efforts

(a) **Hazard Mapping:** It is preferable to prepare a map showing the vulnerable areas expected to be damaged by the floods generated by the tsunami. This should include vulnerable areas, evacuation routes, time taken for mass evacuation, etc., in detail.

(b) **Early Warning System:** A very well-networked system can warn the people residing the coastal areas and alert them as and when a threat is perceived. Tsunami is capable of striking across nations and hence the warning system must be capable of alerting the communities across local, state, and international levels. The local authorities must be informed and alerted to evacuate the people to the planned areas, as decided in the master plan.

(c) **Preparedness:** The communities residing near the coastal areas are vulnerable to the natural disasters and it is imperative that the local community is better prepared to take actions on the threat received and follow emergency actions.

2004 Indian Ocean Tsunami

The Indian ocean was hit by a tsunami on December 2004, known as the Sumatra-Andaman earthquake. The tsunami which hit the coasts killed as many as 2,75,000 people, making it the deadliest disaster in recent history.

The magnitude of tremour was estimated at 9.0-9.3, the second largest in the history, and had ten minutes duration. Normal earthquakes last for few seconds only. This earthquake caused the entire planet to vibrate.

This earthquake originated in the Indian Ocean north of Simeulue Island, off the Western Coast of Sumatra, Indonesia. The resultant tsunami hit the shores of Indonesia, Sri Lanka, Thailand, South India, and other countries, with waves taking height up to 100 feet.

The tsunami affected India's south-east coast, predominantly in the state of Tamil Nadu, as well as the Indian territories of Andaman and Nicobar Islands. In terms of the death toll, India had the third highest total following Indonesia and Sri Lanka. On the Indian mainland, more than 8,800 people are confirmed dead with thousands more still missing. Of this total, almost 8,000 of the deaths were from Tamil Nadu and 600 were from Pondicherry. At least 1,316 of the Andaman and Nicobar islands' 4,00,000 people are confirmed dead and 5,542 are missing – 4,500 from Katchall island alone. At least 1,40,000 Indians, mostly from fishing families, are being sheltered in relief centres.

Of all the countries affected by the tsunami, India was the most developed nation with the strongest economy. This has allowed the nation to be in a strong position to whether such losses, and has led to the government insistence that they bear the brunt of the reconstruction itself, rather than relying on foreign aid. This also holds true for the Andaman and Nicobar Islands where India has military presence on one island, and other islands being inhabited by primitive tribes. India has refused assistance from international aid agencies, because of the presence of a military base on one island, and stone-age tribes on some others.

Here are some of the Tsunami-related Stories Coming out of India

- The cost of the tsunami to India has reached a total of $1.6 billion according to calculations from Citigroup, a figure higher than many officials expected. Officials also estimate damages in the Andaman and Nicobar Islands will exceed $600 million. The Indian government believe they can handle the costs internally without relying too heavily on foreign aid.
- On the Indian mainland, amateur relief workers, dubbed "disaster tourists" have been warned that they may be doing more harm than good. Many established Indian aid organizations see these disaster tourists arriving in large numbers with loads upon loads of relief materials but with no idea as to what they need to do. The organizations believe that their help is needed only if their efforts are organized effectively. There have been numerous reports of people preying on aid supplies that are intended for the real victims.
- Many fishing communities have been devastated by the tsunami, most notably the fishing town of Nagapattinam whose fleet of 10-metre trawlers and long, open boats were once the

pride of the Tamil Nadu coast. Officials estimate that only three of 15,000 fishing vessels along this stretch of coastline escaped damage. Up to $125 million may be needed to fix or replace damaged fishing vessels, buy new nets and lines and generally get the economic lifeblood of this coast flowing again.

- Very little is known about the effects of the tsunami on India's primitive indigenous tribes like the Jarwas, the Onges, the Sentenelese and the Shompens, although officials estimate that they are alright. The Onge are one of the oldest tribes in the Andaman Islands and anthropologists say they could be dated back there 30,00-50,000 years.
- The Onge resemble African bush men in appearance. They're generally short, some four to four-and-a-half feet in height and dark skin colour and curly hair. Today, the Onge tribe are on the verge of extinction with an estimated 98 of them are left.
- Although the tsunami will inevitably slow down the tourism industry, particularly in the Andaman and Nicobar Islands, officials believe that they will get back on track, and may even increase in business due to the exposure the islands have received. The islands, which are known for its spectacular virgin beaches, amazing marine life for scuba diving, and dense forests, were not to heavily affected by the tsunami in tourist and resort areas. Tourism in the Andaman and Nicobar islands has picked up in the last 20 years. There were only 10,000 tourists visiting the islands in 1980. In 2003, the number had increased almost ten-fold, to 93,000. In 2004, it had been expected to cross the 1,00,000 mark before the tsunami hit.
- In the wake of the tragic tsunami, the Indian government have committed to developing a tsunami warning system for the Indian Ocean. The warning system, which will cost $ 27 million, will be up and ready in two to three years says a government minister. The warning system would involve installing Deep Ocean Assessment Reporting Technology at a depth of 6 kms in the Indian Ocean and Bay of Bengal.

2.3 GEOLOGICAL DISASTERS

Earthquake

An earthquake (also known as a quake, tremour, or temblor) is the result of a sudden release of energy in the earths crust that creates seismic waves. The seismic activity of an area refers to the frequency, type, and size of earthquakes experienced over a period of time. Earthquake is one of the most destructive type of natural hazards and it can strike any time within the shortest possible time. They can destroy buildings and infrastructures in few seconds, killing, and injuring communities, and destabilize governments. Earthquake is a sudden shaking of the earth with wild vibrations. They occur in variety of frequencies and velocities and last from 1 second to 1 minute.

Causes of Earthquake

The earths crust is a rocky layer of varying thickness and deepens up to 70 kms under the continents. The crust consists of several pieces called plates, which vary in size from a few hundred to thousand kilometres. These plates are driven by some mechanism and when they contact each other, stress generates. There are movements like, pulling away from each other, sliding sideways and pushing against the other. The areas of stress at plate boundaries which release accumulated energy by slipping or rupturing are known as faults.

There are three main types of fault that may cause an earthquake: normal, reverse (thrust), and strike-slip. Normal and reverse faulting are examples of dip-slip, where the displacement along the fault is in the direction of dip and movement on them involves a vertical component. Normal faults occur mainly in areas where the crust is being extended such as a divergent boundary. Reverse faults occur in areas where the crust is being shortened such as at a convergent boundary. Strike-slip faults are steep structures where the two sides of the fault-slip horizontally past each other; transform boundaries are a particular type of strike-slip fault. Many earthquakes are caused by movement on faults that have components of both dip-slip and strike-slip; this is known as oblique-slip.

Effects/Impacts of Earthquakes

1,755 copper engraving depicting Lisbon in ruins and in flames after the 1,755 Libson earthquake, which killed an estimated 60,000 people. A tsunami overwhelms the ships in the harbour.

The effects of earthquakes include, but are not limited to the following:

Shaking and Ground Rupture

Shaking and ground rupture are the main effects created by earthquakes, principally resulting in more or less severe damage to buildings and other rigid structures. The severity of the local effects depends on the complex combination of the earthquake magnitude, the distance from the epicentre, and the local geological and geomorphologic conditions, which may amplify or reduce wave propagation.

Specific local geological, geomorphological, and geostructural features can induce high levels of shaking on the ground surface even from low-intensity earthquakes. This effect is called site or local amplification. It is principally due to the transfer of the seismic motion from hard deep soils to soft superficial soils and to effects of seismic energy focalization owing to typical geometrical setting of the deposits.

Ground rupture is a visible breaking and displacement of the earth's surface along the trace of the fault, which may be of the order of several metres in the case of major earthquakes. Ground rupture is a major risk for large engineering structures such as dams, bridges, and nuclear power stations and requires careful mapping of existing faults to identify any likely to break the ground surface within the life of the structure.

Landslides and Avalanches

Earthquakes, along with severe storms, volcanic activity, coastal wave attack, and wildfires, can produce slope instability leading to landslides, a major geological hazard. Landslide danger may persist while emergency personnel are attempting rescue. Earthquake can cause avalanches of sizable nature.

The term landslides includes all varieties of mass movements of hill slopes and can be defined as the downward and outward movement of slope forming materials comprising of soils, rocks, artificial fills, etc., and their movement by sliding, falling and flowing, either slowly or quickly from one place to another. Landslides can be falls, flows, debris avalanche, creeping, or toppling type.

Fires

Fires of the 1906 San Francisco Earthquake

Earthquakes can cause fires by damaging electrical power or gas lines. In the event of water mains rupturing and a loss of pressure, it may also become difficult to stop the spread of a fire once it has started.

Soil Liquefaction

Soil liquefaction occurs when, because of the shaking, water-saturated granular material (such as sand) temporarily loses its strength and transforms from a solid to a liquid. Soil liquefaction may cause rigid structures, like buildings, and bridges, to tilt or sink into the liquefied deposits. This can be a devastating effect of earthquakes.

Tidal Forces

Research work has shown a robust correlation between small tidally induced forces and non-volcanic tremour activity.

Human Impacts

Damaged infrastructure, one week after the 2007 Peru Earthquake.

Earthquakes may lead to disease, lack of basic necessities, loss of life, higher insurance premiums, general property damage, road and bridge damage, and collapse or destabilization (potentially leading to future collapse) of buildings. Earthquakes can also precede volcanic eruptions, which cause further problems.

Landslides and Mudflows

A landslide is a rapid shift in land mass that is typically associated with periods of heavy rainfall or rapid snowmelt. Landslides tend to worsen the effects of flooding that often accompanies them. In areas that have been burned by forest and brush fires, a lower threshold of precipitation may initiate landslides. While some landslides move slowly and cause damage gradually, others move so rapidly that they can destroy property and take lives suddenly and unexpectedly.

Areas that are generally prone to landslide hazards include:

(a) Existing old landslides.

(b) The bases of steep slopes.

(c) The bases of drainage channels.

(d) Developed hillsides where leach-field septic systems are used.

Debris flows, sometimes referred to as mudslides, mudflows, lahars, or debris avalanches are common types of fast-moving landslides. Flows usually start on steep hillsides as shallow landslides that accelerate to speeds that are typically about 10 miles per hour, but can exceed 35 miles per hour.

The consistency of debris flows range from watery mud to thick, rocky mud that can carry away items such as boulders, trees, and cars. When the flows reach flatter ground, the debris spreads over a broad area. The most destructive types of debris flows are those that accompany volcanic eruptions.

Lahar

Lahar is a type of mudflow or debris flow composed of pyroclastic material, rocky debris, and water. The material flows down from a volcano, typically along a river valley.

The word "Lahar" originated from an Indonesian word that describes volcanic mudflows or debris flows. Lahars have the consistency of concrete: fluid when moving, then solid when stopped.

Lahars can be deadly because of their energy and speed. Large lahars can flow 100 kms/hr and can flow for more than 300 kms, causing catastrophic destruction in their path. The lahars from the Nevado del Ruiz eruption in Colombia in 1985 caused the Armero tragedy, which killed an estimated 23,000 when the city of Armero was buried under 5 metres of mud and debris.

Lahar is caused by melting the snow or glaciers by the lava or a flood caused by a glacier breakout, or heavy rain. Although lahars are typically associated with the effects of volcanic activity, lahars can occur even without any current volcanic activity, as long as the conditions are right to cause the collapse and movement of mud originating from existing volcanic ash deposits. Earthquakes underneath or close to the volcano can shake material loose and cause it to collapse triggering a lahar.

Sinkholes

A sinkhole, also known as a swallow hole, is a natural depression or hole in the earth's surface caused by karst processes, the chemical dissolution of carbonate rocks or suffusion processes. Sinkholes may vary in size from 1 to 600 metres both in diameter and depth, and vary in form from soil-lined bowls to bedrock-edged chasms. They may be formed gradually or suddenly, and are found worldwide.

Formation Mechanisms

Sinkholes near the Dead Sea, formed by dissolution of underground salt by incoming fresh water, as a result of a continuing sea level drop.

A special type of sinkhole – formed by rain water leaking through the pavement and carrying dirt into a ruptured sewer pipe.

The mechanisms of formation involve natural process of erosion or gradual removal of slightly soluble bedrock by percolating water, the collapse of a cave roof, or a lowering of the water table. Sinkholes often form also through the process of suffusion. Thus, for example, groundwater may dissolve the carbonate cement holding the sandstone particles together and then carry away the lax particles, gradually forming a void.

Occasionally a sinkhole may exhibit a visible opening into a cave below. In the case of exceptionally large sinkholes, a stream or river may be visible across its bottom flowing from one side to the other.

Sinkholes are common where the rock below the land surface is limestone or other carbonate rock, salt beds, or rocks that can naturally be dissolved by circulating groundwater. As the rock dissolves, spaces and caverns develop underground. These sinkholes can be dramatic because the surface land usually stays intact until there is not enough support. Then, a sudden collapse of the land surface can occur.

Sinkholes also form from human activity, such as the rare but still occasional collapse of abandoned mines and more commonly, sinkholes occur in urban areas due to water main breaks or sewer collapses when old pipes give way. They can also occur from the over pumping and extraction of groundwater and subsurface fluids. They can also form when natural water-drainage patterns are changed and new water-diversion systems are developed. Some sinkholes form when the land surface is changed, such as when industrial and runoff-storage ponds are created; the substantial weight of the new material can trigger an underground collapse of supporting material, thus, causing a sinkhole.

Volcanic Eruption

Volcano is an opening, or rupture, in a planet's surface, which allows hot lava, volcanic ash, and gases to escape from below the surface. A volcanic eruption is the point in which a volcano is active and releases its eruptions in various forms. Volcanoes are generally found where tectonic plates are diverging or converging.

Classification of Volcanoes

Active

Volcanoes which erupt regularly are called active. There is no real consensus among volcanologists on how to define an "active" volcano. The lifespan of a volcano can vary from months to several million years, making such a distinction sometimes meaningless when compared to the lifespans of humans or even civilizations. For example, many of earth's volcanoes have erupted dozens of times in the past few thousand years but are not currently showing signs of eruption. Given the long lifespan of such volcanoes, they are very active. By human lifespans, however, they are not.

Scientists usually consider a volcano to be erupting or likely to erupt if it is currently erupting, or showing signs of unrest such as unusual earthquake activity or significant new gas emissions. Presently, there are about 500 active volcanoes in the world and around 50 of these erupt each year.

Extinct

Extinct volcanoes are those considered unlikely to erupt again, because the volcano no longer has a lava supply. Whether a volcano is truly extinct is often difficult to determine. Since "super volcano" can have eruptive lifespans sometimes measured in millions of years, a caldera that has not produced an eruption in tens of thousands of years is likely to be considered dormant instead of extinct.

Dormant

It is difficult to distinguish an extinct volcano from a dormant one. Volcanoes are often considered to be extinct if there are no written records of its activity. Nevertheless volcanoes may remain dormant for a long period of time. The volcanoes, those that have erupted in historical times but are now quite are called dormant.

Avalanche

An avalanche is a rapid flow of snow down a slope, from either natural triggers or human activity. Typically occurring in mountainous terrain, an avalanche can mix air and water with the descending snow. Powerful avalanches have the capability to entrain ice, rocks, trees, and other material on the slope. However, avalanches are always initiated in snow, are primarily composed of flowing snow, and are distinct from mudslides, rockslides, rock avalanches, and serac collapses from an icefall.

Formation and Occurrences

Avalanches only occur when the stress on the snow exceeds the shear, ductile, and tensile strength either within the snow pack or at the contact of the base of the snow pack with the ground or rock surface. A number of the forces acting on a snow pack can be readily determined, for example, the weight of the snow is straightforward to calculate; however, it is very difficult to know the shear, ductile, and tensile strength within the snow pack or with the ground.

Common Elements of Avalanche

All avalanches share common elements:

- A trigger which causes the avalanche, a start zone from which the avalanche originates.
- A slide path along which the avalanche flows.
- A run out where the avalanche comes to rest.
- A debris deposit which is the accumulated mass of the avalanched snow once it has come to rest.

Classification

The nature of the failure of the snow pack is used to morphologically classify the avalanche.

(a) **Slab Avalanche:** Slab avalanches are generated when an additional load causes a brittle failure of a slab that is bridging a weak snow layer; this failure is propagated through fracture formation in the bridging slab. Slab avalanches account for around 90 per cent of avalanche-related fatalities, and occur when there is a strong, cohesive layer of snow known as a slab.

(b) **Loose Snow Avalanche:** Loose snow avalanches occur in freshly fallen snow that has a lower density and are most common on steeper terrain. In fresh, loose snow the release is usually at a point and the avalanche then gradually widens down the slope as more snow is entrained, usually forming a teardrop appearance. This is in contrast to a slab avalanche.

(c) **Isothermal Avalanche:** Wet snow avalanche or isothermal avalanche, which occurs when the snow pack becomes saturated by water. When the percentage of water is very high they are known as slush flows and they can move on very shallow slopes.

(d) **Powder Snow Avalanche:** Powder snow avalanches can exceed speeds of 300 km/hr. and masses of 1,00,00,000 tonnes; their flows can travel long distances along flat valley bottoms and even uphill for short distances. A powder snow avalanche is a powder cloud that forms when an avalanche accelerates over an abrupt change in slope, such as a cliff band, causing the snow to mix with air.

Triggers

The following triggers cause avalanches:

- ❖ Avalanches are always caused by an external stress on the snow pack; they are not random or spontaneous events.
- ❖ Natural triggers of avalanches include additional precipitation, radiative and convective heating, rock fall, ice fall, and other sudden impacts; however, even a snow pack held at a constant temperature, pressure, and humidity will evolve over time and develop stresses, often from the downslope creep of the snow pack.

Human triggers of avalanches include skiers, snowmobiles, and controlled explosive work.

Mitigation

Good avalanche safety is a continuous process, including route selection and examination of the snow pack, weather conditions, and human factors.

- ❖ There are several ways to prevent avalanches and lessen their power and destruction.
- ❖ Explosives are used extensively to prevent avalanches, especially at sky resorts where other methods are often impractical. Explosive charges are used to trigger small avalanches before enough snow can build up to cause a large avalanche.
- ❖ Snow fences and light walls can be used to direct the placement of snow. When there is a sufficient density of trees, they can greatly reduce the strength of avalanches. They hold snow in place and when there is an avalanche, the impact of the snow against the trees slows it down.
- ❖ Artificial barriers can be very effective in reducing avalanche damage.
- ❖ One kind of barrier (snow net) uses a net strung between poles that are anchored by guy wires in addition to their foundations.
- ❖ Another type of barrier is a rigid fence-like structure (snow fence) and may be constructed of steel, wood, or pre-stressed concrete.
- ❖ Finally, there are barriers that stop or deflect avalanches with their weight and strength.

Snow Fence

Do's and Dont's during an Avalanche

- ❖ During the winter, don't venture in the mountain without an adult.
- ❖ If you walk in a trail after a snow fall, don't walk in the middle of it, but rather on the side.
- ❖ Avalanches always fall down in the middle of the path; thus, if you are on the side, the risks of being hit by the avalanche are lower.

- ❖ Once you are caught in the avalanche try to swim to the side with the flow of the snow.
- ❖ Try to stabilize yourself. If at all possible grab a tree or bush. Even a large rock will do, although they are sometimes harder to hang onto.
- ❖ If you become covered with snow you should move your head vigorously side-to-side. This will allow an air space to breathe.

2.4 HUMAN EPIDEMICS AND PANDEMICS

Epidemics

An outbreak of a transmittable disease that rapidly spreads through a community can be described as an epidemic and an epidemic whose spread is global is pandemics.

Management of Epidemics

The word 'Epi' means 'in or on' and the word 'Demic' means 'people'. Some of the epidemic diseases are Plague, Japanese Encephalitis, Cholera, Lyme, Bird flu, Swine flu, etc., occurs when new cases of a certain disease, in a given human population, and during a given period, substantially exceed what is "expected", based on recent experience.

Management of Epidemics

- ❖ Preventing panic and confusion among public.
- ❖ Cautioning the affected or to be affected people about Do's and Dont's.
- ❖ Relaying the measures being taken and monitoring them.
- ❖ Identifying the needy spots and focusing attention on them.
- ❖ Assisting the authorities, voluntary organizations, and volunteers in reaching, informing, and assuring the affected ones of the assistance and the measures taken for their relief.
- ❖ To keep the morale of the people high, to create self-confidence in them.
- ❖ To prevent panic and to maintain order by assuring and making available the necessary help readily and quickly.
- ❖ Appealing to the people to come forward to render help in various ways.
- ❖ Appeal made for relief through the columns and the time slots of the media brings in sizeable aid.
- ❖ To keep a watch and report on some anti-social elements who try to take advantage of such situation.
- ❖ Worst sufferers are weaker sections of the society.
- ❖ They are rarely remembered and the media should discuss their plight.

- ❖ Prompt presentation of real state of affairs.
- ❖ Should counteract the damaging, exaggerated and negative reporting and propaganda in foreign media about disaster.

Famine

Widespread malnutrition, starvation, disease and high mortality rates are part of a social and economic crisis common in any country. A famine is a phenomenon in which a large percentage of the population of a region or country are undernourished and death by starvation becomes increasingly common. In spite of the much greater technological and economic resources of the modern world, famine still strikes many parts of the world, mostly in the developing nations. Famine is associated with naturally – occurring crop failure and pestilence and artificially with war and genocide. In the past few decades a more nuanced view focused on the economic and political circumstances leading to modern famine has emerged.

Modern famines have often occurred in nations that, as a whole, were not suffering a shortage of food. Because herding and agriculture allow for greater population, both in numbers and in density, the failure of a harvest or the change in conditions, such as drought, can create a situation where large numbers of people live where the carrying capacity of the land has dropped radically. Famine is then associated primarily with subsistence agriculture, that is where most farming is aimed at producing enough food energy to survive.

Famine has a strong impact on demographics. For example, it has been observed that periods of extensive famine can lead to a reduction in the number of reported female children in some cultures. There are a number of ongoing famines caused by war or deliberate political intervention.

Today, nitrogen fertilisers, new natural pesticides, desert farming, and other new agricultural technologies are being used as weapons against famine. They increase crop yields by two, three, or more times. Developed nations share these technologies with developing nations with a famine problem. However, since modern famine is usually the result of war and distribution problems, it is questionable how much relevance or impact new agricultural technologies would have on this problem.

Exotic Animal Disease

Animal disease epidemics are harmful to the communities. The increased mobility and globalization are opening up movements, which are no longer safe from exotic animal diseases. In India, the threat from these types of animal diseases are low because of the result of careful management. The warnings and campaigns made from time-to-time, alert people and encourage them to follow precautions. If a fatal disease like foot and mouth disease spreads in India, the situation would result in a big disaster, resulting in threatening our entire economy, even endangering public health. The following are the few exotic animal diseases:

(a) Foot and Mouth Disease.

(b) Avian Influenza.

(c) Newcastle Disease.

(d) Classical Swine Fever.

(e) African Swine Fever.

(f) Swine Vesicular Disease.

The mitigation plan should cover arrangements for dealing with outbreaks and incidents of exotic disease of animals, including Foot and Mouth Disease, Avian Influenza, and Newcastle Disease, which should have two plans, Emergency preparedness plan and Response plan. The emergency preparedness plan envisages how we are prepared for the operational response and response plan includes outlining systems, structures, roles and responsibilities, implementation, etc.

Insect and Vermin Plagues

Insect/vermin complaints involve issues with bedbugs, cockroaches, fleas, mosquitoes, mice, and rats. These species can inhabit human dwellings (except mosquitoes), and since they are potential carriers of human diseases they are regulated by the Health Authority when inhabiting rental property. Although bedbugs are not known to carry any human diseases the Health Authority will investigate complaints about these insects, and issue orders for treatment if necessary. Spiders, ants, termites, sow bugs, and other insects which do not carry human disease are not a health concern, and are not regulated by the Health Authority. Lice are a personal hygiene issue which cannot be addressed by the Health District; however, our public health nurses can provide you with information regarding head lice prevention and treatment.

Types of Insect/Vermin Complaints

(a) Bedbugs.

(b) Cockroaches.

(c) Fleas.

(d) Mosquitoes.

(e) Rats and Mice.

Bedbugs

Bedbugs are small (about ¼ inch), brown, oval-shaped, flat insects which inhabit human dwellings. They hide during the day, and feed on people at night while they are sleeping. Their bite produces white welts which may itch severely. The bugs can be crushed by a sleeper during the night and leave bloodstains on the sheets. If these signs are present the first place to look for the bugs is on the mattress, particularly in the seams.

Bedbugs will hide in every place they can find, behind light switch covers, in electronics, toys, furniture, clothing, picture frames, and knick-knacks. If there is a severe infestation bedbugs may be seen during the day on the walls or ceiling.

Infested items which cannot be treated must be discarded, or sealed in bags and stored 12-18 months until the bedbugs die. Mattresses can be treated with an appropriate pesticide, and then sealed in a plastic mattress bag. Bedbugs can be effectively eliminated from clothing, curtains, and bed linens by washing them in hot water and/or drying for 15-30 minutes on the hot setting. Without treatment bedbugs will spread to every part of a home, so begin treatment as soon as they are discovered.

Cockroaches

As with bedbugs, treatment of cockroach infestations is best left to a professional exterminator. Chemical control measures will be ineffective if poor housekeeping is an issue. Food and garbage in the household should be strictly managed so that vermin such as cockroaches and mice do not have access to it. Floors, food preparation surfaces, cabinets, and appliances should be kept scrupulously clean at all times.

If cockroaches are found in the home control measures should be implemented as soon as possible. In an apartment building surrounding units should be checked for cockroaches, and treated if necessary.

Fleas

Fleas can transmit human diseases, and also tapeworms. A flea bite may produce a small, hard, red, slightly-raised itching spot with a single puncture point in the centre. Flea control is best achieved with a combination of control measures including sanitation, pet treatment, and treatment of the premises (indoors and outdoors). Many pesticides are available on the market for treatment of fleas on pets and the premises. Treat pets and the premises at the same time for successful flea control.

Mosquitoes

Mosquitoes are the biggest carriers of disease and they attack humans drastically. They need to be controlled vigorously and continuously. The eradication of most diseases depends upon the effectiveness of the mosquito control activities.

Rats and Mice

Rats and mice are natural inhabitants of the outdoor environment, and are not ordinarily considered a health nuisance issue as long as they remain outdoors. The Health Authorities cannot control animals in the outdoor environment, but does regulate the storage and disposal of garbage, which can attract rats and other vermin. Rats and mice in the home create a health nuisance issue, and should not be allowed to remain. Setting traps or poisoned bait are the usual control measures, but these will be ineffective if these rodents are not kept out of the building. Holes or other entry points need to be found, and blocked.

Calamities of Extra-terrestrial Origin

These are disasters posed by extra-terrestrial or by a comet on the earth. Although they are a very low risk, could cause major damage to the earth. The impact could be a major regional disaster to a worldwide catastrophe. There are many impacts of this disaster in the world over, including India.

2.5 TECHNOLOGICAL HAZARDS

Power Outage

An interruption in the normal sources of power supply or generation can be called as power outage. Power outages can be short-term and long-term. Short-term outages are more in the order of occurrence and are manageable. Preparedness of the communities for short-term power outages are good and long-term are unhealthy. The excessive power outages result in loss of business, medical facilities, and even lead to civil disturbances.

Fire

Fire is the most common human caused hazard and can be accidental or intentional. Strong fire standards and firefighting measures are used, could result in large-scale human and economic loss. Bush fires, forest fires, mine fires are generally triggered by lightning and also by human negligence and arson. Fire can spread to thousands of kilometres and can result in fire storms.

Hazardous and Toxic Materials

The potential disaster on transportation of hazardous and toxic materials is very high. These can happen upon use and movement of hazardous materials.

Structural Collapse

These are the results of engineering failures and can be design fault or usage of substandard construction materials or a combination of both. A bridge collapse or a dam burst due to leak or a part of the building collapse, are all examples of structural collapse.

Transportation

Transportation disasters could be in the form of mishaps like train, bus disasters or ship wreckage, etc. An important largest mishap could be the Titanic disaster on account of ship collusion with ice berg, killing humans.

Aviation

An aviation accident is defined as an occurrence in the operation of an aircraft, which takes place from the time of boarding, transit time and the time of disembarking, in which a person is seriously injures, aircraft is damaged, missing or is inaccessible. The category of vehicles ranges from helicopter, an airliner, or a space shuttle.

Space Disasters

Space disasters occur during the training, operation of space vehicles. These disasters have killed astronauts, cosmonauts, and civilians. These disasters are the results of malfunctions on ground, during launch, during flight or in the orbit and could result on the deficiencies of technology and natural forces. Unmanned space shuttles could bring in large debris to the earth.

Climate Change

In the history of earth, climate and climate change are common. Today, we are all worried about climate changes taking place too fast and rapid and because it happens rapidly there is larger possibility for dangerous situations. If the earth warms up rapidly, this could result in sea levels rising, due to melting of polar ice. This will result in submerging part of the land into the sea. The changes in atmospheric conditions affect the climate patterns drastically. Such a change in weather pattern will affect agriculture in a big way, as agriculture is depended upon a certain weather pattern.

In addition shifting patterns in weather conditions would result in greater incidents of natural hazards. For example, a location normally dry receives torrential rains, will result in floods.

Global warming generally happens on account of increase in the emission of greenhouse gases.

Some of the indications of global warming is as under:

(a) Glaciers around the world are retreating from Africa.

(b) Severe storm intensity appears to be increasing in Atlantic Ocean.

(c) Carbon dioxide levels are much higher than they are ever before and are rising.

(d) Migratory birds and their breeding patterns have shifted drastically.

(e) Lakes are freezing later and thawing earlier.

(f) Average annual temperatures showing rising tendency.

Radiation Disasters

Any form of energy propagated as waves, rays, or any other energetic particles which can travel through air or any other material medium. The radio active materials contain atoms which are very unstable and give off its excess energy until it becomes stable. The energy is in the form of radiation. Radioactivity is defined as the process by which an atom changes from an unstable state to a stable state by transferring radiation.

The natural radiation exposures from the sun, electronic equipments, soil, rocks, X-ray machines, etc., are sustainable and are normal. The radioactive materials are toxic and harmful and emit radioactive energy harmful to the society.

Solar Flare

Solar flare is a phenomena where the sun suddenly releases more than normal amount of radiation, which is harmful. These are expected to cause damages to the communication systems.

2.6 QUESTIONS

1. Write a short note on the Geological Disasters.
2. Explain the Hydrological Disasters.
3. What are the Meteorological Disasters?
4. Describe the different types of floods and how to mitigate them.
5. What are the types of Avalanches?
6. What is Lahar.
7. Define solar flare.
8. Write a short note on 2004 tsunami.
9. Explain the most destructive earthquake in India.

3 Man-made Disasters

Learning Objectives

- ☞ To know the different types of man-made disasters and how to mitigate them.
- ☞ To explore the possible man made disasters and its threats
- ☞ To educate people to mitigate manmade disasters
- ☞ To develop an attitude to protect the nation
- ☞ To through light on the evil minded behavior of men on earth
- ☞ To facilitate the future generations with adequate power

Structure

3.1 Man-made Disasters and Mitigation Efforts

3.2 Bomb Threat Management

3.3 India and Power Situation

3.4 Forecasting and Casualty Management

3.5 Questions

3.1 MAN-MADE DISASTERS AND MITIGATION EFFORTS

A man-made hazard is a threat having an element of human negligence, intent or an error. This can also be caused by the failure of a human made system. These could be the result of a combination of these factors also.

The man-made disasters can be in the following forms:

Terrorism

Terrorism is an unlawful act of violence. It is also a use of violence or force against people and property for purposes of intimidation, caution, or ransom. The purpose of terrorism is to create fear among people, expose the weakness of the government, and also to achieve political and religious benefits.

Terrorists focus their activities to create mass causalities, disruption of vital services, destabilizing the economy, creation of mass panic, etc., and they involve brutal acts of mass murder against innocent men, women, and children. They target military facilities, government facilities, large cities, international airports, public gatherings, and high-profile landmarks. They create fear through explosives, chemical, biological, and nuclear weapons.

The exploitation of the information technology systems by the terrorist for spread of terrorism is seen increasing. Terrorist groups are learning to use IT for decision making and other organizational destructive purposes. They are using the technology as an offensive weapon to destroy or disrupt. Motivations for cyber attack can be vandalism, anger (insiders), political, curiosity, notoriety, malice, personal gain, potential cyber security risks, hosts running unnecessary services, outdated code, information leakage, misconfigured firewall, weak passwords, inadequate logging, and detecting.

Mumbai Taj Hotel Attack – 26/11/2008

Trade Center Attack – 11/09/2001

Types of Terrorism

Domestic terrorism involves groups whose terrorist activities are directed at elements of our government without foreign involvement. International terrorism involves groups whose terrorist activities are foreign-based and, or directed by countries or groups outside the country.

Different forms of terrorism are:

Cyber Terrorism

"It is a criminal activity committed on the internet. This is a broad term that describes everything from electronic cracking to denial of service attacks that cause electronic commerce sites to lose money."

Cyber means using the computer and the internet to hack system used by others and eventually destroying their systems and data. Latest example can be the hacking of the CBI website by the Pakistani cyber terrorists.

There are four types of cyber crimes.

(a) Cyber Crimes Against Persons: Cyber crimes committed against persons include various crimes like transmission of child pornography, harassment of any one with the use of a computer and cyber stalking. The trafficking, distribution, posting, and dissemination of obscene material including pornography, indecent exposure, and child pornography constitute the most important cyber crimes known today. These threaten to undermine the growth of younger generation and also leave irreparable scars on the minds of the younger generation, if not controlled. Some forms of cyber crimes are:

(i) E-mail Spoofing: A spoofed e-mail is one in which e-mail header is forged so that mail appears to originate from one source but actually has been sent from another source.

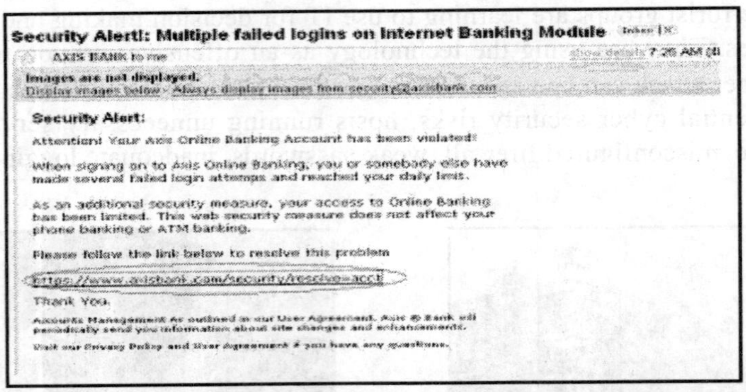

(ii) Spamming: Spamming means sending multiple copies of unsolicited mails or mass e-mails such as chain letters.

(iii) ***Cyber Defamation:*** This occurs when defamation takes place with the help of computers and/or the internet. For example, someone publishes defamatory matter about someone else on a website or sends e-mails containing defamatory information.

(iv) ***Harassment and Cyber Stalking:*** Cyber stalking means following the moves of an individual's activity over internet. It can be done with the help of many protocols available such as e-mails, chat rooms, and user net groups.

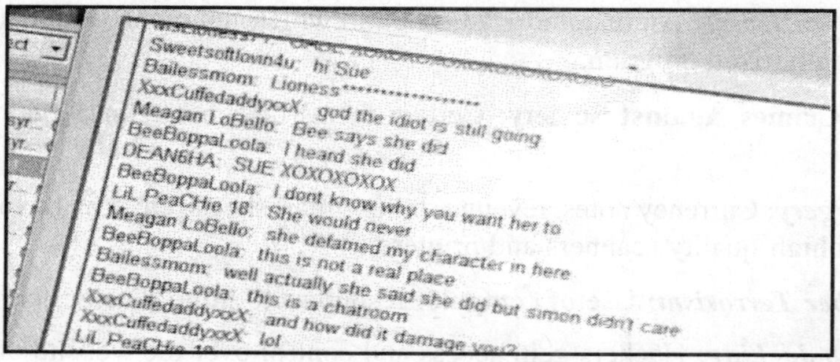

(b) Cyber Crimes Against Property: The second category of cyber crime is against all forms of property and they include unauthorized computer trespassing through cyber space, computer vandalism, and transmission of harmful programs and unauthorized possession of computerized information. Some of the important crimes are:

(i) ***Credit Card Fraud:*** Credit card fraud is a wide-ranging term for theft and fraud committed using a credit card or any similar payment mechanism as a fraudulent source of funds in a transaction. The purpose may be to obtain goods without paying, or to obtain unauthorized funds from an account.

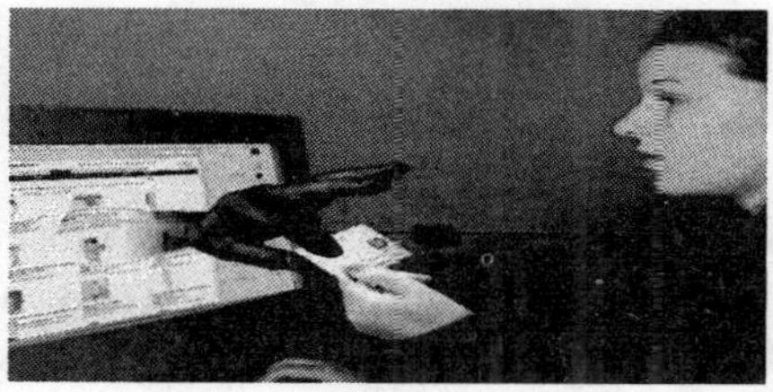

(ii) ***Intellectual Property Crimes:*** These include software piracy and illegal copying of programs, distribution of copies of software, and theft of computer source code.

(iii) ***Internet Time Theft:*** The usage of the internet hours by an unauthorized person which is actually paid by another person.

(c) Cyber Crimes Against Government and Organization: The third category of cyber crimes is cyber crimes against the government and this is the most distinct form of crime in this category. The growth of internet has shown that the medium of cyber space is being used by individuals and groups to threaten international governments as also to terrorize the citizens of a country. This crime manifests itself into cyber terrorism when an individual cracks into a government of military website, for the purpose of perpetuating terror. Some forms of cyber crimes against the government are:

(i) ***Virus Attack:*** A computer virus is a computer program that can infect other computer programs by modifying them in such a way as to including but not limited to hardware and software programs that do not have a reproductive ability.

(ii) ***E-mail Bombing:*** Sending large numbers of mails to the individual or company

(iii) ***Logic Bomb:*** It is an event-dependent program, as soon as the designated event occurs, it crashes the computer, release a virus or any other harmful possibilities.

(iv) ***Trojan Horse:*** An unauthorized program which functions from inside what seems to be an authorized program.

(d) **Cyber Crimes Against Society:** Certain forms of cyber crimes against the society are as under:

(i) ***Forgery:*** Currency notes, revenue stamps, marksheets, etc., can be forged using computers and high-quality scanners and printers.

(ii) ***Cyber Terrorism:*** Use of computer resources to intimidate or coerce others.

(iii) ***Web Jacking:*** Hackers gain access and control over the website of another, and change the content of website for fulfilling political objective or for money.

NBC – Nuclear Biological and Chemical Threats

Nuclear: Biological and chemical sources hazards are present in industrial accidents, war, and terrorism. The world faces the maximum threat from these three popular areas. The Sarin Gas Chemical War in Japan in 1990s and the use of Anthrax in postal covers in 2001, are the deadly examples. The scientists believe that the major nuclear threat could be from a dirty bomb rather than a mega nuclear warhead.

No matter whatever happens, the best strategy would be to seek safe shelter and do anything and everything one can, to reduce exposure.

Nuclear Terrorism

Usage of nuclear weapons by the terrorists would be the most dangerous of all forms of terrorism. It is entirely different from other conventional methods. There will be mass destruction and death, covering wide area of land. Post-disaster could be even disastrous.

There will be large-scale contamination, radiation, etc., posing large-scale health hazards, loss of food crops, loss of land permanently for agriculture, widespread epidemics, etc.

Some forms of nuclear terrorism can be by spreading of radioactive materials through ventilation system or explosion, disabled nuclear reactor cooling system, and causing leakage of radioactive materials, or exploding a nuclear weapon.

The nuclear threats can be spread by direct electromagnetic radiation, nuclear catastrophe, or by dirty bomb detonation.

Experts believe that owning and using nuclear weapons by terrorists are not likely to happen as the system is not easy and the terrorists are not clear about the usage and handling.

(a) **Nuclear:** A nuclear weapon is an explosive device that derives its destructive force from nuclear reactions.

(b) **Threats:** A nuclear blast is an explosion with intense light and heat.

(c) Damaging pressure wave and widespread radioactive material that can contaminate the air, water, and ground surfaces for miles around.

Weapon

Effect

Measures

If there is advanced warning of an attack	If there is no warning
◆ Take cover immediately, as far below ground as possible	◆ Quickly assess the situation ◆ Go inside a building to limit the amount of radioactive material you are exposed to ◆ Shielding ◆ Distance

Biological Terrorism

Biological terrorism can be by use of biological weapons by the terrorists, using infectious biological agents like toxins, biological microbes, to produce illness or death of people, plants, and animals. Terrorists can disperse biological agents as aerosols or airborne particles and release microbes or their toxins to produce illness, death, and terror. The paths of infection can also be contaminated water, food, air, packages, microbes like bacteria, viruses, and toxins.

Biological agents are found in nature and most of them are contagious and their routes of exposure are through inhalation, absorption, and ingestion. Some biological agents are fast and some are very slow to show symptoms. It is also possible that some biological attack takes place and goes unnoticed for sometime. One factor which counters the effect of biological agents is the nature which reduces the impact through heat, light, and other environmental factors.

Biological agents are used only to terrorize an unprotected population and not used against countries even in wars, fearing retaliation, and battlefield contamination.

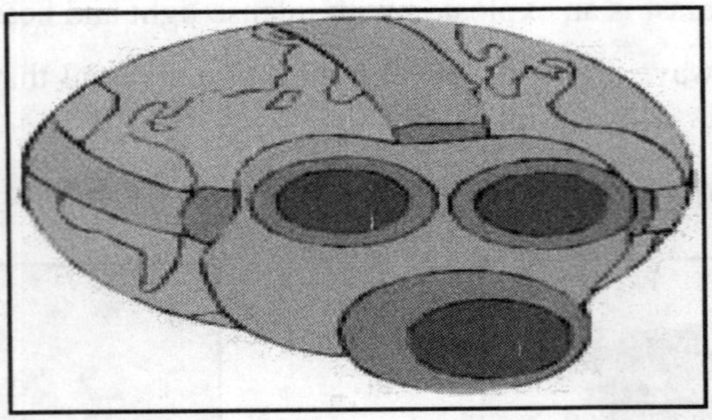

Types of Agents

Category A

- ❖ Agents that can be easily transmitted and disseminated, may cause public panic.
- ❖ Agents that require special action for public health preparedness.

Few examples are anthrax, smallpox, botulinum toxin, bubonic plague, viral fevers, etc.

Category B

- ❖ Agents are moderately easy to disseminate and have low mortality rates.

Category C

- ❖ Easy to produce and disseminate, or may possess high mortality or a major health impact.

Chemical Agents

The ingredients used to produce chemical weapons are found in common products and petroleum products. Terrorists use these materials to produce lethal weapons. Chemical agents kill or incapacitate people, destroy livestock or ravage crops. Some agents are odourless and tasteless and they can have an immediate or a delayed effect.

There are several categories of chemical weapons:

(a) *Riot control agents* cause respiratory distress, tearing, and are designed to incapacitated than killing but will have massive pain. Some of them are tear gas, capsicum, or pepper spray.

(b) *Choking agents* attack the lungs and create breathlessness and suffocation resulting in death. Some of the important agents are chlorine and phosgene.

(c) *Blood agents* are absorbed into the blood stream and reduce the oxygen content and deprive the blood cells of oxygen. This will result in unconsciousness and death and the body becomes bluish. Hydrogen cyanide and potassium cyanide are few examples.

(d) *Blister agents* cause burns, blisters, and other tissue damages and gets spread through liquid or vapour contact on the exposed skin. Some forms of blister agents are mustard, chilly, lewsite, etc.

(e) *Nerve agents* attack the central nerve system of the body and they act most quickly upon exposure. Affected persons suffer from running nose, breathlessness, and weakness. The most important form of nerve agent is the Sarin.

Preparing for Terrorism

The governments and people at large are worried and fed up of watching and hearing terrorist attacks. Terrorists are killing innocent people for reasons best known to them and are striking regularly. What could be done to dissuade the terrorists from acting in such a barbaric manner remains a question. Some measures which could suffice terrorism are:

(a) Making the neighbour countries terrorist free.

(b) Issue of ID cards.

(c) Employment to all.

(d) Making laws more stringent.

(e) Ban on sale of materials used for bomb making.

(f) Reduce poverty.

(g) Reduce gap among haves and have nots.

(h) Use media for better messages of national integration.

(i) Create transparency.

All these measures could help reduce terrorism.

Do's and Dont's

(a) Be aware of your surroundings.

(b) Report to the police of unusual behaviour.

(c) Suspicious packages, and strange devices.

(d) Leave an area if it does not seem right.

(e) Be aware of exits – plan to get out!

(f) Learn first aid and get a first aid kit.

(g) Be familiar with fire extinguishers.

During Bomb Threat

(a) Get as much information as possible.

(b) Notify the police and building management.

(c) Do not touch any suspicious packages.

(d) Clear the area: stay away from glass, windows, and door.

(e) Do not block exits, sidewalks, or streets.

Suspicious Packages and Letters

(a) Unexpected from someone unfamiliar

(b) No return address on it

(c) Marked with "personal" or "confidential"

(d) Strange odours or stains

(e) Unusual weight, irregular or oddly shaped

(f) Inappropriate or unusual labelling

What to Do if There is an Explosion

(a) Leave the area/building

(b) If there is a fire:

- ❖ Stay low
- ❖ Exit quickly
- ❖ Cover your nose and mouth

(c) If trapped:

- ❖ Tap on a pipe
- ❖ Use a whistle if available

IEDs and Bomb Threat Management

With the current growth in economic activity and global challenges, the need for a good security system is relevant, as most organizations focus on security. Bomb threat has assumed importance as most terrorist outfits now rely on bombs to create panic, death and injury.

A bomb or an IED, means improvised explosive devices. A device placed or fabricated in an improvised manner incorporating destructive, lethal, noxious, pyrotechnic, or incendiary chemicals and designed to destroy, incapacitate, harass, or distract. It may incorporate military stores, but is normally devised from non-military components. Bombs can be made to look like anything, from a toy to a pipe piece and can be delivered to their targets in many ways. Following are the latest bombing techniques:

(a) Suicide bomb.

(b) Roadside bomb.

(c) Pipe bomb.

(d) Improvised munitions.

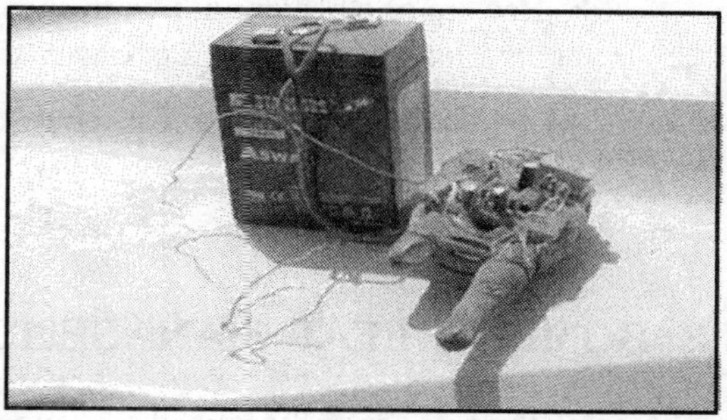

Methods used into Detonate IEDs:

(a) Command detonated devices.

(b) Hard wired (electrical wires between devices and/or leading away from the bomb).

(c) Remote controlled (battery powered doorbell devices (Sega brand), pagers, cellphones as senders and receiving units).

(d) Tall buildings or line of sight observation points will be nearby. Many controllers require a direct line of sight to activate the receiver and detonate.

Materials currently being used for IEDs are 155 rounds, anti-tank mines, diesel fuel in cans, mogas in cans, rockets, mortar rounds, etc., and basically, if it can explode, it's being used.

Forms of IEDs

(a) Black plastic garbage bags (with 130 mm artillery rounds wired in series).

(b) A bus (with a grenade attached to the fuel tank; failed).

(c) Milk cartons, pepsi cans, cigarette cartons (with plastique or C4).

(d) Burlap bags (again using artillery rounds).

(e) A pothole in the road filled in with dirt and an explosive charge.

(f) Refrigerator compressor filled with high explosives and rewelded.

(g) MRE bag (bomb platform; common item; easily disguised).

(h) Cars, trucks, vans (older models, worn so as not to draw attention).

❖ Beware of a beater with worn shocks and springs; overloaded, trash on seats, good tyres on a junk car. This is a one-way trip, driver wants no flats.

(i) Pipe bombs (some of the most renowned IED specialists in EOD have fallen victim to low yield pipe bombs).

(j) Dog carcasses filled with explosives.

3.2 BOMB THREAT MANAGEMENT

A bomb threat is generally defined as a verbal or written threat to detonate an explosive or incendiary device to cause property damage or injuries, whether or not such a device actually exists. Typically delivered by phone or other telecommunication means. The purpose of the bomb threat is to create panic, media attention, to show their power, and to minimize loss.

Guidelines

In the event of a bomb threat, the following guidelines may be followed.

(a) Contact the police, fire department, or other local governmental agencies to determine whether any has a bomb disposal unit.

(b) Establish strict procedures for control and inspection of packages and material entering critical areas.

(c) Inspect the building to determine which areas explosives are likely to be concealed.

(d) Provide adequate protection for classified documents, proprietary information, and other records essential to the operation of the business.

(e) Every telephone operator or receptionist should be trained to respond calmly to a bomb threat call.

(f) Organize and train an evacuation unit. The organization and training of this unit should be coordinated with other tenants of the building.

(g) Consider arranging for temporary relocation of facilities in the event of an explosion and the building being determined to be unsafe.

Handling a Bomb Threat

For Tele Threats

❖ Keep the caller on the line and attempt to get as much information as possible. Ask for the message to be repeated to confirm it. If possible, record the message.

❖ If the caller does not indicate the location of the bomb or the time of possible detonation, ask for this information.

❖ Inform the caller that the building is occupied and the detonation of a bomb could result in death or serious injury to many innocent people.

- ❖ Pay particular attention to background noises which may give a clue as to the location of the caller.
- ❖ Listen closely to the voice (male or female), voice quality (calm or excited), accents, and speech impediments. Immediately after the caller hangs up, report the call to the person designated by management to receive such information. Law enforcement personnel may want to talk first hand with the person who received the call.
- ❖ Report the threat immediately to the appropriate agencies, such as the police or fire department.

Written Threats

- ❖ Save all materials, including envelopes or containers. Once the message is recognized as a bomb threat, further unnecessary handling should be avoided.
- ❖ Every possible effort must be made to retain evidence, such as fingerprints, handwriting or typewriting, paper, and postal marks, which are essential to trace the threat and identifying the writer.

Accidents in Coal Mines

It is an accident which occurs during the mining process and can happen due to various causes, collapsing of mine stones, leak of coal gas, poisonous gases, explosive natural gases, collapsing of mine stoops, seismicity, flooding, and malfunctioning of mining equipments.

With the large-scale exploitation of coal from mines, the safety issues are becoming prominent.

Methods of Mining

(a) Modern Surface Mining

- ❖ Area Mining
- ❖ Contour Mining
- ❖ Mountaintop Removal Mining
- ❖ Room and Pillar Mining

(b) Underground Mining

Major Coal Mines in India

(a) Coal India Limited (CIL)
(b) Eastern Coalfields Limited (ECL)
(c) Bharat Coking Coal Limited (BCCL)
(d) Central Coalfields Limited (CCL)
(e) Northern Coalfields Limited (NCL)
(f) Western Coalfields Limited (WCL)
(g) South Eastern Coalfields Limited (SECL)
(h) Mahanadi Coalfields Limited (MCL)
(i) North Eastern Collieries (NEC)

Mining Accidents

A mining accident is an accident that occurs in the process of mining minerals. Thousands of miners die from mining accidents each year, especially in the process of coal mining and hard rock mining. Most of the deaths today occur in developing countries, especially China, and rural parts of developed countries.

There are various factors which can cause mining accidents and can cause disaster in the mines. Drilling and blasting, heavy machinery, over burden handling, etc., can trigger accidents. The accidents can occur on the surface and underground and can take the following forms:

(a) Underground mining hazards include suffocation, gas poisoning, roof collapse, and gas explosions.

(b) Firedamp explosions can trigger much more dangerous coal dust explosions, which can engulf an entire pit.

(c) Roof fall, inundation, gas explosion, and gas poisoning are also likely.

Damps in Coal Mining

Build up of hazardous gas in the mines are known as damps, which has originated from the German word 'Dampf', meaning vapour or steam.

(a) **Black Damp:** A mixture of carbon dioxide and nitrogen in a mine can cause suffocation, and is formed as a result of corrosion in enclosed spaces so removing oxygen from the atmosphere.

(b) **After Damp:** Similar to black damp, an after damp consists of carbon monoxide, carbon dioxide, and nitrogen, and forms after a mine explosion.

(c) **Fire Damp:** Consists of mostly methane, a flammable gas.

(d) **Stink Damp:** So named for the rotten egg smell of the hydrogen sulphide gas, a stink damp can explode.

(e) **White Damp:** Air containing carbon monoxide which is toxic, even at low concentrations.

Recent Coal Mine Disaster

(a) BEIJING – An electrical fire at an illegal coal mine in central China has left 25 people dead, the latest fatal accident to rock the country's mining industry. (November 2009)

(b) XIANGNING, China – Workers reported underground water leaks days before a flood coursed through a coal mine in northern China, where 153 people remained trapped in potentially one of the country's worst mining disasters, a worker, and state media said.

(c) There has been no communication with the miners since the flood tore through the Wangjialing mine in Shanxi province Sunday afternoon.

(d) Some 1,000 workers are tunneling around the clock to drain away water but appear days away from making any rescue.

(e) World's greatest and largest rescue of miners in Chile in 2010.

Preparedness Plans

(a) Plan operations and systems to eliminate/reduce mining hazards.

(b) Implement statutes.

(c) To improve working conditions by technology upgradation.

(d) Dedicated provision of material and money for safety.

(e) Deploy safety personnel wholly for safety.

(f) Implement worker participation in safety management.

(g) Draw and implement safety plans.

(h) Establish internal safety organization.

(i) Multi-level monitoring of safety.

(j) Senior management to inculcate safety awareness and practice it in their functioning.

(k) Training and retraining to promote safety-oriented skills.

(l) Strive to improve the living conditions and health of employees.

(m) Continuous monitoring through various safety committees.

Technologies Adopted to Reduce Accidents

a. Design of system of support of roof in the development workings in underground mines by scientific support systems based on Rock Mass Rating (RMR) studies.

b. Increased use of Roof Bolting/Roof Stitching methods of support using steel roof bolts/ steel wire ropes with quick setting cement grout to arrest bed separation at early stages to impede deterioration of roof.

c. Introduction of modern drills like mechanized drilling machine to avoid exposure of support personnel to unsupported roof while drilling for roof bolting and greater use of quick-setting cement/resin capsules grouted roof bolts for support in development workings in underground mines.

d. Reduced exposure of workers to mining hazards by mechanization of loading operations by increasing use of SDLs and LHDs in below ground mines, Powered Support Long Wall (PSLW) system of mining, continuous miner technology, etc., are being progressively adopted in suitable areas.

e. Regular monitoring of mine environment by handheld gas detectors/alarms and flame safety lamps for detecting inflammable and noxious gases. Besides, for early detection of situations that could lead to an outbreak of fire or an explosion, highly capital-intensive computerized continuous mine environmental tele-monitoring system (ETMS) have been installed and are in operation in thirteen identified underground mines. Introduction of surface miner, an eco-friendly technology to reduce hazardous operation like drilling, blasting, and crushing wherever applicable.

Crisis in Power Sector

Disaster is defined as a sudden event, which disrupts normal life, including that of power supply. The disaster affect the power supply immediately as they destroy power lines, posts, etc., and result in sudden stoppage of power. Communities have experienced various disasters like cyclone, hurricane, earthquake, floods, etc., during the history of mankind.

Electrical power is the lifeline of any economy and any disruption in the power supply causes economic loss as well as hardships to the human beings and as such a disaster in the power front would impact heavily and needs special attention.

The generation, transmission, and distribution of electricity is focused on large infrastructures, which gets affected in the event of a disaster. It is therefore important to evolve a disaster management strategy and plan to restore generation, transmission, and distribution of electricity as quickly as possible.

Natural calamities like earthquakes, floods, storms, and cyclones are all contributors to a disaster in power sector. The devastating impact of these natural disasters damage the infrastructures of power sector or even destroy them.

Terrorists attacks on power stations, generation units, and installations are another factor. Similarly, fires at electrical installations are another cause of power sector disasters. The most common cause of power sector fires is known to be electrical short circuits and power triggered inflammable materials. Human negligence is another major factor, not following the safety measures, not taking precautions, and not aware of the systems are major examples.

3.3 INDIA AND POWER SITUATION

Power development is the key to the economic development. India is presently positioned as the 11th largest manufacturers of electrical energy. It is also the world's sixth largest electrical energy user. Power generating capacity in 1947 was 1,362 MW and as on January 31, 2008 it was 1,41,079.84 MW (100 times) and plan for 2011 is 1,90,000 MW.

The demand supply gap in India is widening and there is need to augment further generation.

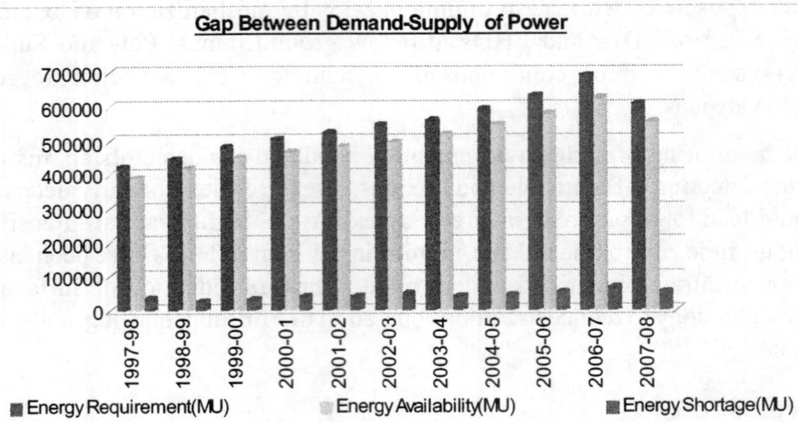

Power Crisis

Power crisis is mainly the gap between Demand and Supply of power and to manage the gap between demand and supply by "load management", which means, power cuts (Outages) to the industries, commercial shops, and domestic usage, etc.

Loss of revenue to the government, loss of production, and loss of capital investment on power generating equipments is the main impact of power crisis. Further power crisis create negative impact on economic growth, unemployment, reduce job opportunity, tax revenue and reduce foreign investment, etc.

Power crisis is caused by slippages in capacity addition targets, high levels of transmission, and distribution (T&D) losses, poor maintenance practices throughout the country resulting in generation as well as transmission outages and power thefts and corruption.

How to Manage Power Crisis

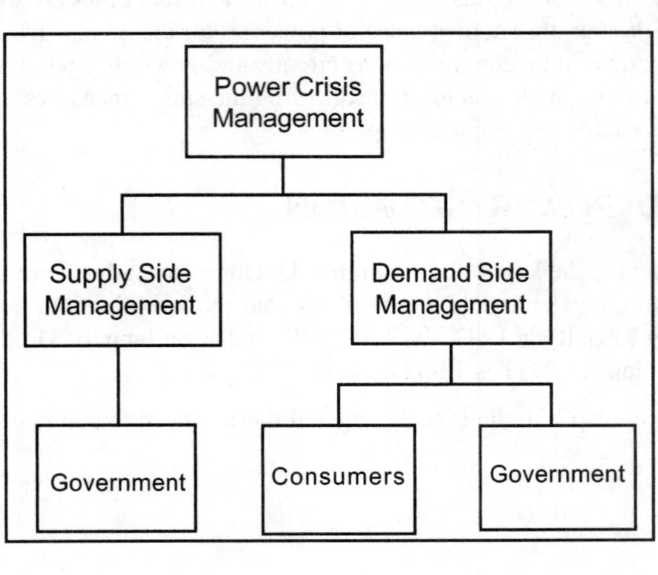

Supply Side Management

- Government should increase the generation capacity.
- Government should encourage private sector to invest.
- In addition to that government should follow some strategies:
  - (i) ***Power Generation Strategy*** towards low cost generation, technology upgradation, and utilization of nonconventional energy sources (Wind, Solar, etc.)
  - (ii) ***Transmission Strategy*** towards optimization of transmission cost.
  - (iii) ***Distribution Strategy*** towards loss reduction, theft control, etc.

Supply Side Management Government Role

- Regulation strategy for consumer interests and making the sector commercially viable.
- Financing strategy is to generate resources for required growth of the power sector.
- Conservation strategy to optimize the utilization of electricity with focus on demand side management,
- Communication strategy for political consensus with media support to enhance the general public awareness.

Demand Side Management

- Management of consumption (demand) at user end.
- Educating consumers to use energy efficient equipment.
- By conducting energy audits to industries.
- Saving of one unit (Kwh) = generation of two units.

Power crisis is a continuing problem, it can be overcome by effective supply side and demand side management only.

Possible Solutions to Power Crisis

Frankly, there are no fast solutions to power crisis. One and the only real solution is to build more power stations and match the demand. Load shedding is not a solution and is practised only when the system is heavily strained.

Short-term solutions could be private participation, solar power, energy saving equipments, and generators. Long-term solutions include, creating facilities, better management, more transparency, proper maintenance of power stations, ensuring supply of raw materials at power stations, retaining skilled employees, and timely technological upgradation.

Forest Fire

The worst hazard in a forest is the forest fire, which destroys a forest area, destroys the wild animals and populace in the area. Forest fires are generally ignited by lightning, but can also trigger from a human negligence or arson and can result in loss of hundreds of acres of forest. Forest fires also known as wild fires, bush fires, etc., are common in United States, Africa, Australia, and Canada, where the climate is on both extremes, allowing vegetation and fire. The forest fires are caused by the drying leafs and branches which becomes highly inflammable and can be ignited by even a small spark. Forest fires not only pose loss of forest wealth but also create ecological and environmental problems, affecting the biodiversity of the region. Forest fires are caused by intentional causes by villagers to scare away animals, tribal in search of animals, miscreants for taking revenge on officials, and illicit traders.

Forest fires result in loss of valuable forest wealth, degradation water catchment areas, loss of biodiversity, animals, loss of wild life habitat, soil erosion, changes in micro climates, global warming, ozone layer depletion, etc.

Forest fires can be of two types: *(a) Surface fire,* primarily starts burning the surface and spreading across the surface of the forest land, engulfed with fire, *(b) Crown fire,* in which the heads and crown of trees and herbs burn. The crown fire is particularly very dangerous in a coniferous forest because the logs burn furiously. The crown fire spreads fast when the fire starts downhill and is less when the fire starts uphill.

Mitigation of Forest Fires

Forest fires are seasonal in nature of occurrence and can be prevented by adequate precautions. They start in dry seasons. It is advisable to burn the litters in isolation and not allow spread. The fire spreads only if there is a continuous fuel supply along its path and hence to prevent it from spreading, by firebreaks can be created in the shape of small clearing of ditches in the forests. The following precautions may be followed against forest fires:

(a) To keep the source of fire under watch.

(b) To keep the source of fire away from inflammable materials.

(c) To arrange firefighting drills regularly.

(d) To adopt safe practices near forest areas.

(e) To adopt firefighting and fire reducing equipments.

Oil Fires

Oil fire presents one of the most severe threats to humanity, as oil is highly inflammable and the products of combustion in concentrated form are most dangerous. Oil wells always pose the greatest risk and oil workers always need to take high precautions. It is very difficult to put out the oil well fire and can burn for months together. This is because of continuous feed of fuel from the well. However, the modern oil wells have cut off valves, which can shut and prevent feed of fuel.

Oil wells, installations, transportations, and spills are always the target of terrorists and wars and hence need high precautions. Oil well fires are oil gushers that catches fire and burn uncontrollably. The crude oil fires pollute the environment and emit toxic gases like carbon dioxide, carbon monoxide, polycyclic, hydrogen sulphide, and other acidic gases. Oil well fires are regarded as extreme and hence firefighting agencies need special skills and training. Oil well firefighters have developed extraordinary methods like blasting the oil well head, covering the well head with mud or concrete blocks, etc.

Human Epidemics and Pandemics

An outbreak of a transmittable disease that rapidly spreads through a community can be described as an epidemic and an epidemic whose spread is global and pandemics.

3.4 FORECASTING AND CASUALTY MANAGEMENT

Post-disaster, the first few days, priority is to treat casualties, the sick or injured. Disasters especially earthquakes often involve the management of mass casualties which require search, rescue, first aid, transport of health facilities, and treatment. This also involves redistribution of patients between hospitals as per exigencies. The demand for curative care is the highest during the emergency stage, especially as the affected population is most vulnerable to the new environment, where basic facilities like water, sanitation, and shelter have been implemented. After this stage, the priority should be to focus on preventive measures, immunization, and other disease control measures to mitigate the possibility of mass spread of diseases like cholera, measles, etc.

Disasters demand for a coordinated response between the curative and preventive health services including food supply, shelter, water, and sanitation. The effectiveness of the above would result in reducing mortality rates. The mass casualties after the disaster would depend upon the ability of the local medical team and their resources to deliver a comprehensive and definite medical care to all the victims.

In fact, the disaster management poses challenges that are distinct from normal surgical practices. It is a situation whereby limited available resources to be put to maximum best use to save patients. This is achieved best by planning and training for disasters, through internal and mock field drills. The best situation is achieved with the best cooperation of all departments in a synchronized manner.

Forecasting Casualties

- Forecasting of disasters is not possible but awareness of calamity (earthquake/flood/cyclones) prone areas is also crucial.
- Any event resulting in number of victims large enough to disrupt the normal course of emergency and health care services.

Handling of Casualties

Handling the casualties is the most difficult stage in the initial phase of management. The following model could be a handy strategy.

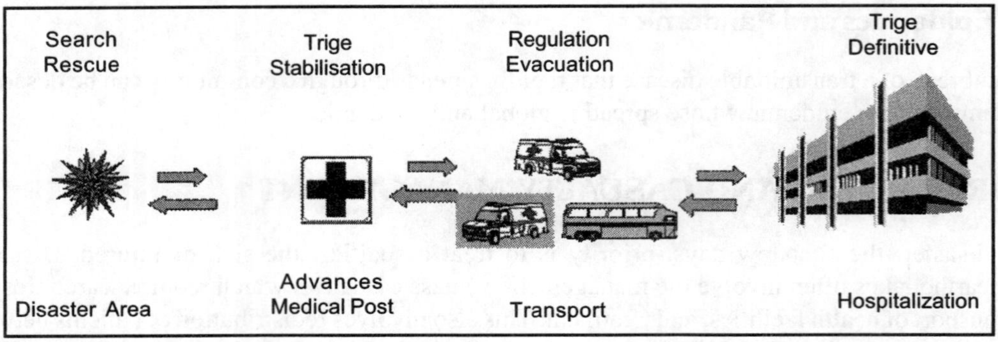

Flow Chart for Disaster Monitoring

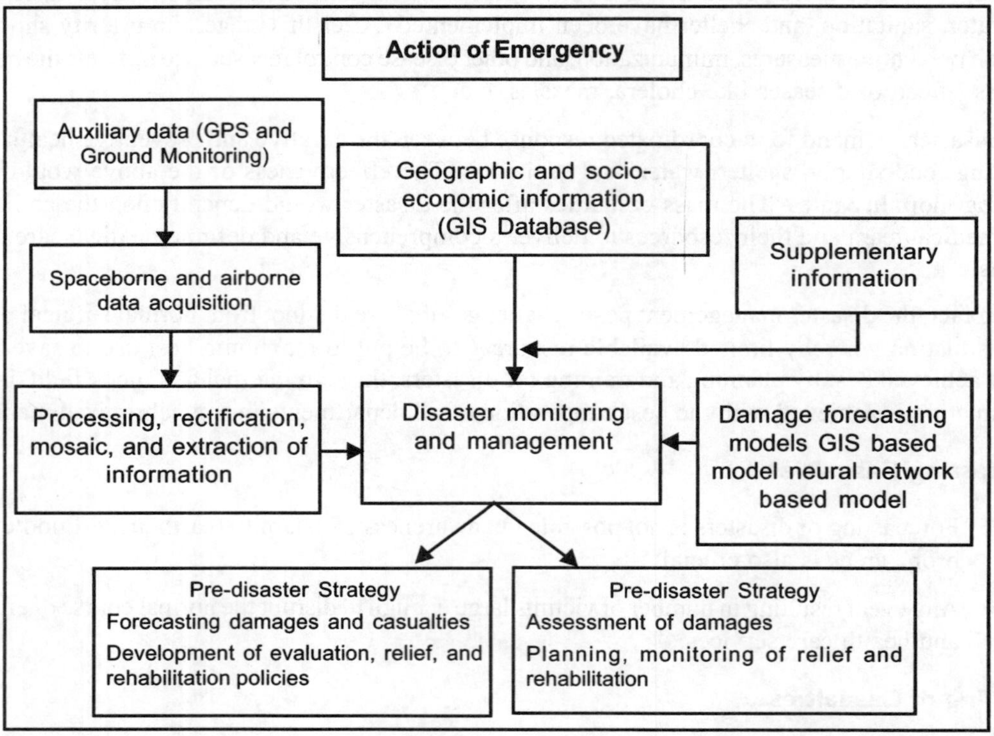

Management of Casualties

There are two phases of casualty management

(a) Pre-disaster phase.

(b) Post-disaster phase.

Pre-disaster Phase

Pre-disaster phase consists of the following areas:

1. Understanding the epidemiology of disasters.

2. Understanding the population health demographics and critical care infrastructure in place.
3. Undertaking risk and hazard assessments.

Capacity development to ensure acute event can be appropriately managed by the affected nation.

Post-disaster Phase

Post-disaster phase include:

1. Ensuring timely response and appropriate response.
2. Logistics.
3. The "field hospital".
4. Needs assessment.
5. Communication and coordination, through incident management team.

This phase includes search, rescue, and first aid of the victims. After a disaster the need for these are so great and improvement in the quality and availability of immediate first aid services depends on training and preparation. Field care is another area of importance. Ideally patients can be transferred to hospitals in a staggered manner and patient should receive field treatments adequately. But normally the patients will converge to whatever medical facilities available through available transport systems, regardless of the facility constraints. The best medical practice, in a disaster situation, relies on triage, whereby the patients are sorted and prioritised based the seriousness of injury and treated. This helps in giving the right attention to the needy at the right time. Triage is a continuous process that begins from the time patients start arriving till their condition improves. Transfer of casualties mean evacuation of casualties from the first aid post to the various hospitals, in designated vehicle, with the facilities for handling. Hospital reception and treatment are very vital and important. At the hospital triage should be the responsibility of a highly experienced clinician, as it may mean life or death to the patient. Lastly, the redistribution of patients between hospitals outside the disaster area, can also be considered. Care must be taken to avoid unnecessary and unplanned shifting.

3.5 QUESTIONS

1. Man act today, the nature react tomorrow – Discuss.
2. What are the different types of man-made disasters?
3. Write short note on power crisis in India.
4. Explain epidemics and pandemics and how will you manage it.
5. Write short notes on oil fires and forest fires.
6. List the important measures in casualty management.
7. What are the evil effects of cyber terrorism?
8. Explain NBC.
9. Elucidate the measures to manage bomb threat.

4 Disaster Operations Management

Learning Objectives

- ☞ To learn about disaster operations through mitigation, preparedness, response, and recovery.
- ☞ To identify, assess, and reduce the risk in disasters.
- ☞ To give knowledge on land use planning, interlinking of rivers and mangroves.

Structure

4.1 INTRODUCTION

Disaster operations management focuses on the application area of management techniques. The focus is on the management of the various operations during the phase, prior to disaster onset, the event impact, and finally the post-impact period. Throughout the disaster operations management phases, the need for an effective and relevant exchange of information is seen as an important part of the service process. The increase in the amount and complexity of information within the process necessitates the need for technology for effective decision making. The use of maps, semantic technology provides opportunity for capture and exchange of contextual information.

Both natural and man-made disasters play a significant and more visible role in today's increasingly global society. Managing the effects of such disasters is an even more complex situation for personnel, volunteers, and other institutions. The service providers have every opportunity for serving, using the analytical tools from engineering, science, and mathematics.

It is important to note that effective delivery of service in disaster management depends upon the ability to share timely and contextually relevant information. It is necessary for the various government, and non-governmenal organizations to work closely, before, during, and post-disaster situations and information sharing among them is most critical and vital for taking multidimensional tasks. There are managerial and technical approaches available for effective decision making.

Today's Quote

What we can or cannot do, what we consider possible or impossible, is rarely a function of our true capability, it is more likely a function of our beliefs about who we are.

— Anthony Robbins

Definition

"Disaster operations management can be defined as the management of activities before, during, and after the occurrence of a disaster with the goal of preventing loss of human life, reducing its impact on the economy, and returning to a state of normalcy."

Phases of DOM

The disaster operations management consists of the following phases. Each of these phases have different timeframe and they differ in the urgency with which information is needed. However, all of them need to share the information for effective and timely service.

(a) Mitigation.

(b) Preparedness.

(c) Response.

(d) Recovery.

Mitigation

Mitigation refers to measures planned to eliminate or reduce vulnerability, the possibility of occurrence of a disaster and the impact of its occurrence. The mitigation phase begins with the identification of hazard and vulnerability analysis. The hazard is first identified and its dangerous impacts on the society and property is analysed. Then mitigation strategies are worked out in detail to reduce the loss. Mitigation is explained in detail in the preceding chapter.

Definition

The most common definition for mitigation is 'actions taken to reduce both human suffering and property loss resulting from extreme natural phenomena'.

Concept of Mitigation

The concept of mitigation stems from the fact that disasters can always happen and mitigation process tries to lessen the impact of the hazard by improving the ability of the communities to deal with its destructive impact. It simply means that mitigation is a risk reduction process.

The scope of mitigation extends to wide range of activities and protection measures that include constructions, agricultural diversification, land use planning, etc.

Saving life and reducing economic disruption has been the vital part of mitigation strategies. Rising population levels across the globe have resulted in making people more vulnerable to risks. This is relevant as the incidents of natural hazards are on the increase. However, the histories of disasters have shown that disasters are largely preventable. There are a number of ways to reduce the impact of a disaster and to mitigate the effects of a possible hazard conflict or accident. The fight against the disasters has to be fought by everyone together, just as we fight against disease. Involvement of public and private sector investment, changes in social attitudes of communities and improvements in overall practices of the individuals are the need of the hour.

While the governments can use public funds to improve and create their country's infrastructure and promote physical environment in disaster-prone areas, private individual must learn how to protect themselves. Just as public health relies on personal hygiene, public protection relies on personal safety as well.

The type of cooking stove public use and their awareness that a sudden earthquake could tip it over is more important in reducing a risk of fire than having a community to maintain a large fire brigade. The location of a house and the type of construction are factors which play an important role than large engineering projects conceived with all precautions.

The dangerous effect of any disasters is the deaths and injuries caused to the population and the loss of property. The justification for mitigation starts from the scale of disasters and the number of people they are capable of killing. Understanding the disaster and understanding the manner in which people are killed and injured is a prerequisite for reducing casualties.

The concept of mitigation is detailed in the first chapter of this book.

Preparedness

Preparedness is a state being ready and prepared to face an emergency situation and to react promptly and effectively. Preparedness really means evolving and developing a complete action plan for meeting the emergency situation. The early warning system gives several hours for planning and acting in the case of hurricanes, floods, etc., however, in the case natural hazards like earthquake, little or no time is available for action. Preparing for an emergency, especially those strikes without time and notice, needs a concrete plan. It is also important to take stock of the resources available and the best manner in which they can be put to best use. An important feature of an emergency plan is that it should work in an emergency situation.

The very purpose of an emergency plan is to evolve a systematic way of responding to an emergency situation. The plan should consider the following elements to make a proper disaster preparedness action plan:

(a) Identifying the vulnerable areas and situations.

(b) Developing a suitable strategy for course of action.

(c) Best use of the resources for optimal benefit.

(d) Identifying and using the government bodies responsible to emergency situations.

(e) Deploying an officer responsible and accountable for actions.

(f) Establishing control room or emergency operation centre (EOC) for quick actions.

Response

The plans ultimate test is the effectiveness of response to warnings and hazard impacts. Various responses will have to be mobilized at different stages of the warning process. The staging of the responses becomes essential for developing a preparedness plan. Response activities occur during and immediately following a disaster. They are indented to provide emergency assistance to the victims of a disaster event and reduce the possibility of a secondary damage.

(a) Warning and notification.

(b) Immediate safety of communities.

(c) Public welfare.

(d) Property security.

(e) Restoration.

(a) Warning: Warning is the first and foremost stage of response. The specific groups which need to be warned of a disaster are the general public, departments, agencies and individuals, who would respond to the emergency. The general public are normally informed through media, radio, and television and those in immediate dangers are either informed directly or through public address system. The people who are likely to be affected must be alerted and told what to do, how to do, and what not to do, in an emergency situation.

(b) Immediate Safety: Immediate public safety involves providing spot emergency medical services, search and rescue operations and evacuation of the mass from the affected area. Therefore, the primary objective should be the safety of people and aid to the injured.

(c) Public Welfare: Public welfare covers the caring for the people after the disaster and assessing the damage. It is mandatory for all agencies to work closely and effectively to get optimum results. Providing shelter, food, clothing, and medical aid are the prime concerns in public welfare.

(d) **Property Security:** This stage deals with the necessary protection to properties and this is the job of the local police. It is the responsibility of the police to see that the property is safe and looting and vandalism does not occur. The fire department, public works department, roads department, rural and urban bodies can also play a significant role in protecting the property.

(e) **Restoration:** Restoration involves repairing and restoring the utility services and further involves removing the debris from the disaster area. In the restoration phase, reconstruction of the infrastructure facilities are taken up.

Recovery

This is the final phase of the disaster management cycle and the process continues till normalcy is restored. The recovery phase is classified into two types namely, short-term and long-term. Short-term recoveries would be immediate reconnection of electrical lines, telephone lines, repairs to buildings, etc., whereas the long-term recovery involves construction process for years together. Long-term recovery extends over a number of years, for complete revamp of the area. A key element in the recovery phase is to develop and implement means and ways to reduce the vulnerability to repeated occurrences of disaster and to build an understanding between State and Central Government for assistance.

Risk Assessment and Disaster Response

Disaster risk management is a new area of social concern and practice. It is an important concern for development cooperation in the field of disaster management. In this fast moving environment, risk identification can be a very difficult task. Identifying the risks, that too the environmental risk, poses great challenge to the governments, especially considering burning issues like cloning, flooding, foot and mouth disease, hurricanes, earthquakes, etc.

Definition

Risk can be defined in a number of ways and one of them is "exposure to the chance of loss" or "degree of probability of such a loss ". It is also important to distinguish between a problem and a risk. A risk is the possibility of something going wrong, whereas a problem is something that has gone wrong. Risk is also defined as the expected loss of life and property. Risk is the probability of particular occurrences and the loss that each is likely to incur. A societal element is said to be at risk or vulnerable, when it is exposed to hazards and is likely to be badly affected as well.

The definition of risk involves one or more of combination of the following:

1. A timeframe over which risks are being considered.
2. A probability of occurrence of events.
3. A measure of the impact of those events.

Hazard and risk are interrelated and differentiation between hazard and risk, helps to understand them better. A hazard is a substance which has the potential to harm the environment, health, etc., whereas a risk is the likelihood of exposure to hazard.

"Risk management is the identification, analysis and economic control of those RISKS which can threaten the assets (property, human) or the earning capacity of an enterprise."

Risk Assessment

Risk assessment is the process of determining the nature and extent of loss or damage caused by a disaster in a particular area during a specified period of time, which can be anticipated and quantified, or in other words scientific quantification of risk and understanding the process involved. Risk evaluation can be the result of social and political judgement of the various risks by the communities which face them, which also involves trading of perceived risks against political benefits. This includes scientific judgements against other factors and beliefs.

The objective of disaster risk assessment is to establish a uniform approach to monitoring and assessing risks which will address disaster risk management planning and disaster risk reduction. Disaster risk assessment is the first step in planning an effective disaster risk reduction programme. It also examines the likelihood of a disaster and its outcomes. This would also include microscoping the hazard, its vulnerability, and chances of loss.

Disaster risk assessment planning includes vertical and horizontal interactions and interpretations with the various agencies and communities and well supported by a good monitoring system. These are essential for:

(a) Effective disaster risk management and risk reduction planning.

(b) Identifying potential threats which can undermine development.

(c) Sustainable development planning.

(d) Identifying high risk periods and risky conditions.

(e) Activating preparedness and response actions.

A very systematic disaster risk assessments are needed prior to the implementation of a national disaster or recovery programme.

To understand better the following will help.

What is a RISK?

1. Risks are simply the future issues which can be avoided or mitigated.
2. Assessment means calculating.
3. Hazard
   (a) Potential to do harm
   - Tornado
   - Hazardous chemical
4. Risk
   (b) Likelihood of defined harm to occur from specific hazard.

How is Risk Assessment Used?

Some examples of usage of risk assessment are:

(a) To set drinking water standards for public water supplies.

(b) Licensing and regulation of pesticides.

(c) Identification and clean-up of hazardous waste sites.

(d) Identification of special handling requirements for chemicals.

Various Risk Assessments

There are two types of risk assessments carried out to study the risks and are:

(a) **Exposure Assessment:** Exposure assessment is the process of estimating or measuring the magnitude, frequency, and duration of exposure to an agent, along with the number and characteristics of the population exposed. Ideally, it describes the sources, pathways, routes, and the uncertainties in the assessment.

(b) **Toxicity Assessment:** Toxicity assessment establishes the relationship between the contaminant/ s of concern and the receptor. It asks the question 'What does the contaminant do to the receptor?' The objective of Toxicity Assessment (also known as hazard assessment) is to determine 'What potential adverse effects might the contaminants of concern cause and at what concentration?

Risk Assessment Process

The disaster risk assessment process is conducted through a systematic staged approach, so that the outcome is synchronized with the planning requirements. Risk assessment is a four-part process and includes the following:

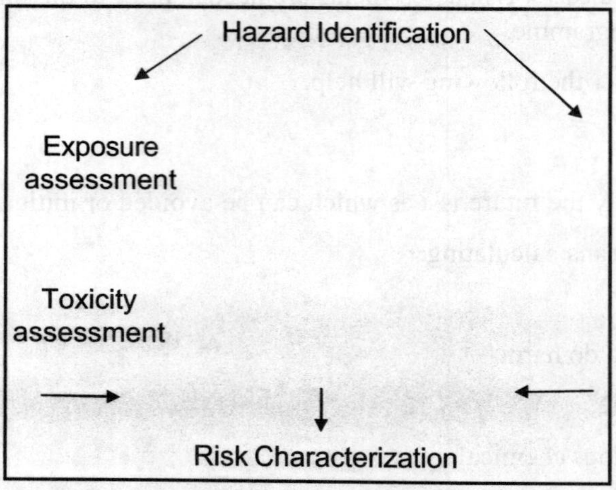

a. Hazard Identification

The first step in risk assessment is to identify the hazard. For example, what chemicals are present and are they likely to be toxic and should be first priority element. This involves an analysis of the likelihood of occurrence of a natural or man-made hazard in a specific future time period, their intensity and area of impact. It also involves estimation of loss consequence to the hazard, and to identify methods and resources available with us to manage the risk by assessing the effectiveness of these gaps, inconsistencies, and inefficiencies of the government and other agencies.

b. Exposure Assessment

Exposure assessment or vulnerability assessment shows, who is exposed, at what concentration, how often, and for how long? This is the process of estimating vulnerability to potential hazards. It is also to estimate the level of risk associated with a specific threat to determine, whether, the resulting risk is a priority matter or not. The estimation of risk levels are done by analyzing the consequences of the disaster in question. This process helps in prioritizing the threats.

c. Toxicity Assessment

Toxicity assessment involves studying the damaging power of the hazard and include knowing how is it toxic and at what exposure levels?

d. Risk Characterization

Risk characterization is nothing but what does the risk assessment tell us about this situation? This stage involves constantly putting disaster risk reduction initiatives to the test. This would further include identifying changing patterns and new developments and risk profiles and updating and disseminating information for planning disaster risk management.

Risk Assessment Measures

The following tools are mainly used in risk assessment:

(a) History of past disasters and natural phenomena

(b) In-depth study on specific geological climatic and other hazards.

(c) Drafting and updating hazard maps and vulnerability profiles.

(d) Systematic survey of vulnerable population.

Limitations of Risk Assessment

The disaster risk assessment process suffers with the following limitations:

(a) **Deficient Outcome:** The risk assessment does not always result in a conclusive outcome regarding corrective measures to be taken, acceptable to all stakeholders. These difficulties could be due to poor identification of the risk problems, target population, area of concern, etc. This further suffers due to insufficient data, resources, and responsibility constraints.

(b) **Lack of Political Will:** The assessment outcomes are generally not politically acceptable to the system. The success of the disaster risk management depends upon the political will of the country. Politicians does not show interest in long-term projects and are interested in short-term immediate results, to gain a political advantage. This is relevant as their tenure of office is for a short period.

4.2 DISASTER RISK REDUCTION

Poverty, vulnerability and disasters are linked – it is most often the poorest that are worst affected and suffer most. Their poverty makes them more vulnerable. Their capacities to cope with disasters and recover from the effects are constrained by their lack of resources.

Disasters rob the poor of their meagre possessions, their homes and livestock and most importantly, their livelihoods. Conversely, droughts, floods, and even earthquakes have impacted on people's lives and livelihoods without being deemed a disaster, when those people were sufficiently prepared and had the capacity to cope and recover quickly.

The practical action approach to disaster management is based on research and operational experience gained over several years in South Asia, Africa, and Peru. The work has convincingly demonstrated that secure and sustainable livelihoods reduce both poverty and susceptibility to disasters. Poor communities have been facilitated to undertake activities which increase their resilience to disasters while strengthening their livelihood strategies, using local knowledge, capacities and resourcefulness, coupled with innovative and appropriate technologies.

Disasters cost lives, destroy infrastructure, disrupt livelihoods and leave a major impact on the survivors' physical and psychological well-being. Over the past decades there has been a substantial increase in the number of people affected by disasters and the subsequent socio-economic losses. In 2007, 414 disasters resulting from natural hazards were reported. They killed 16,847 people, affected more than 211 million others and caused over 74.9 US$ billion in economic damages. Last year's number of reported disasters confirmed the global upward trend in natural hazard-related disasters, mainly driven by the increase in the number of hydro-meteorological disasters. In recent decades, the number of reported hydrological disasters has increased by 7.4 per cent per year on average.

The reality is that developing countries bear the brunt of natural and man-made disasters (90 per cent of the people affected live in Asia) and these countries lack the resources and capacities to respond effectively. Disasters pose a major threat to sustainable development and the attainment of the Millennium Development Goals.

We all live exposed to threats or hazards, so why are disastrous events occurring more frequently and with increasingly severe impacts? Disasters occur when natural or man-made hazards impact on human beings. How much we are affected by a particular hazard and the risks we face depend on two main factors:

(a) The nature of the hazard.

(b) The vulnerability of the affected people.

Poverty, vulnerability, and disasters are linked; it is most often the poorest that are worst affected and suffer most. Their poverty makes them more vulnerable. Their capacities to cope with disasters and recover from the effects are constrained by their lack of resources. Disasters rob the poor of their meagre possessions, their homes and livestock and most importantly, their livelihoods. Conversely, droughts, floods, and even earthquakes have impacted on people's lives and livelihoods without being deemed a disaster, when those people were sufficiently prepared and had the capacity to cope and recover quickly.

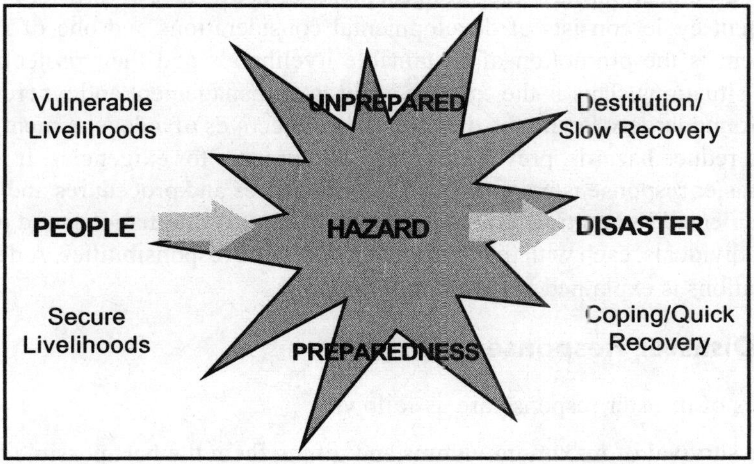

While disasters have traditionally been viewed as dramatic natural occurrences over which passive victims have little or no control, many more poor people are at risk from hazards other than cataclysmic events. Hunger, disease, slow onset, man-made disasters and conflict claim many more lives than floods or earthquakes. Yet these disasters pass largely unnoticed; they are "normal" events in less developed countries. Disasters are rarely just one-off events, but more often the result of deep-rooted long-term failures of development which exacerbate the situation. Very often the impact of several small adversities is all that is required to drive the poor from a state of vulnerability to one of total destitution.

If vulnerability is the key component of both the sustainable livelihoods approach to poverty reduction and disaster risk reduction, then all activities which seek to strengthen livelihoods, increase resilience, and reduce the vulnerability of poor people are risk reduction measures. The sustainable livelihoods framework identifies hazards as an influencing factor which impinges on the assets necessary to attain a sustainable livelihood. All poor people are exposed to risks and hazards and seek ways to cope when their impact overwhelms their normal livelihood strategies.

Disaster risk reduction (DRR) should thus be regarded as part of long-term sustainable development work and should be a core element of development programme planning. DRR contributes to sustainable development by preventing or decreasing the frequency of shocks occurring, or by increasing the capital resource base of a community so that the impact of the shock is less and/or recovery is more rapid. Practical action also works through consultancy, partnership and joint networks in Costa Rica, Bangladesh, Honduras, Guatemala, El Salvador, Columbia, Brazil, the Philippines, and India.

Disaster Response

Disaster response is the combination of actions taken by the agencies and communities in the face of disaster. These actions commends with the warning of a hazard or with the hazard itself, if occurs without warning. The main aim of the disaster response is to provide immediate assistance to save and maintain life, improve health, and to effectively support the morale of the affected communities. Such assistance may range from providing assistance in transportation, shelter, and food. It may further involve initial repair of buildings, and other infrastructure. The main focus in the response face is on meeting the very minimal basic needs of the people, till a permanent sustainable solutions can be found.

Humanitarian organizations have the strongest presence in this face of disaster management cycle. Disaster management cycle consists of developmental considerations and one of the main goals of disaster management is the promotion of sustainable livelihoods and their protection and recovery during emergency situations. This is the essence of disaster management and wherever these are met people have been found largely facing the disasters. The objectives of a development-oriented disaster management are to reduce hazards, prevent disasters, and prepare for exigencies. It is to be noted that each activity in disaster response is governed by a set of policies and procedures and disaster response activities are implemented by multiple government organizations, international and national agencies, local entities and individuals, each with their designated roles and responsibilities. A detailing of the role of various organizations is explained in the ensuing chapters.

Objectives of Disaster Response

The objectives of disaster response are as follows:

(a) To ensure survival of maximum victims and giving them the best possible treatment.

(b) To restore essential services and establish self-sufficiency to cover the needy.

(c) To repair and replace infrastructure and revive economic activity and long-term development.

(d) To provide suitable rehabilitation packages to the displaced people in the quickest possible time.

Disaster Response Activities

The following are the activities of disaster response:

1. **Warning:** Warning is information concerning the nature of the danger and the immediate disaster threats. Warnings must be rapidly disseminated to government officials, institutions, and the communities in the immediate risk areas so that appropriate effective actions can be taken like evacuation, properties, security, etc. Warnings are normally disseminated through television, radio, written press release, telephone systems, and cellular phones.
2. **Evacuation and Migration:** This is a process of relocating a population from risk zones of an imminent disaster to a safer location. The primary concern here is the protection to the communities. Evacuation is commonly associated with hurricanes, and is also nowadays used with technological and industrial hazards. The success of the evacuation system depends on a timely and accurate warning system, identification of escape routes, a responsive community to act on order and a public education programme to make the community aware of the plan.

3. **Search and Rescue (SAR):** This is the process of identify the victims of a disaster location who may be trapped or isolated and bring them to safety and medical care. Normally, after the tropical storms and floods, search and rescue operations include identifying stranded public on the rising water, rescuing them and providing them with first aid, food, and water. In the case of an earthquake, SAR will focus on rescuing people who are trapped in the debris and or injured in collapsed buildings.

4. **Post-disaster Assessment:** The purpose of the post-disaster assessment is to provide a very clear picture of the post-disaster situation, to understand relief needs and to develop recovery strategies. It also determines various options including humanitarian assistance, best utilization of available resources, etc.

5. **Response and Relief:** Immediately upon occurrence of a disaster, response and relief have to take place without delay. This will depend upon the effectiveness of the contingency plan. Relief represents provision on a humanitarian basis of material and medical care necessary to save and preserve human lives. It also enables people to meet their basic needs of food, water, health care, shelter, and clothing. During a disaster, the relief supplies and services are provided free of charge to the communities for sometime. However, in the case of calamities extending over the longer periods, the relief supplies will be extended for a longer time.

6. **Logistics and Supply:** During a disaster, the quickest supply of relief material will be the need of the hour, for which logistics and supply service is very crucial for handling the procurement, storage, and dispatch of relief supplies to the disaster victims.

7. **Communication and Information Management:** The effectiveness of a disaster response system depends on the communication and information system. All the above activities explained are depended on communication. This includes the communication equipments like radio, telephone, etc., and their support systems like satellites and transmission lines. The information management determines the protocol of knowing who will communicate, what information, to whom, and at what priority.

8. **Security:** Security always gets the last priority after a sudden onset of disasters. Normally, it is handled by the local police. However, the protection of the human rights and safety of displaced populations can be of importance requiring greater monitoring.

9. **Rehabilitation:** Consists of actions taken in the post-disaster period to resume emergency services, assist victims, and to facilitate revival of economic activities. The process of rehabilitation helps affected populations to resume normalcy.

10. **Reconstruction:** It is the process of establishing permanent construction or repair of damaged structures, restoration of all services and infrastructure, and the revival of the economy. The reconstruction must go in line with the national development policy or plans and also take into account the future disaster risks. This also should focus on the possibilities of reducing those risks by incorporating relevant mitigation measures.

Insurance in Risk Management

Insurance is a form of risk management primarily used to hedge against the risk of a contingent, uncertain loss. Insurance is defined as the equitable transfer of the risk of a loss, from one entity to another, in exchange for payment. An *insurer* is a company selling the insurance; an *insured,* or policyholder, is the person or entity buying the insurance policy. The *insurance rate* is a factor used to determine the amount to be charged for a certain amount of insurance coverage, called the *premium.* Risk management, the practice of appraising and controlling risk, has evolved as a discrete field of study and practice.

The transaction involves the insured assuming a guaranteed and known relatively small loss in the form of payment to the insurer in exchange for the insurer's promise to compensate (indemnify) the insured in the case of a financial (personal) loss. The insured receives a contract, called the insurance policy, which details the conditions and circumstances under which the insured will be financially compensated. Insurance involves pooling funds from many insured entities (known as *exposures*) to pay for the losses that some may incur. The insured entities are therefore protected from risk for a fee, with the fee being dependent upon the frequency and severity of the event occurring. In order to be insurable, the risk insured against must meet certain characteristics in order to be an insurable risk. Insurance is a commercial enterprise and a major part of the financial services industry, but individual entities can also self-insure through saving money for possible future losses.

The basic difference between disaster insurance and property insurance is that disaster insurance is more specialized and covers your losses against immediate occurrences that have disrupted your business, whereas property insurance covers your property against any number of common property risks, including theft or damage from accidents. There are now various packages that cover property from a wide range of threats and allow you to buy additional coverage for specific concerns such as flooding.

The key today, with so many options, is to first assess exactly what you need and then work with an insurance agent to figure out the best package: one that covers your most significant risks. It is not an either/nor scenario that you want, but a combination of policies that provides protection without duplicating coverage. It is common for business owners to fail to look closely at what is covered by their property insurance and buy another policy that covers many of the same risks. Conversely, many policyholders mistakenly assume disasters such as flooding are covered under one of their policies and do not discover until they're underwater that neither their property insurance nor their disaster insurance covers flooding.

It is also advisable to buy all of your insurance from one carrier because you will usually save money with riders and packages and it is less likely that your coverage will overlap. One way you may notice disaster insurance policies differ from property insurance policies is that often the deductible is not a set fee, but rather based on a percentage of the coverage.

The following are few classes of insurance applicable in disaster risk reduction:

Property insurance provides protection against risks to property, such as fire, theft, or weather damage. This may include specialized forms of insurance such as fire insurance, flood insurance, earthquake insurance, home insurance, inland marine insurance, or boiler insurance. The term property insurance may, like casualty insurance, be used as a broad category of various subtypes of insurance, some of which are listed below:

Aviation insurance protects aircraft hulls and spares, and associated liability risks, such as passenger and third-party liability. Airports may also appear under this subcategory, including air traffic control and refuelling operations for international airports through to smaller domestic exposures.

Boiler insurance (also known as boiler and machinery insurance, or equipment breakdown insurance) insures against accidental physical damage to boilers, equipment, or machinery.

Builder's risk insurance insures against the risk of physical loss or damage to property during construction. Builder's risk insurance is typically written on an "all risk" basis covering damage arising from any cause (including the negligence of the insured) not otherwise expressly excluded. Builder's risk insurance is coverage that protects a person's or organization's insurable interest in materials, fixtures and/or equipment being used in the construction or renovation of a building or structure should those items sustain physical loss or damage from an insured peril.

Crop insurance may be purchased by farmers to reduce or manage various risks associated with growing crops. Such risks include crop loss or damage caused by weather, hail, drought, frost damage, insects, or disease.

Earthquake insurance is a form of property insurance that pays the policyholder in the event of an earthquake that causes damage to the property. Most ordinary home insurance policies do not cover earthquake damage. Earthquake insurance policies generally feature a high deductible rates depend on location and hence the likelihood of an earthquake, as well as the construction of the home.

Fidelity bond is a form of casualty insurance that covers policyholders for losses incurred as a result of fraudulent acts by specified individuals. It usually insures a business for losses caused by the dishonest acts of its employees.

Flood insurance protects against property loss due to flooding. Many insurers in the US do not provide flood insurance in some parts of the country. In response to this, the federal government created the National Flood Insurance Programme which serves as the insurer of last resort.

Home insurance also commonly called hazard insurance, or homeowners insurance (often abbreviated in the real estate industry as HOI), is the type of property insurance that covers private homes, as outlined above.

Landlord insurance covers residential and commercial properties which are rented to others. Most homeowners' insurance covers only owner-occupied homes.

Marine insurance and marine cargo insurance covers the loss or damage of vessels at sea or on inland waterways, and of cargo in transit, regardless of the method of transit. When the owner of the cargo and the carrier are separate corporations, marine cargo insurance typically compensates the owner of cargo for losses sustained from fire, shipwreck, etc., but excludes losses that can be recovered from the carrier or the carrier's insurance. Many marine insurance underwriters will include "time element" coverage in such policies, which extends the indemnity to cover loss of profit and other business expenses attributable to the delay caused by a covered loss.

Supplemental natural disaster insurance covers specified expenses after a natural disaster renders the policyholder's home uninhabitable. Periodic payments are made directly to the insured until the home is rebuilt or a specified time period has elapsed.

Terrorism insurance provides protection against any loss or damage caused by terrorist activities. In the US in the wake of 9/1, the Terrorism Risk Insurance Act, 2002 (TRIA) set up a federal programme providing a transparent system of shared public and private compensation for insured losses resulting from acts of terrorism. The programme was extended until the end of 2014 by the Terrorism Risk Insurance Programme Reauthorization Act, 2007 (TRIPRA).

Volcano insurance is a specialized insurance protecting against damage arising specifically from volcanic eruptions.

Wind storm insurance is an insurance covering the damage that can be caused by wind events such as hurricanes.

Need for Risk Management

The need for risk management rests on the following factors:

(a) Uncertainty in enterprise.

(b) Growing complexity in business environment.

(c) Statutory obligations.

(d) Contractual obligations.

(e) Social obligations.

Insurable Risks

All risks are not insurable, only certain risks are insurable as per the Act and they are:

Insurable Risks

Property Risks

Damage to Physical Assets
- Acts of God
- Accidents
- Breakdown

People Risks

Loss to Employees
- Ill Health and accident
- Death
- Overseas Travel

Financial Risks

Monetary Loss from
- Theft and Burglary
- Business Interruption
- Bad credit

Liabilities Risks

Loss from Operations
- Product Liabilities
- Public Liabilities
- Directors and Officers Liabilities
- Errors and Omissions Liabilities

4.3 THE PROCESS OF RISK MANAGEMENT IN INSURANCE

The process or risk management from an insurance perspective is based on the following factors:

1. **Risk Identification:** It involves an understanding of the area, industry, activities, products, legal, social, and economic environment on which it operates and the relevant hazards associated with the operations. This involves identifying the risk facts and evaluation of the potential loss.

2. **Risk Assessment:** Once the initial process of risk identification is over the next step is the quantification of the potential loss and probability of occurrence of the event. A care must be taken to derive proper assessment, which would help the underwriter to apply judgement to the risk.

3. **Risk Treatment:** The next step after identifying and assessing the risk is to focus on risk treatment methods. The risk treatment methods consists of risk avoidance (non-performance of an activity), risk retention (acceptance of loss), and finally risk transfer.

4. **Risk Reduction:** It is an important factor of risk management, whereby methods are used to reduce the severity of loss. For example, sprinkler system designed to put out a fire to reduce the risk of loss by fire.

4.4 LAND USE PLANNING

Land use planning is the systematic assessment of land and water potential, alternatives for land use and economic and social conditions in order to select and adopt the best land use options. Its purpose is to select and put into practice those land uses that will best meet the needs of the people while safeguarding resources for the future. The driving force in planning is the need for change, the need for improved management or the need for a quite different pattern of land use dictated by changing circumstances.

Land use planning and management leads to communities where people and property are kept out of the vulnerable areas, where development is designed to be a resilient to natural forces and where the mitigative capacity of natural environmental system is not diminished. Land use planning and management can reduce disasters to a level which can be managed by the governments and communities.

Focus of Land Use Planning

The land use planning focuses on the following broad areas:

(a) Planning is for people.

(b) Land is not the same everywhere.

(c) Technology (agronomy, sericulture).

(d) Integration.

Importance of Land Use Planning in Disaster Management

Any disaster is a consequence of a natural hazard and has an impact on human vulnerabilities. Human vulnerability, exacerbated by the lack of prevention and preparedness or lack of response system, leads to human and property loss. The resulting loss depends on their resilience. It is, in this area, a good land use planning prevents disasters to a major extent. This is particularly relevant as land is fundamental to the recovery from disasters. Land provides a site for shelter, livelihood, and access to services and infrastructure. Therefore, land issues are important to the humanitarian sector after a disaster. These sectors include:

Making the Best Use of Limited Resources

Land use planning aims to make the best use of limited resources by:

(a) Assessing present and future needs and systematically evaluating the land's ability to supply them.

(b) Identifying and resolving conflicts between competing uses, between the needs of individuals and those of the community, and between the needs of the present generation and those of future generations.

(c) Seeking sustainable options and choosing those that meet best identified needs.

(d) Planning to bring about desired changes.

(e) Learning from experience.

GOALS

Goals may be grouped under the three headings:

(a) **Efficiency:** Efficiency means different things to different people, however, to the individual land user, it means the greatest return on capital and labour invested or the greatest benefit from the area available. Government objectives are more complex: they may include improving the foreign exchange situation by producing for export or for import substitution.

(b) **Equity and Acceptability:** Land use must also be socially acceptable. Goals include food security, employment, and security of income in rural areas. Land improvements and redistribution of land may be undertaken to reduce inequality or alternatively, to attack absolute poverty.

(c) **Sustainability:** Sustainable land use is that which meets the needs of the present while at the same time, conserving resources for future generations. This requires a combination of production and conservation: the production of the goods needed by people now, combined with the conservation of the natural resources on which that production depends so as to ensure continued production in the future.

Planning at Different Levels

National Level: The national level planning is concerned with national goals and the allocation of resources. National land use planning does not involve the actual allocation of land for different uses, but the establishment of priorities for district-level projects.

A national land use plan may cover:

(a) Land use policy.

(b) National development plans and budget.

(c) Coordination of sectoral agencies involved in land use.

(d) Legislation on such subjects as land tenure, forest clearance, and water rights.

District Level: District level refers not only to administrative districts but also to land areas that fall between national and local levels. Development projects are often at this level.

The kinds of issues tackled at this stage include:

(a) The citing of developments.

(b) The need for improved infrastructure.

(c) The development of management guidelines.

Local Level: The local planning unit may be the village, a group of villages or a small water catchment. At this level, it is easiest to fit the plan to the people, making use of local people's knowledge and contributions. Where planning is initiated at the district level, the programme of work to implement changes in land use or management has to be carried out locally.

(a) The layout of drainage, irrigation, and soil conservation works.

(b) The design of infrastructure – road alignment and the citing of crop marketing, fertiliser distribution, milk collection, or veterinary facilities.

(c) Suggesting of specific crops on suitable land.

4.5 INTER LINKING OF RIVERS

India is blessed with abundant water resources, which are unevenly distributed in space and time. When one part of the country is reeling under severe water scarcity, floods damage another part. This creates the imbalance between the surplus and demand. Hence, we need an inter linking project. Inter linking of rivers means networking the rivers, simply to say joining all the rivers.

Inter Linking of Rivers (ILR) has assumed tremendous importance in our country, with the President of India, the Prime Minister, the Supreme Court, and several officials promoting it as the single panacea not only to recurring problems of drought and floods but also to all water problems. The proposed 'Water grid' is also the biggest project in scope, funds, and impact in Indian history. Increasing water scarcity and crises in our villages and cities are making us more and more desperate to see some 'magic' happen, at least through this project. Many politicians have even made river linking, a campaign issue during the recent elections.

The following factors needs sound answer before we start a river linking project.

1. Is the plan based on a sound understanding of river systems?
2. Will the plan achieve what it claims it will?
3. Has the planning process allowed for sufficient scrutiny from all concerned, and assessment of all available options?
4. What will be the actual cost? What are its implications for the public?
5. What are the lessons to be learnt from similar attempts worldwide?
6. Are there sensible, viable, and sustainable ways of handling our water problems?

National Water Development Agency (NWDA)

The NWP comprises of two components, Himalayan Rivers Development and Peninsular Rivers Development. There are 14 link canals in Himalayan component and 16 link canals in Peninsular component. Storage reservoirs is constructed on the tributaries of Ganga and Brahmaputra along with the canals of Nepal and Bhutan (surplus quantity) transferred to West part. And Peninsular side it is diversion of surplus from Mahanadi to Godavari system and to a further transfer of the surplus from Godavari to Krishna, Krishna to Cauvery, and Cauvery to Vaigai Rivers.

Criteria for Inter Linking of Rivers

Following are the major criteria for linking rivers:

Dams and Reservoirs: While constructing dams and reservoirs, availability of suitable site from the hydrological, topographical, geological, environmental, and ecological impacts must be considered, so as displacement of people.

Barrages and Weirs: Suitability of sites in view of topographical, hydraulic, subsoil conditions, and inundation due to upstream afflux and its impacts are major areas of concern while planning for a construction of weirs and barrages.

Link Channels: These are different from natural channels, which are essentially for drainage and irrigation. However, while constructing link channels, which are primarily for transfer of water, hydraulic demographic suitability needs consideration. The link channels usually carry high discharges and cover over a long distance. Hence, acquisition of substantial land will be required. This may create ecological disturbance in that area. The link channels also cause heavy seepage and result in water logging.

Impact of Inter Linking of Rivers

The inter-linking of rivers create multidimensional impact as detailed below:

Economic Impact: The economic impact of inter linking of rivers will invariably relate to the cost of construction, operation, and maintenance as well as the flood control benefits. The cost for constructing link channels is always higher than the irrigation channels, because the number of cross-drainage works is higher, so as the cost of operating the link channels. On account of the above cost, the cost per unit of water will be substantially high. Depending upon how the cost will be met, whether by subsidy or by beneficiaries, there will be corresponding economic impact on the nation and this may positively or negatively affect regional imbalance.

Environmental and Ecological Impact: Link channels leave huge ecological and environmental impacts, create water logging in the areas they pass through affect dense forests and habitats of wild life, etc.

Social Impact: The link channel may give rise to certain social problems as many a situation it passes through populated areas, causing widespread displacement of people who need to be satisfactorily resettled and rehabilitated. It is important to note that most likely the people to be displaced will not be the beneficiaries which will aggravate social issues and create resistance.

Challenges

The challenges faced by inter linking of rivers are diverse and as under:

1. Normal ecological functions gets disturbed.
2. Hydrological cycle gets disturbed.
3. Changes the composition of sediment load, river morphology, and shape of the delta.
4. Dislocations of villages.
5. Reduces natural fertility.

6. Water-related conflicts between states.
7. High cost.
8. Due to privatization, rights of the people for water resources gets affected.

SWOT Analysis in Disaster Management

All the experts in this field feel that the result of implementation of the policies in the field of disaster management is not satisfactory. There are many opportunities thrown open by the primary and secondary data, which if analysed could bring revolutionary changes in the field of disaster management. A SWOT analysis is prepared to understand the current disaster management position.

Strength

(a) Structured administrative setup.
(b) Opportunity for coordination among departments.
(c) Adequate funds.
(d) Setup for immediate relief and rescue operations.
(e) Opportunity for public and private and international participation.
(f) Availability of experts in every field.

Opportunity

(a) Big scope for research.
(b) Involvement of NGO in pre- and post-disaster.
(c) Involvement of experts in mitigation.
(d) Availability of workforce.
(e) Networking of villages and headquarters.

Threat

(a) Absence of experienced credible NGOs.
(b) Possibility of lethargy and corruption on decentralization.
(c) Lack of monitoring due to decentralization.
(d) Mis-management and poor control.
(e) Lack of control over resources.
(f) Lack of involvement of research.
(g) Impracticability of the models suggested.

Weakness

(a) Focus on rehabilitation negligible.

(b) Poor participation of the local mass.

(c) Poor scope for monitoring and evaluation.

(d) Poor social and psychological treatment.

(e) No connection between disaster management and development.

(f) Poor training to the local in dealing with disasters.

(g) Operational deficiencies.

(h) Slow and poor involvement of research in the field.

A SWOT analysis of the policies and implementation of disaster management gives an idea about the various aspects of the problem and identifies the areas, which need best attention. SWOT analysis of policies and strategies is such that it should not have short comings which may other wise lead to adverse situations. Care should be taken to ensure that no area of disaster management is left untouched or unexplored.

4.6 ANTIFRICTION TECHNIQUES

Antifriction technique is a type of friction reducing or lubricating technology used for preventing disaster events and to be in a safe position against these disasters.

This invention relates to a non-asbestos frictional material composition and more particularly to a break lining and a brake pad which has a desirable lubricant property in a dry or humid atmosphere and which is not affected by temperature or wears out readily and product little noise.

Safety in driving a transportation means, such as an automobile, railway vehicle, or airoplane largely depends on the function of a brake for speed control. The function of a brake is particularly important in case of a vehicle driving at high speed or of vehicle transporting heavy material, equipment. The brake under any conditions should operate punctually.

Any brake having a frictional material attached is a device which converts the kinetic energy of a vehicle into heat and consumes the heat. Accordingly, it is very important to choose a frictional material. Braking ability is limited by the frictional force between tyres and road surface. When the frictional force of the brake is great the tyres are locked completely, resulting in wear of the tyres. When the frictional force of the brake is little, the braking distance of the vehicle gets long, resulting in the braking ability being lost.

In the aspect of stability, a coefficient of action is preferably large. However, an exceedingly large coefficient of friction will cause a great amount of wear and vibration thus producing noise. The great amount of wear of a frictional material will result in the lives of the frictional material being shortened. This requires frequent replacement of the frictional material, which is uneconomical. Furthermore, the production of noise and vibration gives an uneasy feeling to a driver.

In recent vehicles, the engine sound or driving sound produced when the tyres contact with the ground surface is improved greatly, resulting in noise during driving being suppressed. Accordingly, even a slight noise or even a slight sound of a brak will given unpleasant feeling to a driver.

To overcome the above described disadvantages, a lubricant has been added. Presently used lubricants are carbon (graphite) molybdenum disulfide and calcium carbonate. Of these, carbon is more in general use. There are two kinds of friction composition, i.e., semi-metal friction compositions and asbestos friction composition.

The asbestos friction composition comprises 20-60 parts by weight of asbestos power to 5 or 6 grade. 35-65 parts by weight of inorganic filter and 60-40 parts by weight of phenol resin, auxiliary resin or plasticizer cement powder containing 65-80 per cent carbon compound and 20-35 ferric iron components may be substituted for some or the entire inorganic filter.

The inorganic filter refers to conventional calcium carbonate, barium sulfate, aluminium, talc, kaolin, mullite, calcium silicate, silicate in powder form, silica in minute powder form, metal (copper, iron, brass, aluminium, zinc) in powder form and metal oxide.

Conventional frictional materials (semi-metal friction composition) where the main component of the inorganic filler, cement powder contains 25-35 per cent iron component is readily oxidized and corroded when exposed to the atmosphere for a long period resulting in a sudden lowering of the frictional function. Furthermore, the strength and water resisting property of the conventional frictional material will be suddenly lowered by absorbing of moisture. The conventional frictional material is excellent in breaking ability, but generates excessive heat by excessive frictional braking, thus being oxidized readily. Furthermore, since the conventional frictional materials lack frictional stabilization at high temperature, the brake will not be applied smoothly, thus producing noise.

Major Types of Antifriction Techniques

The major types of antifriction techniques which are often used in earthquake and common disaster prevention are as follows:

Self-lubricating Antifriction Material: The present invention proposes a self-lubricating anti-friction material. This material comprises carbon filler in the form of powder of firer oil coke, a powder of artificial graphite or carbon cloth; a binder in the form of epoxy resin having molecular weight of 300-1,560 obtained through condensing of epichlorohydrin with diphenyolopropane, and polyalumophenylsiloxane resin having a molecular weight of 5,000-15,000 with a ratio of the silicon atoms and to the aluminium atoms to 3-8 m chlorinated paraffin having a molecular weight of 500-1,100 and frictional content of 40-70 mole per cent. The proportion of said components is said self-lubricating antifrictional material being as follows (per cent by weight)

(i) Epoxy resin 15-57.

(ii) Polyalumophenylsiloxane 3-10.

(iii) Chlorinated paraffin 2-10.

(iv) Carbon filter – the balance.

The antifriction material can also contain a dry lubricant in the form of powdery boron nitride, natural graphite or molybdenum disulphide in the amount of 5-10 per cent by weight. The above-described self-lubricating antifriction materials has a number of valuable properties, namely good self-lubricating capacity, low friction coefficient, highly wearability, high mechanical strength, and high thermal resistance. These materials can be used for making components of friction units operating without lubricant, as well as for making components of friction units operating in water, kerosene, lubricating oil, and liquid oxygen.

Self-lubricating antifriction material comprising a carbon filler selected from the group consisting of a powder of fired oil coke, a powder of artificial graphite and carbon fabric, a binder in the form of epoxy resin having a molecular weight of 300-1,560 obtained through condensation of epichlorohydrin with diphenylolpropane and polyalumophenylsiloxane resin having a molecular weight of 5,000-15,000 with a molecular ratio of the silicon atoms to the aluminium atoms equal to 3-8 chlorinated paraffin having a molecular weight of 500-1,100 and chlorine content of 40-70 molecular per cent. The proportion of said component is said self-lubricating antifriction material being as follows (per cent by weight).

(i) Epoxy resin 15-57.

(ii) Polyalumophenylsiloxane 3-10.

(iii) Chlorinated paraffin 2-10.

(iv) Carbon filter – the balance.

A self-lubricating antifriction material also contains a dry lubricant selected from the group consisting of powdery boron nitride, powdery natural graphite, and powdery molybdenum disulphide, said dry lubricant being included into the said antifriction material in an amount of 5-10 per cent by weight.

Chemical Reaction Technique

Characterization and antifriction on the solid lubrication. MoS2 films prepared by the chemical ruction technique. The inorganic solid lubricant molybdenum disulphide (MoS2) is a kind of solid lubricant which has been applied extensively for a long time. Its crystalline microstructures tri-biological properties and antifriction mechanisms have been studied deeply. Dunn *et.al.,* investigated the XRD spectrum variation of MoS2 in detail. Feldman *et.al.,* reported the growth pattern of MoS2 which was claded with carbon nano tubes and scientist Chhowalla has studied the tri-biological properties of nano particles of MIS2. There are lots of techniques for preparing of MoS2 film such as magnetron sputtering, ion beam-assisted deposition, anode oxidation combined with heat treatment, chemical reaction and high temperature annealing as well as so gel method. The above techniques are useful, but obviously have the disadvantages such as inaccurate atomic ratio between sulfur and molybdenum and low deposition efficiency, or oxidation after high temperature annealing or poor bonding strength with substrate. To develop the preparation technique for MoS2 film combined the advantages of high deposition efficiency in multi-arc ion plating and the simple low cost low temperature ion sulfuration, the authors adopted a two-step chemical reaction technique.

It is widely accepted that the excellent antifriction property of the MoS2. MoS2 film is associated with the layered crystal structure of the solid lubricant MoS2. MoS2 has a close-packed hexagonal structure with lattice constant of a ZO.316 nm. cZ1.229 nm. In the crystal lattice, the close-packed groups consisting of three layers of S, Mo, and S are formed. The thickness of the group is 0.625 nm and the bonding between the MoS2 layers is weak. Therefore, slippage happens easily along the closely packed plane, resulting in the remarkable antifriction performance is shown.

Conclusion

(i) The solid lubrication composite MoS2 film was successfully prepared by a two-step chemical reaction method, namely multiarc ion plating plus low temp ion sulfuration on the 1,045 steel. The solid lubricant MoS2 is more on the films surface and becomes less and less with the increase of depth.

(ii) The obvious sharp island shape was presented on the MoS2 film and the diameter of each island shape crystal grain was less than 100 nm. The thickness of the MoS2 film was about 2 nm and the bonding strength with substrate was strong.

(iii) The solid lubrication MoS2 film possessed the excellent antifriction property. It is a kind of outstanding solid lubrication film in the future.

Damage Tolerant Fusion Bonded Epoxy Coating

A novel technique has been developed which significantly improves the damage tolerance of epoxy coated components in a variety of corrosive environments. Characterization of these coatings via an array of AC and DC electrochemical techniques has revealed considerable improvements in the overall corrosion performance as a result of this technology. The quality of the protective coating is thereby maintained, despite minor damage, which may occur on the job site. Furthermore, this improved corrosion performance enhances. Cathodic disbonding (CD) performance while the impact resistance and flexibility of the Fusion Bonded Epoxy (FBE) costing are unaffected.

Corrosion is a global problem, consuming 3 -4 per cent of gross national product in the developed countries in the world. Selecting economical and effective techniques for minimizing the effects of corrosion is a critical design decision for pipeline systems. Corrosion protection is essential to prevent leaks, environmental disasters, fire and explosion, personal injury, service disruption, and costly maintenance. Thus, in addition to effectively dictating the lifetime of the pipeline, the corrosion prevention system also significantly influences the pipelines operational costs such as general maintenance, pumping energy, and capacity upgrades. Although these protective measures are critical, they represent only a small fraction of the overall long-term cost of a pipeline system.

Today, higher operating temperature and a host of hostile environmental conditions that the pipelines materials encounter during installation and use require a new generation of coating (2) to protect both the interior and exterior of the pipe. Hydrogen sulfide (H_2S) increased level of carbon dioxide (CO_2) and other factors contribute to a pipeline environment that increases levels of internal corrosion. There are many possible solutions to these problems including use of corrosion resistant alloys, inhibitors and corrosion protective linings and coatings. FBE coatings have offered an effective solution to these problems for nearly 40 years.

As the times and exposure conditions have changed, FBE coatings have evolved as well. More demanding transportation, storage, installation, and pipeline operating conditions require the use of advanced FBE-based worldclass coatings to protect the pipe exterior. In addition, improved field application technology provided comparable quality same system coatings for the girth weld. FBEs have been formulated to operate in these very harsh service environments.

Application of Antifriction Technology in Disaster Prevention/Mitigation

Application of antifriction technology in disaster prevention mitigation especially in case of earthquake scenario for the purpose of risk prevention is as follows:

1. Seismic Vibration Control: Seismic vibration control is a set of technical means aimed to mitigate seismic impacts in building and non-building structures. All seismic vibration control devices may be classified as passive, active or hybrid where:

(i) Passive Control Devices: Passive control devices have no feedback capability between them, structural elements and the ground.

(ii) Active Control Devices: Active control devices incorporate real time recording instrumentation on the ground integrated with the earthquake input, processing equipment and actuators with the structure.

(iii) Hybrid Control Devices: These have combined features of active and passive control systems.

When ground seismic waves reach up and start to penetrate a base of a building, their energy flow density, due to reflections, reduces dramatically usually, up to 90 per cent. However, the remaining portions of the incident waves during a major earthquake still bear a huge devastating potential.

All seismic waves enter a superstructure, there are a number of ways to control them in order to soothe their damaging effect and improve the buildings seismic performance for example,

(i) To dissipate the save energy inside a superstructure with properly engineered dampers.

(ii) To disperse the wage energy between a wider range of frequencies.

(iii) To absorb the resonant portions of the whole wave frequencies band with the help of so-called mass dampers.

Devices of the last kind, abbreviated correspondingly as TMD for the tunnel (passive), AMD for the active, and as HMD for hybrid mass dampers have been studied and installed in high-rise buildings, predominantly in Japan for a quarter of a century. However, there is quite another approach; partial suppression of the seismic energy flow into the superstructure known as seismic on base isolation. For this some pads are inserted into or under all major load carrying elements in the base of the building which should substantially decouple a structure from its substructure resting on a shaking ground.

2. Dry Stone Walls Control: People of Inca civilization were masters of the polished dry stone walls, called ashlar, where blocks of stone were cut to fit together tightly without any mortar. The Incas were among the best stone masons in the world has ever seen and many junctions in their masonry were so perfect that even blades of grass could not fit between the stones.

Peru is a highly seismic land and for centuries the mortar free construction proved to be apparently more earthquake resistant than using mortar. The stones of the dry stone walls built by the Incas could move slightly and resettle without the walls collapsing which should be recognized as an ingenious passive structural control technique employing both the principles of energy dissipation and that of the suppression resonant amplifications.

3. Lead Rubber Bearings: Lead Rubber Bearings (LRB) are a type of base isolation employing a heavy damping. It was invented by Bill Robinson, a New Zealander. Heavy damping mechanism incorporated in vibration control technologies and particularly in base isolation devices is often considered a valuable source of suppressing vibration thus enhancing a buildings seismic performance. However, for the rather plaint systems, such as base isolated structure with a relatively low bearing stiffness, but with a high damping, the so-called damping force may turnout the main pushing force at a strong earthquake. The bearing is made of rubber with a lead core. It was a uniaxial test in which the bearing was also under a full structure load. Many building and bridges, both in New Zealand and elsewhere, are protected with lead dampers and lead and rubber bearings. Te Papa Tongarewa, the national museum of New Zealand and New Zealand Parliament buildings have been fitted with the bearings. Both are in Wellington which sits on an active earthquake fault.

4. Tuned Mass Damper: Typically the tuned dampers are huge concrete blocks mounted in skyscrapers or other structures and moved in opposition to the resonance frequency oscillations of the structures by means of some sort of spring mechanism.

Taipei 101 skyscraper needs to withstand typhoon winds and earthquake tremours common in the area of the Asia-Pacific. For this purpose, a steel pendulum weighing 660 metric tonnses that serve as a tuned mass damper was designed and installed atop the structure. Suspended from the 92nd to 88th floor, the pendulums sways to decrease resonant amplifications of later displacement in the building caused by earthquake and strong gusts.

5. Friction Pendulum Bearings: Friction pendulum bearings (FPB) is another name of friction pendulum bearings systems. It is based on three pillars.

(i) Articulated friction slider.

(ii) Spherical concave sliding surface.

(iii) Enclosing cylinder for lateral displacement restraint.

6. Building Elevation Control: Building elevation control is a valuable source of vibration of seismic loading, pyramid-shaped skyscrapers continue to attract attention of architects and engineers because such structures promise a better stability against earthquakes and winds. The elevation configuration can prevent buildings resonant amplification because a properly configured building disperses the shear wave energy between wide ranges of frequencies. Earthquake or wind quieting ability of the elevation configuration is provided by a specific pattern of multiple reflections and transmission of vertically propagating shear waves, which are generated by breakdowns into homogeneity of story layers, and a taper. Any abrupt changes of the propagating waves velocity result in a considerable dispersion of the wave energy between a wide ranges of frequencies thus preventing the resonant displacement amplification in the building. A tapered profile of a building is not a compulsory feature of this method of structural control. A similar resonance preventing effect can be also obtained by a proper tapering of other characteristics of a building structure, namely, its mass and stiffness. As a result the building elevation control techniques permit an architectural design that may be both attractive and functional.

MANGROVES

Anthropological pressures and natural calamities are the enemies of the ecosystem, so as the growing industrial areas and discharge of industrial and domestic sewage is polluting these areas. Many studies have highlighted these problems and the need for conservation efforts is considered.

It is proved beyond doubt that the presence of mangrove ecosystem on coastal lines, saves lives and property during the onset of hazards like cyclones, floods, landslides, etc., mangroves are salt tolerant plants of tropical and subtropical intertidal regions of the world. The specific regions where these plants grow are called mangrove ecosystem. These plants are known to be highly productive, sensitive and fragile. Mangrove is a plant community which lives between sea and shore where tidal floods are more and they are amazing trees living half way between sea and land. They are unique in the sense that they can survive salt water, whereas others cannot. Another feature of mangrove is the ability to live in a mix of fresh water and sea water and grow rapidly.

The term mangrove refers to a diverse group of salt-tolerant trees and other plant species that are found along sheltered tropical and subtropical shores. Mangroves are buffers between the land and the sea. They are also home to a wide variety of marine and terrestrial life, and serve as nurseries for many coral reef and commercially important fish species. The term "mangrove" may be used more narrowly only for the mangrove family of plants, the Rhizophoraceae, or even more specifically just for mangrove trees of the genus Rhizophora. Mangroves dominate three quarters of tropical coastlines. The geographical location where the mangrove presence is larges are Africa, America, Continetal United States, Central America and Caribbean, South America, Asia, Indo Malasya Ecozone, Middle East, Australia, and Pacific Islands.

There are different types of mangroves and they are:

(a) **Red Mangrove:** These are mangroves which grow along the shoreline and face the toughest condition and are red in colour.

(b) **White Mangrove:** These are mangroves found occupying higher lands than the red and black mangroves.

(c) **Black Mangrove:** Are characterized by long roots and root-like projections and grows in elevated positions. They provide oxygen to underground roots system.

(d) **Buttonwood Mangrove:** Found in the upland transitional zones and has button-like flowers.

Mangroves in India

- ❖ The largest remaining tract of mangrove forest in the world is found in the Sundarbans.
- ❖ The Pichavaram Mangrove Forest near Chidambaram, is the world's second largest mangrove forest.
- ❖ Andaman and Nicobar Islands, the Gulf of Kutch, Bhitarkanika Mangroves, Godavari-Krishna mangroves, Ganges-Surma-Meghna River system are some of the significant mangroves.

Importance of Mangroves

The mangrove system is of greater importance in the preservation of ecological system in a country and covers the following benefits:

- ❖ Mangroves protect costal areas from tsunamis.
- ❖ Mangroves help buffer against cyclones.
- ❖ Act as a catalyst in reclaiming land from seas. This is a very unique phenomenon, since there is a general tendency of water to engulf land.
- ❖ Mangroves protect coastal areas from storm surge (especially during hurricanes).
- ❖ Act as a barrier against typhoons.
- ❖ Mangroves help in preventing soil erosion.
- ❖ The mangroves both shield the land from wind and trap sediment in their roots, maintaining a shallow slope on the seabed that absorbs the energy of tidal surges.
- ❖ In addition, mangroves can buffer coastlines during tsunami events. Mangrove forests reduce the impact of tsunamis by reducing both the height and the velocity of the incoming waves, and by distributing water among the canals and creeks of the mangroves, thus decreasing the level of inundation.
- ❖ Mangroves form a unique ecosystem in the environment and play an important role in governing the coastal areas. In spite of its great importance, degradation of mangroves is an alarming issue.
- ❖ Humans definitely have an enormous influence on how well mangroves survive.

- ❖ Awareness to local people has to be created especially on the importance of mangroves and their management

Role of Mangroves in DM

The use or role of mangroves can be best understood on the following results or situations:

- ❖ Naluvedapathy a village in Tamil Nadu was protected from tsunami destruction – the villagers planted 80,244 saplings in order to get into the Guinness Book of World Records. When the tsunami struck, much of the land around the village was flooded, but the village itself suffered minimal damage.
- ❖ Pichavaram mangrove forest protected hamlets namely, T.S.Pettai, Vadakku Pichavaram, Therkku Pichavaram, Meenavar Colony, MGR Nagar, and Kalaingar Nagar against the fury of tsunami. These hamlets are located between 100-1,000 m from mangroves. In these hamlets seawater has not entered into the village and there is no loss of property.
- ❖ The 1999 'super cyclone' that ravaged Orissa state in eastern India, killing an estimated 10,000 people.

The scientists found that coastal villages in Orissa with the widest mangrove belts suffered fewer deaths, compared to those with narrower or no mangroves.

- ❖ Mangroves minimize the fury of cyclones.
- ❖ Mangroves reduces the fury of tsunami.
- ❖ Mangroves help control floods.
- ❖ Mangroves help prevention of soil erosion.
- ❖ Mangroves act as a buffer zone between land and sea.
- ❖ Mangroves help purify water source.
- ❖ Besides they are important from aesthetic and beauty aspect.

Threats for Mangroves

Like all other areas the mangrove ecosystem is also under threat from various sources and the important sources of threat are from:

(a) Industrial and domestic pollution.

(b) Port development.

(c) Dumping of all kinds of waste and debris.

(d) Deforestation for fuel wood.

(e) Over-harvesting of marine resources.

4.7 QUESTIONS

1. Define disaster operations management.
2. What are the components of disaster operations management?
3. Write short notes on risk assessment in disaster management.
4. What is land use planning and its role in disaster management?
5. What is a mangrove? and what are the major threats for them?
6. Describe the major challenges for inter linking of rivers.
7. Write a note on the role of insurance in disaster risk reduction.

Institutional Awareness and Safety Programmes

Learning Objectives

- To enlighten the role of the state, armed forces, and other institutions and how to create the institutional awareness for disaster mitigation.
- To enlighten the role of state
- To through light on the armed forces and their roles
- To enlist the institutional awareness
- To prepare the institution to mitigate against disasters
- To help the institutions to train their human resources on disaster mitigation

Structure

5.1 Institutional Awareness

5.2 The Government Initiatives

5.3 Institutional Frameworks and Structures

5.4 Role of NGOs in Disaster Management

5.5 Risk Transfer Mechanisms

5.6 Role of Media in Disaster

5.7 Disaster Management Information System

5.8 Questions

Without a community involvement, all the disaster management efforts put up by the various government and non-government agencies are insufficient. Community involvement includes roles of individuals and groups and this involvement makes the relief process and reconstruction process more effective and meaningful. One has to agree that the communities comprise of the poor and in many occasion they fail to understand the different aspects of disaster management and are unable to appreciate the efforts, which in turn, affects effectiveness. Therefore, institutional awareness and safety programmes are very important in fighting disaster.

5.1 INSTITUTIONAL AWARENESS

Creating institutional awareness for disaster mitigation involves the following:

(a) **Strengthening the Institutional Framework:** It is very essential for a strong permanent administrative body, which monitors the development of various schemes across departments and suggest mitigation measures. The national disaster management centre (NMDC) can perform this function with proper legal sanctions and provisions. The director of NMDC can be the authority incharge of the disaster funds. This office can coordinate with all functional experts for a viable strategy.

(b) **Disaster Management Regulation and Rehabilitation Policy:** Any disaster management legislation should include a viable disaster management plan documents at Central, State, District, and Village level and pave the way for local community participation. The policy should include legislation on compensation, resettlement, entitlements, etc., in detail.

(c) **Resources and Incentives:** The disaster mitigation plans require expenditure on developmental activities and relief and this in turn requires resources and incentives. The success of the mitigation plans requires incentives for the communities to encourage mitigation efforts.

(d) **Insurance:** The focus on disaster relief insurance is a matter of paramount importance to cover exposed risks. The introduction of disaster-linked insurance covering both life and property should be actively pursued. It is always possible to have high insurance premiums charged by the insurance companies, in the vulnerable areas depending on the risk, a proper scheme must be laid by the government to subsidize the same.

(e) **Land Use Planning, Hazard Resistant Designs, Structural Alterations to Buildings and Installations:** It is very essential to regulate these areas with proper scientific and legal provisions.

Institutional Safety Management

It is a framework to integrate safety and work and by doing so, it helps in protecting the worker, public, and environment. It is a common sense approach to "Doing Work Safely". Safety measures are measures which are taken proactively to reduce or avoid the impact of risk.

The institutional safety management involves five ISM core functions and they are:

(a) **Define the Scope of Work:** It is the first step in defining the scope of work involved. This will facilitate creating boundaries, job nature, job intricacies, technicalities, risks, etc.

(b) **Identify and Analyze the Hazards:** This is the stage where the identification of hazards associated with the jobs, their properties, etc., are analysed, in detail.

(c) **Develop and Implement Hazard Controls:** In this step, attention is made to develop hazard control measures and implement them properly.

(d) **Perform Work Safety within Controls:** Care is taken to perform the various jobs associated with the project in extreme safety and to perform within the control parameters.

(e) **Feedback and Improvement:** In this stage the various feedbacks of the programmes are analysed and improvement suggested.

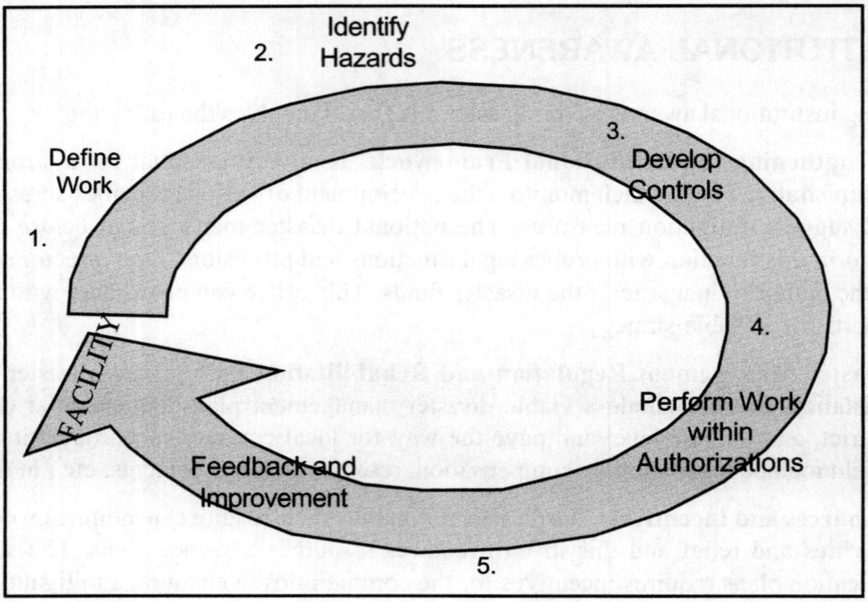

Institutional safety management is applicable always and to all the work and throughout the life cycle of research, design, construction, operations, and maintenance. Similarly, the bottom line applications cover, pre-work screening, plan of the day meetings, pre-job briefings, job site walkthroughs, experimental safety reviews (ESRs)/work permits.

The institutional safety programmes are implemented through the following:

❖ Worker Safety and Health Programme.

❖ Environmental Management System (EMS).

❖ School safety programmes.

❖ City safety programmes.

The institutional safety programmes requires public awareness and cover lot of expectations. By analysing the following a comprehensive ISM is possible.

(a) What kind of work do you perform?

1. Small science and technology – (i.e., basic and applied research)

2. Operations, maintenance, construction, and support – (i.e., electrical, carpentry, mechanical, grounds operator, etc.).

3. Large science and technology machines (i.e., NSLS electrician, RHIC operator, etc.)
4. Skill of the worker activities.

(b) How do you define the scope of work?

1. Job site walk downs, pre-job briefings.
2. Work plans, technical work documents, work permits, radiological work permits, and experimental safety reviews.
3. Work screening to determine if the activity falls within the "Skill of the Worker".
4. Plan of the day meetings – activity discussions and assignment of work activities.
5. Standard operating procedures (SOPs) for operations.

(c) How do you identify hazards associated with your work?

1. Pre-job planning meetings, pre-job walkthroughs, and review of procedure precautions.
2. Experimental safety reviews (ESRs), work permit, and standard operating procedure (SOP).
3. Training, pre-job screening.
4. Job risk assessment (JRA)/facility risk assessments (FRA), environmental process assessments, and job specific work permit reviews.
5. Industrial hygiene and radiological control surveys.
6. Facility use agreements (FUAs) – operating boundary and facility hazards.
7. Job hazard analysis, and radiological work permits (RWPs).

(d) Who do you go to for help?

1. Supervisors, and work control coordinators/managers.
2. ES and H coordinator, facility support representatives, safety and health service representatives.
3. Building managers, and subject matter experts.

(e) What controls are in place to protect you from identified hazards?

1. Controls established in ESRs, work permits, RWPs, and JRAs/FRAs.
2. SOPs are the developed and written such that controls for compliance with safety and health requirements are identified, evaluated, and incorporated into procedures.
3. SBMs subject area requirements (confined space, working with chemicals, lifting safety, lockout/tag out, etc.).
4. Subject matter experts (SMEs).

(f) How are you monitored for exposure to hazards?

(g) Facility support representatives, radiological control technicians (RCTs), safety and health service representatives performance monitoring.

(h) What and/or who authorized you to perform this work?

1. Manager/supervisor verification that adequate preparations have been completed so that work can be performed safely.
2. Work authorization by supervisors and managers approval by issuance of ESRs, work permits, SOPs and RWPs, pre-job briefings by supervisors/managers.
3. Work screening to determine if the activity falls within the "Skill of the Worker".

(i) How do you know you are trained and qualified to perform this work?

1. Assigned job training assessment (JTA) define technical qualifications required.
2. Receive notifications well in advance of qualifications expiring (Brookhaven Training Management System [BTMS]).
3. Meeting the training requirements documented on ESRs, work permits, SOPs, and RWPs.
4. Supervisors, facility support, and work control coordinators verify qualifications before work is authorized to start.

(j) How do you know what personal protective equipment (PPE) is required to do your work? What types of PPE do you use?

1. Standard operating procedure (SOP), ESR, work permit, work plan, RWP, material safety data sheets (MSDS), and thorough training.
2. Safety glasses, safety shoes, double set of anti-contamination clothing, hard hat, ear protection, etc.
3. By speaking to your ES&H Coordinator, Industrial Hygiene Group, or your Facility Support Representative.

(k) Under what conditions are you authorized to stop work?

1. Radiological work that does not meet laboratory requirements or creates a threat of unplanned radiological exposures or releases.
2. Imminent danger exists when you or a co-worker are exposed to a hazard that could result in injury, death, or when there is a significant risk of environmental or equipment damage, and when immediate action is required.
3. Radiological stop work and stop work subject areas.

To issue a stop work order you must have been trained in stop work procedures.

Role of States/Union in Disaster Management

India is one among the Asian nations, vulnerable to the disaster hazards in one way or other. 48.6 per cent of the land mass is prone to earthquakes of moderate to severe intensity, over 48 million hectares of land is prone to floods and around 6,000 kms. is prone to cyclones and hurricanes. In addition most country parts are prone to drought, land slides, etc., and are prone to many man-made hazards. The ever growing population and industrial explosions makes the things even more complex and difficult.

The basic responsibility for undertaking rescue, relief, and rehabilitation measures in the event of a disaster rests with the concerned State Government. The Central Government supplements the efforts of the State Governments by providing the financial support in case of severe natural calamities. In addition, the logistic support extended by the Central, includes deployment of aircrafts and boats, specialist teams of Armed Forces, Central Para Military Forces, and personnel of National Disaster Response Force (NDRF).

The Central assistance also include aarrangements for relief materials and essential commodities including medical stores, restoration of critical infrastructure facilities including communication network and such other assistance as may be required by the affected states to meet the situation effectively.

The Chief Secretary of the State heads a state level committee which is in overall charge of the relief operations in the State and the Relief Commissioners who are in charge of the relief and rehabilitation measures in the wake of natural disasters in their States, function under the overall direction and control of the state level committee. In many states, Secretary, Department of Revenue, is also in-charge of relief. State Governments usually have relief manuals and the districts have their contingency plan that is updated from time-to-time.

State plan should consider the socio-economic and demographic profile of the region and include the vision, theme and objectives of the State Government. The state plans shall be prepared by the SEC in conformity with the guidelines to be issued on related matters by the SDMA having regard to the guidelines laid down in this regard by the NDMA, and after such consultation with local and district authorities and the people's representatives as the SEC may deem fit.

5.2 THE GOVERNMENT INITIATIVES

(a) **High Powered Committee:** The first and the foremost is the constitution of high powered committee for formulating a systematic fail proof approach to disaster. This committee was formed in 1999 at national level.

(b) **National Committee on Disaster Management:** After the Gujarat earthquake, an all party national committee was set up, with the Prime Minister as the Chairman with representatives from national and state level political parties. This was set up to enable preparation of disaster management plans and to suggest best mitigation measures.

(c) **Cabinet Committee on Management of Natural Calamities:** Was set up to oversee all aspects relating to management of natural calamities including assessment, measures identification and programmes for mitigation. The committee was asked to suggest long-term measures for prevention of calamities, formulate and suggest programmes for building public awareness and create resilience. The finance minister heads the committee as Chairman and Agriculture Minister and Dy. Chairman of Planning Commission as members approves the Central assistance to the States.

(d) **Central and State Government:** The primary responsibility for the disaster mitigation plans are state subject. The Central Government initiates coordination, timely help, etc.

(e) **District Administration:** At this level DDMAs will act as planning, coordinating, and implementing body for disaster management, as per guidelines of NDMA and SDMA.

❖ Local Government
  - Local disaster management Group
  - Local Government disaster coordination centre

❖ Disaster – district
  - District disaster management authority
  - District disaster coordination centre

❖ State Government
  - Major incidents group
  - State disaster management authority
  - State disaster coordination group
  - State disaster coordination centre

❖ Central Government
  - National disaster management authority

State Disaster Management Authority (SDMA)/State Executive Committee (SEC) and Departments

Section 23 of the DM Act, 2005 stipulates that there shall be a DM plan for each State. This includes the total plan for the state and provides for review and adjustments and allow for provisioning the finance required for the plans. This also envisages the provision of different plans by the departments of the State Government, in line with the State plan. The State plans are normally prepared by the SEC in line with the guidelines given by the SDMA and NDMA. The State plan prepared by the SEC can be approved by the SDMA.

The main aim of the state disaster management plan is to ensure that the various components are addressed while planning, preparedness, operation, and involvement. While setting the objectives for the DM planning, the following factors may be examined:

(a) Ensure that DM receives the highest priority.

(b) Ensure the importance of community in the DM process.

(c) Prioritizing DM concerns into development planning process.

(d) Ensure forecasting and early warning systems by using the technology.

(e) Ensuring participation of all concerned including the media.

(f) Ensuring efficient response and relief with utmost care.

(g) Ensuring reconstruction.

(h) Ensuring recovery of communities and economy.

The State DM plans should focus on vulnerability and risk assessment of the State in line with the NDMA guidelines. The process is time-consuming and cannot be after the outcome of a disaster. On the basis of the available credible information the state should draw a detailed plan and provide for timely updation. The approach to the preparation of state plan should take into account past history and experiences. The state plan should adopt the generic categorization of disasters with specific state level plans for various departments to handle different disasters. The various levels of disasters are classified into L_0, L_1, L_2, and L_3 according to their power of destruction and the ability with which the authorities could deal with them.

Various colour codes are specified for different levels, they are.

L_0: denotes normal level for close monitoring.

L_1: denotes disasters which can be managed at the District level.

L_2: denotes disasters which may need State participation.

L_3: denotes large-scale involvement of District, State, and Central Government.

It is to be understood that the Central level participation is necessitated in the L_3 level and at all other levels the State and local administration involves.

The State Governments are supported by the following agencies in disaster situations:

(a) Armed Forces.

(b) Central Paramilitary Forces.

(c) State Police and Fire Force.

(d) Home Guards and Civil Police.

(e) State Disaster Response Force.

(f) National Cadet Corps NCC.

Role of Armed Forces

The Indian Armed Forces consists of three divisions namely, The Army, Navy and Air Force. Apart from that there are Para Military forces like the Rapid action force, Central Reserve Police Force (CRPF), Border Security Force (BSF), Central Industrial Security Force (CISF), Police forces, and National Security Guards (NSG).

It is primary responsibility of the State Government to carry-cut the disaster operations using State police resources. Only when the situation is beyond the control of the State administration, the military forces are summoned. The Army resources are the core resource of the Central Government and are the first to respond to the call in a major disaster. The military sources are depended more due to their ability in dealing with complex ground situations and ability to speed up operations and effectively execute tasks. The military resources are very effective in establishing communications systems, search and rescue operations, health and medical facilities, transportation of food and civil supplies, engineering, etc., immediately on post-disaster phase. This is because the Armed Forces are trained to act in emergencies and always prepared. They expertise in providing timely evacuation and relief is the strength of Army. The government and private believe in the Military capabilities more because of their proven capabilities and preparedness.

The disaster management plans always include a major role for the Armed Forces and the need for involving them is based on the following strong situations:

(a) Response in a disaster situation has to be quick and effective.

(b) Catastrophic events cannot be managed by civilian administration.

(c) Lack of training and resource constraints with local civilians.

(d) Military has high level of preparedness for operations.

(e) Extra sensitive ability to work in difficult and adverse situations.

(f) Institutionalization of the disaster response system in India.

Role of Armed Forces/IAF in Disaster Management

(a) The military resource of any country are probably those best organized and managed to provide support to full range of public services such as public work, communication, transport, health and emergency medical services, rescue and support activities.

(b) The armed forces are always in the state of operational readiness to move quickly to any disaster affected areas and they operate in trigger mechanism.

(c) Military aircrafts have always been used in transportation of essential commodities far from places in a short span of time.

(d) Realizing the importance of the service of the armed forces, the government has decided to set up National Disaster Response Force (NDRF) consisting of eight battalions of Central Police Forces to respond to nuclear, biological, and chemical related emergencies.

(e) The Army helps in evacuation and shifting, rescue of stranded people, setting up of relief camps, air dropping of food and water, distribution of food, water and medicines, logistical support, erecting emergency structures for restoration of communication, power, etc., constructing bridges, temporary dams, etc.

(f) The Army helps in maintaining law and order. They use the land, air, and sea medium to locate and provide relief.

(g) The military can utilize the resources of all the three divisions effectively and coordinate functions in a disciplined manner.

(h) In addition, the military can help in survey and damage assessment, set up infrastructure, restore essential services, explosive detection and deactivate it, provide diving support and manage international relief.

(i) The military has the inherent strength of discipline, organizational strength, defined hierarchy, speedy dissemination of orders, versatility of response, etc., and all these strengths make them the best option.

The following agencies extend multi-various help and voluntary services during a disaster.

a. Federal Emergency Management Agency (FEMA).

b. Hospitals/medical associations.

c. Educational institutions to write.

d. Insurance companies.

e. NGOs.

f. Charitable organizations.

g. Voluntary groups like lions club, cannel clubs.

h. NCC.

Important Statutes/Legal Provisions

Legal and regulatory frameworks comprise the laws, executive orders and other legal instruments that set the ground rules for governmental and non-governmental activities relating to disasters and risk reduction. They define the authorities, responsibilities, and roles of officials and organizations, establish legal authority for organizations and programmes, and sometimes create organizations and coordination mechanisms. They may dictate or encourage relevant policies, practices and processes.

Of the 1/19 national reports submitted to the World Conference on Disaster Reduction, Kobe, 2005, 80 per cent included some form of legislation for disaster management. Typically, the national legal and regulatory framework is governed by a core piece of legislation, often referred to as the National Disaster Management Act. The latter is often quite vague and generally requires specific implementing regulations with details on how the law should be implemented in certain areas. The recently adopted Disaster Management Law of Indonesia (April 2007) for example, called for specific implementing regulations to be enacted by the government including one on the role of international institutions and international non-governmental institutions in disaster management in the country.

The important statutes and legal provisions of disaster management are:

(a) Disaster Management Act, 2005: The DM Act, 2005 lays down the legal, financial, institutional, administrative and coordination mechanism at the National, State, District, and Village levels. This new institutional framework is expected to bring in major change from the relief centric approach to a proactive regime, which provides larger emphasis on preparedness, prevention, and mitigation.

(b) National Executive Committee: NEC is headed by the Home Secretary as Chairman and the Secretaries of Agriculture, Defense, Energy, Environment, Forest, Finance, Health, Power, Rural, and Science and Technology. In addition the Chiefs of Army, Navy, and Air Force are also invitees to the committee.

(c) National Disaster Management Authority (NDMA): NDMA is an apex body of the Central Government for disaster management headed by the Prime Minister. It holds the responsibility of laying down policies, plans, and response. It has power to approve the disaster plans of the Central Government and the various ministries. NDMA will over see all functions and matters relating to DM.

NDMA formulate guidelines and facilitate training and preparedness activities.

(d) National Institute of Disaster Management NIDM: It is a premium national level organization engaged in the development of human resources in the field of disaster mitigation and disaster management. The NIDM was established in the year 2003 at New Delhi and will concentrate on developing skills required to combat disaster.

NIDM is expected to gear up National, State, and District level administration to tackle disaster and will coordinate research and training in this field. The objective of NIDM is set to undertake quality research, to work as national resource centre, to professionalize disaster risk reduction, to promote quality training and education, and to promote working partnerships with the various agencies.

(e) All India Disaster Mitigation Institute (AIDMI): AIDMI is a non-governmental resource group based at Gujarat and is a community based action research, action planning and action advocacy organisation. It concentrates towards bridging the gap between policy and practice. As an operational and learning organization, it is able to create a link with the local communities, centre and the international governments on policies of relief and development.

(f) State Disaster Management Authority (SDMA): SDMA is headed by the chief minister and it lays down policies and plans for DM in the State. It has powers to approve the State plan prepared in line with the NDMA guidelines and coordinate the implementation of the plans. It sanctions the funds required for the State plans and coordinates the different departments in preparedness, response, and mitigation.

The SDMA is assisted by an SEC constituted by the State Government for performing its functions. SEC is headed by the Chief Secretary to the State Government which coordinates and controls the implementation of the State plans, National policy, and National plan.

(g) District Disaster Management Authority (DDMA): The DDMA is headed by the District Collector or District Magistrate, with an elected member from the local authority as co-chairperson. DDMA will act as the planning, coordinating, implementing, and monitoring agency at the District level. They act according to the guidelines of NDMA and SDMA and ensure that the prevention, preparedness, mitigation and response measures are followed by the departments, and local authorities.

(h) Local Authorities: Local authorities include Panchayaths, Municipalities, Corporations, Town Planning and the like. The bodies will ensure capacity building of their officers for managing the disasters, relief works, rehabilitation, and reconstruction activities.

5.3 INSTITUTIONAL FRAMEWORKS AND STRUCTURES

Institutional frameworks and structures comprise all organizations or institutions with a recognized role to play in disaster risk management, the mechanism for coordination between them, their human resources, funding, equipment and supplies, leadership and effectiveness. Appropriate institutional frameworks are needed to carry-out policies and legislative measures.

A sound framework will consist of the sections that deal with:

(a) Operational: The operational plan should take into account the socio-cultural and economic realities of the State and should be based on the different needs of the community. It should be in conformity with the national, district, and village level plans and should incorporate implementation strategies, monitoring and evaluation mechanisms. Operational plans include emergency operation plans, medical plans, casualty management plans, funding plans, etc.

(b) **Administrative:** The success of the disaster management plan depends upon the kind of administrative systems created and implemented into the whole system. The administrative measures must be in accordance with the 5-year plans, State DM policy, etc. The systems and institutions for implementation must be clearly understood and spelt out. The system should have in-built facility for accommodating the various agencies, forces, resources, implementations, revisions, and proper documentation and back office procedures.

(c) **Financial:** The DM Act, 2005 makes it mandatory to create a State disaster management fund at the State and District level. The modalities for creation of these funds and the guidelines for utilizing the funds must be clearly spelt out and procedures laid down, for proper and timely drawal of funds. The financial plan must also incorporate details regarding future disaster response and DM concern into the budget. This must reflect the budget for adequate funds for future disaster relief based on past estimation.

(d) **Legal:** This aspect will cover the various legal provisions required for the various projects and agencies and will cover coordination and implementation of national policy, the national plan and the State policy. The legal system should provide the various information to the NDMA relating to the DM plans according to the parameters. The legal system should also ensure revising the building norms, amending the bye-laws and other legislation.

(e) **Process:** This section ensures the flow of the various process and designate the nodal agencies for coordinating the national plan. It identifies the focal points in each group, identifies the officials, trains the officials, and involves the technoadministrative system into the plan. It also describes the nodal agency plans, NGOs, educational institutions, local bodies, media, etc., about their roles and responsibilities.

5.4 ROLE OF NGOs IN DISASTER MANAGEMENT

It is impossible to prevent occurrence of most natural disasters, but it is possible to minimize the impacts of the hazard. It is definitely possible to mitigate the various hazards through measures. The government plays the important role in this disaster management and is supported by other agencies at different stages. One among such agency is NGOs or popularly known as Non-government Organizations.

A specialized unit within the National Health Disaster Management Programme by the name NGOs should coordinate the works of experts in the field of health, public policy and public health, hospital administration, water systems, engineering, planning, and education, etc., NGOs has always been very vibrant in India. They are based on the concept of volunteerism and care for community. Many NGOs undertake DM activities but others take up post-disaster relief work.

The NGOs are seen involved even in the remotest area and their high credibility and acceptability that they enjoy with the local communities, make them a very strong force to reckon with. The NGOs enjoy strong associations with the women group, farmers, youths, and village authorities, etc., which helps them improve their effectiveness and make them the ideal partners in disaster risk reduction plans of the government.

NGOs are defined as "private organizations which conduct and pursue activities to relieve sufferings, promote the interests of poor, provide basic social services or undertake community development".

Generally, NGOs are organized as non-profit corporations (charities) and can be local or international (INGOs). They work independent of government and generally, do not include professional associations, businesses, and foundations.

Examples of NGOs involved in disaster and humanitarian crisis response care are:

(a) MSF.

(b) Oxfam.

(c) Red Cross (not ICRC).

(d) Save the Children.

(e) St. John Ambulance.

(f) World Vision.

Their Core values are:

(a) Neutrality: Aid will not be used for a particular political or religious standpoint.

(b) Impartiality: Aid is given regardless of race, creed, or nationality and is based on need alone.

(c) Independence: Aid agencies shall not act as instruments of government foreign policy.

Who Pays Them?

The NGOs are funded by the private donations from citizens, business men, and foundations and from international Organization (UN) and the National Government. They are monitored by self-regulation, NGO standards, Red Cross Code of conduct, Inter action PVO standards, and sphere minimum standards.

The NGOs generally play an important part in the different phases of disaster management and risk reduction. Their effort does not bear the desired fruit as they are depended on the government agencies which lack effective coordination. However, within the constraints the NGOs put up very high level of performance. NGOs spread their activities in the following areas:

(a) Search and Rescue: Finding those who may be trapped by building collapse and help them and escorting them to safety.

(b) Assessment of Immediate Shelter and Living Needs: Working out what is required, where, in what quantities, and for whom is the right action.

(c) Medical Support: Provision of medical care and preventing the spread of disease through immunization, provision of safe water and food, waste disposal and burial of the dead.

(d) Basic Needs: Procuring and distributing food, shelter, and clothing.

(e) Gender: Understanding the differing requirements of men and women in families and communities to identify needs and ensure fair distribution of recovery resources.

(f) Livelihood and Economy: Assisting people to earn a living to help them recover quicker from adversity.

(g) Emotional Support: Counselling and reuniting separated families.

(h) Logistics: Transportation of people and equipment.

(i) Finance: Obtaining, allocating, and accounting for money.

(j) Communication: Media coverage, information for families, and fund raising.

(k) Infrastructure: Temporary restoration of roads, and electricity.

National NGO Task Force

A national NGO task force was established by the NDMA in 2006 and various actions were taken to consolidate and clarify the efforts of the various agencies in disaster management. NGOs remain as the important resource for the NDMA for any current and future initiatives. Therefore, it is important to define the role of NGOs for a seamless partnership and relationship. It is also important to work with this group through the National NGO Task Force in disaster management, for the formulation of guidelines for pre-disaster, post-disaster, and reconstruction follow-ups.

Following are the objectives of NGO task force:

(a) Mapping of NGOs at state and district levels.

(b) Training the capability building.

(c) Mainstreaming vulnerability reduction through CBDRM.

(d) Guidelines for GO-NGO understanding.

(e) Assistance for building teams.

(f) Integrating CBDRM in development programmes.

(g) Strengthening disaster preparedness, mitigation, and response system.

(h) Setting up working groups on specific areas.

Challenges to NGOs

The working of the NGOs has been seriously affected due to various reasons and they face the following challenges:

1. Weak coordination.
2. Short time spans and relief interventions.
3. Neglect of inaccessible areas.
4. Tendency to rush to the epicentre areas.
5. Inadequate adherence to humanitarian practices.
6. Inadequate transparency of accounting and donors.
7. Neglect of rural urban diversity.
8. Lack of exit strategy during transition.
9. Advocacy role of NGOs.

Role of Corporate in Disaster

Unlike the bounty of nature, its fury is a great leveller. Natural disasters affect everyone alike although the nature of impact varies from region-to-region and including the community, the Corporate sector and others has been brought about for building holistic capabilities for disaster management. The focus has shifted to a balanced approach including pre-disaster aspects such as disaster prevention, mitigation, and preparedness since it is felt that appropriate mitigation measures can substantially, if not wholly, reduce the heavy toll of lives and property, the dissipation of developmental, industrial, and infrastructural gains and the hard-earned socio-economic infrastructure.

For long, the corporate sector had been viewed as a separate entity perennially ranged at the other end of the spectrum *vis-à-vis* the society. Over the past few decades, this perception has undergone a complete metamorphosis and the existence of corporate sector is today intimately intertwined with the safety and well-being of the society. The catastrophic fallout of natural disasters on the community and the people is very well documented by now. At the same time, it is their impact on the existence, survival and viability of the economic muscle of a nation, community, and region, i.e., the corporate sector, which also merits equally focused attention. The critical and catalytic role the corporate sector can play in mainstreaming disaster management into not only its own functioning but also in other sectors and among the community is now being appreciated and duly recognized as an inalienable part of corporate social responsibility.

India has been traditionally vulnerable to natural disasters on account of its unique geo-climatic conditions. In view of India's high vulnerability profile, the recurrent phenomena of a range of geophysical as well as hydro-meteorological hazards impact millions across the country leaving behind a trail of heavy loss of lives, property, and livelihoods. In many areas of the country, disaster losses tend to outweigh the development gains. The economic and social costs on account of losses caused by natural disasters continue to mount year-after-year as disasters occur with unfailing regularity encompassing every segment of national life including the industrial and corporate sector.

The involvement and association of the corporate sector with national risk reduction and risk management initiatives and with dissemination of appropriate and practical structural and non-structural disaster prevention and mitigation measures necessary for their safe and disaster-free functioning has been accorded priority as part of a strategy to systematically mainstream holistic disaster management into the functioning of the corporate sector. The ever-expanding extent, sweep and scale of natural disasters has made it imperative for the ccorporate sector to initiate and integrate disaster risk prevention and mitigation measures in all facets of their functioning and operations with the objective of safeguarding the painstakingly built industrial assets from the impact of natural disasters.

Today, the corporate sector has become an inalienable part of our socio-economic and national life and a vibrant industry is not only better placed to make itself sustainable but can also act as a composite foil to the governmental efforts at holistic disaster management. Recognizing the importance of integrating the corporate sector and their nodal organizations in disaster prevention, mitigation, and preparedness agenda, the National Disaster Management Framework drawn up by the Ministry of Home Affairs, Government of India envisages "involvement of corporate sector in awareness generation and disaster preparedness and mitigation planning" through sensitization, training, and coopting of the corporate sector and their nodal bodies in planning process, and response mechanisms.

The Corporate Role

In keeping with the paradigm shift in its approach to disaster management brought about by the Government of India and the recurring phenomenon of natural disasters impacting all sectors of socio-economic life, including the Corporate sector, and inflicting heavy economic losses, focused attention has been given to risk mitigation endeavors to systematically reduce the vulnerabilities. The new approach stems from the premise that development in any sector, more so in the Corporate world, cannot be sustainable and viable unless risk reduction and mitigation measures are built into the development processes and that investments in mitigation are much more cost-effective than expenditure on relief, rehabilitation, and re-construction. Recognizing the gargantuan proportions of the challenge posed by recurring incidence of natural catastrophes, association and involvement of Corporate sector and their representative nodal organizations for initiating disaster risk management measures has been considered as integral to success of disaster management initiatives. The Corporate in every country have always played a major role in post-disaster relief, rehabilitation, and reconstruction efforts in the affected regions.

One such incident happened in Gujarat in 2001. The industrial and corporate organizations like the Confederation of Indian Industry (CII), the Federation of Indian Chamber of Commerce and Industry (FICCI), the PHD Chambers of Commerce and Industry and other industry and area-specific manufacturers and traders associations have been in the forefront of providing much-needed succor to the affected populace for ameliorating their sufferings.

Apart form addressing natural disasters, CII has established an Environment Management Division (EMD) involved in research and propagation of environmentally sound industrial systems and processes. It has been deeply involved in advising and developing system and methodologies for safer and disaster-free handling of chemicals and other hazardous substances in production processes and procedures. The EMD has also been assisting the Industries in development and implementation of on-site and off-site disaster management plans for ushering into an environment friendly industrial scenario, especially in the light of experience of the Bhopal Gas Tragedy.

It is, therefore, imperative for the success of initiatives in the area of disaster risk management that Corporate sector organizations and their networks are associated with different facets of disaster management.

Corporate Social Responsibility and Disaster Management

Corporate Social Responsibility (CSR) permeates every aspect of the functioning on Corporate sector. The Corporates always look for ways and means to enhance the brand value of their company and their products. It is in this context that corporate social responsibility makes good business sense. It is a business strategy that works.

The business corporations, because of their high visibility, are being adjudged not merely on the basis of their bottom lines but also on their social behaviour. By integrating CSR into its business strategy as a core value, the corporates not only make a significant contribution to a better society but are also recognized for doing so. This has obvious benefits for the company. In fact, enormous rewards are there both for the business/industrial community as well as the society. The companies are motivated to achieve profitability, sustainable growth and human progress by placing corporate social responsibility in the mainstream of their business practice. As part of their corporate social responsibility, the companies are encouraged to conduct business responsibly by contributing to the economic health and development of communities in which they operate; create healthy and safe working conditions to attract and retain a quality workforce; manage risk more efficiently and minimize the negative impact of activities on the environment and its resources; be accountable to all stakeholders through dialogue and transparency regarding economic, social, and environmental impacts of business activities; operate a good governance structure and uphold the highest standards and ethics while conducting business. The corporate sector is also an integral part of the society. As a member of the community, it is its responsibility to contribute to sustainable development and to integrate social and concerns in its business operations as well as in its interaction with other stakeholders.

It can play a leading role in supporting and building the knowledge, capacity and skills of the community in comprehensive risk-based disaster management activities ranging from prevention, mitigation and preparedness to response and recovery. It can offer human and financial resources and can also be a precious source of technical know-how, as for example, in the case of identification and research on technological solutions to prepare for and respond to natural disasters.

Economic Impact of Disasters on Corporate Sector

At the global level, nearly 700 major catastrophes take place every year affecting billions in different countries. The disasters periodically visit the same geographical regions and set the development clock back by decades. It is similar to taking two steps forward and one step backwards. In some countries, this equation even gets reversed. The repeated occurrence of natural catastrophes undermines the economic viability of the communities as well as the corporate sector. It is estimated that 28 developing countries, including India, suffered direct losses of over 1 billion USD each during the past 20 years.

It is estimated that nearly 10,000 industrial units went out of production at the hands of the earthquake and an overwhelming majority of the remaining ones operated at only 50 per cent of their output capacity. The economic loss on account of disruption of industrial and commercial activity for over a month is pegged at more than ₹ 2,000 crore. The earthquake eroded nearly 2 per cent of the GDP of the State of Gujarat – one of the most industrially advanced States in the country.

Industrial and Chemical Disasters

In addition to the onslaught of natural disasters casting a long shadow over the viability of the economic sector, susceptibility to industrial and chemical hazards also poses a major threat to the healthy and safe functioning of corporate sector. The industries employ many production processes involving a wide range of chemicals and hazardous raw materials, intermediates, waste and final products. These disasters, though normally caused by irresponsible handling of hazardous substances or due to their improper and unauthorized use or due to inadequate attention to maintenance of manufacturing undermine the very functioning of industries in the region in the aftermath of any untoward incident since such incidents have widespread ramifications and long-term impact on the environment.

The Confederation of Indian Industry and the National Disaster Management Framework (CII)

Working in tandem with the framework developed by the Ministry of Home Affairs envisioning strengthening and development of capacities at all levels for holistic disaster risk management and sustainable development, the Confederation of Indian Industry (CII) has up-scaled the scope of its association with the national disaster management agenda and has emerged as the flag-bearer of initiatives for integrating the same into the functioning of the corporate sector. Extending its support in the area of disaster management since 1999 especially in disaster response, rehabilitation and reconstruction, CII has partnered with the government initiatives and development organizations like the United Nations Development Programme (UNDP) for effective implementation of disaster risk reduction activities and has been regularly organizing summits and symposiums to promote the same. The "Public-Private-People (PPP) Partnership for Natural Disaster Risk Management" is the off-shoot of these initiatives. In order to vest its initiatives *vis-à-vis* disaster management for corporate sector and the community a greater depth and substance and in consultation with the Ministry of Home Affairs, the CII has delineated a sustained programme of action to deepen and strengthen its work addressing the entire socio-economic sector. It is intended to minimize the impact of natural and man-made disasters and to preclude disruption of economic activity impeding achievement of national developmental goals. The joint work plan evolved with the Ministry of Home Affairs primarily entails association of CII in the entire gamut of issues connected with integrating disaster management concerns in the developmental efforts of the private sector. The broad identified themes are:

Awareness Generation: (i) To make people aware of their vulnerabilities and the need for prevention, mitigation and preparedness measures. (ii) Preparation of a booklet containing information on various hazards and the steps to be taken for mitigating the same by CEOs of industries. (iii) Co-opting CII as a member of the Steering Committee for Mass Media Campaign. (iv) Sponsoring awareness generation capsules in print and electronic media. For awareness generation, a booklet has been designed and developed targeted at the CEO's for inducing a culture of safety and risk management. CII will shortly disseminate the same to its member industries.

Training: (i) Training of industrial personnel, nearby community and volunteers in disaster management. (ii) Development of training modules and identification of Master Trainers. (iii) Linking the trained personnel with the disaster management teams under the District Administration.

Mock Drills: Conducting mock drills at regular intervals to enhance preparedness levels and linkages with the District Administration and other Emergency Support Functions (ESF) departments/ agencies, especially targeted at chemical, mining, and pharmaceutical sectors.

Development of on-site and off-site Disaster Management Plans as per the guidelines issued by the Ministry of Environment and Forests. The development of on-site and off-site plans has also been initiated by industries in consultation with some places, these plans have already been formulated and shared with the administration for linking with the District DM plans. The process of development of on-site and off-site DM plans entails identification of the hazards to which the industry, the neighbouring areas and the region is susceptible; estimation of vulnerable zones using credible worst case scenarios; enumeration of characteristics of socio-economic conditions of human population, *viz.,* number, concentration, health conditions, social infrastructure, and support systems in the vulnerable areas; listing of critical facilities in these areas; analysis of risks posed by each industry based on readily available information on the likelihood of severity of consequences; prioritization of industries on the basis of estimated risks; ranking of risks; compilation of information on community safeguards, response capabilities and previous accident records; assessing probability of occurrence of disasters; enumeration of resources available within the premises in the neighbourhood and likely to be mobilized along with their sources to meet the eventualities likely to occur; conducting mock drills to test the viability of the DM plan, etc.

Preparation of Inventory of Resources, Machinery, equipment, and manpower available with the private sector for mobilization in the event of an emergency for being uploaded on the India Disaster Resource Network. Inventorization of resources is a pre-requisite for mounting a speedy and effective disaster response. An online web-enable resource inventory has been developed and commissioned to capture the resources in terms of specialized equipment, machinery, manpower, etc.

Sensitization Programmes for building a mindset of safety and mitigation among industries and industrial personnel through State Chapters of Confederation of Indian Industry. As per the work plan, a number of sensitization programmes have already been conducted in different provinces (states) in association with the State Government authorities and the Ministry of Home Affairs and over 1,500 senior functionaries and personnel from industries across the country have been sensitized to induce a mindset of disaster risk reduction and mitigation.

The sensitization programmes have primarily concentrated on informing the industries about the hazards and the risks keeping in mind the vulnerability profile of the country; the requisite structural and non-structural mitigation measures necessary to protect industrial assets and infrastructure against earthquakes, cyclones, floods, and others; the need to make the manufacturing processes and procedures inherently safe especially against chemical and fire hazards; importance of developing on-site and off-site disaster management plans and establishing linkages with the district administration as also about the role of corporate sector in overall disaster risk reduction and mitigation initiatives.

5.5 RISK TRANSFER MECHANISMS

Apart from disaster risk management measures to arrest the spiralling cost of disasters and their wider socio-economic import, a nascent beginning has also been made in India towards addressing them through risk transfer mechanisms. One of the major mechanisms for risk transfer is the insurance sector and the proposed instrument is the insurance-linked savings-cum loan-cum-subsidy scheme. The logic behind cross-sectoral risk transfers being that the transferor takes on the risk as a part or consequence of its core business and his incentive being that the cost of transferring or hedging the risk is calculated to be lower than the cost of retaining it.

However, insurance in India is yet to receive due recognition as a socio-economic issue with the result that the insurance market in India, both life and non-life, has not been able to fulfil its potential and achieve higher penetration levels. The cover for natural disasters is today considered as part of the cover against the fire hazard. The need of the hour is to view disaster insurance as a step towards disaster preparedness.

In view of the increasing basic disaster frequency and the rapidly mounting disaster-related monetary losses, the insurance sector can provide the requisite risk transfer instruments. However, the private insurance market is struggling to meet the challenge due to low penetration levels. India's general insurance market is at a nascent stage and is considerably underdeveloped in spite of the fact that it has a huge potential. Yet the catastrophe insurance purchasing is insufficient as major insurers do not have accurate up to date accumulation data. Any insurance programme must strategically aim to dissuade location of industries and buildings in high-risk areas and the pricing mechanism should be as per the level of risk and exposure. In high-risk areas, a pooling together of multiple catastrophe risks would also promote coverage. In view of the underdeveloped nature of India's insurance market, the need is to increase penetration and to optimize catastrophe risk capacity. With shift in approach towards disasters, insurance can and should feature as a means of durable finance. It is a principal tool for hedging against financial loss to make the damage suffered bearable at an affordable minimal premium.

The Road Ahead

In view of the imperative need to meet the gigantic challenge posed by natural hazards, the successes achieved, the experience garnered and the onerous task ahead to secure safety and disaster-free functioning of the corporate sector in the larger interests of the nation and the people, the Confederation of Indian Industry (CII) has decided to upscale and deepen its engagement with integration of disaster management agenda into the corporate sector functioning to minimize losses and prevent disruption of economic activity hampering achievement of developmental goals.

In this context, CII is expanding the scope of its activities in association with the Ministry of Home Affairs and the United Nations Development Programme (UNDP) to facilitate sustainable economic growth through disaster risk reduction and mitigation. This envisages an entire gamut of issues connected with mainstreaming disaster management concerns in the developmental efforts at all levels and across a spectrum of sectors.

The main themes to be addressed are:

- Ensuring that existing and upcoming industrial assets and infrastructure are disaster-resistant.
- Ensuring proper citing of industrial establishments considering hazard parameters.
- Making industrial processes and procedures inherently safe.
- Ensuring that transportation, storage, handling, and usage of chemicals and other hazardous raw materials does not pose a threat to the nearby areas and environment.
- Development of on-site and off-site DM plans by industries in association with the District Administration.
- Conducting mock drills at regular intervals to determine the efficacy of the DM plans.
- Preparation of inventory of corporate resources and uploading them on the IDRN – India Disaster Resource Network.
- Large-scale association with awareness generation initiatives aimed at building the knowledge, attitude and skills of the common people for a safer habitat.
- To move away from relief-centric approach to a pro-active assault on vulnerabilities through risk management measures and capacity building of industrial personnel.
- Assessment and retrofitting of existing industrial infrastructure.
- Training of a core team of structural industries on requisite mitigation measures in association with the Ministry of Home Affairs.
- Mainstreaming private sector participation in disaster management.
- Establishing linkages between private sector and the community.
- Networking knowledge on best practices and tools for effective disaster management.
- Development and implementation of appropriate risk transfer mechanisms.
- The establishment of a sound techno-financial regime would facilitate mainstreaming disaster risk management into all aspects of corporate and industrial sectors.

Sustainable Development

It is becoming an accepted practice to integrate sustainable development into the planning and measurement systems of business enterprises. Sustainable development for corporates would entail adopting and implementing business approaches which meet the needs of the industry and its stakeholders while at the same time protecting, sustaining, and enhancing the human and natural resources for the future. It means that economic development must while satisfying the needs of the enterprise protect the community by ensuring that the natural and human resources are not exploited to their detriment. There is an umbilical bond between sustainable development and disaster risk management and the business organizations are recognizing it so. Risk management measures have to be an all-pervasive activity by the corporates across the industrial spectrum and must not remain a one-off activity. It would seek minimization of expenditure on rehabilitation and reconstruction to obviate dissipation of precious developmental resources and help interweave a culture of safety and preparedness in every walk of national life and more so in the corporate sector so that the development efforts are both socially safe and commercially viable and sustainable.

The need is to bring about a change in perceptions, attitudes, pre-conceived notions and mindsets among the corporate sector about the way the things are approached now. Sustainable development envisions integration of economic and social development with environment protection as interdependent and mutually reinforcing pillars. The overarching objective being to change the existing unsustainable patterns of production and consumption.

The World Summit on Sustainable Development (WSSD) defines sustainable development as *"development that meets the needs of the present without compromising the ability of future generations to meet their own needs"*.

For the corporate sector, it is imperative to usher into not only sustainable but also safer development for which harmonization of socio-economic and environment concerns is a must. A multi-hazard approach addressing the disaster management concerns in the corporate sector and the corporates in turn complementing the disaster management endeavours at all levels will ensure a strong and concerted attack on our vulnerabilities.

Conclusion

Disaster management being an all-encompassing and multi-disciplinary activity spanning across all sectors of development, a coordinated action in conjunction with all stakeholders including the corporate sector is a *sine qua non* for overcoming the vulnerabilities and minimizing the risks. It will not only help pooling of resources but would also facilitate exchange of information and expertise across sectors, learn from each others' experience and best practices. The objective of disaster management initiatives is to consciously move towards strengthening the national capabilities in accordance with the status acquired by India as a self-sufficient and self-respecting nation well-positioned to mount an effective and substantive disaster response and to take care of the concerns *vis-à-vis* disaster management across different sectors.

However, effective disaster management is a long-drawn battle against the formidable forces of nature and necessitates devising a comprehensive strategy and work plan based on the lessons learned and experiences gained from every disaster. The shortcomings and gaps need to be addressed and successes built upon. The Government of India as well as other stakeholders including the corporate sector have reaffirmed their commitment and resolve to achieve the objective of moving towards a disaster resilient and safe nation. The task is arduous and the challenge ominous. However, the road map is well-defined and clear. No effort will be spared and no constraint would be allowed to impede the progress towards creating a safe and disaster-free nation and the challenge thrown by successive disasters will be converted into an opportunity for further strengthening disaster risk management measures.

5.6 ROLE OF MEDIA IN DISASTER

The media throughout the world play a vital role in educating the public about disasters, warning of hazards, gathering and transmitting information about affected areas, alerting government officials, relief organizations, and the public to specific needs, and facilitating discussions about disaster preparedness and response.

For the media to fill these roles most effectively, the scientific and disaster mitigation organizations need to establish and strengthen working relationships with the media. One vital factor in effective communications is the creation and repetition of precise and effective messages, both through the mass media and in other alternative forms of communication.

Such messages can empower people to take practical steps to protect themselves from natural hazards and to demand attention by private and governmental organizations to disaster prevention, mitigation, and response.

National Meteorological and Hydrological Services (NMHSs) have a unique responsibility in early warning system (EWS) of states. Their responsibility is mostly concentrated on forecast and warning services both for natural and some of the man-made disasters. In any case, NMHSs should always work in a close cooperation with other organizations involved in a wider state EWS. The state EWS involves, besides NMHS, parts carried out by other authorities such as the river basin boards, civil defence outfits, fire brigades, and local administration at various levels. Besides the "professional way" of dissemination of warnings also media, especially of electronic type, can play important role in dissemination of warnings to the public. This contribution will concentrate on the role of media in early warning leaving their importance in other parts of general disaster management and prevention, e.g., giving general information to people about the danger of disasters, how to prepare to be able to face disasters, etc.

In many countries rather detailed schemes of an overall disaster management have been released often without stressing the importance of "switching on" of such systems by issuing the first warning. Such warning alerts all responsible bodies in the state EW system. If the first warning is sufficiently accurate and timely then a successful alert and response of responsible authorities and of the population can be achieved. Moreover, the follow-up dissemination of forecasts and warnings within an EW system and also dissemination by the media and the mitigation run usually smoothly. On the other hand, an inaccurate or delayed first warning could lead to a panic and increase the damages and losses caused by disaster. As a result, the credibility of an NMHS could decrease significantly. Good preparedness and functioning of NMHS is always critical as "nobody" alarms NMHS!!!

Dissemination of Flood Warnings

Warnings issued mostly by NMHSs are in all cases disseminated to the public via "professional" part of distribution system (covered by a 24 h/day service) by means of Civil Protection and/or Fire Protection Services, flood protection authorities, regional and local administrations. NMHS should always be in a direct contact with dispatchers of river basin boards.

However, in some cases, when rapid dissemination to public is urgent, electronic media (TV, radio, internet) can advantageously be used for warning dissemination from NMHS directly. A continuous contact and cooperation of NMHSs with national and local TV and radio stations as well as newspapers should lead to a smooth functioning of the EW system. Detailed conditions for direct broadcast of warnings from forecasting offices in radio and TV should preferably be included in an agreement between NMHSs and media. These problems have been discussed many times.

It is rather difficult to issue public warnings in media in the case that the threat to affected communities is imminent only. At the same time, so-called under warning should also be avoided. In many countries, the concept of a "watch", "alert", or "advice" has been employed preliminary to the issuance of warnings.

Very important is the use of a single official issuing authority for warnings (single voice principle) to avoid public confusion – it is recommended that NMHSs should always act as such official authorities. Then, warnings and forecasts issued publicly by commercial providers would be consistent with those issued by NMHSs. When warnings should be disseminated quickly then electronic media like radio and TV have to be preferred.

Radio Broadcast

The SDMA can interrupt current radio broadcast and present fresh warning message. Other possibility is to utilize standard broadcasting sequences delivered directly from forecasting room of CHMI several times in morning broadcast. During some disasters also extended news showing the situation and warnings for further development of the disaster and direct talk with meteorologist from forecasting office could also be used.

Television

With the TV another possibility for dissemination of warnings consisting of so-called crawler with a brief warning appearing on the TV screen during a current TV programme could be applied in urgent cases and quickly approaching disasters. Before and during a disaster TV could advantageously show more sophisticated graphical products like radar and satellite images, precipitation forecast from numerical weather models in the form of images, maps in GIS showing flooded areas and predictions from hydrological models, etc. Also interviews of meteorologists and hydrologists dealing with a current disaster and actual situation have always been very beneficial. Anyway, all presentation of warnings in TV and other electronic media should be done very carefully with precise wording. As big damages of property and especially losses of lives could often occur media reporters should be very careful and keep a certain standard in their presentations.

Internet

Modern telecommunication and information means like internet, internet via mobile phones, SMS messages, and warnings should also be applied. There might be a problem that users should be "active" and open "specific pages" first themselves to get warning or other urgent information. On the other hand, these modern means can be used with advantage for graphical presentation of warnings and other useful information not only for public but also for professionals involved in the whole EW system. In some cases also Teletext (accessible by more people than internet) should be used for warning dissemination. Printed media like newspapers can be used to supply more detailed additional information – but they are generally to slow for direct warning in urgent and quick events.

The role and benefits of the various medium of broadcast are detailed below:

Channel	Benefits	Challenges
Radio and Television	Widespread	Takes time to get the warnings Limited use at night
Telephone (Fixed and mobile)	Messages delivered quickly	Problems of authenticity does not reach non-users Congestion
SMS	Quick Messages can be sent to groups	Congestion does not reach non-users Local language problems
Cell Broadcasting	No congestion Can address a group simultaneously	Does not reach non-users Local language problems
Satellite Radio	High reachability	Cannot be used to educate masses Only good for specific points
Internet/E-mail	Interactive Multiple sources can be checked for accuracy of information	Not widespread
Amateur/Community Radio	Excellent for rural, poor, and remote communication	Not widespread People lose interest if used only in case of disaster
Sirens	Can be used even at night. Good in rural areas	Maintenance of the system cannot disseminate a detailed message.

Legal Support of Early Warning

The DM Act, 2005 provides for new laws for treating crisis management in India. This group of laws will contain – crisis management law, integrated rescue system law and also the law about Fire and Rescue Service. The laws treat all aspects of crisis including natural disasters in a systematic way by defining strictly and rather simply competencies of main "players" like the government, NGOs, and other agencies. Laws also include a certain limitation of some "human" rights during crisis just enabling better operability of bodies involved in crisis management and rescue activities.

The group of laws strictly defines a key role of the ministry in coordination of preparations for crisis events and their solutions, unification of handling of events by other ministries, regional, county and community organs and companies, organization of training and education of all crisis management organs.

Effective Working Relationship

(a) Effective working relationships require the media, NGOs, scientists, government agencies, and international organizations to recognize that, while they have much in common, they also often have distinct objectives and needs.

(b) It is also important to recognize differences among media (print vs. broadcast, radio vs. television, domestic vs. international, etc.), and to take into account their distinct characteristics, potential, and needs.

(c) The media and relief organizations at times, challenge each other and ask difficult, penetrating questions.

(d) After all, "it is through the media that the agencies are accountable to the public".

(e) Many participants in the conference expressed hope that disaster mitigation organizations would focus more on their public information efforts, and that the media would focus more of its coverage, on disaster prevention and reduction, instead of loss of life and damage to property.

(f) Both disaster mitigation agencies and the media, for example, should identify and communicate to the public specific measures that have either succeeded or failed to reduce the impact of natural hazards.

Media Roles in Different Stages of a Disaster

The media has different roles to play in the different stages of a disaster.

- **Before Disaster:** The media will give warnings and information about the disaster and will educate the people to avoid panic and guide how to respond to the disaster.
- **During Disaster:** Will facilitate with the information, current status, what to do next, etc.
- **After Disaster:** Will help the people by giving informations about the people affected. Will help the people to identify their near and dear ones and also involve in collection of money, materials from the public and distribute among the victims.

Conclusions

The role of media before and during disasters can often be important and very helpful. However, there have been some drawbacks and mistakes which should be avoided whenever possible. For instance, the above mentioned and strongly recommended "single voice" principle have been violated many times especially by small media companies like local radios, TVs, etc. Some media often present warnings not issued by NMHS but "produced" by reporters and their information suppliers!

Other problems might be connected with wrong timing of warning dissemination or very vague or incorrect localization of the event. Sometimes, graphical images have been incorrectly presented and explained to the public. Also wording itself plays very important role and should be done very carefully by taking into account not only technical and scientific aspects but also estimation of possible psychological effects on people in areas facing disaster. It occurs very often that during important time media people present lot of irrelevant and temporary unimportant information instead of efficient use of time for better warning and more detailed explanation of the event.

It has always been recommended to prefer a presentation of positive aspects and side of the event showing good performance of rescue teams and other people involved instead of looking for sensations and pinpointing some drawbacks and errors in disaster warning and prevention. Such discussions should be left for later time after the event. Other problem might be connected with warnings and forecasts prepared by "amateurs" or unreliable sources and, as it have been stressed several times, "single voice" principle and the use of warnings originating from NMHS should be used.

However, NMHSs should care about proper and "up to date" forecasting and warning service capable of dissemination of warnings not only to official "channels" but also, when necessary, directly to media. In any case, efficient and well-defined crisis management system within a state including involvement of media should be used and backed up by related legislation. Precise definition of the role of NMHS in a state EW system and connection to a crisis management by a law and related norms should be preferred. However, NMHSs should be very active in this direction to find its place in a state early warning systems. Only then, a sufficient financing of such services and technical and scientific progress of NMHSs can be ensured.

5.7 DISASTER MANAGEMENT INFORMATION SYSTEM

Introduction

To effectively mitigate against natural hazards, it is essential that a well-defined disaster management information system is in place. Such a system should be capable of addressing the various aspects and phases of disasters. It should meet the requirements of the users at various levels.

The success of disaster management largely depends on availability, dissemination, and effective use of information. The information needs will include current information on weather, climate, infrastructure (roads, hospital, markets, administrative boundaries), socio-economic data, etc., to use in assessing natural hazards. Currently, such data are being generated by multiple users; government departments, NGOs, the UN agencies, and the private sectors. Data is fragmented, stored in multiple locations, and formats, making it difficult to bring together to support disaster management activities. In addition, there is a need to assess the disaster in terms of location, extend and likely impact so as to plan relief and recovery actions.

An integrated disaster management information system, highly structured, developed and installed, adequately equipped with the necessary infrastructure and expertise to constantly monitor the risk profiles of possible disasters is relevant.

One of the crucial elements of disaster management is the availability of timely and reliable information made available to decision makers. Information helps in minimizing damages by warning the affected population, helping in planning of relief and adopting tangible solutions for rehabilitation and recovery. The disaster management information system should have a solid networking between those who provide the data, administrators, and affected population, government ministries, and the humanitarian community. Disaster management calls for synergy of technologies and interaction of different agencies. Networking and multi-agency interface will lead to institutionalization of disaster management.

Definition

MIS is a set of information subsystem which are rationally interrelated and which transform data into meaningful information for the recipient in order to enhance his productivity according to his styles and characteristics.

Overall Objective

(a) To develop a Disaster Management Information System (DMIS) to collect and classify data from local levels as well as relevant organizations. The DMIS not only collect information on damage but also support disaster preparedness and prevention activities and identify relief needs.

(b) Further objective is to establish operational mechanism to exchange information at Central and village levels.

(c) Establish a disaster management information network based on information and communication technology applications such as internet, GIS, SMS, etc.

(d) Disseminate natural disaster information via website and facilitate the information sharing mechanism from Central level to villagers, communities, and management agencies.

(e) Strengthen IT application capacity for staffs , support them in accessing and using technologies in order to meet the high demand for efficiency and quality of work.

National Disaster Management Information Systems and Networks

An Asian Overview

Over the last few decades, the importance of effective management of information is being increasingly recognized in the disaster management sector in Asia and Pacific regions. A number of countries have set up disaster management information systems according to their own specific needs. The applications of these systems range from emergency response planning to short-range early warning to long-range mitigation and prevention planning.

Information Needs in Disaster Management

The information needs of disaster managers fall into two distinct, but closely related, categories of activities, *viz:*

1. **Pre-disaster Activities:** Analysis and research (to improve the existing knowledge base), risk assessment, prevention, mitigation, and preparedness.

2. **Post-disaster Activities:** Response, rehabilitation, and reconstruction. Accordingly, there are two categories of disaster-related data:

   (a) Pre-disaster baseline data about the country and risks.

   (b) Post-disaster real-time data about the impact of a disaster and the resources available to combat it.

The ability of leaders and administrators to make sound disaster management decisions – to analyze risks and decide upon appropriate counter-measures – can be greatly enhanced by the cross-sectoral integration of information. For example, to understand the full short- and long-term implications of floods and to plan accordingly requires the analysis of combined data on meteorology, topography, soil characteristics, vegetation, hydrology, settlements infrastructure, transportation, population, socio-economics, and material resources. This information comes from many different sources and at present it is difficult in most countries to bring it all together.

There are two essential preliminaries to establishing a disaster management information system:

1. **Defining the Purpose of the System:** Ask who will be the main users and what end product do they require? The system must be appropriate to the level of management at which it is used. Failure to have a very clear idea of the purpose of the system is likely to lead to the creation of an unnecessarily elaborate one which attempts to do more than is really necessary, with the attendant risks of it being costly, time-consuming to maintain, the data being out of date and the system itself being inappropriate to the real needs of its users.

2. **Investigating the Existing Databases and Integrating with Them:** Often the information needs of disaster managers overlap those of other organizations and the data may, therefore, already be stored elsewhere. Disaster managers should resist the temptation to establish their own all embracing database. At the national level there are almost certainly existing databases for a wide variety of purposes. An example of a disaster-related international database is a commercially developed one on hazardous substances. UNEP is planning to introduce a similar one for environmental matters.

Components of a National Disaster Management Information System

Key components of a disaster management information system would be a database of:

(a) Hazard assessment mapping.

(b) Vulnerability assessment.

(c) Demographic distribution.

(d) Infrastructure, lifelines, and critical facilities.

(e) Logistics and transportation routes.

(f) Human and material response resources.

(g) Communication facilities.

The usage of Disaster Management Information Systems (DMIS) would be in three contexts.

1. Preparedness planning.
2. Mitigation.
3. Response and recovery.

The hazard and vulnerability assessments and mapping components of a DMIS are the cornerstone of preparedness planning as well as planning and implementation of a mitigation programme. All data is of critical use in the preparedness plan as well as in the actual response operations. It must be recognized that the development of these databases in the country has to be built bottom up from the lowest administrative unit in the country, i.e., the sub-district and district corresponding to the level of the disaster preparedness plan. The district databases would feed into the state/provincial database and then into the national database.

Examples of Some of the Existing Information Systems in Asia and Pacific Countries

Indonesia

Indonesia Disaster Management Information System (SIPBI)

Developed by the National Disaster Management Coordinating Board in the context of the UNDP funded project on Strengthening Disaster Management in Indonesia. SIPBI is aimed at enhancing Bakornas PB's decision making capability besides increasing and ensuring flows of reliable and up to date information on various disaster events and related disaster management measures. The main objectives of SIPBI component were: (i) formulate concept and design, (ii) establish operational mechanism on pilot basis at national level and in four project areas, (iii) standardize disaster management information/data, (iv) formulate standard operating procedures for system operations, and (v) facilitate development of similar system in other disaster-prone districts and provinces. The scope of SIPBI development are: (i) development of computer networking system, (ii) development of database for disaster management, and (iii) development of Geographic Information System (GIS) for disaster management. The GIS component aims at developing risk maps at the national, provincial and district level. The national (1:500,000) and provincial (1:250,000) level maps are used to determine priority provinces and areas for disaster management activities, planning and installation of early warning systems. The district level maps (1:50,000) are used for district contingency planning. Under this project, a number of modules on forest fires, earthquakes/tsumani, volcanic eruption, and social unrest, for building database system in an internet mode have been underway. A need to synthesize these modules has also been identified.

India

(a) National Natural Disaster Knowledge Network: In 1999, the Government of India has established a high-powered committee to address the multiple facets of natural disasters in India. One of its major decisions in 2000 has been to set up a National Natural Disaster Knowledge Network (Nanadisk-Net). This Knowledge Network is being planned as a "network of networks". It will be a platform to facilitate an interactive dialogue with all government departments, research institutions, universities, community-based organizations and even individuals. The network will act as a digital library service and will facilitate access to global databases and early warning systems in a significant way. The Knowledge Network is designed to give a fillip to technical cooperation among developing countries and to expand international relationships to include exchange of information and transfer of technology. Nanadisk-Net will also promote e-training and will have the feature of many languages through a translation software.

(b) Vulnerability Atlas of India: In 1997 the Government of India, Ministry of Urban Affairs and Employment constituted an Expert Group to prepare a Vulnerability Atlas taking into account three natural hazards which are the most common and damaging to India, namely earthquakes, cyclones and floods. The zoning maps on macro level for the three hazards are available on small-scale for the country as a whole. To make this information readily available to the planners, administrators and disaster managers, these maps were prepared on larger-scale, state-wise, showing all the administrative units, namely, the district boundaries, for easy identification of the areas covered by the zones of various intensity levels. The Vulnerability Atlas contains the following information for each State and Union Territory of India:

1. Seismic hazard map.
2. Cyclone and wind hazard map.
3. Flood-prone area map.
4. Housing stock vulnerability table for each district, indicating for each house type, the level of risk to which it could be subjected sometime in the future.

The Vulnerability Atlas has been published by the Building Materials and Technology Promotion Council (BMTPC) and is an important input into the State Level Disaster Management Planning. Given that a DMIS would require digitization and information collection on key indicators at various levels, the Atlas is an important step in the establishment of DMIS and represents the kind of work required to be done in each country.

(c) State Level Disaster Management Communication, Network and Information System in Maharashtra, India: The Maharashtra Emergency Earthquake Rehabilitation Programme (MEERP) implemented from 1995 to 1998 after the Latur earthquake, India with World Bank funding included a component of developing a Disaster Management Plan for the State of Maharashtra supported by a communication network and DMIS.

The Communication Network comprised of: (1) State Level VSAT network, and (2) Intra District VHF Network. The VSAT network with 37 fixed network stations in each District Control Room (DCR) provides a direct link with a variety of Telecom services linking each DCR with the State level EOC including videoconferencing facilities. The VHF network has been established within 11 districts of the State, comprises 600 base stations, 56 repeater stations, and 190 mobile stations.

The GIS-based Disaster Management Information System was created on 1:250,000 and 1:50,000 scale for all the districts of Maharashtra. The creation of DMIS was primarily meant to compile, store and update information related to hazards, facilitating integrated analysis of the spatial and non-spatial data and generation of hazard maps for flood and epidemics, earthquake, accidents, industrial hazards, fire, and cyclone.

The DMIS on 1:250,000 scale for all the districts has been completed. The digitization of data on 1:50,000 scale has been completed for 17 districts. In a second phase, the digitization of remaining districts will be completed and elaborate query design too will be taken up.

The MRSAC secured the remote sensing data from the National Remote Sensing Applications Centre, and got it interpreted through a number of subcontractors in the private sector. Once the thematic maps were made available, the experts checked these maps and validated it with the ground level findings. After the validation, the digitization of these maps would be done in the MRSAC, and the physical and socio-economic data attributed to the maps. Another round of validation takes place, before the database is finally approved. The important inputs in this exercise are the remote sensing maps and physical and socio-economic data. Further, it required an intensive work to digitize these data, and validate them.

Although the primary objective of the DMIS is to plan for disasters, the database has been organized in such a way that it could be extensively utilized for resource planning. A number of departments, like the water supply, water conservation, PWD, forests, etc., are using the database for their own applications.

The Maharashtra programme is a forerunner of such a programme at the national level and has become a model for other states in the country. A similar programme is now under implementation in the state of Uttar Pradesh. Significantly, it was implemented in the course of an externally funded rehabilitation program, and linked to a program of undertaking state and district level disaster preparedness plans.

Sri Lanka

Under the Ministry of Social Services (MOSS), Sri Lanka has established a disaster management information system called Social Management Information System (SOMIS). The National Disaster Management Centre (NDMC) of Sri Lanka is developing a database which will incorporate various aspects of disaster management integrated with SOMIS and the software would be compatible to commonly used operating platforms.

5.8 QUESTIONS

1. Write a note on institutional safety programmes.
2. Describe the role of states in disaster management.
3. Armed Forces plays a major role in DM – discuss.
4. Write a short note on NGO in disaster management.
5. Discuss the role of corporate sector in DM.
6. Media plays a vital role in the three phases of disasters – discuss.
7. Elucidate the disaster management information system.

6 Psychological and Social Dimensions in Disasters

Learning Objectives

- ☞ To have a detailed understanding about the psychological and social impacts of disasters and the measures to overcome these evil effects
- ☞ To highlight the psychological dimensions of disasters
- ☞ To educate people to reduce social impact of disasters
- ☞ To enlighten the measures to overcome the evil effects
- ☞ To develop humanitarian attitude among people

Structure

6.1 Psychological Dimensions of Disaster

6.2 Psychiatric Disorders

6.3 The Disaster Response

6.4 Emotional and Psychological Trauma

6.5 Emotional Intelligence

6.6 Social Dimensions of Disaster

6.7 Rehabilitation

6.8 The Role of Building Materials and Services Banks

6.9 From Shelter to Housing

6.10 Disaster Information Provider

6.11 Questions

6.1 PSYCHOLOGICAL DIMENSIONS OF DISASTER

The occurrence of major disasters all over the world in recent decades has fuelled interest in emergency psycho-social interventions. The psychological consequences of catastrophes are generally underestimated even though they are often much greater than the physical effects. There is therefore unequal, and sometimes insufficient, planning when it comes to the psycho-social component of comprehensive emergency response plans.

Disasters are defined as situations whose impact can overwhelm the adaptive capacity of affected populations and groups, to a varying extent and for more or less extended periods of time, depending on the circumstances. There are two major types of disasters: natural disasters (e.g., floods) and disasters resulting from human action, whether intentionally (e.g., shootings) or unintentionally (e.g., toxic spills).

Disasters can have a significant psycho-social impact because they bring substantial loss for the victims: loss of loved ones, of bodily integrity, of material goods, of places they have made their own, of a sense of safety and security, etc. Natural disasters usually have a beginning and an end, which helps make psychological recovery easier. Disasters linked to human activity, particularly those of an intentional nature, are more disturbing because they generate feelings of psychological threat and uncertainty about the associated risks. In such conditions, it is not unusual to see more long-term reactions of stress and demoralization set in.

The majority of persons exposed to a disaster do well and have only mild, transitory symptoms. However, some individuals develop psychiatric illness post-disaster. Such illnesses include those that are secondary to physical injury and sickness as well as specific trauma-related psychiatric disorders such as acute stress disorder. The extent of the psychiatric morbidity and mortality that develops in individuals in the community depends on the type of disaster, the degree of injury sustained, the amount of life threat, and the duration of community disruption.

Disasters can be natural or human-made. Human-made disasters such as industrial accidents, airplane crashes, terrorist acts, and war can be more deadly than natural ones. For example, the leak of poisonous gas from a Union Carbide Corporation plant in Bhopal, India, killed 3,800 people and injured over 3,00,000 more.

Psychiatrists must use a wide spectrum of skills in providing care to disaster victims. They need to diagnose and treat the disorders associated with trauma (e.g., Post-traumatic stress disorder [PTSD], depression); they must also provide consultation to medical and surgical colleagues on these psychiatric disorders as they present in a general medical clinic among patients injured in the disaster. Psychiatrists are essential in educating other physicians and the community about the "normal" responses to "abnormal" events; they also assist in the development of disaster plans for hospitals and communities. Psychiatrists contribute to the primary prevention of psychopathology by using epidemiological training, as well as their traditional skills of diagnosis, treatment, and consultation.

TRAUMA

Any injury, whether physically or emotionally inflicted. Medically, "trauma" refers to a serious or critical bodily injury, wound, or shock. In psychiatry, "trauma" has assumed a different meaning and refers to an experience that is emotionally painful, distressful, or shocking, which often results in lasting mental and physical effects.

Physical Trauma

Physical trauma refers to a physical injury, generally of a considerably severe degree emotional and psychological trauma. Emotional and psychological trauma is the result of extraordinarily stressful events that shatter your sense of security, making you feel helpless and vulnerable in a dangerous world. It is the feelings of intense fear, helplessness, loss of control and threat of annihilation. The emotional wound or shock that creates substantial lasting damage to the psychological development of a person. Psychic trauma effects are Emotional: Fear, shock, horror, anxiety, sadness, anger, and guilt.

Responses to Trauma and Disaster

The behavioural and psychological responses seen in disasters are not random; they frequently have a predictable structure and time course. For most individuals, post-traumatic psychiatric symptoms are transitory. For some, however, the effects of a disaster linger long after its occurrence, rekindled by new experiences that remind the person of the past traumatic event. A rainstorm can become the reminder of a flood; the flash of lightning and the crash of thunder, the reminder of an explosion; a bumpy ride in an airplane, the reminder of a plane crash; and a small earth tremour, the reminder of a major earthquake. Even normal life events can cause anxiety and bring to mind destroyed home or deceased loved ones. The factors influencing resilience and vulnerability to catastrophic events are only now being identified. Although several empirical studies have investigated psychiatric response to disaster, few have addressed interventions. Such studies are very difficult to do and will probably not be undertaken in sufficient number to guide clinical work. However, understanding responses to disaster can provide the basis for developing interventions.

Although exposure to disasters and other trauma has been associated with debility that can persist for decades, the effects of traumatic events are not exclusively bad. For some people, trauma and loss facilitate a move towards health. A traumatic experience can become the centre around which a victim reorganizes a previously disorganized life, reorienting values and goals. Traumatic events may function as psychic organizers for memory, i.e., psychic glue linking event-related feelings, thoughts, and behaviours that are later accessed *en bloc* following symbolic, environmental, or biological stimuli.

The study of emotional reactions to disasters began with observations of the oldest human-made disaster. During the American Civil War, combat psychiatric casualties were thought to be suffering from "nostalgia", which was considered to be a type of melancholy, or mild type of insanity, caused by disappointment and longing for home. In World Wars I and II, terms such as "shell shock," "battle fatigue," and "war neuroses" were more common descriptors of the emotional responses to trauma.

Post-traumatic stress disorder (PTSD), however, is not the only psychiatric disorder associated with disasters. Major depression, substance abuse, generalized anxiety disorder, and adjustment disorder have also been diagnosed in individuals exposed to a disaster. In addition, psychological reactions to physical injury and illness as well as psychological resiliency are important post-disaster responses.

Common Psychiatric Responses to Disaster

Following are some of the common psychiatric responses to a disaster.

Psychiatric Diagnoses

(a) Organic mental disorders secondary to head injury, toxic exposure, illness, and dehydration.

(b) Acute stress disorder.

(c) Adjustment disorder.

(d) Substance use disorders.

(e) Major depression.

(f) Post-traumatic stress disorder.

(g) Generalized anxiety disorder.

(h) Psychological factors affecting physical disease (in the injured).

Psychological/Behavioural Responses

(a) Grief reactions and other normal responses to an abnormal event.

(b) Family violence.

The severity of a disaster is perhaps the single best predictor of both the probability and the frequency of post-disaster psychiatric illness. Physical injury – the number of injured and the type of injury – is one indicator of the severity of a disaster. Physical injury also appears to increase the risk of psychiatric disorder.

6.2 PSYCHIATRIC DISORDERS

Stress

Modern life is full of hassles, deadlines, frustrations, and demands. For many people, stress is so commonplace that it has become a way of life. Stress isn't always bad. In small doses, it can help you perform under pressure and motivate you to do your best. But when you're constantly running in emergency mode, your mind and body pay the price.

If you frequently find yourself feeling frazzled and overwhelmed, it's time to take action to bring your nervous system back into balance. You can protect yourself by learning how to recognize the signs and symptoms of stress and taking steps to reduce its harmful effects.

The Body's Stress Response: When you perceive a threat, your nervous system responds by releasing a flood of stress hormones, including adrenaline and cortisol. These hormones rouse the body for emergency action.

Your heart pounds faster, muscles tighten, blood pressure rises, breath quickens, and your senses become sharper. These physical changes increase your strength and stamina, speed your reaction time, and enhance your focus – preparing you to either fight or flee from the danger at hand.

Stress is a normal physical response to events that make you feel threatened or upset your balance in some way. When you sense danger — whether it's real or imagined — the body's defenses kick into high gear in a rapid, automatic process known as the "fight-or-flight" reaction, or the stress response.

The stress response is the body's way of protecting you. When working properly, it helps you stay focused, energetic, and alert. In emergency situations, stress can save your life — giving you extra strength to defend yourself, for example, or spurring you to slam on the brakes to avoid an accident. The stress response also helps you rise to meet challenges. Stress is what keeps you on your toes during a presentation at work, sharpens your concentration when you're attempting the game-winning free throw, or drives you to study for an exam when you'd rather be watching TV. But beyond a certain point, stress stops being helpful and starts causing major damage to your health, your mood, your productivity, your relationships, and your quality of life.

Effects of Chronic Stress

The body doesn't distinguish between physical and psychological threats. When you're stressed over a busy schedule, an argument with a friend, a traffic jam, or a mountain of bills, your body reacts just as strongly as if you were facing a life-or-death situation. If you have a lot of responsibilities and worries, your emergency stress response may be "on" most of the time. The more your body's stress system is activated, the easier it is to trip and the harder it is to shut off.

Long-term exposure to stress can lead to serious health problems. Chronic stress disrupts nearly every system in your body. It can raise blood pressure, suppress the immune system, increase the risk of heart attack and stroke, contribute to infertility, and speed up the aging process. Long-term stress can even rewire the brain, leaving you more vulnerable to anxiety and depression.

Many health problems are caused or exacerbated by stress, including: pain of any kind, heart disease, digestive problems, sleep problems, depression, obesity, auto immune diseases, skin conditions, such as eczema.

How Much Stress is Too Much?

Because of the widespread damage stress can cause, it's important to know ones own limit. But just how much stress is "too much" differs from person-to-person. Some people roll with the punches, while others crumble at the slightest obstacle or frustration. Some people even seem to thrive on the excitement and challenge of a high-stress lifestyle. Ones ability to tolerate stress depends on many factors, including the quality of your relationships, your general outlook in life, your emotional intelligence, and genetics. The stress levels are influenced by the following factors:

Support Network: A strong network of supportive friends and family members is an enormous buffer against life's stressors. On the flip side, the more lonely and isolated you are, the greater your vulnerability to stress.

Sense of Control: If one has confidence in himself and his ability to influence events and persevere through challenges, it's easier to take stress in stride. People who are vulnerable to stress tend to feel like things are out of their control.

Attitude and Outlook: Stress-hardy people have an optimistic attitude. They tend to embrace challenges, have a strong sense of humour, accept that change is a part of life, and believe in a higher power or purpose.

Ability to Deal with One's Emotions. You're extremely vulnerable to stress if you don't know how to calm and soothe yourself when you're feeling sad, angry, or afraid. The ability to bring your emotions into balance helps you bounce back from adversity.

Knowledge and Preparation: The more you know about a stressful situation, including how long it will last and what to expect, the easier it is to cope. For example, if you go into surgery with a realistic picture of what to expect post-op, a painful recovery will be less traumatic than if you were expecting to bounce back immediately.

Causes of Stress

Stress can be caused by the many events such as spouse's death, divorce, marriage separation, jail term, death of a close relative, injury or illness, marriage, fired from job, retirement, etc.

The situations and pressures that cause stress are known as stressors. However, anything that puts high demands on you or forces you to adjust can be stressful. This includes positive events such as getting married, buying a house, going to college, or receiving a promotion. What causes stress depends, at least in part, on your perception of it. Something that's stressful to you may not faze someone else; they may even enjoy it. Common external causes of stress are major life changes, work, relationship difficulties, financial problems, being too busy and children and family. Common internal causes of stress are inability to accept uncertainty, pessimism, negative self-talk, unrealistic expectations, perfectionism, and lack of assertiveness.

How do one Respond to Stress?

There are three most common ways people respond when they're overwhelmed by stress:

Foot on the Gas: An angry or agitated stress response. You're heated, keyed up, overly emotional, and unable to sit still.

Foot on the Brake: A withdrawn or depressed stress response. You shut down, space out, and show very little energy or emotion.

Foot on Both: A tense and frozen stress response. You "freeze" under pressure and can't do anything. You look paralyzed, but under the surface you're extremely agitated.

The following table lists some of the common warning signs and symptoms of stress. The more signs and symptoms you notice in yourself, the closer you may be to stress overload. The most common symptoms are: cognitive symptoms, emotional symptoms, memory problems, inability to concentrate, poor judgement, seeing only the negative, anxious or racing thoughts, constant worrying, moodiness, irritability or short temper, agitation, inability to relax, feeling overwhelmed, sense of loneliness and isolation, depression or general unhappiness.

The physical symptoms and behavioural symptoms are aches and pains, diarrhoea or constipation, nausea, dizziness, chest pain, rapid heartbeat, loss of sex drive, frequent colds, eating more or less, sleeping too much or too little, isolating yourself from others, procrastinating or neglecting responsibilities, using alcohol, cigarettes, or drugs to relax, and nervous habits (e.g., nail biting, pacing). Keep in mind that the signs and symptoms of stress can also be caused by other psychological and medical problems.

Dealing with stress and its symptoms are very important in stress management. While unchecked stress is undeniably damaging, there are many things you can do to reduce its impact and cope with symptoms.

It is equally important to learn how to manage stress. You may feel like the stress in your life is out of your control, but you can always control the way you respond. Managing stress is all about taking charge: taking charge of your thoughts, your emotions, your schedule, your environment, and the way you deal with problems. Stress management involves changing the stressful situation when you can, changing your reaction when you can't, taking care of yourself, and making time for rest and relaxation.

Strengthen your relationships and a strong support network is the greatest protection against stress. When you have trusted friends and family members you know you can count on, life's pressures don't seem as overwhelming. So spend time with the people you love and don't let your responsibilities keep you from having a social life. If you don't have any close relationships, or your relationships are the source of your stress, make it a priority to build stronger and more satisfying connections. Tips for reaching out and building relationships are: help someone else by volunteering, have lunch or coffee with a co-worker, call or e-mail an old friend, go for a walk with a workout buddy, schedule a weekly dinner date, take a class or join a club, and learn how to relax.

You can't completely eliminate stress from your life, but you can control how much it affects you. Relaxation techniques such as yoga, meditation, and deep breathing activate the body's relaxation response, a state of restfulness that is the opposite of the stress response. When practised regularly, these activities lead to a reduction in your everyday stress levels and a boost in your feelings of joy and serenity. They also increase your ability to stay calm and collected under pressure.

Reading is a relaxation techniques for stress relief: relaxation exercises to reduce stress, anxiety, and depression. Invest in your emotional health, most people ignore their emotional health until there's a problem. But just as it requires time and energy to build or maintain your physical health, so it is with your emotional well-being. The more you put into it, the stronger it will be. People with good emotional health have an ability to bounce back from stress and adversity. This ability is called resilience. They remain focused, flexible, and positive in bad times as well as good. The good news is that there are many steps you can take to build your resilience and your overall emotional health. Laughter is the best medicine, and the health benefits of humour and laughter are huge.

Acute Stress Disorder (ASD)

Since ASD is a new diagnosis, no specific investigations are available on its course or outcome. However, recent studies of war suggest that acute combat-related stress reactions predict an adverse outcome and are associated with increased rates of somatic complaints. Numerous investigations also document that acute symptoms of intrusion, avoidance, and dissociation, part of the symptom complex of ASD, predict the development of later psychiatric disorders.

Post-traumatic Stress Disorder (PTSD)

PTSD has been widely studied following both natural and human-made disasters. The diagnostic criteria for PTSD closely resemble those of ASD, with the primary difference being time course: for a diagnosis of ASD the symptoms must occur within four weeks of the traumatic event and resolve within four weeks. The diagnosis of PTSD applies to a similar constellation of symptoms if the symptoms persist longer than one month or if the onset of symptoms begins later than one month after the traumatic event. Studies have examined post-traumatic psychiatric responses in survivors of airplane crashes, volcanic eruptions, tornadoes, floods, and other disasters.

The most frequent predictor of PTSD is the degree of exposure to the disaster. Although the prevalence of PTSD after a disaster varies greatly depending on the type of disaster and the degree of exposure, well-controlled studies, suggest that 10 to 30 per cent of highly exposed individuals develop the disorder. The greatest risk is in persons exposed to life threat, the grotesque (e.g., handling human remains or viewing mangled bodies), or similar situations evoking intense, overwhelming revulsion or fear. Persons who are injured are at higher risk, reflecting both their high level of exposure to life threat and the added persistent reminders and additional stress burden accompanying an injury.

Treatment of PTSD, when it has become persistent, can be complicated, and several different approaches have been used. Psychopharmacological and behavioural techniques have been reported to be successful in treating PTSD symptoms.

Psychiatric Illness and Physical Disease

Often overlooked after a disaster are the psychiatric disorders attributable to head trauma and metabolic disturbances following crush injuries and burns. Co-occurring psychological symptoms are frequently seen in injured victims who may be dealing with the stress of their injury, the loss of family members, and an absence of resources and social supports with which to plan recovery. Since most studies indicate a high rate of psychiatric disorder in the physically injured, a proactive consultation liaison plan is a necessary part of a hospital emergency response plan."Major depression, generalized anxiety disorder, substance abuse, and adjustment disorders in disaster victims have been less often studied than ASD and PTSD, but available data suggest that these disorders also occur at higher than average rates. Major depression, substance abuse, and adjustment disorders (anxiety and depression) may be relatively common in the 6-12 months after a disaster and may reflect survivors' reactions to their injuries, to affects and feelings stimulated by the disaster, and/or to their attributions of the cause of the disaster. The occurrence of these psychiatric disorders may also be mediated by secondary stressors (i.e., the problems associated with disaster recovery, such as negotiations with insurance companies for reimbursement, or unemployment secondary to destroyed businesses) following a disaster. Major depression and substance abuse (drugs, alcohol, and tobacco) are frequently co-morbid with PTSD.

Other symptoms and psycho-social problems may warrant psychiatric attention and intervention. Grief reactions are common after all disasters. One investigation indicated that single parents may be at high risk for developing psychiatric disorders since they often have few resources to begin with, and they lose some of their social supports after a disaster. Over time, when resources remain limited and employment and financial resources are scarce in the community, family violence, spouse abuse, and child abuse increase, with high morbidity and significant mortality. Primary care and emergency room services must remain alert to these problems for many months after a disaster.

Post-disaster chronic sleep disturbances are common clinical problems that may require treatment. Sleep difficulties can be due to anxiety related to recurrent disaster events (e.g., after shocks) or to underlying psychiatric disease such as depression or PTSD. Somatization is common after a disaster and must be managed both in the community and in individual patients. Primary care providers must recognize that somatization is a frequent presentation of anxiety and depression in patients seeking care in medical clinics. Such recognition can help in the appropriate diagnosis and treatment of these psychiatric disorders, thereby minimizing inappropriate medical treatments.

Hostility, with its accompanying social disruption, feelings of frustration, and perception of chaos, is also common. Although in some cases it is helpful for individuals to recognize that the return of anger can be a sign of a return to normal, in others hostility should remind the care provider to assess the risks of family violence and substance abuse.

6.3 THE DISASTER RESPONSE

Time Course

Although individual patterns of response vary, several phases generally emerge over time. There are four phases in the response to disaster.

The first, the impact phase, immediately following a disaster, generally consists of strong emotions, including feelings of disbelief, numbness, fear, and confusion. People tend to cooperate, and heroic deeds are sometimes seen. These reactions are best understood as "normal responses to an abnormal event". Rescue personnel, family, and neighbours are generally the support systems that are most heavily used.

The second, early aftermath phase usually lasts from a week to several months after the disaster. At this juncture, assistance flows in from agencies external to the community, and the cleanup/rebuilding process begins. In this phase of adaptation, denial alternates with intrusive symptoms. The intrusive symptoms generally arise first and consist of unbidden thoughts and feelings accompanied by autonomic arousal (e.g., a heightened startle response, hyper vigilance, insomnia, and nightmares). Towards the end of the adaptation phase, denial is more prominent. This is often accompanied by an increase in visits to physicians for complaints of somatic symptoms such as fatigue, dizziness, headaches, and nausea. Anger, irritability, apathy, and social withdrawal are often present.

The third, short-term phase lasts up to a year and is marked by disappointment and resentment when expectations of aid and restoration are not met. During this period, the strong sense of community may weaken as individuals focus on their personal concerns.

The final, long-term phase, reconstruction, may last for years. During this period, disaster survivors gradually rebuild their lives, making homes, and finding work. Recovery from a disaster involves the resolution of the initial psychological and somatic symptoms through reappraisal of the event, assignment of meaning, and integration into a new concept of self.

Mediating Factors of Disaster Response

To understand the nature and degree of trauma sustained by patients, it is also useful to examine the mediating characteristics of disasters along the following dimensions:

(a) Threat: The higher one's perceived risk of death or injury, the more likely one is to suffer an adverse psychological response.

(b) Physical Harm or Injury: Crush injuries and burns (and later, illnesses due to loss of sanitation systems and to accumulated debris and waste) are a part of the disaster's destructive impact.

(c) **Exposure to the Grotesque:** Exposure to the dead or mutilated increases the risk of psychiatric illness. This particular dimension is of special importance when one is treating hospital personnel, rescue workers, police officers, and mortuary volunteers.

(d) **Sudden, Violent Loss of a Loved One:** The death of a family member or friend is a powered stressor that gives rise to bereavement issues. Although such deaths are a normal part of life, unexpected, violent death is especially difficult to confront. The bereaved individual may experience intrusive images surrounding the death.

(e) **Witnessing or Learning of Violence to a Loved One:** Observing or hearing of violence to a loved one can cause traumatic stress. A good example of this phenomenon occurs in the aftermath of a violent crime such as rape. It is not uncommon for the victims partner to develop intrusive thoughts about the crime, creating a mental image based on reports.

(f) **Learning of Exposure to a Noxious Agent:** Exposure to toxins (e.g., radiation) often goes undetected, sometimes for decades. Revelation of the exposure carries the threat of death, illness, injury, or property loss. The knowledge itself is the stressor. The potential for information and, similarly, news reports to create distress in the listener or viewer needs further study in our media-intensive age.

(g) **Causing Death or Severe Harm to Another:** Technological disasters (e.g., plane crash, Three Mile Island, Chernobyl) are often caused by human error. The effects of natural disasters may be worsened by people as well — for example the builder who used substandard building practices 20 years prior to a devastating hurricane or earthquake may "cause" substantial loss of life. Stress is caused by the belief that the disaster could have been prevented.

(h) **Intentional Injury/Harm:** As evidenced in the Oklahoma City bombing, perpetrating deliberate injury or death is seen as especially heinous and provokes strong emotions.

In addition to these dimensions, another important factor influencing individuals' responses to a disaster is the degree to which the disaster disrupts their community. The community serves as the person's physical and emotional support system. The larger the scale of the disaster, the greater the potential disruption of the community. It is instructive to contrast the challenges facing the hypothetical survivor of an airplane crash with those confronting the victim of a larger-scale disaster such as a tornado or flash flood. If family members were not on the same aircraft, the plane crash survivor can return home to family, friends, and co-workers. He or she will most likely go back to a structurally intact house, to a community unaffected by the accident, to the same job with the same financial security, and so forth. By contrast, a tornado involves additional factors that amplify the trauma. Although the tornado survivor may experience and witness comparably gruesome sights, the recovery environment is markedly different: home and work site may have been destroyed, and relatives, friends, and co-workers may be dead, injured, or displaced. Thus, in considering the impact of a trauma, the degree to which the community is affected is an important consideration in estimating potential psychiatric morbidity.

Clinical studies suggest that the meaning ascribed to the disaster by individuals, families, and communities influences its psychiatric consequences. Beliefs community consultation, treatment, and prevention about the cause of the disaster and the ramifications of these beliefs (such as self-blame, the shattering of assumptions about human nature, and rage at "those responsible" when the event is viewed as preventable) are important to assess in psychiatric evaluation and represent potential areas for intervention. The meaning of a disaster to any one person results from the interaction of his or her past history, present context, and physiological state. The ascribed meaning will then direct individual behaviours of what to do, what to fix, and whom or what to blame.

Epidemiological Model

For many psychiatrists, disaster psychiatry requires a shift from the traditional focus on psychopathology. Preventive medicine's epidemiological model offers a useful paradigm for psychiatric assessment and intervention as it does for other medical responses to disaster. The epidemiological model is a traditional medical model used to investigate outbreaks of infectious disease. Adapting this model to understanding the mental health effects of disasters includes determining the individual's level of exposure to the toxins (e.g., was there exposure to the dead and the gruesome, were family members killed), identifying individuals at higher risk for illness, and monitoring behavioural and psychological responses over both the short-term and the long-term. Recovery from a disaster often takes months or years rather than days.

Consultation to the community can facilitate recovery and limit disability. In the wake of a disaster, the psychiatric consultant attempts to identify high-risk groups and behaviours, foster recovery from acute stress, decrease the development of persistent disorders, and minimize pain and suffering. Both acute and long-term effects of the disaster must be considered. Initial interventions include consultation to the disaster community's leaders, teachers, and care providers to maximize their understanding of the responses to trauma and disaster. Because disaster victims rarely present to traditional mental health services, psychiatric care must be organized around outreach programmes into the community. Identifying high-risk groups is one of the most important aspects of the consultation to the disaster community.

The Disaster Consultation Team in a Disaster

After a disaster, consultation teams must mobilize quickly, often without prior warning. Frequently, they must carry their own resources. Even before beginning the consultation, the psychiatric consultant must design the team. Its composition is usually based on many factors, including the availability of trained consultants. The need to train new ones, characteristics of the disaster (e.g., scope, type of community affected), and financial resources. Ideally, the team is multidisciplinary, including psychiatrists, psychologists, social workers, psychiatric nurses, chaplains, and/or mental health para-professionals. When the consultation team comes from a distant site, practitioners from the affected community must be included; this facilitates entree into the community as well as continuity of care.

The initial tasks of the team are to gain an understanding of the disaster and to establish contacts for collaboration. The team must integrate smoothly into the disaster environment at a time when outsiders are often experienced as intrusive. Liaison with primary care providers and disaster workers is critical for effective intervention. The consultants must be knowledgeable of the culture and customs of the group they wish to help, whether that be a hospital, a school system, the police, firefighters, disaster workers, community leaders, or a foreign nation.

Members of a consultation team, like other disaster workers, experience the stresses of the disaster. The team leader must stay alert to the signs of stress in the team to maintain its health and functioning. Team leaders regulate the working hours and ensure adequate rest and respite for team-members and themselves. Excessively long work hours are to be avoided if at all possible. Dedication to the mission is important, but over dedication – working extraordinarily long hours or exposing oneself to extreme psychological and physical suffering – is a problem. The team leader must recognize that asking a team-member to take time out may cause him or her to feel devalued but may be necessary.

Initial Interventions

Disaster sites can look remarkably calm shortly after the event, even when the destruction and loss have been intense. Individuals feel chaos around them and can experience dissociation and a pervasive sense of unreality. During this time, rest and respite can be importantly. The initial interventions following a disaster must focus on the establishment of safety, the provision of food and water, and protection from the environment. In times of disaster, the most important aspect of psychological care is the social provision of physical care. Fears of loss and separation should be addressed by establishing reliable communications and casualty identification and notification procedures. The following summarizes important interventions to consider during the early phases of disaster response. In a large-scale disaster, physicians will first intervene using public health and medical skills, such as their knowledge about sanitation and injury care.

a. Establishing safety, respite, and physiological recovery for victims.

b. Relieving symptoms of post-disaster stress.

c. Prescribing sleep medication.

d. Providing reality orientation.

e. Encouraging ventilation of feelings.

f. Establishing outreach programmes to provide community support and social-intervention programmes to decrease chronicity.

g. Educating medical personnel and community groups (media, schools, PTAS, hospitals, and corporations) on normal responses to trauma and loss.

h. Consulting with community.

Often the initial focus of the community consultant needs to be on communication within teams and on providing information to the public. The loss of communications during and after a disaster is the norm. Disaster planning includes identifying alternative communication modalities for the days or weeks following a disaster when communication may be limited. It is important to reestablish communications in the disaster community as soon as possible: newspapers, office bulletins, television, and radio can provide information as well, as emotional help. Radio often plays a particularly important part in these communication systems since radios are more easily distributed and are widely available.

Fear of loss of control is not uncommon in individuals who experience major disaster. Disasters make one feel that the normal rules of life are not operating. The stress on families, particularly the persistent problems of loss of housing, income, and employment secondary to a disaster, results in increased rates of child and spouse abuse. Educating primary care providers about these problems is important to case identification. Establishing caretaker respite services – child care and elder care – may decrease the incidence of such violence and warrants scientific investigation.

Within the first hours or days, psychiatrists located in a hospital setting should begin a consultation-liaison outreach programme to injured victims who are at increased risk of PTSD. The psychiatric consultant and treating psychiatrists need to be alert to the physical health effects of any disaster (e.g., crush injuries, burns, head trauma, metabolic disturbances due to poor food and water intake, and infections, and to problems caused by such issues as lost medications.

The initial impact of a disaster is often much wider than anticipated. Those affected by a disaster may be widely dispersed. One cannot think of the disaster community as including only those directly affected. Modern transportation and information flow by telephone, television, and radio often help the disaster community to span the globe.

Identifying High Risk Groups

In a review of the literature on disaster responses, several groups (including rescue workers, the injured, heroes, and children) emerge as being at greater risk for traumatic stress-related sequelae. Children are a unique population during times of disaster. Often community leaders and teachers notice how wonderfully quiet children are being and are thankful, given their own level of distress. However, the inhibition of children's normal activity is an indicator of their degree of stress. Teachers must be alert to social withdrawal in their students as a possible sign that the stress is continuing. Sometimes, children's distress may be more evident.

Exposure to death and the dead is part of most disasters and one of the risk factors for the development of psychiatric illness. The number of dead and injured and the sight and smell of dead bodies were among the most stressful aspects of the disaster. Usually these symptoms abate over several weeks or months.

The loss of a child in a disaster carries particular meaning and brings high risk. Disaster and rescue workers often experience the symptoms of PTSD or ASD and other psychiatric illnesses. Such workers can become forgotten victims of a disaster. They are repeatedly exposed to mutilated bodies, mass destruction, and life-threatening situations while doing physically demanding work that in itself creates fatigue, sleep loss, and often great danger. Workers also experience the stresses of their role as help providers. They often must exercise their long-practiced skills while ignoring their own risk. At times, they are forced to abandon pleading victims when their skills are needed elsewhere to assist a greater number of individuals. Such conflict is inherent in the job but can become a source of guilt or the focus of persistent feelings of helplessness or incompetence.

Disaster workers who do not participate directly in the disaster recovery are also frequently overlooked. These include medical personnel and individuals who staff telephone hotlines. Other often-forgotten persons are those who handle the personal effects (such as wallets, photographs, and jewellery) of the dead — a task that is particularly stressful because of constant reminders of the victims' lives. Supervisors and community leaders also experience great stress in a disaster. They must make rapid decisions with little or no information and provide hope no matter what they fear. Interacting with the media may also be stressful for community leaders following a disaster. Having one appointed individual manage the media can substantially decrease this strain.

Heroes are part of nearly every disaster. Empirical observations suggest that they are often overlooked as a highly stressed group. Heroes are expected to carry the burden of idealization placed on them by the community. They are required to be away from their homes and families, always to be good, and to be able to tell a story that brings hope and courage to those around them. They are rarely allowed to express their own despair, worry, and fear or to recall the feelings that they overlooked in order to perform their heroic acts.

Community Consultation

The psychiatrist can play an important role in communitywide recovery through consultation with community leaders and the media based on knowledge of community responses to disaster. Rumours are prominent in disaster communities and represent the community's attempt to understand events that are not fully explained or do not fit previous patterns. Rumour management is an important task of community leaders and an area in which the psychiatric consultant can assist. Recognizing rumours as the attempt of the community to explain the disaster and its aftermath can assist a community leader in responding appropriately. Community leaders should actively provide information and their interpretation of events in order to quell rumours and assist the disaster victims in recovery through managing the meaning of the event for the community.

After the initial impact of the disaster is over, those involved in rescue operations should be given time off and encouraged to talk. The psychiatric consultant can provide assistance in helping these individuals to process the meaning of their experiences. Rescue workers must feel free to discuss their experiences. Symbols are an important part of the recovery process. Commendations and awards to rescue workers and to those who have distinguished themselves are important components of the community recovery process. Memorials to the victims or the heroes of the disaster are part of the healing process and should be encouraged. Leaders are powerful symbols themselves. Leaders should be encouraged to express their own grief in order to lead the community in recognizing the appropriateness of grieving losses.

Post-disaster Psychiatric Interventions

(a) Differential diagnosis.

(b) Debriefing.

(c) Psychotherapy: individual, couples, and family.

(d) Appropriate treatments for disorders, including psycho-social supports and interventions to deal with disaster stressors.

(e) Media-based education on recovery.

(f) Education of medical personnel on likely presentations of psychiatric disorders to primary care physicians: somatization, grief reactions, depression, substance abuse, family violence, spouse, and child abuse.

The recognition of a disaster by outside authorities, such as the president or the governor, is an important part of recovery. When a community is recognized and its distress acknowledged, it often feels less alone and more joined by others. These "others" offer the hope of additional resources as well as emotional support. The consultant, who may at first feel like an "outsider," fills some of these same functions, serving as an indicator of outside concern, providing hope for the return of "normal" life, and allowing a brief respite from the ongoing issues of disaster stress and recovery.

6.4 EMOTIONAL AND PSYCHOLOGICAL TRAUMA

What is Psychological or Emotional Trauma?

The ability to recognize emotional trauma has changed radically over the course of history. Until recently, psychological trauma was noted only in men after catastrophic wars. The women's movement in the sixties broadened the definition of emotional trauma to include physically and sexually abused women and children. Recent research has revealed that emotional trauma can result from such common occurrences as an auto accident, the breakup of a significant relationship, a humiliating or deeply disappointing experience, the discovery of a life-threatening illness or disabling condition, or other similar situations. Traumatizing events can take a serious emotional toll on those involved, even if the event did not cause physical damage.

Regardless of its source, an emotional trauma contains three common elements:

(a) It was unexpected.

(b) The person was unprepared.

(c) And there was nothing the person could do to prevent it from happening.

"It is not the event that determines whether something is traumatic to someone, but the individual's experience of the event. And it is not predictable how a given person will react to a particular event. For someone who is used to being in control of emotions and events, it may be surprising — even embarrassing — to discover that something like an accident or job loss can be so debilitating."

What Causes Emotional or Psychological Trauma?

Our brains are structured into three main parts, long observed in autopsies:

❖ The cortex (the outer surface, where higher thinking skills arise; includes the frontal cortex, the most recently evolved portion of the brain).

❖ The limbic system (the centre of the brain, where emotions evolve).

❖ The brain stem (the reptilian brain that controls basic survival functions).

Because of the development of brain scan technology, scientists can now observe the brain in action, without waiting for an autopsy. These scans reveal that trauma actually changes the structure and function of the brain, at the point where the frontal cortex, the emotional brain and the survival brain converge. A significant finding is that brain scans of people with relationship or developmental problems, learning problems, and social problems related to emotional intelligence reveal similar structural and functional irregularities as is the case resulting from PTSD.

What is the Difference between Stress and Emotional or Psychological Trauma?

Trauma is stress run amuck. Stress disregulates our nervous systems — but for only a relatively short period of time. Within a few days or weeks, our nervous systems calm down and we revert to a normal state of equilibrium. This return to normalcy is not the case when we have been traumatized. One way to tell the difference between stress and emotional trauma is by looking at the outcome —

how much residual effect an upsetting event is having in our lives, relationships, and overall functioning. Traumatic distress can be distinguished from routine stress by assessing the following:

- ❖ How quickly upset is triggered.
- ❖ How frequently upset is triggered.
- ❖ How intensely threatening the source of upset is.
- ❖ How long upset lasts.
- ❖ How long it takes to calm down.

If we can communicate our distress to people who care about us and can respond adequately, and if we return to a state of equilibrium following a stressful event, we are in the realm of stress. If we become frozen in a state of active emotional intensity, we are experiencing an emotional trauma — even though sometimes we may not be consciously aware of the level of distress we are experiencing.

What Causes Psychological Trauma?

Psychological trauma can result from events we have long recognized as traumatic, including:

- ❖ Natural disasters (earthquakes, fires, floods, hurricanes, etc.).
- ❖ Physical assault, including rape, incest, molestation, domestic abuse.
- ❖ Serious bodily harm.
- ❖ Serious accidents such as automobile or other high-impact scenarios.
- ❖ Experiencing or witnessing horrific injury, carnage, or fatalities.

Other potential sources of psychological trauma are often overlooked including:

- ❖ Falls or sports injuries.
- ❖ Surgery, particularly emergency, and especially in first three years of life.
- ❖ Serious illness, especially when accompanied by very high fever.
- ❖ Birth trauma.
- ❖ Hearing about violence to or sudden death of some one close.

In addition, traumatic stress in childhood that influences the brain is caused by poor or inadequate relationship with a primary caretaker. Sources of this developmental or relational trauma include the following:

Forced separation very early in life from primary caregiver; "chronic mis-attunement of caregiver to child's attachment signals ("malattachment") or reasons such as physical or mental illness, depression, or grief.

It is acknowledged that early life trauma creates vulnerability for experiencing future traumatic responses.

Why can an event cause an emotionally traumatic response in one person and not in another?

There is no clear answer to this question, but it is likely that one or more of these factors are involved:

- The severity of the event.
- The individual's personal history (which may not even be recalled).
- The larger meaning the event represents for the individual (which may not be immediately evident).
- Coping skills, values and beliefs held by the individual (some of which may have never been identified).
- The reactions and support from family, friends, and/or professionals.

Anyone can become traumatized. Even professionals who work with trauma, or other people close to a traumatized person, can develop symptoms of "vicarious" or "secondary" traumatization. Developing symptoms is never a sign of weakness. Symptoms should be taken seriously and steps should be taken to heal, just as one would take action to heal from a physical ailment. And just as with a physical condition, the amount of time or assistance needed to recover from emotional trauma will vary from one person to another.

What are the Symptoms of Emotional Trauma?

There are common effects or conditions that may occur following a traumatic event. Sometimes, these responses can be delayed, for months or even years after the event. Often, people do not even initially associate their symptoms with the precipitating trauma. The following are symptoms that may result from a more commonplace, unresolved trauma, especially if there were earlier, overwhelming life experiences:

Physical

- Eating disturbances (more or less than usual).
- Sleep disturbances (more or less than usual).
- Sexual dysfunction.
- Low energy.
- Chronic, unexplained pain.

Emotional

- Depression, spontaneous crying, despair, and hopelessness.
- Anxiety.
- Panic attacks.
- Fearfulness.
- Compulsive and obsessive behaviours.
- Feeling out of control.
- Irritability, angry, and resentment.
- Emotional numbness.
- Withdrawal from normal routine and relationships.

Cognitive

- Memory lapses, especially about the trauma.
- Difficulty making decisions.
- Decreased ability to concentrate.
- Feeling distracted.
- ADHD symptoms.

The following additional symptoms of emotional trauma are commonly associated with a severe precipitating event, such as a natural disaster, exposure to war, rape, assault, violent crime, major car or airplane crashes, or child abuse. Extreme symptoms can also occur as a delayed reaction to the traumatic event.

Re-experiencing the Trauma

- Intrusive thoughts.
- Flashbacks or nightmares.
- Sudden floods of emotions or images related to the traumatic event.

Emotional Numbing and Avoidance

- Amnesia.
- Avoidance of situations that resemble the initial event.
- Detachment.
- Depression.
- Guilt feelings.
- Grief reactions.
- An altered sense of time increased arousal.
- Hyper-vigilance, jumpiness, an extreme sense of being "on guard".
- Over reactions, including sudden unprovoked anger.
- General anxiety.
- Insomnia.
- Obsessions with death.

What are the Possible Effects of Emotional Trauma?

Even when unrecognized, emotional trauma can create lasting difficulties in an individual's life. One way to determine whether an emotional or psychological trauma has occurred, perhaps even early in life before language or conscious awareness were in place, is to look at the kinds of recurring problems one might be experiencing. These can serve as clues to an earlier situation that caused a dysregulation in the structure or function of the brain.

Common personal and behavioural effects of emotional trauma:

- Substance abuse.
- Compulsive behaviour patterns.
- Self-destructive and impulsive behaviour.
- Uncontrollable reactive thoughts.
- Inability to make healthy profession or lifestyle choices.
- Dissociative symptoms ("splitting off" parts of the self).
- Feelings of ineffectiveness, shame, despair, and hopelessness.
- Feeling permanently damaged.
- A loss of previously sustained beliefs.

Common effects of emotional trauma on inter-personal relationships:

- Inability to maintain close relationships or choose appropriate friends and mates.
- Sexual problems.

- ❖ Hostility.
- ❖ Arguments with family members, employers or co-workers.
- ❖ Social withdrawal.
- ❖ Feeling constantly threatened.

What if Symptoms don't go Away, or Appear at a Later Time?

Over time, even without professional treatment, symptoms of an emotional trauma generally subside, and normal daily functioning gradually returns. However, even after time has passed, sometimes the symptoms don't go away. Or they may appear to be gone, but surface again in another stressful situation. When a person's daily life functioning or life choices continue to be affected, a post-traumatic stress disorder may be the problem, requiring professional assistance.

How is Emotional Trauma Treated?

Traditional approaches to treating emotional trauma include talk therapies, Cognitive Behavioural Therapy (CBT) — intentionally changing one's thoughts and actions — and systematic desensitization to reduce reactivity to a traumatic stressor. These approaches to healing trauma were developed without brain science information, and therefore have varying degrees of success. Recent developments in the treatment of emotional trauma include new, effective forms of psychotherapy and somatic (body) therapies that were developed with new brain science information in mind. Although often intensely interpersonal, these therapies are also psychological and neurological in their focus and application. This group of therapies relies on innate instinctual resources, rather than medications, to bring about healing. They differ in some ways, but the one thing they have in common is combining talk therapy with a focus on the body. As with any therapy, but especially due to the intensity of the emotions involved, it is important to find a therapist with whom one feels trust and a strong bond. They include:

Eye Movement Desensitization/Reprocessing (EMDR) was developed by psychologist, Francine Shapiro, after she noticed her own stress reactions diminishing when her eyes swept back and forth as she walked through a park. It is conducted by licensed mental health professionals who have taken specific training in this complex approach. It combines elements of a range of therapeutic approaches with eye movements or other forms of rhythmical stimulation, such as hand taps or sounds. EMDR has been most effective with single-incident trauma, but its uses continue to evolve in addressing longer histories of emotional or physical trauma, and in balancing other aspects of a person's life.

Somatic Psychotherapies: The term somatic, means mind/body or more precisely brain/body. The idea is that to change the body, we have to engage the brain and change the brain – not only how we think and feel, but also the neurological connections themselves. The body, its sensations, and direct sensory experience are referenced throughout the therapeutic process. Somatic therapies include:

- ❖ **Somatic Experiencing:** This approach evolved in part from observations of how animals literally "shake off" traumatic experiences, allowing the body to process stress chemicals completely until they return to normal levels. The SE therapist may be a licensed professional or unlicensed but with some mental health training. All SE therapists complete an extensive training programme, in which they learn to observe the body, facial expressions and gestures carefully and to help the person "thaw" a response that was "frozen" in a traumatic situation (illustration: the person might be observed to make short gestures that almost appear to be a "pushing" motion, but that stop abruptly – the therapist might have the person complete the gesture in full, and notice how the body's tension level changes).

- **Hakomi Method:** This system is based on five therapeutic principles – mindfulness, organicity, non-violence, the mind-body connection, and unity. It is a body-centred approach for which, in part, the therapist helps the client experiment with small changes in gesture or other movements, to see what differences occur in the processing of emotionally charged content (illustration: the person might be observed to always make a certain gesture or have a certain posture when talking about the attacker – the therapist might suggest the gesture or posture be changed to a different one as an experiment, and then to notice the changes in feelings or thoughts).
- **Somatic Psychology:** This treatment merges somatic therapies, neuroscience, attachment theory, and cognitive approaches, as well Hakomi Method. The approach often uses physical expression to process the energy stored in the body following a trauma, to reset the neurological system into better balance (illustration: the person might be asked to push the attacker away by forcefully pushing against a wall or against a pillow held by the therapist, to allow the body's neurological and musculature systems to reset themselves to a more normal level).
- **AEDP (Accelerated Experiential Dynamic Psychotherapy):** This approach brings the elements of secure attachment into her work with adults. The talk therapy she practices focuses on the mutual exchange of all deeply-seated emotions, bodily awareness and joyous playful exchange.

Injury as a Problem

Road-traffic accidents are increasing at an alarming annual rate of 3 per cent. In 1997, 10.1 per cent of all deaths in India were due to accidents and injuries. A vehicular accident is reported every three minutes and a death every ten minutes on Indian roads. During 1998, nearly 80,000 lives were lost and 3,30,000 people were injured. Of these, 78 per cent were men in the age group of 20-44 years, causing significant impact on productivity. A trauma-related death occurs in India every 1.9 minutes. The majority of fatal road-traffic accident victims are pedestrians, two-wheeler riders, and bicyclists.

No credible data is available to ascertain the outcome of trauma victims; it is generally perceived that outcomes in patients with single system injury (e.g., musculoskeletal trauma) have improved. Unfortunately, the same cannot be said for polytrauma. There is a high mortality rate amongst those with multi-system injuries, which can be attributed to the primitive state of trauma-care systems, lack of pre-hospital care, and inadequate critical care. It is established that the mortality in serious injuries is six times worse in a developing country such as India compared to a developed country.

Administrative Components

Despite trauma being a major public-health problem with high morbidity and mortality, the Ministry of Health does not have a designated unit to deal with issues related to trauma. There is no Central Government agency to integrate policymaking, planning, financing, drafting legislation, or establishment of minimum standards for the performance of a trauma-care system. No reliable institutional arrangement exists to lead the development of such a system in any Indian state. In 26 per cent of the systems surveyed, the overall responsibility for leading the system was undefined. The Centralized Ambulance

Transport Service (CATS) of the Government of the State of New Delhi is the only noteworthy state initiative in this direction. This is restricted mainly to pre-hospital care. Only 28 per cent of respondents identified the presence of a unified leadership coordinating various components and agencies.

The existing systems for trauma care are elementary in nature, predominantly restricted to cities and semi-urban areas, without integration of region or statewide systems. No such systems exist in rural and remote areas to offer prompt life-saving treatment and safe transfer to an appropriate facility. Consequently, fatal accident rate (expressed per kilometre of travel) in India is estimated to be seven-fold worse compared to most advanced states.

No law exists to ensure prompt access to life-saving treatment for trauma victims. Statutory provisions to aid national, state, or interstate planning and implementation of trauma-care systems, regardless of jurisdictional boundaries, are yet to evolve. Issues such as the accreditation of trauma centres and critical care units, specialist licensing of health personnel and mandatory training of physicians lack national guidelines. The publication of ISCCM guidelines for ICUs is an important step in that direction. Legislative provisions for the minimum qualification of ambulance personnel, the type and quality of ambulance equipment and essential hospital capabilities are not in place.

Clinical and Operational Components

In the absence of guidelines, the workforce available for pre-hospital and hospital-based critical care varies enormously. Available personnel and their skills often do not match the needs of the patients. The optimal number and type of pre-hospital personnel for ambulances is not defined. The concept of a dedicated trauma team is not accepted at all levels. At a majority of hospitals in the public health system, the casualty medical officer is the only one to respond to a demand for major resuscitation. This paradox is striking, resulting in the most seriously injured patients frequently being dealt with by the most junior and inexperienced staff. There are no plans for dynamic and flexible responses to the optimal management of trauma patients. The lack of precise and predetermined role allocation during peak periods of activity stresses the fragile current systems and workforce.

Education

The state medical and nursing councils control the educational and licensing requirements for physicians and nurses. However, formal education and speciality training (in emergency medicine, trauma surgery, and critical care) are not mandatory for personnel involved in trauma care and available at selected private institutions. The standardized education in trauma life-support skills is made available through the efforts of Academy of Traumatology (India) under the 'National Trauma Management Course' (NTMC). Currently, this training is available mainly in larger centres and is intended for doctors. So far over 2,500 doctors have received training through this programme.

The issues of educational standards, certification and continuing education and evaluation requirements for doctors involved in trauma-care are yet to be addressed. The National Board of Examinations has recently begun registering courses in trauma-care, though in a very limited manner. There are no minimum stipulated educational standards for paramedic and ambulance personnel.

Pre-hospital Care

Pre-hospital care is virtually non-existent in most rural and semi-urban areas in India, and implementation of the 'golden hour' concept is still an unachieved goal. The concept of a coordinating agency and a designated authority is restricted mainly to cities where trauma systems are operational in some form. Quite often there is an overlapping of private and public facilities and ambulance services in an urban geographical area. Gross discrepancy is seen in pre-hospital services between urban and rural settings, as well as between paying and non-paying patients. In the absence of guidelines and trained paramedical staff, decisions about evacuation of the victim and the choice of the destination hospital are made on an individual case basis. These choices are often made at the behest of patients or their kin.

Formal licensing to run an ambulance service is not mandatory. Ambulance services are run by a multitude of organizations including government, police, fire brigades, hospitals, and private agencies. Some facilities surveyed even had to rely, at times, on waterways to transport injured victims.

The absence of minimal educational and training standards for paramedics brings in unskilled labour to handle the most delicate of tasks. Many private hospitals in large cities offer efficient pre-hospital care, but this covers too small an area and too small a segment of the population. No national or regional guidelines exist for triage, patient-delivery decisions, pre-hospital treatment plans and transfer protocols. Policies, procedures and regulations governing medical directions are in place only in some city systems. There are recent attempts to provide one-time formal training in pre-hospital care to the ambulance personnel in various parts of the country.

Communication System

Despite technological advances, communication in trauma systems in India remains rudimentary and inefficient. Only 14 per cent of the systems have a dedicated central telephone number for incident reporting. Some 30 per cent of the trauma systems, mainly in cities, are equipped with wireless communication. Only 4 per cent of systems have a comprehensive network operational between hospitals and ambulances.

Disaster Preparedness

India is a disaster-prone country with frequent floods, cyclones, landslides, and earthquakes. Train accidents and industrial mishaps are not uncommon. Government plans are in place, in general, to deal with disasters. However, regular drills to test preparedness are not carried out. Only 26 per cent of the systems in the survey reported a well-documented disaster management plan. The rest of the systems have plans underdevelopment, or no plans. This deficiency has resulted in excessive numbers of deaths in natural disasters. In 1999, there was an increase of 20.8 per cent in fatalities due to such disasters compared to the previous year. This figure for 2001 is likely to rise even further as a result of a killer earthquake in Gujarat, causing over 12,000 deaths.

Definitive Trauma-care Facilities

Definitive care for trauma victims is offered by government hospitals, corporate hospitals, and a large number of small clinics across the country. Facilities that offer treatment for trauma victims, at different levels, report 10-30 per cent of their beds occupied by people injured in road accidents.

Most government hospitals offer free care, but the quality of that care differs from one centre to another. Most university hospitals provide a reasonable level of care; these hospitals are able to fulfil the role of tertiary trauma centres but critical care continues to remain the weak link in such settings for a variety of reasons. Private and corporate hospitals, located mostly in large cities, are equipped with modern diagnostic and imaging facilities, good operating environments, and intensive-care units. Some of them also run dedicated trauma services. However, there are no norms to govern their standards and their relations with the public trauma system. On the other hand, the district hospitals often lack trained staff, adequate infrastructure for management of polytrauma, and supply of consumables. Small hospitals and clinics mushrooming across India are simply unable to cope with polytrauma, due to lack of multi-disciplinary support, particularly the critical care units. Such small establishments struggle to manage severely injured patients, resulting in substandard care and high mortality.

Only 54 per cent of the hospitals have set protocols for triage. In 30 per cent of the hospitals, the casualty medical officers are the only physicians available to provide resuscitation. Their level of training and experience in providing life support is not uniform. The concept and practice of forming dedicated trauma-response teams is yet to percolate beyond tertiary-care hospitals.

There are no dedicated trauma surgeons in India. Orthopaedic surgeons lead the trauma response in 50 per cent of facilities. In the remainder, the responsibility is not clearly defined. Clinical decisions are often delayed, in the absence of clear perceptions of clinical responsibility among specialists, putting patients with multi-system injury at a greater risk.

Interfacility Transfer

Nearly half of the systems surveyed have no protocol for interhospital transfers. Linkages between rural and urban facilities do not exist in most regions. The availability of specialist care (e.g. spinal trauma, burns, head injuries, childhood injuries, etc.), is restricted to major cities and teaching hospitals. Transfer to such a speciality centre in an emergency is often difficult and time-consuming, resulting in delay in decision making and management.

Rehabilitation

Rehabilitation, though an integral element of any trauma-care system, is a neglected area in India. It is restricted to physiotherapy in most centres. Although 76 per cent of the facilities offer physiotherapy services, only a third offers occupational rehabilitation and psychological counselling. The surveyed hospitals failed to demonstrate strong links and transfer agreements between acute facilities and rehabilitation units. Social security, retraining, as well as employment and other support schemes from the government for the rehabilitation of the injured, are limited; only a few voluntary organizations offer such assistance.

Information Systems

It is widely known that not all accidents are reported to the police, for a variety of reasons. It is estimated that for every one death, nearly 10-20 people will get hospitalized and 50-100 will receive emergency care in hospitals. The information systems in most places are manual and rudimentary. There is no Central trauma registry in any state. Most hospitals have reliable data on trauma admissions, but only 40 per cent have data on the clinical outcome of the trauma patients. This lack has a negative impact on development and implementation of an effective public policy on trauma-care.

Evaluation and Research

In the wake of the gross disparity between accessibility and affordability of trauma-care; quality assurance is a major casualty. In the absence of a lead agency and with a poor information system, evaluation and research on trauma systems is a difficult proposition. Monitoring of the performance of the system and its individual components, and any quality improvement programme, is far away. Very little work has been done to evaluate the working of trauma systems in India.

The Future

The future appears both daunting and challenging. It is estimated that from its present position of the ninth leading cause of deaths in India, trauma will move up to third position by 2020. It is also estimated that in the developing countries over 6 million will die and 60 million will be injured, or disabled, in the next 10 years. India will have a large share in this, with an estimated economic loss of around 2 per cent of GDP. To meet this challenge several efforts are required: resource creation, education, legislation, upgrading pre-hospital and hospital-based care, public awareness and a change in the attitude of the policymakers. The public health institutions will also benefit from adopting WHO Essential Trauma Care guidelines for trauma-care, which is aimed at low cost improvements to the trauma-care. There are already some ongoing efforts in that direction.

Although the overall picture in trauma care is not as dismal as it used to be three decades ago, 'trauma care for all' continues to remain a distant dream in India. Despite significant overall progress in many other fields, trauma systems in India continue to remain at a formative stage for various reasons. A concerted effort from all the parties involved, as well as the society, is the need of the hour.

Conclusions

The psychiatrist should work closely with primary care physicians; following disaster trauma many patients with psychiatric disorders will present with somatic complaints. Family practitioners, internists, paediatricians, obstetrician/gynaecologists, and other physicians need to be especially vigilant for symptoms of family violence, substance abuse, depression, and somatization. By making use of radio, newspapers, and television, psychiatrists can provide outreach to large segments of the population. Discussions of normal responses to disaster trauma as well as symptoms that should prompt medical attention can broaden outreach efforts substantially. When psychiatric disorders are identified, referrals should be made and the disorder-specific treatment(s) initiated.

The majority of persons exposed to a disaster will do well and will not develop psychiatric illness. The development of psychiatric disease depends on the type of disaster, the degree of injuries, the amount of life threat, and the duration of community disruption. Psychiatric intervention after disaster is based on the principles of preventive medicine and includes disaster consultation and outreach programmes to identify high-risk groups, aid in community recovery, and minimize social disruption. High-risk behaviours (e.g., family violence, substance abuse, somatization) and inappropriate treatment must be assessed and remedied to decrease their impact on morbidity and mortality.

Further study of individual resilience after disasters will help to predict under what conditions and in which people post-traumatic psychiatric illness develops. The formal recognition of ASD is an important step in this process and will facilitate the systematic study of the relationship between acute and chronic post-traumatic health outcomes. Long-term follow-up studies of post-traumatic grief reactions and depression are needed in order to clarify the natural course and duration of these syndromes. The design of future studies of any disaster-related disorder should include examining the time course of and differences between acute and chronic symptoms.

6.5 EMOTIONAL INTELLIGENCE

Emotional intelligence is the innate potential to feel, use, communicate, recognize, remember, describe, identify, learn from, manage, understand, and explain emotions.

We probably all know people, either at work or in our personal lives, who are really good listeners. No matter what kind of situation we are in, they always seem to know just what to say – and how to say it – so that we are not offended or upset. They are caring and considerate, and even if we do not find a solution to our problem, we usually leave feeling more hopeful and optimistic.

We probably also know people who are masters at managing their emotions. They do not get angry in stressful situations. Instead, they have the ability to look at a problem and calmly find a solution. They are excellent decision makers, and they know when to trust their intuition. Regardless of their strengths, however, they are usually willing to look at themselves honestly. They take criticism well, and they know when to use it to improve their performance.

People like this have a high degree of emotional intelligence or EI. They know themselves very well, and they are also able to sense the emotional needs of others. As more and more people accept that emotional intelligence is just as important to professional success as technical ability, organizations are increasingly using EI when they hire and promote.

Although "regular" intelligence is important to success in life, emotional intelligence is key to relating well to others and achieving your goals. Many people believe that emotional intelligence is at least as important as regular intelligence, and many companies now use EI testing to hire new staff.

Emotional intelligence is an awareness of your actions and feelings – and how they affect those around you. It also means that you value others, listen to their wants and needs, and are able to empathize or identify with them on many different levels.

We all have different personalities, different wants and needs, and different ways of showing our emotions. Navigating through this all takes tact and cleverness – especially if we hope to succeed in life. This is where emotional intelligence becomes important.

Emotional intelligence is the ability to recognize your emotions, understand what they're telling you, and realize how your emotions affect people around you. Emotional intelligence also involves your perception of others: when you understand how they feel, this allows you to manage relationships more effectively.

People with high emotional intelligence are usually successful in most things they do. Why? Because they are the ones that others want on their team. When people with high EI send an e-mail, it gets answered. When they need help, they get it. Because they make others feel good, they go through life much more easily than people who are easily angered or upset.

Characteristics of Emotional Intelligence

There are five elements that define emotional intelligence:

Self-awareness: People with high emotional intelligence are usually very self-aware. They understand their emotions, and because of this, they do not let their feelings rule them. They are confident — because they trust their intuition and do not let their emotions get out of control. They are also willing to take a honest look at themselves. They know their strengths and weaknesses, and they work on these areas so they can perform better. Many people believe that this self-awareness is the most important part of emotional intelligence.

Self-regulation: This is the ability to control emotions and impulses. People who self-regulate typically do not allow themselves to become too angry or jealous, and they do not make impulsive, careless decisions. They think before they act. Characteristics of self-regulation are thoughtfulness, comfort with change, integrity, and the ability to say no.

Motivation: People with a high degree of emotional intelligence are usually motivated. They are willing to defer immediate results for long-term success. They are highly productive, love a challenge, and are very effective in whatever they do.

Empathy: This is perhaps the second-most important element of emotional intelligence. Empathy is the ability to identify with and understand the wants, needs, and viewpoints of those around you. People with empathy are good at recognizing the feelings of others, even when those feelings may not be obvious. As a result, empathetic people are usually excellent at managing relationships, listening, and relating to others. They avoid stereotyping and judging too quickly, and they live their lives in a very open, and honest way.

Social Skills: It is usually easy to talk to and like people with good social skills, another sign of high emotional intelligence. Those with strong social skills are typically team players. Rather than focussing on their own success, they help others develop and shine. They can manage disputes, are excellent communicators, and are masters at building and maintaining relationships.

Emotional intelligence can be a key to success in your life — especially in your career. The ability to manage people and relationships is very important in all leaders, so developing and using your emotional intelligence can be a good way to show others the leader inside of you.

How to Improve Your Emotional Intelligence

The good news is that Emotional Intelligence (EI) can be taught and developed. Many books and tests are available to help one to determine his current EI, and identify where one may need to do some work. The following tips are useful:

Observe how you react to people. Do you rush to judgement before you know all of the facts? Do you stereotype? Look honestly at how you think and interact with other people. Try to put yourself in their place, and be more open and accepting of their perspectives and needs.

Look at your work environment. Do you seek attention for your accomplishments? Humility can be a wonderful quality, and it does not mean that you're shy or lack self-confidence. When you practice humility, you say that you know what you did, and you can be quietly confident about it. Give others a chance to shine — put the focus on them, and don't worry too much about getting praise for yourself.

Do a self-evaluation. What are your weaknesses? Are you willing to accept that you're not perfect and that you could work on some areas to make yourself a better person? Have the courage to look at yourself honestly — it can change your life.

Examine how you react to stressful situations. Do you become upset everytime there's a delay or something doesn't happen the way you want? Do you blame others or become angry at them, even when it's not their fault? The ability to stay calm and in control in difficult situations is highly valued – in the business world and outside it. Keep your emotions under control when things go wrong.

Take responsibility for your actions. If you hurt someone's feelings, apologize directly — don't ignore what you did or avoid the person. People are usually more willing to forgive and forget if you make a honest attempt to make things right.

Examine how your actions will affect others — before you take those actions. If your decision will impact others, put yourself in their place. How will they feel if you do this? Would you want that experience? If you must take the action, how can you help others deal with the effects?

Advantages of Emotional Intelligence

- **Improvement in Relationship:** EI is helpful in improving relationships and is important while working with colleagues and friends.
- **Improvement in Inter-personal Communication:** When a person is acting with EI, he is expected to behave very smoothly and improve communication with others. The understanding of EI helps them develop a whole set of skills and strategies which allow for more meaningful communications.
- **Better Empathy Skills:** This is one of the core skill required in effective communication. This gives a person the ability to know how others feel and this thought gives them develop close relationship.
- **Acting with Integrity:** Integrity is another core of EI ability, means behaving in a way that is consistent with his core beliefs, being true to himself and honest with others.
- **Respect from Others:** Respect is always give and take and when a person behaves with EI, he gets respected by people for his act.
- **Change Management with Confidentiality:** It is found that people with low EI always resist change. They lack the self-confidence to adopt change and they tend to turn their face at things and eventually lose out as progress happens around them.

Disadvantages of Emotional Intelligence

- **EI is too Vague a Subject:** The terminology is so vague that many researchers tend to take it in its different form. Most of us cannot accept that being self-aware or having empathy is a matter of intellect. The researchers also focus on different skills and make it difficult proposition.
- **EI cannot be Measured:** Many researchers feel that EI cannot be measured as it is a form of intelligence where the right and wrong answers are not measurable and validity questionable.

- **Validity of EI is Suspicious:** The critics argue that because EI is so closely related to intelligence and personality, once you control for these factors, EI has nothing unique to offer. EI is correlated with measures of personality, especially emotional stability and there is no answer for EI beyond measures of personality and general intelligence in predicting job performance.

6.6 SOCIAL DIMENSIONS OF DISASTER

Introduction

"Natural" disasters are nature's judgement on what humans have wrought. Natural disasters destroy more than lives and infrastructure – they violently and suddenly rip apart social interaction patterns and cohesiveness. Recovering from a disaster, then, requires more than burying the dead, caring for the injured, and rebuilding structures. It must also ensure that social structures knit together. This is a substantial challenge, and one that is rarely addressed with great success by any of the many institutions that respond to disasters, in large part because the character of the initial response may make doing so more difficult.

Disaster responses resemble military operations in their heavy reliance on command and control systems that historically have been effective in making a chaotic situation more manageable. With such an approach, however, there is little room for participation. The sense of urgency when lives are at stake works against such a process, which takes time to implement. The perceived need for haste also makes it easier to take short cuts to solving problems. Local power structures may be sidelined rather than engaged. People and institutions that might help rebuild affected communities may be left out of the relief response, often because the responding institutions have limited knowledge of the communities affected by the disaster. An immediate response that ignores local power structures, social groups, and differences in vulnerability risks makes recovery more difficult by undercutting the very factors that helped create social cohesion in the first place. And when the pressures of the response are allowed to carry over to the later stages of rebuilding and mitigation, too little may be done to ensure that the social and livelihoods needs of the affected populations are considered. It may also leave the poor and other vulnerable groups even more disadvantaged than they were before the disaster. IEG examined several issues with social development dimensions: poverty reduction, gender-specific impacts, shelter, and housing. Underlying all of these issues, however, is the larger concern about the inadequacy of participation in the response to natural disasters.

Participation in Natural Disaster Response

Low levels of public participation in the planning, design, and in many cases implementation of recovery activities is a common and worrying theme across the case studies. Project evaluations fairly consistently raise community participation as an issue of importance. All project plannings advocated that communities should participate in planning, designing, implementing, managing, supervising, maintaining, and (sometimes) financing a project. Efforts to restore livelihoods may founder because of inadequate beneficiary participation.

Following the Gujarat earthquake, the borrower's priority was to provide housing for earthquake victims, and the restoration of the damaged public markets in the centre of Bhuj was postponed until the completion of long-term urban planning. While urban roads were widened and dead-end streets connected, reconstruction was moving quickly outside the city centre. Shopkeepers and vendors could not wait for the project to attend their needs: they moved to the periphery where new markets sprang up spontaneously.

Beneficiary participation is especially important when it comes to shelter and housing, because the nature of the place where people live has significant impact on their feeling of security, and hence on their ability to rebuild community. Emergency shelter and housing reconstruction efforts should always embody the bank's priority concern with benefiting the poor by providing priority assistance to those unable to afford it by other means.

Participation occurs rarely but can enhance sustainability and ownership. When stakeholders' views are not considered, the solution they are provided often fails to solve their problems. Rebuild apartment buildings and commercial areas without specifying clearly who will manage and maintain them. Worse, they may leave vulnerable groups even more disadvantaged than they were before the disaster. Some projects that provided shelter have encountered difficulties brought about by the risk of breaking up social networks, dislocating people from their extended families and jobs. The sheer numbers of people in need of housing have been daunting in some cases. Also an issue is the difficulty beneficiaries may have keeping up with maintenance of units handed over (even if the unit was free).

From the government's perspective, the goal is to help the disaster homeless get back on their feet as quickly as possible, while focusing on the poorest, and encouraging mitigation measures to help reduce the impact of future disasters. What works? Preserve and secure existing social relationships when providing emergency shelter financing expensive temporary shelter should be avoided unless the areas involved face severe winters or weather conditions are life-threatening. People are able to provide themselves with adequate temporary shelter using materials from damaged buildings, and families that did not lose their dwellings take in friends and relatives. When shelters are called for, efforts need to be made to keep families and neighbourhood groupings intact. The layout of temporary shelter structures can reduce crime if care is taken during the relocation process to ensure that as many doors as possible face a common and well-lit area — thus avoiding the creation of passages and alley ways that are dark and not well-observed.

Shelter and Housing

Emergency efforts to help the homeless should avoid undermining good housing sector policies, and seek to incorporate best practice prescriptions of such policies whenever possible. Emergency shelter and housing reconstruction efforts should always embody the priority concern with benefiting the poor by providing priority assistance to those unable to afford it by other means. Reconstruction projects commonly rebuild apartment buildings and commercial areas without specifying clearly who will manage and maintain them. Worse, they may leave vulnerable groups even more disadvantaged than they were before the disaster.

Several approaches to shelter have been taken in the emergency context – building emergency shelters, relocating victims to safer areas, and facilitating self-help construction of temporary shelter while simultaneously preparing house for the homeless with housing reconstruction. Where it has not been feasible or desirable to relocate people, the bank will support dedicated shelters and strengthened warning systems.

The goal is to help the disaster homeless get back on their feet as quickly as possible, while focusing on the poorest, and encouraging mitigation measures to help reduce the impact of future disasters. The bank finances temporary housing for disaster victims and learned through that process that such shelters are sometimes occupied for long periods of time, and often become permanent.

Key Consideration of Shelter and Housing

Following points should be considered in relation to shelter and housing:

(1) Preserve and Secure Existing Social Relationships when Providing Emergency Shelter: Financing expensive temporary shelter should be avoided unless the areas involved face severe winters or weather conditions are life-threatening. People will be able to provide themselves with adequate temporary shelter using materials from damaged buildings, and families that did not lose their dwellings take in friends and relatives. Emergency shelter and housing reconstruction should reflect the bank's priority concern with the poor.

Social relationship sustain people during disasters and should be considered at all stages of the response.

(2) Build to Higher Standards: Temporary housing is rarely temporary and should be built accordingly. Temporary housing is sometimes occupied for long periods of time. For this reason, temporary shelter was build to slightly higher standards after the Marmara earthquake so that the structures could become another form of housing for the poorer once the new housing was completed. Moreover, if shelters are built using disaster-resistant construction techniques, not only are they safer for the displace living in them, but such construction also serves as an example that people will see, that will then potentially inform their future construction choices. Simplicity of message is essential to the adoption of disaster-resistant construction technologies. The Maharashtra Emergency Earthquake Project promoted simple earthquake-resistant features for non-engineered masonry construction based on three short rules that could be understood, adopted, and applied by the villagers. Their simplicity made wide dissemination possible and benefited a much larger population than originally targeted.

(3) Consider the Social Context when Providing Sites and Services: The approach of providing beneficiaries with a "wet core" of plumbing in cooking and bathroom facilities and having them invest in building up around that start has had mixed success. This is, in part because without a place to sleep, beneficiary families find it difficult to move to the site. For example, in EL Salvador, following the October 1986 earthquake, the sites and services aspect of the Popayan, Colombia project met with considerable success, however. The project's infrastructure components, which carefully targeted poor households, had a lasting positive impact on urban development.

(4) Provide Incentive to Complete Rural Housing: Funding for disaster-resilient rural housing has worked on an incremental "you finish one stage and you will get money for the next" basis. Such an approach was successful in Turkey and India.

(5) Relocation: Much of the huge loss of life from a disaster can be attributed to people living in makeshift homes on land not appropriate for such structures. Vulnerability can be reduced with relocation, but this rarely takes place because too little care is taken to prevent reoccupation and to preserve social relationships. To reduce vulnerability in the future, cities must relocate people away from and that is vulnerable to disasters and ensure that new families do not create informal settlements. Often old historic districts have structures that have been built unsafely and too close together, increasing the susceptibility to collapse in a disaster. Safety considerations during the reconstruction phase invariably will call for better designed housing and infrastructure to protect citizens and allow communities to be more resistant to disasters. In relocation programmes a balance needs to be their previous dwellings (in terms of location, social infrastructure, and access to jobs and services) but are less vulnerable to disaster risk, while also allowing flexibility in families choose where to live.

Key Considerations of Relocation

(1) **Use Urban Reconstruction to Enhance Cultural or Historic Districts:** After the Lijiang earthquake in China, high-rise apartment complexes were torn down and single family houses were reconstructed in a traditional style. This helped Lijiang achieve UNESCO (United Nations Educational, Scientific, and Cultural Organization) designation as a World Heritage Site, which increased the city's attractiveness for tourists, creating additional employment.

(2) **Consider Employment Patterns when Relocating:** After the EL Salvador earthquake, squatters were relocated from the city centre to a Northern suburb some 15 kms., away from the centre, where most of them had been employed. A survey conducted by the project showed those years after the disaster, economic conditions had worsened for 6 per cent of the resettled families. In India's Maharashtra Emergency Earthquake. Reconstruction Project, some villages were relocated so farway that peasants gave up farming because they could not reach their fields.

Drawbacks Shelter and Housing

Over the past so many years, people rendered homeless by natural disasters or living on at-risk land were relocated in different projects, with varying levels of success. In majority cases, people were relocated to a safer area. In seven cases (all earthquake-related), a lack of technical expertise coupled with victims' anxieties and opportunism led to a suboptimal result, and in four cases the area that disaster victims vacated received a higher value use once they were gone. In almost all cases, the vulnerability of the relocated families in these projects was reduced, if for no other reason than that they moved into more disaster-resilient houses. However, in majority cases relocation sites were quite distant from the original settlements, and commercial transport costs were therefore involved.

In most of the projects, resettled people moved back to their former location, either to go back to where their roots were, or to cash in their benefits by selling their new home and moving back to the hazardous area. A well known drawback to relocation is the difficulty of preserving social networks in the process. The Beneficiary Analysis performed by the project reports: "Beneficiaries reported a strong preference for rebuilding their own damaged houses, rather than moving to the assigned houses in new neighbourhoods. Moving means dissolving social networks that often had generations of history."

Much of the huge loss of life from a disaster can be attributed to people living in makeshift homes on land not appropriate for such structures. Vulnerability can be reduced with relocation, but this rarely takes place because too little care is taken to prevent reoccupation and to preserve social relationships. To reduce vulnerability in the future, cities must relocate people away from and that is vulnerable to disasters and ensure that new – families do not create informal settlements. Often old historic districts have structures that have been built unsafely and too close together, increasing the susceptibility to collapse in a disaster. Safety considerations during the reconstruction phase invariably will call for better designed housing and infrastructure to protect citizens and allow communities to be more resistant to disasters. In relocation programmes a balance needs to be their previous dwellings (in terms of location, social infrastructure, and access to jobs and services) but are less vulnerable to disaster risk, while also allowing flexibility in families choose where to live.

Drawback of Relocation

(1) **Provokes Social Disruption:** A well known drawback to relocation is the difficulty of preserving social networks in the process. More significantly, at least on the part of those being relocated, it provokes social disruption and upheaval when people are bundled into an alien environment. Notwithstanding the influence of structural/social forces, people are also reluctant to be relocated far from relatives, friends and their place of work.

(2) **Plans to Relocate are Costly:** Relocation is unpopular, as plans to relocate entire communities are costly, mainly because of the need to acquire alternative locations and the provision of housing for those resettled.

(3) **Worst Option:** In disaster management, relocation/resettlement is more often seen as the worst option as it gives the impression that nothing else can be done about the hazard and people have to be moved.

Vulnerable Groups

Each type of disaster has impacts related to the nature of the event (earthquakes knockdown buildings) and another set of impacts on sectors of society that are particularly vulnerable. The uneven impacts of disaster arise from differences in income status, culture, gender, location of home, and land tenure. Essentially, disaster impacts on people vary, depending on the levels of social vulnerability and risk. The unevenness of the impacts is often highly visible because of media attention, but the recovery process is potentially more uneven, and it tends to be less visible, at least to those on the outside, because their attention has turned elsewhere. For example, absence of explicit determination to deal with the situation of renters made homeless by disaster, public money may end up being used to provide multiple housing replacements for the wealthy. Another common inequity occurs when the immediate cash needs of the poor are ignored in the immediate post-disaster period and they have to sell their productive assets, including their land, to the better-off.

The government's various approaches to pre- and post-disaster assistance have affected economic and social recovery in different ways. The following sections discuss approaches used when dealing with the special situations of the poor and women in the complex context of post-disaster recovery.

Poverty and Disaster

Poverty alleviation measures of all kinds, if successful, can lower levels of vulnerability to disaster because of the tightly interwoven nature of the two issues. The World Development Reports underscores the importance and connection of poverty levels and vulnerability to natural disasters and highlights the importance of putting poverty reduction and vulnerability reduction high on the list of development priorities. While experts note that the poorest countries and their weakest groups are the hardest hit in terms of direct and indirect losses from natural disaster, there is little quantitative analysis of how the poor are treated during the recovery, and little research on how the impact of reconstruction work spreads across socio-economic groups.The impact of disaster is uneven, and without careful planning, the recovery can exacerbate existing social and economic inequalities.

Key Considerations for Poverty

The key considerations for poverty are as follows:

(1) **Ensuring Beneficiary Views:** Beneficiaries should be involved in the project design and implementation phases through involvement of local leaders, formal social assessments, and open meetings where all are welcome. The involvement of beneficiaries in the project design and implementation plays a part in greater project success.

(2) **Cash Support:** It stabilizes the situation of the poor in the early recovery stage. During the recovery process, getting cash support to victims quickly has positively affected people's sense of safety and security. It has been a prominent first sign of the government's support in a time of acute need. When promptly provided, cash support enabled people to survive and get local economies moving again and was reported as highly preferable to in-kind support by beneficiaries.

(3) **Providing Livelihood Opportunities:** Approaches to livelihood generation have been tried in disaster projects, giving the affected people a chance to take part in the rebuilding and

maintenance, while providing much needed income sources. For example, North China Earthquake Reconstruction Project included income generation schemes that were introduced to help facilities to repay loans received for reconstruction. This was of particular benefit to affected poor farmers who did not have funds to repair or rebuild their home. Local economic activity was not only restored to pre-earthquake, levels, but has been growing since projects completion.

(4) **Working at the Finer Textured, Smaller-scale Level:** Following a disaster, solutions that will directly benefit the poor are found at the micro level. As one disaster expert interviewed by the study team put it, government has "thick fingers for such fine-scale work". Building major infrastructure will eventually benefit the poor indirectly, but programmes that are effective in reaching the neediest people within the recovery process are located close to the ground and are designed with stakeholder input.

(5) **Mitigate to Reduce the Impact of Disaster:** The best way to address the needs of the poor in natural disaster projects – to develop prevention and mitigation programmes so that their homes did not fall down in the first place.

Providing Livelihood Opportunities

Approaches to livelihoods generation have been tried in disaster projects, giving the affected people a chance to take part in the rebuilding and maintenance while providing much-needed income sources. There are few examples of success, however. Preparation for the North China Earthquake Reconstruction Project included income-generation schemes that were introduced to help families repay loans received for reconstruction. This was of particular benefit to affected poor farmers who did not have funds to repair or rebuild their homes. Local economic activity was not only restored to pre-earthquake levels but also has been growing since project completion.

Working at the Finer-textured, Smaller-scale Level

Governments have "thick fingers for such fine scale work". Building major infrastructure, as the government tends to do after a disaster, will eventually benefit the poor indirectly, but programmes that are effective in reaching the neediest people within the recovery process are located closer to the disaster area. Following a disaster, solutions that will directly benefit the poor are found at the micro level ground and are designed with stakeholder input.

Historically, the governments have suffered working at this level, and when new structures to deal with the problem must be set up, the process slows down. In addition, the learning curve for working at that new level is steep. Civil society organizations already on the ground are more adept at targeting and working with communities, the poor in particular. Disaster assistance becomes a matter of increasing the scale of what they are already doing.

Gender and Disasters

The uneven impacts of disaster are sometimes starkest between the genders, to the extreme that gender and survival rates can be closely tied. Only one woman for every three men survived the December 2004 tsunami in one district in Aceh. Women and men have different vulnerabilities, and they cope with disasters differently. A number of factors contribute to the particular vulnerability of women before, during, and after natural disasters: a lack of information about evacuation warnings and shelter options, culturally restricted mobility, and responsibilities within the family to care for the young and the elderly. The literature stresses the importance of assessing women's vulnerabilities separately because of the potential for vulnerability differences and the relationship between these differences and a number of cultural and social factors.

Key Consideration of Gender and Disasters

Some key considerations of gender and disasters are as follows:

1. **Improve Data Gatherings:** After disaster and during recovery, lack of data can impede equitable distribution of compensation. The damage assessment can help to ensure equity by disaggregating mortality and morbidity by gender and taking into account losses suffered in the informal sector.
2. **Target Female-headed Households:** Gender projects stressed that single-headed households are especially vulnerable to natural disasters since caregivers are less mobile. The women's needs and vulnerabilities are called "gender projects". Gender projects stressed that single-headed households are especially vulnerable to natural disaster since caregiver are less mobile. The increase in poverty in the aftermath of a disaster and the increase in the number of female-headed household after a disaster make women more vulnerable to a subsequent disaster.
3. **Provide Support to Lighten Workload:** Women shoulder much of the burden of care for children and the elderly and disabled, as well as such household tasks as provision of water and fuel wood. Disasters can increase the intensity of this work, and informal networks among neighbours and the extended family, an important coping mechanism for women in times of crisis, have often dissolved. Reconstruction programmes need to try to preserve social networks and find ways to lower the workload of women.
4. **Ensure Equity of Treatment in Employment:** Women are often discriminated against in food for work programmes, services, and employment opportunities during disaster recovery. Another area in which women's contributions are often neglected is the agriculture sector. Women's agricultural labour often goes unrecognized, and they are not compensated tools and agricultural inputs after disasters.
5. **Ensure Access to Training:** Training and capacity building for women following a disaster has proved more difficult than employment creation. Although women often provide labour in the agricultural sector, they usually do not receive advice on improved practices because of cultural taboos in rural areas. To overcome this problem, recent projects aimed to train female extension workers to reach women in rural areas.
6. **Look for Opportunities to Create Equity in Land Ownership:** Some projects have influenced gender relations by modifying land rights. In many developing countries, women are not allowed to own land or houses. In Tonga, after a disaster in 2002, any woman whose house was not damaged by the cyclone had to give up her home to a male relative who had lost his house.

Projects financed by the government banks have elevated the status of women in society by providing land titles in the names of both men and women. Unprecedented in this region, even widows received houses in their own names, and *ex gratia* payments for lost relatives were disbursed to them.

6.7 REHABILITATION

Natural disasters are crises, and a crisis is a time-limited period of psychological disequilibrium in victims, precipitated by a sudden and significant change in individual life situations. That life situation change can be represented by loss of home, which leads to feeling of insecurity and vulnerability in the loss of privacy and treasured possessions. These persons are thrown into situations where they must lodge themselves in temporary shelters, without restrooms or cooking arrangements, and with poor sleeping conditions. The loss of home can extend to loss of community and employment, with concomitant loss of support and income.

The injury and death associated with natural disasters makes an imprint on the person's mind, with that imprint taking the nature of guilt for not doing enough, or of fear and anxiety it is pointed out that denial and anger are frequent concomitants of disasters. The denial is especially common where lost relatives are involved, and the anger seems to be directed towards public officials for not having prevented dislocation, for rescuers who did not react fast enough, or to insurance companies for not paying a claim. Some major concerns of rehabilitation are discussed below.

The goal of appropriate disaster rehabilitation is to support the affected society while working as an agent of positive change for disaster-prone elements. Rehabilitation is a long haul effort and requires strength, energy, and stamina. We need to understand the difference between temporary and permanent shelter. We need to identify the kind of people who would be interested in such long run work. Finally, the kind of people and materials need to be resourced for a particular disaster area. Then there are the little appreciated and understood issues of coordination with government departments and the importance of proper project reports which are pivotal to get funding.

One of the most widely-held myths regarding earthquakes, cyclones, floods, and other natural disasters is that they are 'great equalizers'. They bring to mind the wrath and power of an untamed nature that hits men and women, young and old; rich and poor alike. Infact, natural disasters are not great equalizers. There is sufficient evidence for the fact that they affect populations selectively. The poor are the most vulnerable, the least prepared and the hardest hit. Among them, the most seriously threatened by mortality and morbidity are often those already known to be greatest risk even in normal times; women, children and the elderly.

Issues in Rehabilitation

If a society is to return the economic systems, damaged by a disaster, to normal, physical facilities and distribution networks must be restored as quickly as possible. In the succeeding phases, the issues are essentially economic. They deal with housing, reconstruction, and agricultural recovery, restoration of jobs, small businesses, and governmental services. The development issuers, most overlooked during rehabilitation are:

1. **The Need to Facilitate Cooperative Action.** It has been shown that if a society is to develop socially or economically, it must attain a degree of sophistication in conducting cooperative action in future programmes.
2. **Participation in Decision Making.** An NGO, that offers a pre-determined plan or one prepared without the full participation of the disaster victims, misses the opportunity to help people make choices and attain self-confidence in decision making. For example, housing planned in

the aftermath of the Kutch earthquake, had toilets with 12-litre flushing system. This provision, of a 12-litre flushing system was ridiculous, given the fact that it was as good as impossible to so much as get a bucket of water in this context.

3. **Dependency Relationships.** The degree of dependency, on institutions or resources beyond the control of a low-income population, is a major contributor to social and economic underdevelopment. The dependency relationship may involve leadership, money or materials. Generally, dependency relationship are either one-sided or are highly loaded in favour of the provider.

4. **Fostering Unrealistic Expectations.** Many relief programmers have led unrealistic expectations on the part of recipients. For example, the provision of free housing for a relatively small number of people, following the Andhra Pradesh cyclone or the Odisha cyclone, created the expectation that everyone, who had lost a house, would receive a pucca (brick and cement) house from either the government or a relief agency. In fact, it was impossible for the government to provide housing of this type for even one-tenth of the total number of affected families.

Disaster rehabilitation should be seen in a more holistic manner and the problem should be dealt with in its entirety. The issues that need the attention of policymakers, administrators, planners and professionals associated in this activity must be identified for further consolidation. The major issues related to disaster rehabilitation are :

1. Disaster rehabilitation should be part of the total development perspective of an area. To achieve this, the development needs, for different disaster-prone areas, should be assessed and specific planning approaches should be evolved keeping in mind things like resource endowments, population pressure, and the types of disaster in the area.
2. Area-specific plans should be prepared and the disaster reduction activities and socio-economic development of the area should be integrated appropriately.
3. There should be a specific settlement and housing policy for the disaster areas so that the concentration of people in high risk areas can be checked in the future. Disaster-proof housing designs and technologies should be strictly enforced.
4. There should be a well-organized and scientific databased system, networking and information sharing. Detailed guidelines and appropriate techniques should be evolved. The organizational and administrative network should be improved further.
5. Rural development programmers should be specifically designed for disaster areas. Programmes like those of drinking water supply; construction of roads and school buildings; and housing should be planned and implemented keeping in view their vulnerability to disaster.

Hindrances to Normalization

Many a time, disaster relief operations can create a second round of after shock or disaster within the community. Humanitarian aid after a disaster can, in fact, be harmful to the beneficiary. Rehabilitation volunteers have no understanding of the resources existing within a society. Nor do they have an understanding of the role these coping mechanisms play. This is due to their lack of familiarity with the social and anthropological background of the locality and their desire to respond to short-term needs. Therefore, every NGO must learn to identify the coping mechanisms that exist in society and how they relate to outside help. They must learn to use these built-in disaster response systems and to encourage a collective response. Failure to do this can:

1. Undermine the authority and prestige of local leaders.
2. Become a disincentive to self-help.
3. Undermine confidence in local agencies whose resources, are compared to those of outdide agencies, are fairly limited.

Most experienced relief agencies feel that their foremost responsibility is to avoid inflicting harm. Unfortunately, however, examples of the detrimental effects of ill-conceived assistance on painfully achieved progress abound. Example includes:

1. Immediately following a disaster, large amounts of food and essential items are brought in. A distribution system is set up by government agencies and NGOs, which operate through local working groups or committees. The relief packets are then given away to disaster victims. In the meantime, because the relief packet distribution system is divorced from the normal distribution system, local merchants are stuck with the items that would have been of great use of victims.
2. Inability to resolve problems impedes the re-establishment of normalcy. The can lead to new problems that must be overcome to attain pre-disaster development objectives within the affected locality.
3. Relief and reconstruction programmes compete with development programmes for funds, with the likelihood of the former gaining precedence.

Rehabilitation Approaches

Inevitably, a rehabilitation strategy must include the means and tools necessary to achieve its goals. Rehabilitation through the identification and definition of needs, goals, and priorities will contribute greatly to target of achieving the best possible future for a given territory, community or society. It is a creative process intended to attain a certain course of action based on the characteristics of each place and the prioritization of issues according to their importance, urgency, and resources availability. The process focuses particularly on aspects that are pivotal to future development.

What is needed now is a well-coordinated multidisciplinary effort on the part of planners, policy-makers, scientists, and implementers. These are some of the approaches used by authorized NGOs to attain rehabilitation and relief targets.

1. **The *Ad hoc* Approach:** NGOs provide aid in as many different sectors – health and housing – as possible. The problem is that these activities are neither well-coordinated nor linked and thus, do not supplement each other.
2. **The Single Sector Approach:** In this approach, an NGO focuses all of its efforts and resources in one sector, which could perhaps be that of housing. It may, however, conduct a variety of projects and use a number of different methods to make provision for building materials and housing loans and grants. In this way various activities are designed to contribute to the long-term objective of rehabilitation.

3. **The Integrated-recovery Approach:** If conducted properly, integrated-recovery programmes afford an NGO the most opportune method of introducing measures that will prove beneficial to a small locality.

The main impediment to accomplishing a comprehensive rehabilitation process our *ad hoc* approach to matters. The aim is to bride the gap between humanitarian aid and reconstruction, and to gear post-disaster recovery programmes to a stage where they can remove the source of risk altogether through comprehensive local sustainable development management.

Opportunity for Change after Disaster

Vulnerability persists and in many cases is exacerbated by the prevailing short-term vision of disaster relief operations, which focus only on the consequence of disasters; and not on the root of the matter. As a result, not too much attention is paid risk-reduction measures. Even after a disaster, the primary focus is on the emergency itself; or humanitarian assistance; and at the most, on re-instating basic services and restoring normalcy. In a way, this is tantamount to rebuilding vulnerability and helps perpetuate the same 'development paradigm'.

Disaster rehabilitation must be closely linked to and incorporated into different areas of economic, social, political, and environmental development. The system has to understand that a sustainable disaster rehabilitation programme must begin with a prevention-oriented approach and culture. This perspective must be included in risk studies and analyses; land-use planning and risk reduction activities; mitigation efforts; preparedness and early warning efforts; emergency management; and reinstatement, recovery, and reconstruction process. Activities preceding, during, and following a devastating event must be strengthened and synergized to enable linkages and continuity among projects.

Our record of success, for building a model society after a disaster, has been low. This does not mean that opportunities for modest change are not present. Rather, it means that a subtle approach, patience and long-term commitment on the part of the government and NGOs are required. There are three broadly recognized ways by which change can occur:

1. **Invisible Change:** Making improvements without outwardly affecting appearance or performance. For example, improving traditional building – techniques to enable housing to withstand earthquakes better.
2. **Substitute Method:** For example, the introduction of a new type of seed – that is post-resistant, but required no basic change in normal cropping patterns – is a measure worth-striving for in a post-disaster situation where crops have been destroyed.
3. **Building Block Method:** An organization can introduce changes slowly by first working to re-establish a semblance of normalcy, and then introducing limited innovations.

In some of the most severe disaster, the single greatest loss (after human suffering) is that of housing. The reconstruction of damaged or destroyed houses is the most expensive part of the disaster recovery process.

The objectives of the rehabilitation programme should be:

- To help disaster victims repair or rebuild safe houses at affordable rates,
- To improve the building skills of local carpenters, masons, and other building tradesmen so that they can continue to build safe houses,

- To lower the disaster vulnerability of housing in the community,
- To stimulate economic recovery as well as physical reconstruction,
- To stimulate the development of small enterprises in the housing sector to reduce building costs and to provide a basis for improving the standard of housing in the project area,
- To establish a basis for vulnerability reduction in areas outside the disaster-affected zone.

Generally, in a shelter-to-housing programme, a variety of post-disaster shelter and housing services are offered by NGOs to low-income disaster victims. Many badly hit high-income groups are simply left out the loop. After sometime many families from low-income group move to pucca houses but families belonging to pre-disaster high-income groups continue to temporary shelters. There should be programmes which enable them to rebuild their houses. In this programme, building materials may be sold to them at a subsidized price. The housing programme should be designed in such a manner that it allows each and every family to move on to the long-term recovery phase.

The reconstruction programme should also involve victims, in a more participatory way in the repair and rebuilding of their housing.

Given below is a sequential list of the measures required for a housing rehabilitation programme:

1. **Disaster Assessment:** An assessment of needs and resources available in the area.
2. **Rehabilitation Planning:** The planning process sets out a framework for the initial stages of implementation. As the project proceeds, plans may be revised or changed.
3. **The Acquisition of Materials:** The materials, necessary to help people rebuild or repair houses, are identified and acquired during this phase.
4. **Public Awareness:** As the programme commences, an extensive methodology for informing the public about how they can participate in the programme is carried out.
5. **Construction Training:** The key element of the programme is that of providing training in methods of improved disaster-resistant construction.
6. **Participation:** NGOs should help victims to participate more effectively in rehabilitation programmes. Special attention is given to collaborative work as families help each other build as a means of reducing costs and speeding up construction.

Material Distribution for Rehabilitation

The sustainability of infrastructure reconstructed after disaster is always in doubt when long-term measures to address disaster mitigation are absent. Reaching agreement on the mitigation measures, within the first three months, is very important because it is much harder to focus on the disaster once the memory of the emergency recedes.

Once these agreements are reached they need to be translated into some form of commitment. Options to be considered, within the context of what affordable, include financial incentives, land use, a review of land tenure patterns, upgraded building codes, training of construction craftsmen, and other non-structural measures to lessen vulnerability. Once these issues are sorted out it is important to create a system for the distribution of building materials. Material distribution activity has four components.

1. **Material Acquisition:** These are usually procured either from commercial supplies, on-site building materials, or salvaged material.

2. **Logistics:** It consists of the equipment procedures, and means of moving the materials from the source of acquisition to the point of distribution.

3. **Materials Distribution:** It consists of direct sales to the beneficiary, grants-in-aid, materials-for-work.

4. **Credit:** In some cases it may be necessary to provide loans to enable families to puchase building materials.

Relief and reconstruction operations should be conducted within the context of development. The process, through which a family obtains disaster assistance, may be that much more important than the actual aid received. People can do it and they know how to. People usually prefer private and informal solutions to rehabilitation can provide a strong stimulus to recovery and a base for positive changes.

6.8 THE ROLE OF BUILDING MATERIALS AND SERVICE BANKS

Building Materials Service Bank – An Introduction

A Building Materials Service Bank (BMSB) provided the dual advantage of rapid response to re-construction needs and continuity in community-managed habitat and infrastructure improvement. In addition, it generated local employment and enhances local capacities to manage the supply and delivery of contextually relevant, safe habitat solutions.

The Post-disaster Context

Any natural disaster – be it tsunami, cyclone or earthquake – causes major devastation. The loss of shelter and livelihood makes people more vulnerable to poverty. There is some confusion regarding reconstruction, as people often do not know how to build better and safer homes for the future. Since reconstruction; at a mass scale, is an urgent and immediate priority matter, traditional construction methods cannot cope up with the pace of work due to longer processing time. Moreover, monitoring the quality of construction is difficult due to the large-scale and highly decentralized nature of construction. In addition, the dearth of supplies makes the demand for traditional building materials and skilled manpower more urgent and more expensive.

Need for a Post-disaster Systematic Delivery of Habitat Products and Services

BMSB is designed to facilitate supply and augment availability of high-quality pre-fabricated building elements at a rapid pace. These pre-fabricated elements have a standard quality and accelerate the process of reconstruction, while providing jobs to those hit by disaster. Moreover, the BMSB helps in guiding bewildered houseowners about how best to construct an appropriate house, thus keeping them away from touts and opportunity-seeking unscrupulous contractors. Due to its large-scale of operations, a BMSB can also become a supply chain for providing bulk building materials, like cement and steel and trained masons, for speedy reconstruction. Supported by mobile units and village construction centralized production centres, are delivered to needy families and their construction queries and dilemmas are responded to.

A Long-term Habitat and Livelihood Process

Beyond the goal of immediate reconstruction, the BMSB also serves as a one-stop for building materials, infrastructure and services. BMSBs can enhance its portfolio by not looking only at the supply side of materials and skills but also the demand for more access to financial and professional services such as structural and architectural guidance; and sanitation and domestic energy facilities. The reconstruction project/programme provides an opportunity for setting up, establishing the business of, and establishing the credibility of BMSB services. Such centres can attract the attention of booth cement companies and housing finance companies.

Functions of BMSB

The functions of a Building Materials and Service Banks are as follows:

(a) Production and supply of building elements.

(b) Training in production of building elements to producers and for construction to artisans.

(c) Training to masons, bar-benders, welders, carpenters, and other affiliated tradesmen.

(d) Demonstration of building technologies would include equipment and products, production processes and applications.

(e) Provision of building elements for community accessing the bank.

(f) Keeping a record of skilled masons and artisans trained in construction and building – materials production and network with them as and when the need arises.

(g) Providing expert construction services through teams of trained artisans.

In addition, these centres become the nodal points for facilitating habitat and livelihood finance by connecting rural users to local banks and other financial institutions. The BMSB response model builds up and strengthens local knowledge and capacity for safe construction practices.

Management

The primary components of the habitat and livelihood delivery system the BMSB include infrastructure building and helping local building material production enterprises link mobile building units and entrepreneurial village construction teams.

The BMSB requires the management of both infrastructure and production units. While the basic infrastructure can be managed by the panchayat or the local community group; the production units can be treated as microenterprises located at the BMSB site. In this way, local entrepreneurship is encouraged and supported.

A technical team, on-site, or linked resource, provides the technology support initially required. The quality assurance and training and associated services can be provided by this technical team of the BMSB. Local production enterprises become the primary production and delivery agents. Construction services are provided by local masons trained at the BMSB and linked to it for regular jobs and employment prospects.

6.9 FROM SHELTER TO HOUSING

This study of residential rehabilitative shelters for victims of disaster is based on a review of the literature addressing residential shelters, protection, and rehabilitation for victims of disasters; and interviews with individuals engaged in rescue and relief work including government officials, scholars, and representatives of non-governmental and international organizations. It addresses the major types of residential shelters, the constraints that affect shelter operations, and a series of issues and challenges to effective shelter care, and includes examples of good practices and recommendations.

No two shelters are alike: Location, size, cost, length of stay, and the population that the shelter serves differ from place-to-place and from shelter-to-shelter. The services shelter facilities offer must be flexible enough to address each population's range of needs, including the different situations in which trafficking victims have been held; the type of exploitation they have experienced; and the victims' age, gender, and nationality. The size of the group residential facility is usually determined by the location, the demand for shelter, security considerations, the type of services offered, and availability of external support. Shelters can be small enough to serve only a dozen individuals or big enough to serve well over 100 or 200 people, with no one optimal size.

The cost of establishing and maintaining group residential rehabilitative facilities varies significantly from shelter-to-shelter. Funding may come from local or international sources. Finding a viable long-term means of self-support is difficult for most shelters and requires creative approaches. Activities contributing to sustainability may include enterprises that both increase former victims' job skills and generate income to support the shelter.

Factors that influence the type and geographic location of shelters include the needs of the victims, as well as security issues. Shelters located in border areas may be equipped to provide short-term services to recently rescued victims but may not be an appropriate site for mounting a rehabilitative care programme. Longer-term shelters are more likely to be located where the trafficked victims can access services while working towards obtaining legal employment. Security is a concern for all shelters and includes protection against outside break-ins and escape from the shelter by victims.

Group Residential Facilities

Emergency Shelters. Emergency shelters are usually the first destination for victims of disaster, following a rescue, or escape, and typically provide for stays of a few nights to a month. They emphasize the immediate provision of medical and physical security for the victims.

Transit Centres. Transit centres are similar to emergency centres but are distinguished by their strategic location at significant areas and migration border crossings. They provide assistance to victims of disaster. An effective transit centre needs strong coordination between service providers and local law enforcement.

Short-term Shelters. Short-term shelters commonly provide assistance to victims of disaster from one week to three months.

Long-Term Shelters. Long-term shelters prepare disaster victims for reintegration into society, whether within their families or in new communities. The length of stay in long-term shelters varies; most provide support and assistance for six months or more.

Rehabilitation, Recovery, and Reintegration. Critical factors in rehabilitation, recovery, and reintegration include the victims' age, physical and psychological health, background, family life, culture, extent of damage, etc. The long-term recovery, rehabilitation, and reintegration of victims can involve educational and economic opportunities, as well as extended psycho-social care.

Education. Many shelters provide a range of educational opportunities, including formal and non-formal education, life skills, and vocational training.

Economic Opportunities. To live, victims need the skills to earn an adequate income. Skills training programmes should be created to match the needs of the local job market. Some shelters have included income earning ventures to provide vocational skills to former victims as well as to supplement shelter resources.

Psycho-social Support. Victims of disasters commonly experience severe physical and psychological trauma as a result of the event. Psycho-social support and counselling can help victims free themselves from the anxiety and depression and start rebuilding their self-confidence.

Reintegration. The reintegration of victims often is a difficult, complex, and long-term process. It is different for each victim, and it involves not only the victim but also the environment and culture within which the reintegration is to take place. The organization providing support may need to make a long-term commitment to the victim to help in this process.

Security: Security is a concern for all shelters and includes protection against outside break-ins and escape from the shelter by victims. The practice of holding victims against their will in shelters is an issue in some places. In a country with a number of shelters, victims may be kept against their will by some shelters and not by others.

6.10 DISASTER INFORMATION PROVIDER

Introduction

Disaster has little regard for existing boundaries, whether geographical, political, or professional. When a disaster strikes, everyone needs to make informed decisions about when to do to protect their facilities, their business, and their community. Disaster managers and responders suddenly become very important but so do emergency responders such as physicians, firefighters, and law enforcement personnel. As rebuilding proceeds, architects, engineers, financiers, construction workers, building inspectors and many others play critical roles. Thus, much of the disaster management community is involved full-time, while many of those affected are involved only part-time. Disaster involves the public and private sectors, government and business professionals and volunteers, practitioners, academia and the research community.

The challenge for a disaster information provider is to meet the widely varying needs of a very broad spectrum of users during all phases of disaster management. In addition to the needs for basis situational awareness and resource management information, there are needs for information to make critical decisions, needs for training community throughout the world must continually be improved and benefit from technical assistance, training and the latest technologies so that it is ready to take crisis reparation and mitigation actions. The need to integrate across many boundaries, all phases of disasters, and the many different user requirement make designing a disaster information network a formidable task.

Information on hazards should be accurate, reliable, and comprehensible to planners. It must also cover all significant hazards. Planners will seek to obtain as much existing hazard information (proceed or raw data) as possible for their assessment, drawing upon a variety of information providers. A high level of accuracy, and detail is often possible in hazard assessment, for example, visually, through maps, remote sensing, and GIS technology and in prediction such as complex flood models that model rainfall to run-off, the movement of flood waters through waterways and flood plains, and inundation areas. Also, laser scanning is used to gather data about an object or environment which can be used to create a 3D model for details reconstruction.

Key Features of Disaster Information

Information on the following key features of natural hazards is needed to indentify past, present and potential hazards and their effects are as follows:

1. **Location and extent.** Is the programme or project are affected by one or more natural hazards, what types of hazard and where?
2. **Frequency and probability of occurrence.** How often hazard events likely to occur (in both the short-term and long-term)?
3. **Intensity/severity.** How severe are the events likely to be (e.g., flood levels, speed of wind, and volume/rate of rainfall during hurricanes, magnitude and intensity of an earthquake).
4. **Duration.** How long will the hazard event last (from a few seconds or minutes in the case of earthquake to months or even years in the case of drought)?
5. **Predictability.** How reliably can we predict when and where events will happen? Information about the speed of onset of hazard event is principally relevant to disaster preparedness and early warring systems but may also have a bearing on planning decisions (e.g., planning, secure evacuation routes).

Types of Disaster Information Providers

Following are the main types of hazard information providers:

1. Vulnerable communities and other local stakeholders, whose environmental knowledge can be obtained through surveys and particularly appraisal.
2. State disaster management agencies, planning, organizations other ministries and departments, and public utilities (which generate hazard risk, vulnerability and disaster impact data sets and maps). The military often have good hazard data, although it may not be easy to obtain.
3. National and international scientific research and monitoring institutions such as meteorological offices, volcano observatories, geological surveys (which produce maps showing hazards and hazard-prone zones, install and operate monitoring systems and maintain the data sets collected, and carry-out surveying research and modelling), and space investigation agencies (which collect remote observation data).
4. International Development and Disaster Management Organizations, notably Regional Management Disaster Agencies and documentation centres and United Nations (UN) operational agencies (which produce diverse information materials including maps, disaster impact data research studies and field reports).

5. Other non-state organizations such as libraries, archives, the media, universities, research institutes, insurance companies and non-governmental organizations (also with varied information products).

Recent Trends in Disaster Information Provider

Disaster management is a complex domain and effective disaster management, from risk assessment and mitigation to response and recovery requires the right information to be delivered to the right people at the right time to make the right decisions at the right level at the right time. Since all events happen somewhere, at sometime, information provider forms the backbone of the information requirement. Since many organization are involved data sources required are many and varied information sharing and integration is therefore of paramount importance. While developments in technology have made data capture easier, the total information spare has become more complex and the task of data management harder. This has also changed the nature and demands placed on geographic information (GI).

But this information revolution is still in its infancy, foretelling opportunities that will improve ability to mitigate the impacts of natural disasters. However, recent and anticipated development in spatial databases, GPS, wireless, mobile, and computing technologies have changed and will continue to change, the way in which GI can be collected, maintained, analysed, integrated, and delivered to the end-user in disaster management and other domains. Electronic warning systems, Geo Informatics, and Laser Scanning are the result of such technological innovations and they are defining the recent trends in disaster information provider.

Within the disaster management, domain actors and decisionmakers use information providers to carry-out tasks and activities. They are not interested in GI as an end in itself but as a means to an end in making the right decision at the right time in order to carry-out tasks or activities effectively and efficiently. GI is one ingredient required to make an informed decision in order to carry-out a task. Other ingredients may include resources, costs, and time.

GI adds value when it meets those conditions when it contributes to informed decision making allowing more effective execution of tasks and activities and the saving of time, costs, resources, and lives. GI loss value if it adds nothing to the decision making or when there are barriers to accessing the right information, at the right time. Example of such barriers could include time taken to manipulate the required data, inappropriate scales, poor accuracy, etc.

While technological advances have (and will continue to) made data collection easier, contributing to an explosion of potential information availability, they have made the information management task more complex, hence the need for information management frameworks, stands and governing principles.

1. Understanding user needs and behaviours in order to identify what, when, where, and how GI adds a value to the task-identifying moments of value by applying techniques of user-centred design and human factors.

2. Enabling the meaning of GI to be understood by human and machines through the development of ontology and semantic reference systems.

3. Generalizing information appropriate to the users task.

4. Developing spatial and spatio-temporal database structures that represent the dimensionally and event-based nature of the real world.
5. Using continual development in technology to provide the right information to the user appropriate to their task (personalizing information according to context) at their location, at that time.

6.11 QUESTIONS

1. Define trauma?
2. What are the psychological impacts of a disaster?
3. Describe the major causes of stress? and what are the measures to overcome stress?
4. Write short notes on the different types of trauma? What are the psychiatric interventions to overcome this?
5. Narrate the rehabilitation approaches in disaster management.
6. What is the importance of emotional intelligence in disaster management?
7. Write short notes on social dimensions of disasters.
8. What are the various types of disaster information provider?

7 Applications in Disaster Management

Learning Objectives

- To understand the various applications in disaster management viz.,
- Statistical seismology
- Reconstruction technologies
- Remote sensing
- Electronic warning systems
- Geo informatics
- GIS and GPS
- Laser scanning

Structure

7.1 Application of Statistical Seismology in Disaster Management

7.2 Application of Quick Reconstruction Technologies in Disaster Management

7.3 GEO Informatics in Disaster Studies

7.4 Electronic Warning System

7.5 Global Positioning System (GPS)

7.6 Laser Scanning

7.7 Questions

7.1 APPLICATION OF STATISTICAL SEISMOLOGY IN DISASTER MANAGEMENT

Introduction

Seismology is *science dealing with all aspects of earthquakes.* Statistical seismology is the application of rigorous statistical methods of earthquake science with the goal of improving our knowledge of how the earth works. Within statistical seismology, there is a strong emphasis on the analysis of seismology data in order to improve our scientific understanding of earthquakes and to improve the evaluation and testing of earthquake forecasts, earthquake early warning, and seismic hazards assessments.

There are currently multiple commercial seismography applications available including mineral or hydrocarbon prospecting, groundwater investigations, environmental and hazardous waste site studies, archaeology, and civil engineering.

Seismography is based on transmitting pressure wages from source through the earth or sea, receiving these waves using a network of distributed sensors, and deducting the sub-surface composition and features from the received signals. The cost and complexity of seismological survey vary widely, but the two main drives are.

1. The cost, reliability, and weight of cables connecting the sensors.
2. The cost of large numbers of seismographic sensors.

Global Navigation Satellite System (GNSS) broadcast very precise timing signals that can be used to derive an extremely accurate absolute time reference. This information can be received by seismography sources and sensors equipped with GNSS received. Time tagging both transmitted and received seismic signals with this absolute time reference, and combining it with the measured GNSS position of the sources and sensors, will remove the need for connecting cables. A single sensor connected to a PC carried in a backpack could be used to perform seismographic surveys.

This will considerably reduce the minimum cost of seismography surveys, and open up the lower end of the seismography market. It could be used, e.g., by development agencies to locate sites for water wells, to survey potential archaeological sites before starting digs, or by local councils to perform hazardous waste site studies.

The system also has potential application in scientific seismology and natural disaster management. The accuracy of the GNSS timing signals will allow detailed variations in sub-surface stress or composition to be measured over time. Installing a GNSS seismography network in earthquake/tsunami-prone or volcanic areas could help to predict earthquake or volcanic activity and reduce the impact of these events on the local population.

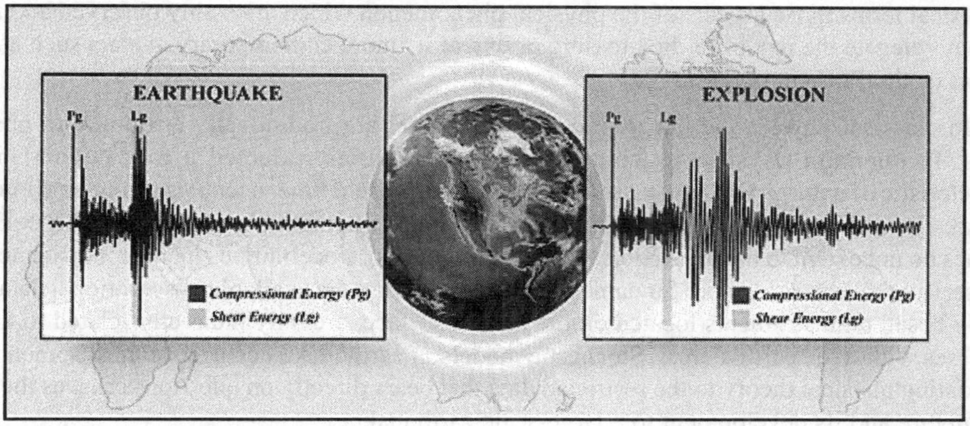

Statistical Seismology Models

The following four types of models are used in statistical seismology:

1. Physical and stochastic models.
2. Conceptual models.
3. Descriptive models.
4. Engineering models.

1. Physical and Stochastic Models: The terminology 'stochastic model' means a model in which some stochastic or random elements appear. "Statistical model' is used almost synonymously, but it is preferred to use the term. 'Stochastic' because it draws attention to the key element – the appearance of some features whose behaviors cannot be predicted exactly, but can be summarized in probability terms.

The difference between physical and stochastic model is commonly taken to mean that the physical model embodies no random components, whereas the stochastic model embodies no physical components. Both are exaggerated views and neither touches on the real requirements of useful models in a field such as seismology. Of course, there is a difference between deterministic and stochastic models, but neither seems to be more physical than the other. Both are physical to the extent that they succeed in describing and predicting the physical processes they purport to represent.

A physical model which contains no stochastic component deprives itself of the possibility of making any statement concerning the uncertainties of predictions based on the model . In a famous statement, Sir Jeffery, who is also regarded as a pioneer in inferential statistics, argued that to be worthy of its name, every physical theory should contain within itself the means not only of predicting the relevant observed quantities, but also of predicting their uncertainties. He was arguing that every physical theory should include some stochastic component.

From a philosophical point of view, the basic feature of a stochastic model is that it accepts that some aspects of the physical processes are out of range, at least for practical purposes, and must be replaced in the model by some unknowable and hence random process. The model should incorporate in physical terms those aspects of the physical phenomenon which are stably observed and repeatable, but may relegate the rest of or dice-tossing or one of its more contemporary avatars such as Browman motion or the Poisson process.

In classical physics the uncertainties in the model are traditionally attributed to observational errors. In quantum physics, by contract, the uncertainties reflected a fundamental, irrefutable characteristic of nature. Earthquake seismology, at the present time, occupies an uncomfortable middle ground. General patterns of behaviours may be predicted qualitatively from physical theories, but the theories do not extent to the prediction of local earthquakes. Uncertainties include, but are not restricted to observational errors. A more fundamental difficulty is that the available observational data, wholly or largely based on instruments located on the earth's surface, are only indirectly related to the physical processes within the earth's crust. Stochastic models of earthquake occurrence must somehow manage the existing physical theory to the restricted data that bears directly on questions crust as the intimation of a rupture and its development to a large-scale earthquake.

Under such circumstances, quantifying the uncertainties in the model predictions represents a major and formidable challenge. It is believed that it is fundamentally for this reason that the stochastic models for earthquake occurrence often appear to reflect the physical picture in such a limited way. They reflect the gap in the ability to observe and hence to understand the crucial physical processes at the microscopic level.

But such general statements are too glib. In actual practice, a wide variety of models, both stochastic and otherwise, are used for a wide range of different purposes.

Different Types of Stochastic Models. Across these diverse fields of application in the natural sciences, two broad roles for stochastic models may be distinguished.

(i) The first is epitomized by statistical mechanics. Here the stochastic model plays an integral role in understanding the physical process themselves. Large-scale macroscopic behaviours are deduced from the statistical properties of the interactions of large numbers of microscopic entities. Many details governing the behaviours of the microscopic entities do not need to be known precisely, as they do not affect the macroscopic effects. Hence very simple ("toy") models may suffice at the microscopic level, provided they capture the key aspects which influence behaviours at the macroscopic level.

(ii) In the second, by far more common, type of application, the stochastic model is used as a basis for planning, prediction, or decision making. In this case, whether or not it adequately represents the underlying physical process may not be the crucial aspect. What is important is such application is to know the reliability of the forecast values; not just the forecast values themselves, but some measures of their variability, given the information on which they are based.

It is also vital, since the model may be largely empirical in character, that the parameters in the model can be fully determined from the available data. Even if better models exist in principle, they will be of little practical value if they rely on information that cannot be obtained from the available data.

2. Conceptual Models: Within seismology, a role of this kind is implicit when the fracture processes within the earth's crust are described as 'frozen turbulence'. It is also present in models for the fracture strength of materials as functions of the density and size distribution of micro cracks within the material. Indeed, statistical models of this character have long played a role in fracture mechanics, from the time of Griffiths and Weibull forward. Weibull attributed the variations in strength from otherwise similar laboratory specimens to the random distribution of micro crack lengths in the specimen. The Weibull distribution takes its name from his studies of these variations.

The branching process, percolation, and cellular automata interpretations of the earthquake process all start from the underlying idea that, instead of progressing smoothly, as would a fault or fracture in a homogeneous elastic medium, the movement of an earthquake rupture is irregular, controlled by its essentially random progress from one weakness to another.

My own interest in this area was stimulated by the possibility of applying branching process ideas to the development of an earthquake rupture. This leads to a stochastic model which predicts a G-R law with *b* value around 2/3 in the critical case, and to Tapered Pareto distributions ('Kagan distribution') when the process is sub-critical.

It is remarkable that very similar branching process concepts reappear in Ogata ETAS model, lending credibility to one of Yan Kagan's old thesis (e.g., Kagan Knopoff) that the distinction between stages of the rupture itself, and the associated events which accompany or follow it, are due more to the characteristics of the recording instruments than they are to the physical processes causing the motions.

It is also of interest to compare the roles of stochastic models for earthquake occurrence, such as the ETAS model or the branching model for fracture, with models for complex systems, whether stochastic, such as cellular automata, or deterministic, as in block-and-slider and related mechanical models for fault systems.

Under a wide range of conditions, many such models show characteristic features of earthquake occurrence – a GR law, long-range correlations, after shock sequences, etc. In this sense there may be no overriding reason for preferring one type of model over another. Each provides a different insight into the circumstances under which these features can be produced.

The merit of a model such as the branching model for crack propagation lies in the extent to which it can explain a complex phenomenon from simple premises. It is viewed as negligible as in modelling a complex physical phenomenon by a model whose complexity approaches that of the phenomenon itself, particularly when both may be adequately predicted by a simple stochastic model, and only the model is known in detail at the microscopic level.

3. Descriptive Models: The term 'descriptive model' seems clear enough to require little further explanation although a geophysicist might prefer the term 'empirical model' to denote much the same concept, in any case, the aim of the model is to describe, in the sense of being able to reproduce, the broad features of the observed data.

Within seismology, the canonical example would have to be the Gutenberg Richter frequency-magnitude law. From the outset its purpose was purely descriptive, and in this it succeeds, very well. The tragedy is that Gutenberg and Richter, following bad habits common among the physicist, first described their data in terms of numbers rather than proportions, then used the most familiar logarithm tables to base 10 and finally compounded their errors by fitting a least squares regression lines to the cumulative data. This led them to the familiar form.

$\log_{10} (M) = a + b (M-M_0) + E_M$ ...(1)

Or equivalently

$N(M) = 10\ a + b (M-M_0) + E_M$ ...(2)

Where,

N and M are the number of events in the data set under study which have magnitudes above M, M the magnitude threshold for reliable statistics, E_M the error term which, to quote Harold Jeffery's once more, 'is quick forgotten or altogether disregarded in physical theories'.

Had it been regarded more carefully, the unsuitability of the above formulation might have been more apparent. Just think how different elementary textbooks in seismology might appear if, instead of numbers Guttenberg and G = Richter had phrased their discovery in terms of the proportions, p(M) of events above magnitude M:

$\log p(M) = 10^{-b\,(M=M_a)}$ ...(3)

The pseudo parameter 102 disappears, being revealed as nothing more than normalization constant (here the total number of events above the threshold magnitude). Nor is it any great step to replace the decimal logarithms by natural logarithms, and so to recognize the exponential distribution. Finally the term, EM is revealed as nothing like the error in a regression problem, but as the discrepancy between the true and empirical distribution functions at a particular point M on the cumulative curve, a least of a totally different character.

Our personal view on this issue is that anyone pretending to the title of an up to date seismologist should be required an oath to forsake the use of the traditional form of the G – R law (other than in its historical context) and to persuade their colleagues to do likewise, to rid both textbooks and current practice of a misleading, unhelpful, and totally unnecessary anachronism.

Within the revised formulation, i.e., as a distribution function which gives a good fit to the data, the Guttenberg – Richter law is a clear example of a purely descriptive stochastic model. It has no pretence at being a physical law – the reasons why the distribution should be exponential are nowhere mentioned, let alone tied back to some physical theory.

The second obvious example is the Omori law, at least when described, as Poisson process with time dependent rate of the form.

$\lambda (t) = A(c + t)^{-p}$ ...(4)

Where, A, c, and p are the parameters and t is the elapsed time since the main shock. This formulation of Omori's law is perfectly adequate for simulating a set of aftershocks with the same broad characteristics as the data set to which the parameters were fitted, and permits estimates of the errors in the parameters as well as in any prediction made from the model. Once again, however, it has no physical content beyond the central fact that it describes a physical phenomenon.

4. Engineering Models: This means models developed in order to resolve a particular practical question in some planning decision making, or forecasting context.

There is a broad overlap between such models and descriptive models. The main difference is in the purpose of the model. In a descriptive model, the main purpose is simply to describe the data effectively. In an engineering model, the main purpose is to meet the specified practical end.

Traditional uses of such models in seismology have been those relating to earthquake zoning, earthquake engineering design, and earthquake insurance. For example, for many decades, the Poisson model has played just such a role in the applications to earthquake zoning. Nobody now pretends that the model fits earthquake data well, but its application to zoning schemes are easy to understand, and lead to recommendations which are reasonable and even conservative in many cases, although it is clear that they ignore certain key features of earthquake occurrence such as aftershocks.

However, it appears to that the major class of models in this category may now comprise the models used to produce earthquake probability forecasts. The task of the model is clear. It cannot be undertaken without a stochastic model. The question is whether the models are effective for the purpose in view. Recent developments such as the establishment of forecast testing centres testify to the perceived relevance of testing the models against the purpose for which they were designed, rather than against more general purpose.

Before addressing this issue in detail, it may be helpful to formulate a few guiding principles for the development of engineering models in general, which then can be applied to models for earthquake forecasts in particular. These are as follows:

(i) The level of detail of the model should match the purpose in view. There is no point in modelling details that is not needed for the purpose in hand. Moreover, a simple model is likely to be more helpful than a complex one in understanding and communicating the issues involved, and also in avoiding nonsense recommendations.

(ii) The model must be able to be estimated from the available data. There is no room in this context for an elegant model that relies on unavailable data.

(iii) The model may 'borrow strength' from data outside the immediate context. Example, by using Bayesian methods to make partial use of parameter values found from previous studies. Bayesian methods are almost unavoidable in decision making context, and are likely to be used in most real-life applications of earthquake probability forecasts.

(iv) Even though following the physics may not be the main aim, a model which is based on a good, if simplified physical picture is likely to be safer for prediction than a model which is purely descriptive or *ad hoc* model cannot be trusted outside the range of the data to which it has been fitted.

(v) Models used for limited term forecasts may lack the long-term satisfactory properties commonly required of time series models. Such models also should be used with caution in making longer-term forecasts.

Benefits of Statistical Seismology

The main benefits of the statistical seismology are as follows:

1. **Cost, Weight, Reliability, and Portability:** Only one portable sensor and a seismic source, each with a GNSS receiver, are required. No cables are needed.
2. **Compatibility with Existing Systems:** The system is compatible with existing sensor technologies and processing software.
3. **Flexibility and Accuracy:** Sensors can be placed wherever desired, instead of being restricted to rectangular cable-based array grids.

4. **Real Time Investigation:** The operator can increase survey resolution in real time by adding extra measurement points.
5. **Reduced Environmental Impact and Constraints:** Survey can be performed in areas covered by vegetation or building.

To see how earthquakes really occur, we first need to learn about constitution of the Earth!

The earth comprises of three major chemical radial divisions as:

- Crust
- Mantle
- Core

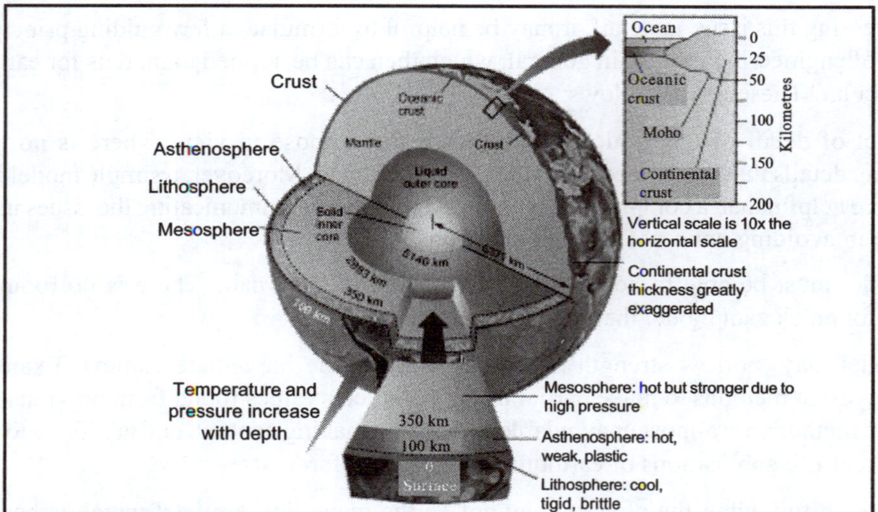

Crust

The shallowest layer of the earth is known as the crust. The crust is the most heterogeneous layer in the earth. The crust is on an average 33 km thick for continents and 10 km thick beneath oceans and it varies from just a few km to over 70 km globally.

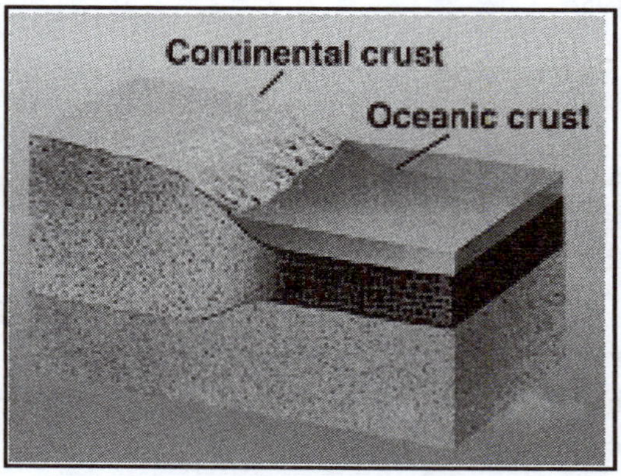

The boundary between the crust and the mantle is mostly chemical. The crust and mantle have different compositions. This boundary is referred to as the Mohorovicic discontinuity or "Moho". It was discovered in 1910 by the Croatian seismologist Andrija Mohorovicic.

Middle Earth: The Mantle

Earth's mantle exists from the bottom of the crust to a depth of 2,891 km (radius of 3,480 km) – Gutenberg discontinuity and it is further subdivided into:

- ❖ The uppermost mantle (crust to 400 km depth)
- ❖ The transition zone (400-700 km depth)
- ❖ The mid-mantle (700 to 2,650 km depth)
- ❖ The lowermost mantle (2,650 to 2,891 km depth)

The uppermost mantle is composed dominantly of olivine; lesser components include pyroxene, enstatite, and garnet.

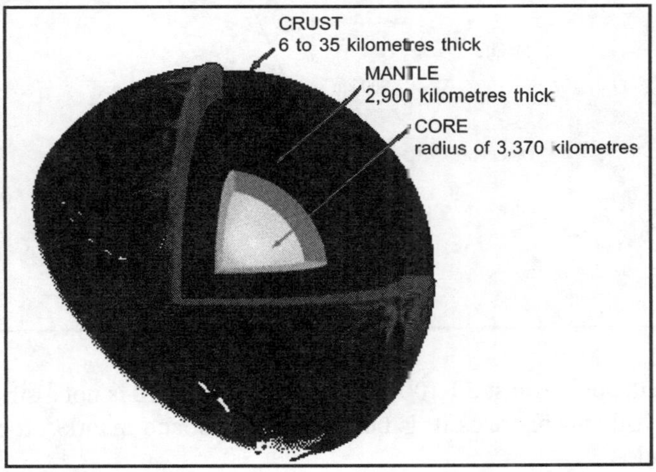

Earth's Core

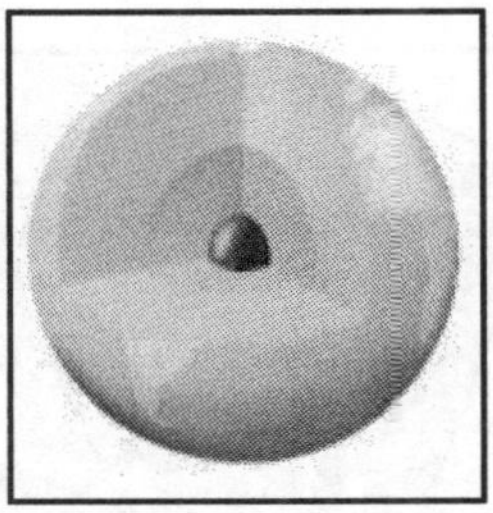

Owing to the great pressure inside the earth, the earth's core is actually freezed as the earth gradually cools. The boundary between the liquid outer core and the solid inner core occurs at a radius of about 1,220 km – Lehman discontinuity, after Inge Lehman from Denmark. The boundary between the mantle and outer core is sharp.

The viscosity of the outer core is similar to that of water, it flows kilometres per year and creates the earth's magnetic field. The outer core is the most homogeneous part of the earth and is mostly an alloy of iron and nickel in liquid form.

Mechanical Layers

1. Lithosphere
2. Asthenosphere
3. Mesosphere

Lithosphere

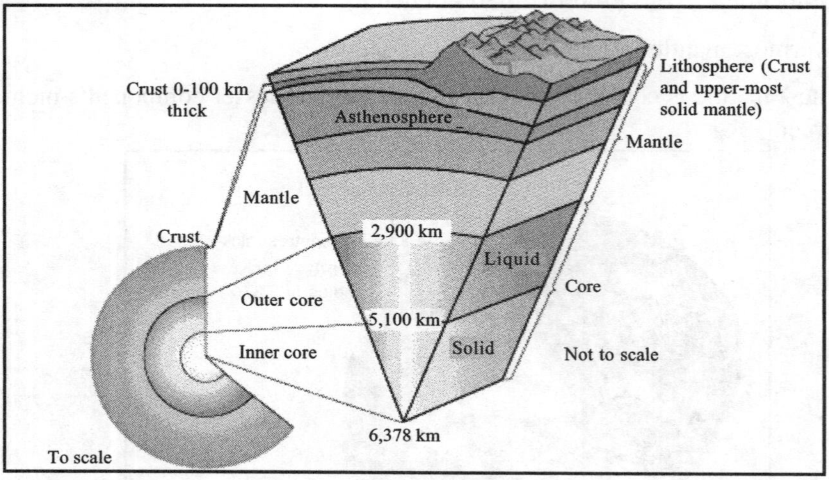

The lithosphere is the uppermost 50-100 km of the earth. There is not a strict boundary between the lithosphere and the asthenosphere as it is between the crust and mantle. It consists of both crust and upper parts of mantle.

Asthenosphere

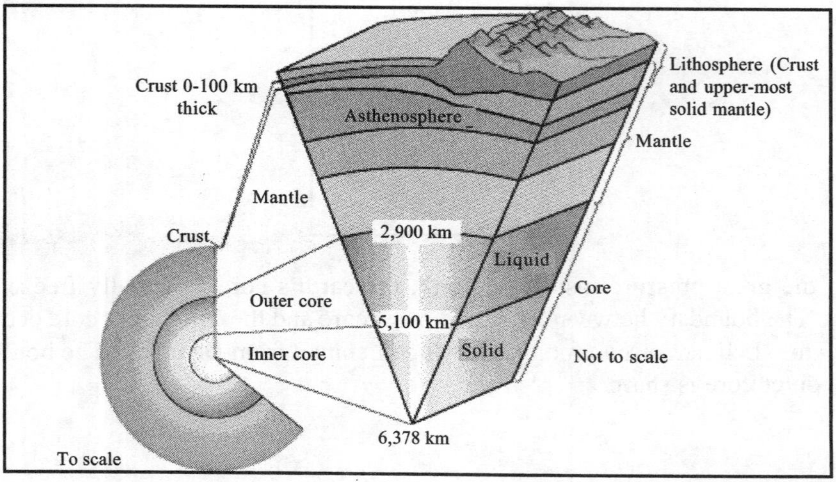

The asthenosphere exists between depths of 100-200 km. It is the weakest part of the mantle. It is a solid over short time scales, but behaves like a fluid over millions of years. The asthenosphere decouples the lithosphere (tectonic plates) from the rest of the mantle.

Major Tectonic Plates

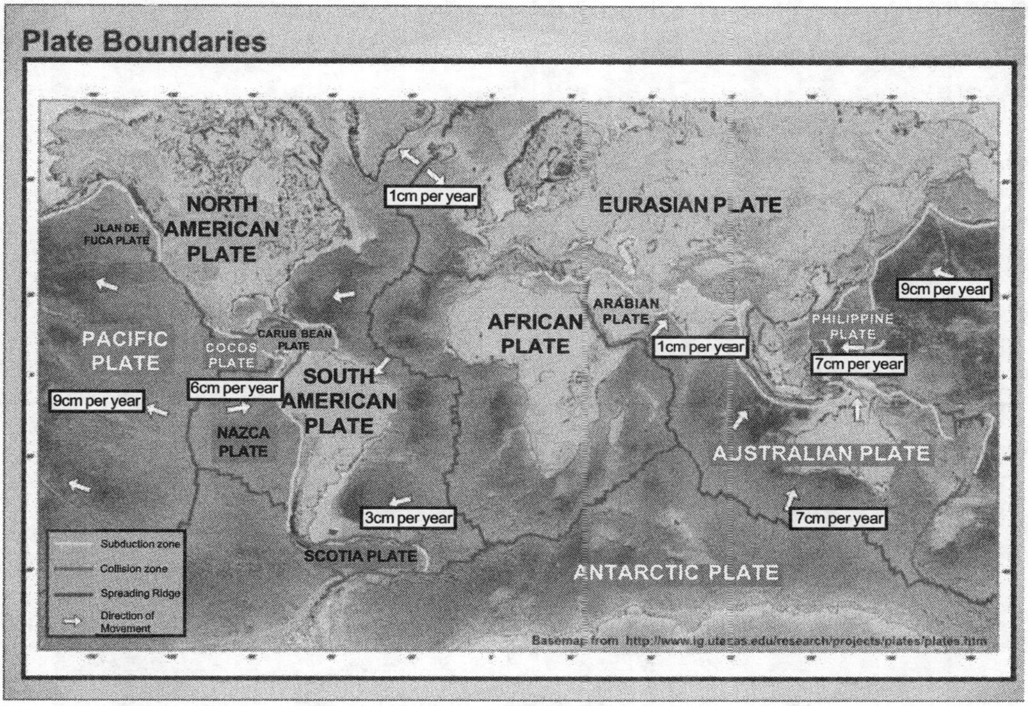

How Earthquakes Occur?

Earthquakes occur at FAULTS. Fault is a weak zone separating two geological blocks.

Tectonic forces cause the blocks to move relative one to another.

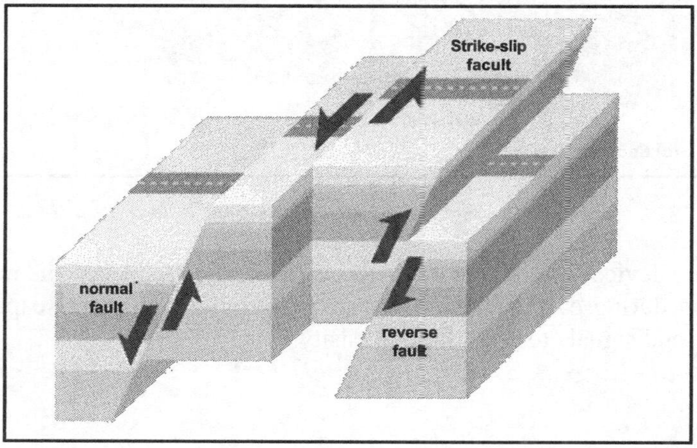

Elastic Waves – Body Waves

Longitudinal Waves

- They are faster than transversal waves and thus arrive first.
- The particles oscillate in the direction of spreading of the wave.
- Compressional waves
- P-waves

Transversal Waves

- The particles oscillate in the direction perpendicular to the spreading direction.
- Shear waves – they do not propagate through solids (e.g., through the outer core).
- S-waves

Elastic Waves - Body Waves

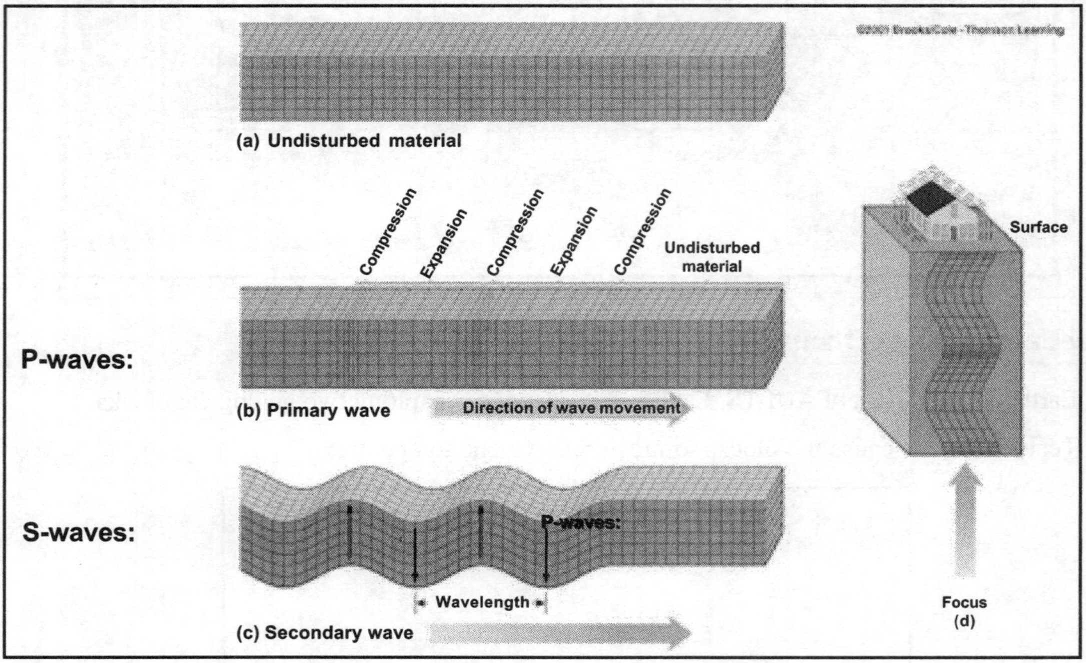

Seismographs

Seismographs are devices used to record the occurrence of earthquakes and measure the intensity of the ground motion during earthquakes. They are electronic equipments capable of sensing the ground motions and send signals to record the intensity.

- Seismographs are devices that record ground motion during earthquakes.
- The first seismographs were constructed at the very end of the 19th century in Italy and Germany.

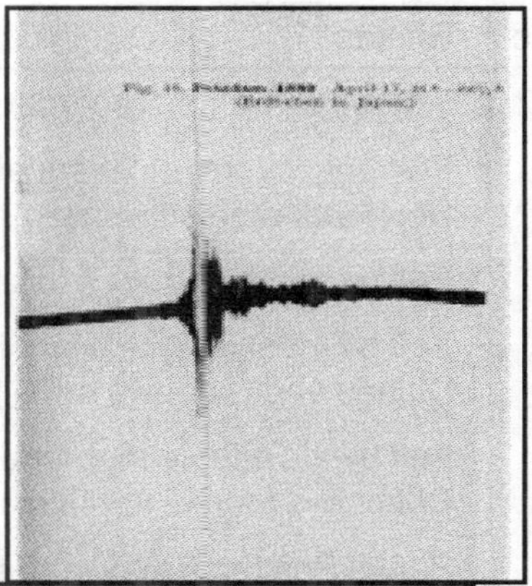

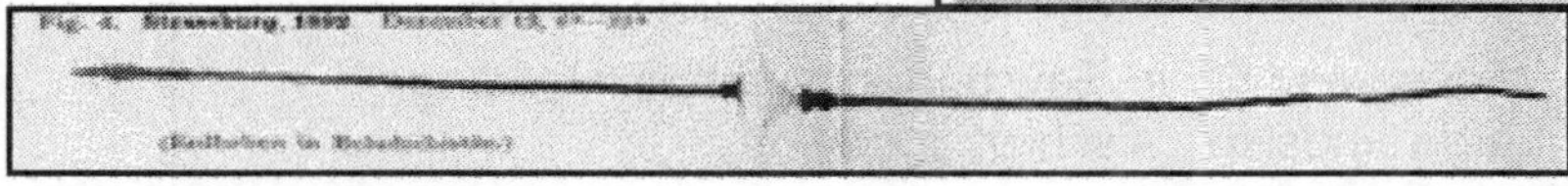

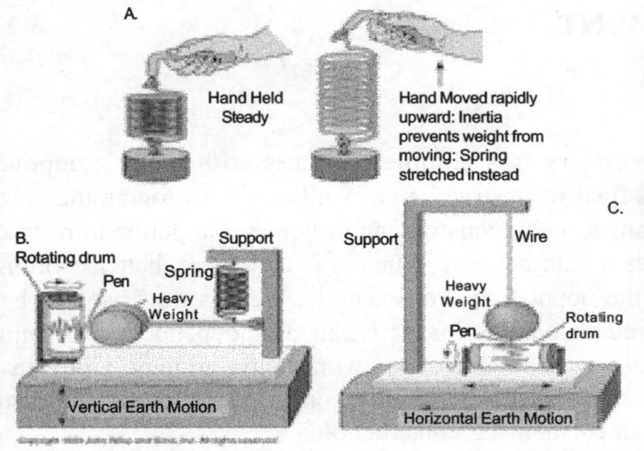

Horizontal 1000 kg Wiechert Seismograph in Zagreb (built in 1909)

Modern digital broadband seismographs are capable of recording almost the whole seismological spectrum (50 Hz-300s). Their resolution of 24 bits (high dynamic range) allows for precise recording of small quakes, as well as unsaturated registration of the largest ones.

The following table gives the magnitude reading in earthquake and the earthquakes are classified according to the table.

Magnitude	Effects	Number per year
less than 2	Not felt by human recorded by instruments only	Numerous
2	Felt only by the most sensitive. Suspended objects swing	>10,00,000
3	Felt by some people. Vibration like a passing heavy vehicle	1,00,000
4	Felt by most people. Hanging objects swing. Dishes and windows rattle and may break	12,000
5	Felt by all; people frightened. Chimneys topple; furniture moves	1,400
6	Panic. Buildings may suffer substantial damage	160
7 – 8	Widespread panic. Few buildings remain standing. Large landslides; fissures in ground	20
8 – 9	Complete devastation. Geound waves	2

7.2 APPLICATION OF QUICK RECONSTRUCTION TECHNOLOGIES IN DISASTER MANAGEMENT

Introduction

Post-disaster reconstruction and recovery is a complex process with many components. Emergency aid, transitional measures and final reconstruction, as well as other programmes such as livelihood support, work for food programmes, and reconstruction of homes and public infrastructure are closely interconnected. Some measures would be more efficient if they were, better coordinated and backed up by more information for the population. For example, there is no reason to handle emergency relief, transitional shelters, and reconstruction or repair as independent programmes. Integrating the transitional structures into permanent houses would save money. Coordinating infrastructure repairs (that is the first step to be done with the whole reconstruction process is important), as transport and water supply problems hamper housing construction.

It is assumed that reconstruction normally has many advantages compared with resettlement. There is consent within the expert community that resettlement should never be forced and should be limited to the evacuation of highly hazardous sites and to relieve overcrowded settlements.

However, once the damage assessment has confirmed the extent of structural damage, one is left facing two different possible solutions which are as follows:

1.Controlled destruction of damaged structure. Any structure that is damaged beyond possible repairs or retrofitting, which has to be removed, posses quite a difficult problem if placed in the urban area where the uncontrolled destruction can induce to a significant damage to any neighbouring structure. Infact, it is more difficult to destroy the partially damaged structure in a controlled manner, that to understand the damage mechanisms and carry-out the damage assessment not only the reliable estimates of the damage mechanisms accounting for possible heterogeneities are needed, but it is also needed to carry-out the simulation of the complete structural failure in post-stable regime.

It is important to understand that the problems of this kind calls for the numerical modelling and simulation tools capable of going beyond the non-linear structural mechanics applications into the area of multibody dynamics, so that the post-critical path of the failing structure can be predicted. Moreover, the computational tools for handling the contact problems are also needed in order to predict the final position of the failing structure produced upon hitting the ground. These three phases carried out for the chosen building and the corresponding analyses are carried out by computer codes like (FEAP, MBS-code, and LS-DYNA, respectively).

However, there is still one important phase missing from the analysis of this kind, which concerns any debris from the fallen structure big enough to induce potential damage in the neighbouring structures in the urban zone. However, this last phase of computation would again require a change of the computational model in that the discrete rather that finite element should be used for the debris trajectories computations.

2.Quick repair and reconstruction. If the structural damage is reparable, one should carry-out this kind of following procedures by using modern materials such as ultra high performance fibre reinforced concrete or carbon fibre, which can help us recover the structural integrity to a desired level. Several keynote lectures are focusing on this particular class of problems.

If the structure, however, are damaged beyond the reparation and would take much longer period of time to rebuild, then the temporary structures can be employed, which can re-establish the operations in the urban zones.

Basic Considerations

Physical reconstruction itself has many dimensions which can roughly be summarized under:

1. Procedures (documentation, assessment, funds, payment, etc.). An idealized procedure that does not allow enough time for reconstruction within a reasonable time will end in meagre results as people remain unhoused. Idealized technology, which does not take time or funds into account, hampers, implementation and quick reconstruction or leaves many people out. This is certainly not a good approach.
2. The attempt to bring one component to perfection reduced the overall result. It is much better to aim at simple approach which are really applied and reach all beneficiaries. This is the way to optimize the total project. The procedures must be fast established and well manageable.
3. Technology (technical rules, reasonable safety standards, and training): The technology needs to be efficient and each to handle, and timing must always be kept in mind as a patient that died gets no help from a potentially perfect treatment. Forward thinking is necessary, which could produce now the better approach for the next disaster.
4. Time: Time is an important consideration in reconstruction as delays have a negative impact.

Technology for Reconstruction

Safety is a fundamental consideration. The design for acts of nature (especially flood, wind, earthquakes, and tsunami) is based on statistics, first the real magnitude of conceivable events is not known; second, one could not afford to build for any worst case. For example, one designs bridge pillars to withstand the impact of truck, but not for all houses along a road. This is based on the likelihood and the consequences of such an accident.

Remote Sensing

Meaning of Remote Sensing

Remote sensing is the use of electromagnetic (EM) wave radiation to acquire information about an object or phenomenon, by a recording device that is not in physical contact with the object. In other words, remote sensing is the acquisition of information about an object by a recording device that is not in physical or intimate contact with the object.

Remote sensing in the context of disaster management usually refers to the technology, that includes man-made sensors that are attached to aircrafts or satellites, instead of viewing a far away planet from earth, the sending equipment is usually high above looking down at our 'distant planet-earth'. Distinct in this contest can mean just a few hundred feet overhead or miles above the earth's surface.

The space technology evolve as a suitable strategy for disaster preparedness and operational framework for monitoring, assessment, and mitigation which identifies gap areas and recommends appropriate strategies for disaster mitigation *vis-à-vis* likely development in space and ground segments. While communication satellites help in disaster warning, relief mobilization, and tele-medicinal support, earth observation satellites provide a required database for pre-disaster damage assessment, and reconstruction, and rehabilitation.

Classification of Remote Sensing

Remote sensing is classified by three wavelength regions.

1. **Visible and reflective infrared remote sensing.** This device use everyday light and infrared lasers, with wavelength ranging from approximately 0.4-0.8 micrometers. Usually regular cameras or videorecorders are attached to aeroplanes to provide real photos. This is the most common and inexpensive form of remote sensing. Visible remote sensing allows before and after comparisons in the event of a disaster.
2. **Thermal infrared remote sensing.** Night goggles are made from a type of infrared sensor. Infrared sensors allow to image temperature differences, such as thermal pollution in rivers which cannot be seen with naked eyes or to gauge the temperature difference near volcanoes. Infrared sensors exploit the fact all objects emit a type of EM radiation called "blackbody radiation" at a wavelength proportion to their surface temperature. These sensors allow seeing a particular part of the electromagnetic spectrum that would not be able to be seen with naked eyes. The term electromagnetic spectrum refers to the range of electromagnetic waves with different wavelengths. In terms of wavelengths, electromagnetic waves range from gamma rays to radio waves.
3. **Microwave remote sensing.** Another type of remote sensing uses microwave radiation. An important property of microwaves is that they are seldom affected by atmosphere conditions. Although useful property of microwave radiation is that it can often image beneath or through objects (just like an X-ray – another type of electromagnetic wave that is used in everyday lives). Microwaves can also image differences in the earth's surface due to the absorption level of water or chemicals.

Remote sensing can also be categorized into two broad categcries:

(i) **Passive Remote Sensing:** It makes use of sensors that detect the reflected or emitted electromagnetic radiation from natural sources (usually sunlight).

(ii) **Active Remote Sensing:** It makes use of sensors that detect reflected responses from object that are irradiated from artificially generates energy sources, such as radars.

Use of Remote Sensing in Disasters

The data gathered from remote sensing can be used in a variety of ways to accomplish several objectives. It is usually combined with information from other data sources, and with information from on-the-ground observations to get a full picture of water, lad, or ground activities. Remote sensing data is often integrated with GIS. There exist a wide variety of commercial and free software that allow users to view data collected from the many observing satellites.

As new technologies emerge, and with the increased incidents of natural and man-made disasters, it is necessary to employ as many of these technological advancements as possible to mitigate against the effects of disasters. They are as follows:

1. **Remote Sensing and Flooding:** Flooding is one of the most frequently occurring hazards. With flooding comes the risk of damage or disruption to normal living including communication, transportation, the environmental, and infrastructure. Given the magnitude of disruption that can take place, it may be difficult for disaster managers to gain access to remote areas or areas that have been cut-off as a result of the disaster. Remote sensing as a technological tool would greatly assist this process as it would allow users of the technology the opportunity to view what is taking place in an affected area, without jeopardizing the safety of the user since they will not actually be at the site.
2. It is always going to be difficult, if not impossible for planners to identify all the areas likely to experience flooding in any location. The use of technology, however, in determining flood potential could highlight features of the geography that could make the community susceptible to the hazard. Types of flooding such as flash flooding which usually take place in a relatively short time, with little or no warning could prove potentially dangerous for disaster managers if they attempt to physically go into an area that has been experiencing continuous rainfall. While the task of providing assistance to victims is critical and time-dependent, a physical presence in the affected area could increase the person at risk. Using remote technology, however, would allow response workers to stay away from the danger zone while at the same time gather pertinent information to facilitate time response, rescue, and relief efforts.
3. Flood-plain mapping is a useful indication of flood possibilities in an area and remote sensing can aid the process of identifying flood-plains. The technology would generate satellite imagery of the area in question, which would allow for proper planning and timely rescue efforts should the need arise. The detailed photography produced from remote sensing provides accurate information and can restrict efforts to the affected area. Other characteristics that could be identified about a geographic region using remote sensing include land use classification, historical data, soil coverage, and soil moisture.

4. **Remote Sensing and Hurricane:** Hurricane forecasting over the last century has improved dramatically, with experts being able to estimate the likely number of storms for a given year, intensity and possible levels of destruction. Today, this process is made even easier with the use of remote sensing technology. Trackers are able, even, while the storm is in progress, to go to the core of the system in search of information. This tool at any stage of the hurricane threat is useful in mitigating against the deadly effects that could take place. Remote sensing can allow planners to ascertain data about the features of watersheds to include drainage and density. Once obtained, this is useful information as to provides information on the capacity of the watershed to deal with the volume of water flow that could result from rains associated with the storm.

   High-resolution technology, a feature of remote sensing is useful in providing spatial data on hurricanes. Because of the scales of geographic areas in remote sensing can be manipulated, users will be in a position to zoom in one specific areas for study. Storm surges and coastal flooding which often accompany hurricanes can be better mapped using remote sensing and provide information on the level of flooding that has been experienced.

5. **Remote Sensing and Earthquake:** Development in any area with high seismic risk is always going to be problematic. Given the high volume of fault lines that extend across the breadth of geographic areas, it is inevitable that there are going to be human settlements in these areas. Considering also that there is no early warning system in place for earthquakes, emphasis must be placed on hazard mitigation to reduce the likely impact from earthquakes on lives or properties. Extensive use of remote sensing (and especially the use of satellite imaging) is critical to the planning process for earthquake preparedness. This technology will help in identifying the structural and nonstructural earthquake hazards that are present and employ the most appropriate tool for minimizing these risks. Landsat imagery is one tool that is effective for this purpose given availability and cost.

   After an earthquake has taken place, visibility with the naked eyes, as well as accesses to worst affected areas may be restricted. When this happens, it becomes difficult for emergency personnel to gain access to survivors in a short period of time. Using remote sensing technology, however, would significantly improve the timeliness and quality of aid that can be provided. Activities, such as search and rescue, are best affected after major earthquakes using remote sensing. Since there will be considerable amount of debris from collapsed structures, it would be advantages to employ the service of remote sensing for deep searching.

6. **Remote Sensing and Volcanic Eruptions:** On the spot seismic monitoring of volcanoes is the most effective way to monitor volcanic activity. However, it may not be practical or safe to be on site at all times. In the light of this, remote sensing is crucial to the monitoring process. Remote sensing technology can allow disaster managers to observe volcanic activities on a continuous basis without being physically on site especially at times when it would be dangerous.

7. **Remote Sensing and Landslides:** Landslides usually occur with other hazards, such as flooding, hurricanes, and earthquake, but can also happen independently. Once major portions of land shift out of the place, access to and general visibility of the area affected usually severely restricted. Remotely sensed images under these conditions are useful tools in assisting planners. It presents a picture of what has taken place and aids in the decision making process regarding the future of the affected area.

Table below shows the applications of Remote Sensing in Disaster Management

Disaster	Prevention	Preparedness (warning)	Relief
Earthquake	Mapping geographical land use	Geodynamic measurements of strain accumulation	Locate stricken areas, map damage.
Volcanic eruption	Topography and land use maps	Detection/measurement of gaseous emissions	Mapping lava flows, ash falls and lahars, map damage
Landslides	Topographic and land use maps	Rainfall, slope stability	Mapping sliding area
Flash flood	Land use maps	Local rainfall measurements	
Major flood	Flood-plain maps land use maps	Regional ra nfall, evaporation, transcription	Map flood damage
Storm surge	Land use and land cover maps	Sea state, ocean surface, wind velocities	Map extend of floods
Hurricane		Synoptic weather forecasts	Map extent of damage
Tornadoes		Nowcasts; local weather, local weather observations	Map amount, extent of damage
Drought		Long ranged climate models	Monitoring vegetation biomass

Advantages of Remote Sensing

Following are the advantages of remote sensing:

1. Save time.
2. Users of the technology do not have to be in direct contact with danger zones.
3. Shows image of very large area of land or space.
4. Detect features at wavelengths not visible to the human eye.
5. Data can be regularly and routinely acquired and archived.
6. The most cost-effective data set for monitoring change over large areas.
7. Can assist with damage assessment monitoring.
8. The imagery obtained using remote sensing can be useful for forward planning and reconstruction of an affected area.
9. Helps to prevent the recurrence of the same disaster in future.

Disadvantages or Remote Sensing

Following are some of the disadvantages of remote sensing:

1. It can be costly to build and operate a remote sensing system.
2. Small size activities cannot be delineated on remote sensing imagery or through areal photography.

3. Data can be difficult to interpret and may acquire expert skills.
4. Resolution is often coarse.

7.3 GEO-INFORMATICS IN DISASTER STUDIES

Meaning and Definition of Geo-informatics

Geo-informatics synonymously used as geo-matics, is a powerful tool to create maps, integrate information, visualize scenarios, solve complicated problems, and develop effective solutions. The discipline that deals with all aspects of spatial data handling is called geo-informatics.

It is defined as 'the integration of different disciplines dealing with spatial information'. Geo-informatics has also been described as "the science and technology dealing with the structure and character of spatial information, its capture, its classification and qualification, its storage, processing, portrayal and dissemination including the infrastructure necessary to secure optimal use of this information".

According to Ehlers and Amer, "Geo-informatics is the art, science, or technology dealing with the acquisition, storage, processing production, presentation, and dissemination of geo-information".

According to Goodchild, "GIS research is the research on the generic issues that surround the use of GIS technology, impede its successful implementation or emerge from an understanding of its potential capabilities".

Geographic information technology was used to manipulate objects in geographic, space, and to acquire knowledge from spatial facts. Spatial information theory provides a basis for GIS by bringing together fields that deal with spatial reasoning, the representation of spare and human understanding of space.

Tools of Geo-informatics in Disaster Studies

The scientific and technological advancement has improved tremendously the human capabilities of understanding the complex physical processes of nature operating on a varying scale. Remote sending, Geographic Information System (GIS) and Globe Positioning System (GPS) are the result of the revolution in the field of geo-computational techniques. Remote sensing is the science and art of gathering information about an area, object, or phenomenon with the help of a sensor that is not in physical contact with the area or object under investigation. Such sensors are generally on broad satellites, sending images of different areas in their path. The advantages that remote sensing data have over other forms of data are its uniformity over a large area, synoptic view and repetitive coverage. The characterization helps in real time and near real-time monitoring of the various natural disasters. Satellite remote sensing is very effective in mapping flood affected areas. Microwave data can provide information on flood inundated areas even under cloud, which is not possible with optical data.

The remote sensing satellites use high-resolution cameras and they have a host of applications which include the mapping of natural resources, cropping patterns, and monitoring ocean currents (India has eight such satellites in orbit).

Remote sensing data when used within a GIS package becomes a highly powered tool. GIS is used to capture, store, retrieve, analyze, and display geographically referenced data. Infact, remote sensing and GIs are used to complement each other. Using GIS, any area can be suitably represented into a falser image of vector form with its various physical and socio-economical characteristics. With the use of GIS and remote sensing, areas vulnerable to both natural and man-made disasters along with their varying degree of vulnerability can be established and previously made maps can be updated very easily. Such processes make planning and policy very easy for implementation. With the use of remote sensing satellites, the path of cyclones can be monitored and they can provide ample time with warning for evacuation and preparedness in advance for incoming hazards.

Role of Geo-informatics in Disaster Studies

Thus, the role of geo-informatics in disaster management can be summarized as follows:

1. In general remote sensing, GIS and GPS provide databases which can be interpreted and analyzed to produce hazard maps, which have immense value in any kind of activities related to disasters.
2. Many types of disasters have precursors, which can be detected at an early stage by orbiting satellites and can be used for the prediction of both rapid and slow disasters.
3. When a disaster occur. The aerospace media is the quickest mode of information collection and can be utilized for monitoring during the event. Finally, geo-informatics can also assist in damage assessment and aftermath monitoring, providing a quantitative base for relief operations.
4. Finally geo-informatics can also assist in damage assessment and aftermath monitoring, providing a quantitative basis for relief operations.

7.4 ELECTRONIC WARNING SYSTEM

Introduction

The first important step towards reducing impact is to correctly analyze the potential risk and identify measures that can prevent mitigate or prepare for emergencies. This can be done through early electronic warning. Warning is the communication of information of a hazard or threat to a population at risk in order for them to take appropriate actions to mitigate any potentially negative impacts on themselves, those in their care and their property.

An electronic warning system comprises a signal generator, a power amplifier, and at least one loudspeaker. Means may be provided to adjust the overall acoustic output of the amplifier, to adjust the level of each loudspeaker and to vary the overall level with the time of day. A plurality of loudspeakers which are preferably directional, can be arranged to operate sequentially by means of a multiplexing operation. The system can give audible warning of the imminent start up of machinery or plant while minimizing the noise level at the works or site boundary.

Information and communication technologies can play a significant role in highlighting risk areas, vulnerabilities and potentially affected population by producing geographically referenced analysis through for example, a geographic information system (GIS). The importance of time disaster warning is mitigating negative impacts can never be underestimated. For example, although damage to property cannot be avoided, developed countries have been able to reduce loss of life due to disaster much more effectively than their counterparts in developing world. A key reason for this is the implementation of effective disaster warning system and evacuation procedures used by the developed countries and the absence of such measures in the developing world.

Importance of Electronic Warning System

Electronic warning is important amongst due to the following reasons:

1. Effective electronic warning allows population at risk to take necessary actions that will reduce the impact on their lives and property. Not having a warning system that have disruptive effects on a society, causing chaos and confusion during as well as in the aftermath of an emergency, including large-scale displacement of people, disease outbreaks, disruption of schooling, etc. Early public warning enables seedier disaster recovery than otherwise. It also provide citizens with a sense of security and provides order to society.
2. Effective warning can prevent much economic loss to individuals, businesses, and industries. Warning enables these groups to prepare for and mitigate the impacts of hazards that may affect them. Furthermore, the lack of mechanisms for early warnings can harm investors (local and foreign) and business confidence and hence stifle economic development of a country. Added to this, public warning can also be a protector of the poor, giving that the sectors of the economy most vulnerable to disaster are often the poorest.

GIS Technology: Meaning of Geographic Information System

A geographic information system (GIS) is a powerful set of tools for collecting, storing, retrieving, transforming, and displaying spatial data from the real world for a particular set of purposes. Advanced techniques like remote sensing and global positioning systems, if integrated with GIS, can provide valuable information about earth surface features and processes involved. GIS has an important role to play in landside hazard assessment because of its spatial modelling. Models can be created and displayed to reflect hazards or the implication of a hazard in terms of risk and planning which can be depicted. The maps are based on various variables for analyzing landslides like slope angle, bed, rock lithology, distance from fault, slope aspects, vegetation density, presence of settlements, rainfall and water, sediment type, and water depth of dams.

Thus, GIS are information systems capable of integrating, storing, editing, analyzing, sharing, and displaying geographically referenced information. In a more generic sense, GIS is a tool that allows users to create interactive queries (user-created searches), analyze the spatial information, edit data, maps and present the results of all these operations. It can be considered as an information technology, which stores, analyses, and displays both spatial and nonspatial data.

One of the main advantages of GIS is that it can be used as a decision support system involving the integration of spatially referenced data in a Problem-solving environment. For example, it can be used to assess several hazards and risk scenarios, while taking a decision about the future development of an area, and the optimum way to protect it from natural disasters. Due to the above reasons, there has been an explosion of the use of GIS in various stages of natural disaster management.

Geographic information system (GIS), Remote sensing (RS), and Global positioning system (GPS) have gained much attention for their application in disaster management and are increasingly being utilized throughout the entire disaster management cycle as a tool to support decision making. GIS is commonly recognized as a key support tool for disaster management. The visualization capabilities of these systems have almost become expected by policymakers, disaster manager and even the public.

Uses of GIS Technology

GIS applications can be useful in the following activities:

1. **To Create Hazard Inventory Maps:** At this level, GIS can be used for the pre-feasibility study of development projects at all inter-municipal or district level.
2. **Locate Critical Facilities:** The GIS system is quite useful in providing information on the physical location of shelters, drains, and other physical facilities. The use of GIS for disaster management is intended for planners in the early phase of regional development projects or large engineering projects. It is used to investigate where hazard can be a constraint on the development of rural, urban, or infrastructural projects.
3. **Create and Manage Associate Database:** The use of GIS at this level is intended for planners to formulate projects at feasibility levels, but it is also used to generate hazard and risk maps for existing settlement and cities and in the planning of disaster preparedness and disaster relief activities.
4. **Vulnerability Assessment:** GIS can provide useful information to boost disaster awareness with government and the public, so that (on a national level) decision can be taken to establish or expand disaster management organizations. At such a general level, the objective is to give an inventory of disaster and simultaneously identify high risk or vulnerable areas within the country.
5. **Emergency Shelters:** GIS technology can be used by shelter operators to capture specific personal details of persons being housed at the shelter. It would also facilitate the process of stock, demands, and distribution. The technology would capture information on the general make up of the shelter, i.e., the number of children, adults, disabled, or any other special occupants.
6. **Distribution of Relief:** "Food drops" in affected areas after a disaster is always likely to take place. The process can be done with the use of GIS, as maps can be generated which identify the specific areas, where clusters of victims are located and the unique needs of persons within these clusters.
7. **GIS and Data Gathering:** With GIS, disaster managers are placed in a position where they have diagrammatic presentations of the specific location of disabled or elderly persons, e.g., that reside within a community. This will make organized assistance on their behalf more efficient and time-saving. Maps can be produced to highlight more "high risk" areas that are particularly prone to disasters. These kinds of information help with planning (before occurring of the disaster) and also facilitate the coordination of efforts during and after the event.

GIS Technology and Disaster Management Cycle

GIS technology plays an important role in various phases of DM cycle which are as follows:

1. **Mitigation:** The use of GIS in disaster management can help with structural and non-structural mitigation. GIS allows to spatially representing areas at risk and the level of risk associated with a particular hazard, which can be a guide in decision making. It will facilitate the implementation of necessary mechanisms to lessen the impact of a potential emergency. With GIS, disaster managers are in a better position to determine the level of mitigative structures that should be in place given the vulnerability of an area of population.
2. **Preparedness:** As a tool, GIS can help with the identification and location of resources and "at risk" areas. It establishes a link between planners and critical agencies, which allow disaster managers to know where relevant partner agencies are stationed. In the context of disaster management, GIS maps can provide information on the human resources present in an Emergency Operation Centre, as well as on the ground personnel such as security, health providers, and other key responders. This is particularly useful since the technology can help with strategic placement of emergency personnel where it matters most. GIS helps to answer the question of who is to be used where and at what phase during the emergency. It can help to determine whether or not road infrastructure and communications network are capable of handling the effects of disaster and, if necessary, guide in the placement of resources.
3. **Response:** GIS technology can provide the user with accurate information on the exact location of an emergency situation. This would prove useful as less time is spent trying to determine where the trouble areas are. Ideally GIS technology can help to provide quick response to an affected area once issues (such as routes to the area) are known. In the case of a chlorine explosion, e.g., GIS can indicate the unsafe area as well as point rescue workers to resources that are closest to the affected areas. GIS can be used as a floor guide for emergency response to point out evacuation routes, assembly points, and other evacuation matters.
4. **Recovery:** Mapping and geo-spatial data will provide a comprehensive display on the level of damage or disruption that was sustained as a result of the emergency. GIS can provide a synopsis of what has been damaged, where and the number of persons or institutions that were affected. This kind of information is quite useful to the recovery process.

Benefits of GIS Technology

1. GIS has the ability to represent spatial information over a wide geographic area. GIS accommodates three dimensional graphics which will provide a more detailed view of its contents.
2. GIS technology facilitates the integration of different geo-spatial information, which can include models, maps, and other graphic forms.
3. GIS effectively analyzes, collect, manages, and distributes up to date information.
4. GIS is a versatile and easy to use – this requires little training to get individuals involved in the process.

5. Attribute table which forms a database – given that information from GIS can be easily tabulated, it provides a comprehensive pictorial overview of what is happening in the country. For example, GIS can show the exact location of shelters across the country, or sites where search and rescue operations have taken place.

Challenges of Using GIS Technology in Disaster Management

1. Major impacts on life of people, economy, and environment. In the context of emergency management, GIS can impact people's lives in a significant way as it reveals sometimes personal and people specific information.
2. Crucial decisions based on the information obtained from GIS mapping, it may require taking critical (sometimes hard) decisions in the best interest of the affected area.
3. GIS being a technological tool can be a complex and a bit difficult to grasp initially.
4. Large amounts of information (input) is usually required to get useful output from the system.
5. Time is critical during an emergency. The decision making process may be stalled during an emergency due to:
   (i) The large volume of information required by the GIS system.
   (ii) The vast amount of time requires for analyzing the information before a decision is finally made.

7.5 GLOBAL POSITIONING SYSTEM (GPS)

Meaning

The term Global Positioning System (GPS) is used to refer to the Global Navigation Satellite System (GNSS) developed by the United States Department of Defense. The proper name is The Navigation System with Timing and Ranging Global Positioning System (NAVSTAR GPS). However, the acronym GPS is typically used. Though initially intended solely for US military purposes the GPS system was extended for civilian use in the 1980s. Popular applications include automobile and marine navigation tracking, farming and research.

GPS is a grouping of 24 well-spaced satellites that orbit the earth and make it possible for people with ground receivers to pinpoint their exact geographic location with great accuracy.GPS equipment is widely used across the globe and is sufficiently low cost so that anyone can own a GPS receiver.

The GPS make use of the Time-of-Arrival (TOA) of the GPS signal to determine positions on the earth's surface. The availability of GPS has made it very easy to locate and map one of the most difficult terrains on the earth such as mountains and dense rain forests. It also has a vital role to play in determining the extent of hazards and disasters. With the spatiotemporal analysis of GPS readings for a particular place, various geological/tectonic movements can be detected and necessary warnings can be issued in case of predicting earthquakes, and disasters, such as volcanic eruptions. These spatial information technology systems, i.e., remote sensing, GPS, and GIS will help in creating framework and models for creating and understanding the complex nature of disasters involving physical as well as socio-economical dimensions.

Applications of GPS

1. GPS is particularly useful during disasters because it operates in any weather anywhere and at all times. While it functions simply to give the location of the receiver, the level of precision of GPS makes it quite useful in disaster management. In many instances, GPS data is integrated with GIS to overlay realtime activity during emergency. GPS find its greatest utility during the response and recovery phases; however, it can also be utilized during preparedness and mitigation phases.
2. An important application of GPS is tracking of emergency vehicles or supplies. In this application, the GPS receiver attached to the vehicle and the location is overlaid into a map. Other applications include the monitoring the height of waves. GPS units are fixed to buoys the height of the unit can be determined to within centimetres. Any significant change in wave height or velocity can trigger an alarm for a tsunami or sea surge. Volcanoes can also be monitored using GPS. By measuring the deformation of the ground, inferences about volcanic activity can be made.

7.6 LASER SCANNING

Meaning of Laser Scanning

Laser scanning is a technique which can be used to gather data about an object or environment which can be used to create a 3D model or detailed reconstruction. There are a huge number of applications for laser scanning, ranging from the highly specialized laser scanning confocal microscopy used in scientific labs to the 3D scanning of objects of historical value which cannot be personally studied due to worries about damage, but can be studied in a reconstructed form with the assistance of a laser scanner. Several companies make laser scanners for various purposes.

Laser scanners can operate in several different ways, including a triangulation method and a "time of flight" method. In all cases, the laser is low powered, so that it will not damage the object being scanned, and number of beams are shot at the object are recorded. Some objects scan better than others, with light objects tending to reflect more light, creating greater detail, and shiny objects causing refraction, which distorts the image. The data from a laser scanning session takes the form of a point cloud, a collection of tiny data points which can be used together to map an object.

The raw data from laser scanning can be run through a computer program which will use the point cloud to establish a 3D model. Because a laser scanner can only see what is visible, it is common to move the scanner around the object or to rotate the object during scanning to get a complete image of all sides and all angles. The computer program can stitch the data together, and information like colour can also be added, if desired.

Features of Laser Scanning

1. Instant tracking technology.
2. Compact and lightweight handheld scanner.
3. Large measurement volume.
4. Integrated touch probing.
5. Dynamic referencing.

Use of Laser Scanning

Following are some of the uses of laser scanning:

1. One use of laser scanning is in architecture and construction where laser scanning can be used to model environments and landscapes make 3D models of proposed structures, and in other activities.
2. Laser scanning is also used to record objects so that they can be replicated and to make copies of objects of historical value. The ability of laser to scan an object and create a 3D model also allowed museums to share their collections around the world without having to endanger the objects they are preserving; people can log on to a museum website and explore 3D models of objects of interest.
3. Archaeologists use 3D laser scanners to construct as-built plans. The information collected through 3D laser scanners to digitize historical sites and previous remains. The data files are reserved for future study and information management.
4. Surveyors use 3D laser scanners to construct as built plan. The information collected through 3D laser scanners in long-term monitoring such as the displacement of a high voltage transmission tower is used to estimate the wind and earthquake damage to structure. Managerial steps can be taken once related information is provided.
5. Tunnel and bridge engineers use 3D laser scanner to build up polygonal models of structures to quantify construction progress. The total volume of earth removed and placed in the construction sites can be estimated through 3D laser scanners. As for bridge engineer, a monitoring system using 3D scanner can provide vital information on bridge long-term performance under the influence of change environment.
6. Preservation of infrastructure can be done using 3D laser scanning techniques providing information in relation to the strengthening and reconstruction.

7.7 QUESTIONS

1. Define statistical seismology.
2. Write a note on the application of statistical seismology in disaster management.
3. What is GIS and explain its advantages?
4. Disasters pave the way for development – discuss with reference to reconstruction technologies.
5. What are the advantages and disadvantages of remote sensing?
6. Write a note on laser scanning.
7. What is the role of Geo-informatics in disaster studies?
8. Describe the importance of electronic warning systems.

8 Disaster Management in India

Learning Objectives

- To facilitate the knowledge on the disaster management – preparedness, risk assessment, DM Act 2005, warning system in India, and disaster mitigation.
- To make people aware on the knowledge on disaster preparedness in India
- To help people to assess risk
- To highlight the disaster management Act in India
- To make awareness on warning systems in India
- To educate people to mitigate disasters in Indian context.

Structure

8.1 Culture of Preparedness for Disaster Management in India – An Initiative by National Disaster Management Authority

8.2 Disaster Mitigation

8.3 Early Warning System

8.4 Annexure-I: Ministry of Home Affairs (NDM Division)

8.5 Annexure-II: Disaster Management the Development Perspective

8.6 Annexure-III: Guidelines to State Governments

8.7 Ministry of Home Affairs (NDM Division)

8.8 Information Technology and Natural Disaster Management in India

8.9 Disaster Management Act, 2005

8.1 CULTURE OF PREPAREDNESS FOR DISASTER MANAGEMENT IN INDIA – AN INITIATIVE BY NATIONAL DISASTER MANAGEMENT AUTHORITY

Introduction

Disasters are not new to mankind. However, in recent times, owing to their increased frequency as well as the intensity, disaster management (DM) has attracted immense public interest at the national and international level.

More than half of the disasters in the world occur in Asia, making this region the world's most vulnerable area. Indian continent account for 24 per cent of all disasters in Asia. 58.6 per cent of India is prone to earthquakes and 12 per cent to river floods, affecting more than 1 million people every year. 7,200 kms out of 7,516 kms of Indian coastline is prone to cyclones and tsunami and 3 per cent of landmass is vulnerable to landslides. Snow avalanches are frequent and drought occur almost every alternate year. More than 80,000 people get killed in road accidents alone and India stands at number two position, after Iraq, in number of people who died due to terrorist related activities during 2008. There is no known disaster, natural or man-made, which is not taking place in India. Some of the reasons for increase in the frequency of natural disasters are population explosion, rapid and uncontrolled urbanization leading to mushrooming of not so well-planned growth of cities, unplanned land use and global warming. Rapid industrialization and the menace of terrorism have also added new dimensions to man-made disasters.

The poor and marginalized sections of the society are the worst hit. Among those affected, pregnant, and lactating women, children below 5 years, aged, sick, and differently abled groups suffer the most.

Global Trends

Keeping in view the death and destruction wrought by devastating disasters, the decade of 1990s was observed, by the United Nations, as the International Decade for Natural Disaster Reduction. A number of initiatives were taken globally, prominent among them being the Kyoto Protocol, under which the United Nations Framework Convention on Climate Change has been ratified by 175 countries. Under this protocol, industrialized countries were to reduce the collective emissions of greenhouse gases by 52 per cent compared to the base year 1990. The new millennium began with the launch of International Strategy for Disaster Reduction to build up disaster resilience in vulnerable areas. The Hyogo Framework for Action (2005-2015) was adopted by 168 governments at the World Conference on Disaster Reduction at Kobe, Japan in January 2005. India is one of the signatories to these declarations.

Transition in India

Government of India, in recognition of the importance of disaster management as a national priority, after the horrific experience of Latur earthquake in 1993 and the Orissa Super Cyclone in October 1999, had set up a High Powered Committee (HPC) in August 1999 and a National Committee on Disaster Management (DM) after the Bhuj earthquake for making recommendations on the preparation of DM plans and for expediting laying down the framework for disaster mitigation and management in India.

Even while the recommendations of the HPC report were being analysed by the government, as an interim measure, the management of disasters was shifted from the Ministry of Agriculture to the Ministry of Home Affairs, pending finalization of an arrangement at the National level. Indian Ocean Tsunami acted as the catalyst and the Government of India (GoI) took a defining step in the legislative history of the country by enacting DM Act, 2005.

Disaster Management (DM) Act, 2005

The DM Act (2005) formalized the institutional framework for DM in India, at national, state, district, and at the local levels. National Disaster Management Authority (NDMA) was constituted as the single window, apex body for DM, at the Centre, under the chairmanship of the Prime Minister.

Similar arrangements came up at the State level under the Chief Minister. This enabling system was taken down to grassroot level by having District Disaster Management Authority (DDMA) headed by the District Collector.The most notable feature is that the co-chairman of the DDMA is the elected representative of the Zilla Parishad. This brings in the much required public interface at the cutting edge level. The fact that these authorities are headed by the Heads of the Government themselves indicate the national resolve to tackle this problem. The Act envisages a paradigm shift, from the erstwhile response-centric syndrome to a pro-active, holistic, and integrated management of disasters with emphasis on prevention, preparedness, and mitigation. These efforts are aimed at conserving developmental gains and also minimizing losses to lives, livelihood, and property. The Act also created 10,000 strong eight battalions of the National Disaster Response Force (NDRF) as a specialized response and the National Institute of Disaster Management (NIDM) for institutional capacity development. The NIDM works within the broad guidelines of the NDMA which ensures complete synergy at the national level. The entire DM arrangement is backed by institutional, financial, and legal mechanism. These institutions are not parallel structures but complimentary and will work in harmony with existing organizations which ensures complete synergy at the national level.

National Vision

The national vision is "to build a safer and disaster resilient India by developing a holistic, pro-active, multi-disaster, and technology-driven strategy for DM. This will be achieved through a culture of prevention, mitigation, and preparedness, to generate a prompt and efficient response at the time of disasters. The entire process will centre-stage the community and will be provided momentum and sustenance through the collective efforts of all government agencies and non-governmental organizations (NGOs)."

National Disaster Management Strategy

While formulating national DM strategy, NDMA took into consideration the contemporary imperatives, the lessons learnt from the past, the commendable work in management of disasters by the Armed Forces, the motivated and selfless role of the NGOs and volunteer organizations, the innate resilience of the communities to live with disasters, the significant role of the corporate sector in providing relief, the capacity of academic and scientific institutions in providing innovative and futuristic inputs and above all to take off from the good work already done in this field. The national strategy for DM is based on six pillars of prevention, mitigation, preparedness and capacity development, awareness generation, rapid operationalization of NDRF and further strengthening of the NIDM.

It was also decided to centre-stage the community which bear the brunt of disasters as immediate responders. Necessity of making them aware of the various types of disasters they are vulnerable to, the elementary preparedness measures and training they must undertake, to provide themselves immediate succour and to save their own and their families lives before specialized response is activated, are the cornerstone of national DM strategy.

Culture of Preparedness — An Initiative by NDMA

NDMA is mandated by DM Act, 2005, to lay down national policy and plan on DM and issue guidelines for various types of natural and man-made disasters. One of the tasks also envizages monitoring and coordinating the implementation of the policies and plans. It is in this regard, an initiative has been taken by NDMA to conduct tabletop and mock exercises on various types of disasters, initially in the most vulnerable areas of the country. The aim of the initiative is to inculcate a culture of preparedness and secure effective participation of the community and other stakeholders. Some of the objectives for conduct of the mock exercises are, to highlight the roles and responsibilities and enhance the coordination among the stakeholders, identify gaps in the resources, communications and systems, identify areas for public-private partnership and empower the community to face disasters squarely. Mock exercises on natural and man-made disasters (except chemical industrial disasters) are conducted at districts level. The chemical (industrial) disaster mock exercises are organized in most accident hazardous industries.

Four-step Mock Exercises

The mock exercises are conducted in four steps. In step one, during orientation-cum-coordination conference, sensitization of the participants takes place. Need for conduct of the mock exercises, the aim, objectives, and scope of the particular exercise, the exercise organizing committee, the participants, the nodal officers, detailment of independent observers and media coverage are delineated during this step. In Tabletop exercise, initially the key stakeholders, like the collector, superintendent of police, district medical officer, district fire officer, and the managing directors of the short listed industries (in case of chemical industrial disasters) are requested to present their emergency response plans. In certain cases, State Disaster Management Secretary, Director General (DG) Fire and Emergency Services, State DG Police, and DG Health Services also present their respective State DM plans.

The worst case scenarios are thereafter painted in a bottom up approach, from preparedness to rescue and relief and through injects, the responses of the concerned stakeholders are elicited. The roles and responsibilities of each stakeholder, in mitigating the disasters get clarified. The control and coordination of the disaster is managed through the concept of incident command system. Independent observers are detailed for each stakeholder department/organization, to report on the gaps and deficiencies. Observers are given a detailed format to report on. Safety officer is also nominated for avoiding mishaps/accidents during actual conduct of the mock exercise. In step three, the observers are briefed on their roles. They are asked not to interfere in the functioning of the organization being observed. Thereafter, the mock exercise is conducted by mobilizing resources, according to developing situations, to derive certain lessons.

Additional resources from the State/Centre are released as per the demand and availability. During conduct of mock exercises on chemical disasters, both 'on-site' and 'off-site' plans are activated. Incident Command Post is established at district level for command and management of the disaster.

Incident Commander and Emergency Support Functionaries (ESF) work in close coordination and synergy. Immediate response by the community for search and rescue is seen and the response time of the first responders get tested. Specialized response is activated. Medical response includes rescue, triaging, evacuation, hospital preparedness, and creating surge capacity. The police response includes, cordoning, law and order, traffic control, directing the first responders to their assigned tasks, conducting the VIP visits and handing over the dead bodies to the relatives, after 'panchnama'. The fire and emergency services activate their resources for fighting fires and for emergency situations. Other ESF play their roles according to the standard operating procedures given in the DM plan. At the end of the mock exercise, detailed debriefing is carried out where the observers and heads of all participating organizations participate and give their observations and share experiences. Step four involves documentation.

All the mock exercises are documented by filming them as also recording the lessons learnt for future references and for training purposes. The gaps identified during the mock exercise are evaluated at NDMA and sent to the Chief Minister/Chief Secretary/MDs of the concerned State/industries, for follow-up action.

Participants in Mock Exercises

The participants include departments and stakeholders dealing with disasters at the State and districts levels, with emphasis on community participation in large numbers. The stakeholders at State level include, Secretary Disaster Management, Secretary Health/DG Health, DG Police/IG (Law and Order), DG Fire and Emergency Services, Bomb Disposal Squads, Chief Inspector of Factories and Boilers and Pollution Control Board (for chemical industrial disasters), Armed Forces columns , NDRF teams and Para Military Forces. At district level, they comprise of Revenue Depatment led by the Collector, police force headed by SP/SSP, Fire and Emergency Services, led by the District Fire Officer, Medical Services, headed by the District Medical Officer, NGOs, District Supply Officer, Municipal Corporation, District Public Relation Officer, Civil Defence, Home Guards, Red Cross, NCC, NYK, NSS, Resident Welfare Associations, and PRIs. In chemical (industrial) disaster, the short-listed industries take part in full strength at operational, supervisory and management levels. In major exercises like in earthquake, cyclones the participation go up to 15,000 to 20,000 and in minor disasters like urban fires and chemical (industrial) disasters the participations ranges between 3,000 to 5,000.

Types of Mock Exercises

The mock exercises are conducted on natural and manmade disasters.The range includes earthquakes, floods, cyclones, landslides, urban fires, chemical (industrial) , mass causalty management, terrorist attacks, bomb blasts, gas leaks, etc.

In conclusion, this initiative of the NDMA has elicited overwhelming and positive response from the States/Districts/MAH industries. The community has also started feeling involved. Post-Mumbai attacks 26/11, there has been tremendous demand even from the private entrepreneurs for assisting them in preparedness and mitigation measures. India may, perhaps be the only country in the world, to have taken the initiative, to conduct so many mock exercises at national level, on so varied disasters from earthquake to terrorist-related disasters, with utmost commitment, sincerity, and social responsibility. Hopefully, in the next 2-3 years time, we may claim to be among the most prepared countries for managing all types of disasters.

8.2 DISASTER MITIGATION

Introduction

India has been traditionally vulnerable to natural disasters on account of its unique geo-climatic conditions. Floods, droughts, cyclones, earthquakes, and landslides have been a recurrent phenomena. About 60 per cent of the landmass is prone to earthquakes of various intensities; over 40 million hectares is prone to floods; about 8 per cent of the total area is prone to cyclones and 68 per cent of the area is susceptible to drought. In the decade 1990-2000, an average of about 4,344 people lost their lives and about 30 million people were affected by disasters every year. The loss in terms of private, community, and public assets has been astronomical.

At the global level, there has been considerable concern over natural disasters. Even as substantial scientific and material progress is made, the loss of lives and property due to disasters has not decreased. Infact, the human toll and economic losses have mounted. It was in this background that the United Nations General Assembly, in 1989, declared the decade 1990-2000 as the International Decade for Natural Disaster Reduction with the objective to reduce loss of lives and property and restrict socio-economic damage through concerted international action, specially in developing countries.

The super cyclone in Orissa in October 1999 and the Bhuj earthquake in Gujarat in January 2001 underscored the need to adopt a multidimensional endeavour involving diverse scientific, engineering, financial, and social processes; the need to adopt multidisciplinary and multisectoral approach an incorporation of risk reduction in the developmental plans and strategies.

Over the past couple of years, the Government of India have brought about a paradigm shift in the approach to disaster management. The new approach proceeds from the conviction that development cannot be sustainable unless disaster mitigation is built into the development process. Another corner-stone of the approach is that mitigation has to be multidisciplinary spanning across all sectors of development. The new policy also emanates from the belief that investments in mitigation are much more cost-effective than expenditure on relief and rehabilitation.

Disaster management occupies an important place in this country's policy framework as it is the poor and the underprivileged who are worst affected on account of calamities/disasters.

The steps being taken by the government emanate from the approach outlined above. The approach has been translated into a National Disaster Framework (a road map) covering institutional mechanisms, disaster prevention strategy, early warning system, disaster mitigation, preparedness and response, and human resource development. The expected inputs, areas of intervention and agencies to be involved at the National, State, and district levels have been identified and listed in the road map. This road map has been shared with all the State Governments and Union Territory Administrations. Ministries and Departments of Government of India, and the State Governments/UT Administrations have been advised to develop their respective road maps taking the national road map as a broad guideline.There is, therefore, now a common strategy underpinning the action being taken by all the participating organizations/stakeholders. A copy of the road map is explained in annexure-I.

Institutional and Policy Framework

The institutional and policy mechanisms for carrying out response, relief, and rehabilitation have been well-established since independence. These mechanisms have proved to be robust and effective insofar as response, relief, and rehabilitation are concerned.

At the national level, the Ministry of Home Affairs is the nodal Ministry for all matters concerning disaster management. The Central Relief Commissioner (CRC) in the Ministry of Home Affairs is the nodal officer to coordinate relief operations for natural disasters. The CRC receives information relating to forecasting/warning of a natural calamity from India Meteorological Department (IMD) or from Central Water Commission of Ministry of Water Resources on a continuing basis. The Ministries/ Departments/Organizations concerned with the primary and secondary functions relating to the management of disasters include:

India Meteorological Department, Central Water Commission, Ministry of Home Affairs, Ministry of Defence, Ministry of Finance, Ministry of Rural Development, Ministry of Urban Development, Department of Communications, Ministry of Health, Ministry of Water Resources, Ministry of Petroleum, Department of Agriculture and Cooperation, Ministry of Power, Department of Civil Supplies, Ministry of Railways, Ministry of Information and Broadcasting, Planning Commission, Cabinet Secretariat, Department of Surface Transport, Ministry of Social Justice, Department of Women and Child Development, Ministry of Environment and Forest, and Department of Food. Each Ministry/Department/ Organization nominate their nodal officer to the Crisis Management Group chaired by Central Relief Commissioner. The nodal officer is responsible for preparing sectoral action plan/emergency support function plan for managing disasters.

National Crisis Management Committee (NCMC)

Cabinet Secretary, who is the highest executive officer, heads the NCMC. Secretaries of all the concerned Ministries/Departments as well as organizations are the members of the Committee. The NCMC gives direction to the Crisis Management Group as deemed necessary. The Secretary, Ministry of Home Affairs is responsible for ensuring that all developments are brought to the notice of the NCMC promptly. The NCMC can give directions to any Ministry/Department/Organization for specific action needed for meeting the crisis situation.

Crisis Management Group

The Central Relief Commissioner in the Ministry of Home Affairs is the Chairman of the CMG, consisting of senior officers (called nodal officers) from various concerned ministries. The CMGs functions are to review every year contingency plans formulated by various ministries/departments/ organizations in their respective sectors, measures required for dealing with a natural disasters, coordinate the activities of the Central Ministries and the State Governments in relation to disaster preparedness and relief and to obtain information from the nodal officers on measures relating to above. The CMG, in the event of a natural disaster, meets frequently to review the relief operations and extend all possible assistance required by the affected states to overcome the situation effectively. The Resident Commissioner of the affected State is also associated with such meetings.

Control Room (Emergency Operation Room) an Emergency

Operations Centre (Control Room) exists in the nodal Ministry of Home Affairs, which functions round the clock, to assist the Central Relief Commissioner in the discharge of his duties. The activities of the Control Room include collection and transmission of information concerning natural calamity and relief, keeping close contact with governments of the affected states, interaction with other Central Ministries/Departments/Organizations in connection with relief, maintaining records containing all relevant information relating to action points and contact points in Central Ministries, etc., keeping up to date details of all concerned officers at the Central and State levels.

Contingency Action Plan

A National Contingency Action Plan (CAP) for dealing with contingencies arising in the wake of natural disasters has been formulated by the Government of India and it has been periodically updated. It facilitates the launching of relief operations without delay. The CAP identifies the initiatives required to be taken by various Central Ministries/Departments in the wake of natural calamities, sets down the procedure and determines the focal points in the administrative machinery.

State Relief Manuals

Each State Government has relief manuals/codes which identify that role of each officer in the state for managing the natural disasters. These are reviewed and updated periodically based on the experience of managing the disasters and the need of the State.

Funding Mechanisms

The policy and the funding mechanism for provision of relief assistance to those affected by natural calamities is clearly laid down. These are reviewed by the Finance Commission appointed by the Government of India every five years. The Finance Commission makes recommendation regarding the division of tax and non-tax revenues between the Central and the State Governments and also regarding policy for provision of relief assistance and their share of expenditure thereon. A Calamity Relief Fund (CRF) has been set up in each State as per the recommendations of the Eleventh Finance Commission. The size of the Calamity Relief Fund has been fixed by the Finance Commission after taking into account the expenditure on relief and rehabilitation over the past ten years. The Government of India contributes 75 per cent of the corpus of the Calamity Relief Fund in each State. 25 per cent is contributed by the State. Relief assistance to those affected by natural calamities is granted from the CRF. Overall norms for relief assistance are laid down by a national committee with representatives of States as members. Different States can have State specific norms to be recommended by State level committee under the Chief Secretary. Where the calamity is of such proportion that the funds available in the CRF will not be sufficient for provision of relief, the state seeks assistance from the National Calamity Contingency Fund (NCCF) – a fund created at the Central Government level. When such requests are received, the requirements are assessed by a team from the Central Government and thereafter the assessed requirements are cleared by a High Level Committee chaired by the Deputy Prime Minister. In brief, the institutional arrangements for response and relief are well established and have proved to be robust and effective.

In the federal set-up of India, the basic responsibility for undertaking rescue, relief, and rehabilitation measures in the event of a disaster is that of the State Government concerned. At the State level, response, relief, and rehabilitation are handled by Departments of Relief and Rehabilitation. The State Crisis Management Committee set up under the Chairmanship of Chief Secretary who is the highest executive functionary in the State. All the concerned Departments and organizations of the State and Central Government Departments located in the State are represented in this Committee. This Committee reviews the action taken for response and relief and gives guidelines/directions as necessary. A control room is established under the Relief Commissioner. The control room is in constant touch with the climate monitoring/forecasting agencies and monitors the action being taken by various agencies in performing their responsibilities. The district level is the key level for disaster management and relief activities.

The Collector/Dy. Commissioner is the chief administrator in the district. He is the focal point in the preparation of district plans and in directing, supervising, and monitoring calamities for relief. A District Level Coordination and Relief Committee is constituted and is headed by the Collector as Chairman with participation of all other related government and non-governmental agencies and departments in addition to the elected representatives. The Collector is required to maintain close liaison with the district and the State Governments as well as the nearest units of Armed Forces/Central police organizations and other relevant Central Government organizations like Ministries of Communications, Water Resources, Drinking Water, Surface Transport, who could supplement the efforts of the district administration in the rescue and relief operations. The efforts of the government and non-governmental organizations for response and relief and coordinated by the Collector/Dy. Commissioner. The District Magistrate/Collector and Coordination Committee under him reviews preparedness measures prior to a impending hazard and coordinate response when the hazard strikes. As all the departments of the State Government and district level report to the Collector, there is an effective coordination mechanism ensuring holistic response.

New Institutional Mechanisms

As has been made clear above, the existing mechanisms had based on post-disaster relief and rehabilitation and they have proved to be robust and effective mechanisms in addressing these requirements. The changed policy/approach, however, mandates a priority to full disaster aspects of mitigation, prevention and preparedness and new institutional and policy mechanisms are being put in place to address the policy change.

It is proposed to constitute a National Emergency Management Authority at the National level. The High Powered Committee on Disaster Management which was set up in August 1999 and submitted its Report in October 2001, had *inter alia* recommended that a separate Department of Disaster Management be set up in the Government of India. It was, however, felt that conventional ministries/departments have the drawback of not being flexible enough specially in terms of the sanction procedures. The organization at the Apex level will have to be multidisciplinary with experts covering a large number of branches. The National Emergency Management Authority has, therefore, been proposed as a combined Secretariat/Directorate structure – a structure which will be an integral part of the government and, therefore, will work with the full authority of the government while, at the same time, retaining the flexibility of a field organization. The National Emergency Management Authority will be headed by an officer of the rank of Secretary/Special Secretary to the Government in the Ministry of Home Affairs with Special Secretaries/Additional Secretaries from the Ministries/Departments of Health, Water Resources, Environment and Forests, Agriculture, Railways, Atomic Energy, Defence, Chemicals, Science and Technology, Telecommunications, Urban Employment and Poverty Alleviation, Rural Development and India Meteorological Department as members of the Authority. The Authority would meet as often as required and review the status of warning systems, mitigation measures and disaster preparedness. When a disaster strikes, the Authority will coordinate disaster management activities. The Authority will be responsible for:

(i) Coordinating/mandating government's policies for disaster reduction/mitigation.

(ii) Ensuring adequate preparedness at all levels in order to meet disasters.

(iii) Coordinating response to a disaster when it strikes.

(iv) Coordination of post-disaster relief and rehabilitation.

The National Emergency Management Authority will have a core permanent secretariat with three divisions – one for disaster prevention, mitigation and rehabilitation, the other for preparedness, and the third for Human Resource Development.

At the State level, as indicated in para-disaster management was being handled by the Departments of Relief and Rehabilitation. As the name suggests, the focus was almost entirely on post-calamity relief. The Government of India is working with the State Governments to convert the Departments of Relief and Rehabilitation into Department of Disaster Management with an enhanced area of responsibility to include mitigation and preparedness apart from their present responsibilities of relief and rehabilitation. The changeover has already happened in eight State Governments/Union Territory Administrations. The change is under process in other States.

The States have also been asked to set up Disaster Management Authorities under the Chief Minister with Ministers of relevant Departments (Water Resources, Agriculture, Drinking Water Supply, Environment and Forests, Urban Development, Home, Rural Development, etc.) as members. The objective of setting up an authority is to ensure that mitigation and preparedness is seen as the joint responsibility of all the departments concerned and disaster management concerns are mainstreamed into their programmes. This holistic and multidisciplinary approach is the key to effective mitigation.

At the district level, the District Magistrate who is the chief coordinator will be the focal point for coordinating all activities relating to prevention, mitigation, and preparedness apart from his existing responsibilities pertaining to response and relief. The District Coordination and Relief Committee is being reconstituted/redesignated into Disaster Management Committees with officers from relevant departments being added as members. Because of its enhanced mandate of mitigation and prevention, the district heads and departments engaged in development will now be added to the Committee so that mitigation and prevention is mainstreamed into the district plan. The existing system of drawing up preparedness and response plans will continue. There will, however, also be a long-term mitigation plan. District Disaster Management Committees have already been constituted in several districts and are in the process of being constituted in the remaining multihazard-prone districts.

Similarly, we are in the process of creating Block/Taluq Disaster Management Committees in these 169 multihazard-prone districts in 17 States. At the village level, in 169 multihazard-prone districts, we are constituting Disaster Management Committees and Disaster Management Teams. Each village will have a Disaster Management Plan. The process of drafting the plan has already begun. The Disaster Management Committee which draws up the plans consists of elected representatives at the village level, local authorities, government functionaries including doctors/para-medics of primary health centres located in the village, primary school teachers, etc. The plan encompasses prevention, mitigation and preparedness measures. The Disaster Management Teams at the village level will consist of members of voluntary organizations like Nehru Yuvak Kendra and other non-governmental organizations as well as able bodied volunteers from the village. The teams are provided basic training in evacuation, search, and rescue, etc. The Disaster Management Committee will review the disaster management plan at least once in a year. It would also generate awareness among the people in the village about do's and dont's for specific hazards depending on the vulnerability of the village. A large number of village level Disaster Management Committees and Disaster Management Teams have already been constituted.

The States have been advised to enact Disaster Management Acts. These Acts provide for adequate powers for authorities coordinating mitigation, preparedness, and response as well as for mitigation/ prevention measures required to be undertaken. Two states (Gujarat and Madhya Pradesh) have already enacted such a law. Other states are in the process. The State Governments have also been advised to convert their relief codes into disaster management codes by including aspects of prevention, mitigation, and preparedness.

In order to further institutionalize the new approach, the Government of India have decided to enunciate a National Policy on Disaster Management. A draft policy has accordingly been formulated and is expected to be put in place shortly. The policy shall inform all spheres of Central Government activity and shall take precedence overall existing sectoral policies. The broad objectives of the policy are to minimize the loss of lives and social, private, and community assets because of natural or man-made disasters and contribute to sustainable development and better standards of living for all, more specifically for the poor and vulnerable sections by ensuring that the development gains are not lost through natural calamities/disasters.

The policy notes that State Governments are primarily responsible for disaster management including prevention and mitigation, while the Government of India provides assistance where necessary as per the norms laid down from time-to-time and proposes that this overall framework may continue. However, since response to a disaster requires coordination of resources available across all the Departments of the Government, the policy mandates that the Central Government will, in conjunction with the State Governments, seek to ensure that such a coordination mechanism is laid down through an appropriate chain of command so that mobilization of resources is facilitated.

Broad Feature of National Policy of DM

The broad features of the draft national policy on disaster management are enunciated below:

(i) A holistic and pro-active approach for prevention, mitigation, and preparedness will be adopted for disaster management.

(ii) Each Ministry/Department of the Central/State Government will set apart an appropriate quantum of funds under the plan for specific schemes/projects addressing vulnerability reduction and preparedness.

(iii) Where there is a shelf of projects, projects addressing mitigation will be given priority. Mitigation measures shall be built into the ongoing schemes/programmes.

(iv) Each project in a hazard-prone area will have mitigation as an essential term of reference. The project report will include a statement as to how the project addresses vulnerability reduction.

(v) Community involvement and awareness generation, particularly that of the vulnerable segments of population and women has been emphasized as necessary for sustainable disaster risk reduction. This is a critical component of the policy since communities are the first responders to disasters and, therefore, unless they are empowered and made capable of managing disasters, any amount of external support cannot lead to optimal results.

(vi) There will be close interaction with the corporate sector, non-governmental organizations and the media in the national efforts for disaster prevention/vulnerability reduction.

(vii) Institutional structures/appropriate chain of command will be built-up and appropriate training imparted to disaster managers at various levels to ensure coordinated and quick response at all levels; and development of inter-state arrangements for sharing of resources during emergencies.

(viii) A culture of planning and preparedness is to be inculcated at all levels for capacity building measures.

(ix) Standard operating procedures and disaster management plans at State and district levels as well as by relevant Central Government departments for handling specific disasters will be laid down.

(x) Construction designs must correspond to the requirements as laid down in relevant Indian Standards.

(xi) All lifeline buildings in seismic zones III, IV, and V – hospitals, railway stations, airports/airport control towers, fire station buildings, bus stands major administrative centres will need to be evaluated and, if necessary, retro-fitted.

(xii) The existing relief codes in the states will be revised to develop them into disaster management codes/manuals for institutionalizing the planning process with particular attention to mitigation and preparedness.

With the above-mentioned institutional mechanism and policy framework in position and the actions taken to implement the policy guidelines, it is expected that the task of moving towards vulnerability reduction will be greatly facilitated.

8.3 EARLY WARNING SYSTEM

Cyclone Forecasting

Tropical cyclones are intense low pressure systems which develop over warm sea. They are capable of causing immense damage due to strong winds, heavy rains and storm surges. The frequency of the TC in the Bay of Bengal is four to five times more than in the Arabian Sea. About 35 per cent of initial disturbances in the north Indian ocean reach TC stage of which 45 per cent become severe.

Indian Meteorological Department (IMD) is mandated to monitor and give warnings regarding Tropical Cyclone (TC). Monitoring process has been revolutionized by the advent of remote sensing techniques. A TC intensity analysis and forecast scheme has been worked out using satellite image interpretation techniques which facilitate forecasting of storm surges

Data resources are crucial to early forecasting of cyclones. Satellite-based observations are being extensively utilized. Satellite integrated automated weather stations have been installed on islands, oil rigs, and exposed coastal sites. Buoys for supplementing the surface data network in the tropical ocean have been deployed. The government have also started a National Data Buoy Programme. A set of 12 moored buoys have been deployed in the northern Indian ocean to provide meteorological and oceanographic data.

Dynamic forecasting of TCs requires knowledge of the vertical structure of both the cyclone and the surrounding environment. The Rawin Sonde remains the principal equipment for sounding. The Doppler Radar wind profiler provides hourly soundings. A mesosphere, stratosphere, troposphere (MST) radar has also been installed at Thirupatti. Another profiler is being developed and will be deployed at IMD Pune. Another important source of upper level data is the aircraft reports. Increasing number of commercial jet aircraft are equipped with the Aircraft Meteorological Data Relay system. This data is being made available is also being used by the IMD for analysis and predictions.

Radars have been used to observe TCs since long. Surveillance of the spiral rain bands and the eye of the TC is an important function of the coastal radars. Ten Cyclone Detection Radars have already been installed. These radars are providing useful estimates of storm centres up to a range of 300-400 km. Doppler Radars provide direct measurements of wind fields in TCs. Due to range limitation, Doppler wind estimates are usually within a range of about 100 km. IMD has deployed Doppler Radars at three sites on the east coast. Another set of three Doppler Radars are being deployed in Andhra Pradesh in near future.

The meteorological satellite has made a tremendous impact on the analysis of cyclones. All developing cloud clusters are routinely observed through satellite cloud imagery and those showing signs of organization are closely monitored for signs of intensification. TC forecasters everywhere use the Dvorak technique to estimate storm location and intensity. It has been found to provide realistic estimates for TCs in the Bay of Bengal as well as Arabian Sea. INSAT data has also been used to study the structures of different TCs in the Bay of Bengal. IMD is also producing Cloud Motion Vectors (CMVs). Very High Resolution Radiometer (VHRR) payload onboard INSAT-2E which have been improved upon to provide water vapour channel data in addition to VIS and IR onboard INSAT-2E. A separate payload known as charged couple device (CCD) has also been deployed onboard this satellite.

The goal of any warning system is to maximize the number of people who take appropriate and timely action for the safety of life and property. All warning systems start with detection of the event and with people getting out of Harm's way. Such warning systems encompass three equally important elements namely detection and warning, communication, and response.

The two-stage warning system has been in existence since long in IMD. Recently it has been improved upon by introducing two more stages – the 'pre-cyclone watch' and the 'post-landfall scenario'. This four stage warning system meets the requirements of public administrators and crisis managers. The 'pre-cyclone watch' stage, contains early warning about the development of a cyclonic disturbance in the form of monsoon depression which has a potential to threaten the coast with cyclone force winds. The coastal stretch likely to be affected is identified. This early warning bulletin is issued by the IMD before the cyclone-alert stage. This provides enough lead time for the crisis managers to undertake preparedness actions.

After the early warning on the 'pre-cyclone watch' the Collectors of coastal and few immediate interior districts and the Chief Secretary of the concerned maritime State are warned in two stages, whenever any coastal belt is expected to experience adverse weather (heavy rain/gales/tidal wave) in association with a cyclonic storm or a depression likely to intensify into a cyclonic storm.

The second stage of "Cyclone Alert" is sounded 48 hours in advance of the expected commencement of adverse weather over the coastal areas. Forecasts of commencement of strong winds, heavy precipitation along the coast in association with arrival of cyclone are issued at the alert stage. Landfall point is usually not identified at this stage. The third stage warning known as "Cyclone Warning" is issued 24 hours in advance. Landfall point is forecast in this stage of cyclone warning. In addition to the forecasts for heavy rains and strong winds, the storm surge forecast is also issued. Since the storm surge is the biggest killer so far as the devastating attributes of a storm are concerned, information in this regard is most critical for taking follow-up action for evacuation from the low lying areas likely to be affected by the storm.

After the landfall of the cyclone the strong winds with gale force speeds continue over certain interior districts of the maritime states hit by the cyclone. To take cognisance of that, a fourth stage known as 'Post-landfall Scenario Stage' is now identified usually as a part of the 'Cyclone Warning Stage' either at the time of landfall of the disturbance or about twelve hours in advance of it. It includes warnings of strong winds and heavy rains likely to be encountered in the interior districts.

For communications, the IMD makes use of 97 point-to-point teleprinter links connecting different field offices. Switching computers have been provided at five regional centres. These computers are linked to the Central Regional Telecom Hub Computer at New Delhi. In addition, 69 centres have been provided with 85 telex connections. Besides, 27 field offices have been provided with Radio Teletype facility. IMD also utilizes VSAT technology which has been installed at field offices. In addition, there are a number of HF/RT and VHF links.

Cyclone warnings are communicated to crisis managers and other concerned organizations by high priority telegrams, telex, telephones, and police wireless. Cyclone warning are provided by the IMD from the Area Cyclone Warning Centres (ACWCs) at Kolkata, Chennai, and Mumbai and Cyclone Warning Centres (CWCs) at Visakhapatnam, Bhubaneswar, and Ahmedabad.

There is also a satellite-based communication system called the Cyclone Warning Dissemination Systems (CWDS) for transmission of warnings. There are 250 such cyclone-warning sets installed in the cyclone prone areas of east and west coast. The general public, the coastal residents and fishermen, are also warned through the government machinery and broadcast of warnings through AIR and television.

Flood Forecasting

Flooding is caused by the inadequate capacity within the banks of the rivers to contain the high flow brought down from the upper catchments due to heavy rainfall. It is also caused by accumulation of water resulting from heavy spells of rainfall over areas, which have got poor drainage characteristics.

Flooding is accentuated by erosion and silting leading to meandering of the rivers in plains and reduction in carrying capacity of the river channel. It is also aggravated by earthquakes and landslides, leading to changes in river course and obstructions to flow. Synchronization of floods in the main rivers and tributaries and retardation of flow due to tidal effects lead to major floods. Cyclones bring in their wake considerable loss of life and property.

The flood forecasting and warning system is used for alerting the likely damage centres well in advance of the actual arrival of floods, to enable the people to move and also to remove the moveable property to safer places or to raise platforms specially constructed for the purpose.

A beginning in scientific flood forecasting was made in November 1958 by Central Water Commission (then known as Central Water and Power Commission) when a Flood Forecasting Centre was set up at its Headquarters at Delhi, for giving timely Forecasts and Warnings of the incoming floods to the villages located in the river areas around the National Capital, Delhi. The network has been expanding and by now the Flood Forecasting Network of the Central Water Commission (CWC) covers all the major flood-prone inter-state river basins in the country.

At present there are 166 flood forecasting stations on various rivers in the country which includes 134 level forecasting and 32 inflow forecasting stations.

The Flood Forecasting involves the following four main activities:

(i) Observation and collection of hydrological and hydro-meteorological data,

(ii) Transmission of data to forecasting centres,

(iii) Analysis of data and formulation of forecast,

(iv) Dissemination of forecast.

On an average, 6,000 forecasts at various places in the country are issued during the monsoon season every year. The analysis of the forecasts issued during the last 25 years (1978-2002) indicates that accuracy of forecasts has consistently increased from around 81 per cent to 98 per cent. Forecast is considered accurate if forecast water level is within ± 15 cm of actual water level of the inflow forecast (i.e., discharge) is within ± 20 per cent of actual discharge.

In monitoring the floods, severity of floods are placed in the following four categories by the Central Water Commissions:

(i) **Low Flood Stage:** It is that flood situation when the water level of the river is flowing between warning level and danger level of the forecasting stations.

(ii) **Medium Flood Stage:** The river is called in medium floods when its water level is at or above the danger level of the forecasting station but below 0.50 of its highest flood level (HFL).

(iii) **High Flood Stage:** When the water level of the river is below the HFL but within 0.50 m. of the HFL of the forecasting stations.

(iv) **Unprecedented Flood Stage:** The river is called in unprecedented floods when it attains water level equal to or above its previous HFL at any forecasting station.

A computerized monitoring system has been developed under which daily water levels as observed at 08:00 hrs. and forecasts issued by field units are transmitted to CWC headquarters in New Delhi. Based on the compilation of all such data received from field divisions, daily water level and flood forecast bulletins in two parts for stage and for inflow forecasting stations, respectively.

Special Yellow Bulletins are issued whenever the river stage at the forecasting site attains a level within 0.50 m of its previous HFL. Red Bulletins highlighting security of the problem are also issued whenever the water level at the forecasting stations equals or exceeds previous HFL.

Disaster Prevention and Mitigation

The Yokohama message emanating from the international decade for natural disaster reduction in May 1994 underlined the need for an emphatic shift in the strategy for disaster mitigation. It was *inter alia* stressed that disaster prevention, mitigation, preparedness, and relief are four elements which contribute to and gain, from the implementation of the sustainable development policies. These elements along with environmental protection and sustainable development, are closely interrelated. Therefore, nations should incorporate them in their development plans and ensure efficient follow-up measures at the community, subregional, regional, national, and international levels. The Yokohama Strategy also emphasized that disaster prevention, mitigation, and preparedness are better than disaster response in achieving the goals and objectives of vulnerability reduction. Disaster response alone is not sufficient as it yields only temporary results at a very high cost. Prevention and mitigation contribute to lasting improvement in safety and are essential to integrated disaster management.

The Government of India have adopted mitigation and prevention as essential components of their development strategy. The Tenth Five-Year Plan document has a detailed chapter on Disaster Management. A copy of the said chapter is enclosed at Annexure-II. The plan emphasizes the fact that development cannot be sustainable without mitigation being built into developmental process. Each State is supposed to prepare a plan scheme for disaster mitigation in accordance with the approach outlined in the plan. In brief, mitigation is being institutionalized into developmental planning.

As indicated in the earlier chapter, the Finance Commission makes recommendations with regard to devolution of funds between the Central Government and State Governments as also outlays for relief and rehabilitation. The earlier Finance Commissions were mandated to look at relief and rehabilitation. The terms of reference of the Twelfth Finance Commission have been changed and the Finance Commission has been mandated to look at the requirements for mitigation and prevention apart from its existing mandate of looking at relief and rehabilitation. A memorandum has been submitted to the Twelfth Finance Commission after consultation with States. The memorandum proposes a Mitigation Fund.

The Government of India have issued guidelines that where there is a shelf of projects, projects addressing mitigation will be given a priority. It has also been mandated that each project in a hazard prone area will have disaster prevention/mitigation as a term of reference and the project document has to reflect as to how the project addresses that term of reference. A copy of the guidelines is at Annexure-III.

Measures for flood mitigation were taken from 1950 onwards. As against the total of 40 million hectares prone to floods, area of about 15 million hectares have been protected by construction of embankments. A number of dams and barrages have been constructed. The State Governments have been assisted to take up mitigation programmes like construction of raised platforms, etc. Floods continue to be a menace, however, mainly because of the huge quantum of silt being carried by the rivers emanating from the Himalayas. This silt has raised the bed level in many rivers to above the level of the countryside. Embankments have also gives rise to problems of drainage with heavy rainfall leading to water logging in areas outside the embankment.

Due to erratic behaviour of monsoons, both low and medium rainfall regions, which constitute about 68 per cent of the total area, are vulnerable to periodical droughts. Our experience has been that almost every third year is a drought year. However, in some of the states, there may be successive drought years enhancing the vulnerability of the population in these areas. Local communities have devised indigenous safety mechanisms and drought-oriented farming methods in many parts of the country. From the experience of managing the past droughts particularly the severe drought of 1987, a number of programmes have been launched by the government to mitigate the impact of drought in the long run. These programmes include Drought-prone Area Programme (DPAP), Desert Development Programme (DDP), National Watershed Development Project for Rainfed Areas (NWDPRA), Watershed Development Programme for Shifting Cultivation (WDPSC), Integrated Water Development Project (IWDP), and Integrated Afforestation and Eco-development Project Scheme (IAEPS).

A comprehensive programme has been taken up for earthquake mitigation. Although, the BIS has laid down the standards for construction in the seismic zones, these were not being followed. The building construction in urban and suburban areas is regulated by the Town and Country Planning Acts and Building Regulations. In many cases, the building regulations do not incorporate the BIS codes. Even where they do, the lack of knowledge regarding seismically safe construction among the architects and engineers as well as lack of awareness regarding their vulnerability among the population led to most of the construction in the urban/suburban areas being without reference to BIS standards. In the rural areas, the bulk of the housing is non-engineered construction. The mode of construction in the rural areas has also changed from mud and thatch to brick and concrete construction thereby increasing the vulnerability. The increasing population has led to settlements in vulnerable areas close to the river bed areas which are prone to liquefaction. The government have moved to address these issues.

A National Core Group for Earthquake Mitigation has been constituted consisting of experts in earthquake engineering and administrators. The Core Group has been assigned with the responsibility of drawing up a strategy and plan of action for mitigating the impact of earthquakes; providing advice and guidance to the States on various aspects of earthquake mitigation; developing/organizing the preparation of handbooks/pamphlets/type designs for earthquake resistant construction; working out systems for assisting the states in the seismically vulnerable zones to adopt/integrate appropriate Bureau of Indian Standards codes in their building byelaws; evolving systems for training of municipal engineers as also practicing architects and engineers in the private sector in the salient features of Bureau of Indian Standards codes and the amended bye-laws, evolving a system of certification of architects/ engineers for testing their knowledge of earthquake resistant construction, evolving systems for training of masons, and carry-out intensive awareness generation campaigns.

A committee of experts has been constituted to review the building bye-laws. The State Governments have been advised to ensure rigorous enforcement of existing bye-laws. A national programme for capacity building for earthquake mitigation has been finalised for imparting training to 10,000 engineers in public and private sectors. Since earthquake engineering is not a part of course curriculum in engineering colleges at undergraduate level at present, it is proposed to select three to four leading engineering colleges in each State and train the faculty members of the civil engineering departments in earthquake engineering at the Indian Institutes of Technology and few other apex level institutes which have the requisite capabilities. These faculty members will take up training of municipal engineers as well as the training of engineers/architects in the private sector in RCC and masonry construction. The first phase of this programme for imparting training to 10,000 engineers will be completed within a period of three years. The trained faculty members of the leading engineering colleges will also assist the State Governments in the detailed evaluation of lifeline buildings and their retrofitting, wherever necessary.

It has been decided to include earthquake engineering education in the engineering colleges at undergraduate level. The course curriculum for this purpose has already been finalized by a group of experts taken from IITs and will be introduced in the engineering colleges within an year. A system of special audit of buildings is being put in place with a view to ensuring that the new constructions conform to the latest building bye-laws, which have been reviewed and revised recently by Bureau of Indian Standards.

While these mitigation measures will take care of the new constructions, the problem of unsafe existing buildings stock would still remain. It will not be possible to address the entire existing building stock, therefore the lifeline buildings like hospitals, schools, or buildings where people congregate like cinema halls, multistoried apartments are being focused on. The States have been advised to have these buildings assessed and where necessary retrofitted. The Ministry of Finance have been requested to advise the financial institutions to give loans for retrofitting on easy terms. Insofar as the private housing stock is concerned emphasis is placed on awareness generation.

An earthquake mitigation project has been finalized for reducing the vulnerability to earthquakes. The programme includes detailed evaluation and retrofitting of lifeline buildings such as hospitals, schools, water and power supply units, telecommunication buildings, airports/airport control towers, railway stations, bus stands, and important administrative buildings. The programme also includes training of more than one hundred thousand masons for earthquake resistant constructions. Besides, assistance will be provided under this project to the State Governments to put in place appropriate techno-legal regime.

An accelerated urban earthquake vulnerability reduction programme has been taken up in 38 cities in seismic zones III, IV, and V with population of half a million and above. Sensitization workshop for engineers/architects, government functionaries, and voluntary organizations have already been held in 36 of the 38 cities. Disaster mitigation and preparedness plans are under preparation in these cities. Awareness generation campaign has already been undertaken. The orientation courses for engineers and architects have been organized to impart knowledge about seismically safe construction and implementation of BIS norms. This programme will be further extended to 166 earthquake-prone districts in seismic zones IV and V.

Rural housing and community assets for vulnerable sections of the population are created at a fairly large-scale by the Ministry of Rural Development under the Indira Awas Yojna (IAY) and Sampooran Grameen Rojgar Yojna (SGRY). About 2,500 small but compact units are constructed every year, besides community assets such as community centres, recreation centres, anganwadi centres, etc. Technology support is provided by about 200 rural housing centres spread over the entire country. The Ministry of Rural Development are now under the process of revising their guidelines for construction of such dwelling units by incorporating appropriate earthquake/cyclone resistant features. Training to the functionaries in the rural housing centres will be organized through the Ministry of Home Affairs. This initiative is expected to go a long way for the construction and popularization of seismically safe construction at village/block level.

A National Core Group on Cyclone Monitoring and Mitigation has been constituted. Experts from Indian Meteorological Department, National Centre for Medium Range Weather Forecasting, Central Water Commission, National Remote Sensing Agency, and Indian Space Research Organization have been made the Members of the Core Group, besides administrators from the relevant ministries/departments and State Governments vulnerable to cyclones. The group has been assigned with the responsibility of looking warning protocols for cyclones, coordination mechanism between different Central and State Ministries/Departments/Organizations, mechanism for dissemination of warning to the local people, and cyclone mitigation measures required to be taken for the coastal states. The group will also suggest short-term and long-term measures on technology upgradation.

A cyclone mitigation project has been formulated. The project *inter alia* includes components on strengthening of monitoring/warning systems, coastal shelter belt plantation, mangrove plantation, construction of cyclone shelters, storm surge modelling, and water envelope studies. The focus will be on regeneration of coastal shelter belt plantation and mangrove plantation where these have degenerated. The location of the cyclone shelters will be decided in such a manner that no person in the vulnerable zone is required to walk more than 2 kms to reach a cyclone shelter. The cyclone shelters will be multi-purpose units to be run as schools or community centres in normal times and will have capacity to house 3,000-5,000 persons with adequate number of toilets, community kitchen, and other facilities. Areas will be identified for providing shelter to livestock.

In the engineering designs for construction, special attention will be paid to the attachment of roof to the dwelling units so as to make such units cyclone proof, besides incorporating earthquake resistant features. The project will be taken up shortly and is expected to be completed over a period of five years.

A Disaster Risk Management Programme has been taken up with the assistance from UNDP, USAID and European Union in 169 most hazard-prone districts in 17 States including all the eight North Eastern States. The implementation of the project commenced from October 2002 and is expected to be concluded by December 2007. The programme components include awareness generation and public education, preparedness, planning and capacity building, developing appropriate policies, institutional, administrative, legal and techno-legal regime at State, district, block, village, urban local body, and ward levels for vulnerability reduction.

Under this programme, Disaster Management Plans have been prepared for about 3,500 villages, 250 grama panchayat, 60 blocks, and 15 districts. Elected representatives of over 8,000 panchayati raj institutions have already been trained, besides imparting training to members of voluntary organizations. Over 20,000 government functionaries have been trained in disaster mitigation and preparedness at different levels. About 600 engineers and 220 architects have been trained under this programme in vulnerability assessment of lifeline buildings. Training is being imparted to master trainers under the programme. More than 600 master trainers and 1,000 teachers have already been trained in different districts in disaster mitigation. Disaster Management Committees consisting of elected representatives, civil society members, civil defence volunteers, and government functionaries have been constituted at all levels including village/urban local body/ward levels. Disaster Management Teams have been constituted in villages and are being imparted training in basic functions of first aid, rescue, evacuation and related issues. The thrust of the programme is to build up capabilities of the community since the community is invariably the first responder. During the last 15 months, it has been experienced that the capacity building of the community has been very helpful even in normal situations when isolated instances of drowning, burns, etc., take place. With the creation of awareness generation on disaster mitigation, the community will be able to function as a well-knit unit in case of any emergency. Mock drills are carried out from time-to-time under the close supervision of Disaster Management Committees. The Disaster Management Committees and Disaster Management Teams have been established by notifications issued by the State Governments which will ensure that the entire system is institutionalized and does not disintegrate after the conclusion of the programme. The key points being stressed under this programme are the need to ensure sustainability of the programme, development of training modules; manuals and codes, upscaling partnerships in excellence, focused attention to awareness generation campaigns; institutionalization of disaster management committees and disaster management teams, disaster management plans and mock drills and establishment of techno-legal regimes.

Human Resource Development at all levels is critical to institutionalization of disaster mitigation strategy. The National Centre for Disaster Management at the national level has been upgraded and designated as the National Institute of Disaster Management. It is being developed as a Regional Centre of Excellence in Asia. The National Institute of Disaster Management will develop training modules at different levels, undertake training of trainers and organise training programmes for planners, administrators and command functionaries. Besides, the other functions assigned to the National Institute of Disaster Management include development of exhaustive National level information base on disaster management policies, prevention mechanisms, mitigation measures formulation of disaster management code, and providing consultancy to various states in strengthening their disaster management systems and capacities as well as preparation of disaster management plans and strategies for hazard mitigation and disaster response.

Disaster management faculties have already been created in 29 State level training institutes located in 28 States. These faculties are being directly supported by the Ministry of Home Affairs. The State Training Institutions take up several focused training programmes for different target groups within the State. The Disaster Management faculties in these institutes are further strengthened so as to enable them to develop as Institutes of Excellence for a specific disaster. This system has already been institutionalised and is being further strengthened so as to make it a focal point in each State for development of human resources in disaster mitigation and preparedness. Assistance to the State level training institutes will be provided by the National Institute of Disaster Management in the development of training/capsules training modules for different functionaries at different levels.

Large-scale awareness generation bringing out specific do's and dont's is crucial to disaster mitigation. A steering committee on mass media campaign has been constituted for this purpose. The Committee is in the process of developing a profile for taking up mass media campaign through audio, video and print media as well as publicity through pamphlets, posters, buyback panels at all levels. The posters would be prominently displayed at buildings like Primary Health Centres, Community Centres, schools, and such other places where villagers normally congregate for community activity. The corporate sector is also being associated with the dissemination of campaign.

Disaster management as a subject in Social Sciences has been introduced in the school curriculum for Class VIII from the current academic year. The Central Board of Secondary Education has introduced the curriculum, which runs a very large number of schools throughout the country and the course curriculum is invariably followed by the State Boards of Secondary Education. Several State Governments have already introduced the same curriculum in Class VIII from the current academic year. Syllabus for Classes IX and X has been finalized and will be introduced in the course curriculum from April 2004 and April 2005 respectively.

In order to assist the State Governments in capacity building and awareness generation activities and to learn from past experiences including sharing of best practices, the Ministry of Home Affairs has compiled/prepared a set of resource materials developed by various organizations/institutions to be replicated and disseminated by State Governments based on their vulnerabilities after translating it into the local languages. The voluminous material which runs in about 10,000 pages has been divided into four broad sections in seven volumes. These sections cover planning to cope with disasters; education and training; construction toolkit; and information, education and communication toolkit including multi-media resources on disaster mitigation and preparedness. The planning section contains material for analysing a community's risk, development of preparedness, mitigation and disaster management plans, coordinating available resources and implementing measures for risk reduction. The model bye-laws, DM Policy Act and model health sector plan have also been included. Education and Training includes material for capacity building and upgradation of skills of policymakers, administrators, trainers, engineers, etc., in planning for and mitigating against natural disasters. Basic and detailed training modules in disaster preparedness have been incorporated along with training methodologies for trainers, for community preparedness and manuals for training at district, block, panchayat, and village levels. For creating a disaster-resistant building environment, the construction toolkit addresses the issue of seismic resistant construction and retrofitting of existing buildings. BIS codes, manuals and guidelines for RCC, masonry and other construction methodologies as also for repair and retrofitting of masonry and low-rise buildings have been included.

IEC material seeks to generate awareness to induce mitigation and preparedness measures for risk reduction material and strategies used by various States and international organizations, including tips on different hazards, have been incorporated along with multimedia CDs on disasters. The material has been disseminated to all the State Governments/UT Administrations with the request to have the relevant material, based on the vulnerability of each district, culled out, translated into local languages and disseminate it widely down to the village level.

The various prevention and mitigation measures outlined above are aimed at building up the capabilities of the communities, voluntary organizations, and government functionaries at all levels. Particular stress is being laid on ensuring that these measures are institutionalized considering the vast population and the geographical area of the country. This is a major task being undertaken by the government to put in place mitigation measures for vulnerability reduction. This is just a beginning. The ultimate goal is to make prevention and mitigation a part of normal day-to-day life. The above mentioned initiatives will be put in place and information disseminated over a period of five to eight years. We have a firm conviction that with these measures in place, we could say with confidence that disasters like Orissa cyclone and Bhuj earthquake will not be allowed to recur in this country; at least not at the cost, which the country has paid in these two disasters in terms of human lives, livestock, loss of property, and means of livelihood.

Preparedness

Mitigation and preparedness measures go hand-in-hand for vulnerability reduction and rapid professional response to disasters. The Bhuj earthquake in January 2001 brought out several inadequacies in the system. The search and rescue teams had not been trained professionally; specialized dog squad to look for live bodies under the debris were not available; and there was no centralized resource inventory for emergency response. Although army played a pivotal role in search and rescue and also set up their hospital after the collapse of government hospital at Bhuj, the need for fully equipped mobile hospitals with trained personnel was felt acutely. Despite these constraints, the response was fairly well organized. However, had these constraints been taken care of before hand, the response would have been even more professional and rapid which may have reduced the loss of lives. Specialist search and rescue teams from other countries did reach Bhuj. However, precious time was lost and even with these specialist teams it was not possible to cover all severely affected areas as quickly as the government would have desired. It was, therefore, decided that we should remove these inadequacies and be in a stage of preparedness at all times.

The Central Government are now in the process of training and equipping 96 specialist search and rescue teams, with each team consisting of 45 personnel including doctors, paramedics, structural engineers, etc. Ten teams have already been trained. These teams will be located at various centres around the country for specialised response. These teams will have the latest equipment as also dog squads for locating survivors in the debris.

Apart from specialist search and rescue units, it has been decided that personnel of Central Police Organizations should also be imparted training in search and rescue so that they can be requisitioned to the site of incident without loss of time. Pending arrival of the specialist teams, the battalions located near the site of incident would be deployed immediately. For this purpose, a curriculum has been drawn up and integrated into the training curriculum of CPMFs.

The States have also been advised to set up their own specialist teams for responding to disasters. Assistance will be provided to the State Governments for training their trainers at the national institutes already designated for this purpose. The State Governments' search and rescue teams to be constituted from the State Police will be equipped to meet the requirement. For this purpose, the State Governments have been authorised to utilize ten per cent of the annual allocation made under the Contingency Relief Fund for purchase of equipments.

Fourteen Regional Response Centres are being set up in different parts of the country. These centres will have response teams and equipment and resources for being able to response to any hazard/calamity in the neighbouring States.

A Steering Committee has been constituted in the ministry to oversee the creation of capabilities for emergency response.

A 200-bedded mobile hospital, fully trained and equipped is being set up by the Ministry of Health and attached to a leading government hospital in Delhi. Three additional mobile hospitals with all medical and emergency equipments are proposed to be located in different parts of the country. These mobile hospitals will also be attached to the leading government hospitals in the country. This will enable the mobile hospitals to extend assistance to the hospitals with which they are attached in normal time. They will be airlifted during emergencies with additional doctors/para-medics taken from the hospitals with which the mobile hospitals are attached to the site of disaster.

It is proposed to purchase dedicated aircraft and helicopters with a view to reducing the response time. The issue is pending for consideration and approval of Empowered Group of Ministers on Disaster Management. Once the airlift facilities are developed for exclusive use for disaster management, it will be possible to provide airlift facilities to specialist search and rescue teams, mobile hospitals, and equipments.

In order to professionalize the response, it is proposed to introduce the Incident Command System in the country. This system provides for specialist incident command teams with an Incident Commander and officers trained in different aspects of incident management – logistics, operations, planning, safety, media management, etc. The Incident Command System has been finalized keeping in view the systems and procedures prevalent in our country by dovetailing it in the existing governmental machinery already in position. The training of trainers in the Incident Command System has already commenced at Lal Bahadur Shastri National Academy of Administration at Mussoori which has been designated as the nodal training institutes for this purpose.

A web-enabled centralized database for the India Disaster Resource Network has been operationalized. The network will ensure quick access to resources to minimize response time in emergencies. The list of resources to be updated in the system has been finalized. It has 226 items. About 60,000 records in 481 districts throughout the country have already been uploaded since September 1, 2003 when the India Disaster Resource Network was formally inaugurated. The system will give, at the touch of the button, location of specific equipments/specialist resources as well as the controlling authority for that resource so that it can be mobilized for response in the shortest possible time. The database will be available simultaneously at the district, State and national levels.

The States are being persuaded to set up control rooms/emergency operation centres at the State and district level. Assistance for construction and purchase of equipments for control rooms is being provided. The control rooms, which will function round the clock, will be composite control rooms to look after law and order issues as well as disaster management. Equipments are also being provided for these control rooms under the disaster risk management programme.

Communication is a major bottleneck in case of any major disaster particularly when the traditional network system already in force brakedown. In order to strengthen communications, it has been decided that police network (POLNET) will also be used for disaster management. For this purpose, POLNET communication facility will be extended to District Magistrates, Subdivisional Magistrates as well as the Control Rooms. For emergency communication, mobile satellite based units which can be transported to the site of the disaster are being procured. A group was constituted to draw a comprehensive communication plan for disaster management and the report has since been received. This provides for a dedicated communication system for disaster management with built in redundancies.

The Geographical Information System (GIS) database is an effective tool for emergency responders to access information in terms of crucial parameters for the disaster affected areas. The crucial parameters include location of the public facilities, communication links and transportation network at national, State and district levels. The GIS database already available with different agencies of the government is being upgraded and the gaps are proposed to be bridged. A project for this purpose is being drawn up with a view to institutionalizing the arrangements. The database will provide multilayered maps on district-wise basis. Three maps taken in conjunction with the satellite images available for a particular area will enable the district administration as well as State Governments to carry-out hazard zonation and vulnerability assessment, as well as coordinate response after a disaster.

In order to further strengthen the capacity for response, the fire services are proposed to be developed into multihazard response units as is the normal practice in several other countries. It is proposed to provide rescue tenders in addition to fire tenders to each fire unit and fill up all gaps up to subdivisional level. Hazmat vans will be provided to State capitals and metropolitan cities. This will necessitate recruitment of additional fire men and drivers and intensive training required to be provided to enable them to function as efficient of all purpose response units. A project for development of fire service into all hazard response units has also been finalized and submitted for obtaining necessary financial approval.

India has a large network of Civil Defence and Home Guards volunteers. The existing strength is about 1.2 million. However, this organization has not so far been associated with disaster mitigation, preparedness, and response functions. It is proposed to revamp the civil defence organization to enable them to discharge a key responsibility in all the facets of disaster management including preparedness. A proposal in this regard has been finalized and is under consideration of the government.

Standard operating procedures are being laid down to ensure all the steps required to be taken for disaster management are put in place. The standard operating procedure will also in encompass response, besides preparedness.

With the development of disaster management committees and disaster management teams at all levels including village/urban local body/ward level, the stage will be set for comprehensive preparedness measures to be taken with active participation of the community and non-governmental organizations.

With the mitigation and preparedness measures outlined in this and earlier sections in position, it is expected that natural hazards could be handled more efficiently so as to ensure that these hazards did not get converted into disasters.

8.4 ANNEXURE-I: MINISTRY OF HOME AFFAIRS [NDM DIVISION]

1. A review of the disaster management mechanism was carried out by the Government of India after the Bhuj earthquake. It was noted that there was need for building up holistic capabilities for disaster management – so as to be able to handle both natural and man-made disasters. It was accordingly decided that the subject of Disaster Management be transferred from the Ministry of Agriculture to the Ministry of Home Affairs (excluding drought and epidemics and those emergencies/disasters which were specifically allotted to other ministries). The Government (Allocation of Business) Rules, 1961 were accordingly amended in February 2002. The actual transfer of work took place in June 2002.
2. India has been very vulnerable to natural hazards and calamities. The Bhuj earthquake accounted for 13,805 deaths, the super cyclone in Orissa accounted for 9,885 deaths. The government are of the view that if appropriate mitigation measures had been taken these casualties could have been reduced significantly.
3. Each year disasters also account for loss of thousands of crore in terms of social and community assets. It is clear that development cannot be sustainable without building in mitigation into the planning process. Keeping the above factors in view, the Government of India have brought about a change in policy which emphasises mitigation, prevention and preparedness. With the approval of Dy. Prime Minister, a strategic road map as given in the succeeding pages has been drawn up for reducing the country's vulnerability to disasters. Action for reducing our vulnerabilities to disasters shall be taken in accordance with the road map. The road map will be reviewed every two years to see if any change in direction is necessary.

National Disaster Management Framework

I. Institutional Mechanisms

Expected Output Areas of Intervention Agencies/Sectors to be Involved and Resource Linkages.

Nodal agency for disaster management at the national level with appropriate systems: (i) Constitution of National Emergency Management Authority with appropriate legal, financial, and administrative powers. (ii) Roles and responsibilities of the NEMA: (1) Coordinating multihazard mitigation, prevention, preparedness and response programmes. (2) Policies for disaster risk reduction and mitigation-preparedness at all levels. (3) Coordination of response. (4) Coordination of post-disaster relief and rehabilitation. (5) Amendment of existing laws, procedures, instructions. Ministries/Departments of Health, Water Resources, Environment and for Railways, Atomic Energy, Defence, Chemicals, Science and Technology, Rural Development, Road Transport, and Highways, etc. 47 Creation of State Departments of Disaster Management Departments of Relief and Rehabilitation to be redesignated as Department of Disaster Management with enhanced areas of responsibility to include mitigation, prevention and preparedness State Governments/UT Administration. Setting up State Disaster Management Authorities: (i) State Disaster Management Authority to be headed by the Chief Minister. (ii) The Authority to lay down policies and monitor mitigation, prevention, and preparedness as also oversee response. Ministers for Agriculture, Home, Disaster Management, Water Resources, Health, Road and Transport, Civil Supplies, Environment and Forests, Rural Development, Urban Development, and Public Health Engineering Departments as Members.

II. Disaster Mitigation/Prevention

Disaster Mitigation/Prevention to be Mainstreamed into the Development Process

(i) Each Minister/Department which has a role in mitigation prevention will make appropriate outlays for schemes addressing mitigation/prevention.

(ii) Where there is a shelf of projects schemes, projects/schemes contributing to mitigation to be given a priority.

(iii) Wherever possible Ministries/Department of Government of India/State Governments/UT Administration schemes/projects in areas prone to natural hazards to be so designed as to contribute to mitigation and preparedness.

(iv) Projects in vulnerable areas/areas prone to natural hazards to be designed to withstand natural hazards. Techno-legal regime: (i) regular review of building codes and its dissemination (ii) construction in seismic zones III, IV, and V to be as per BIS codes/National Building Codes. (iii) Construction in areas vulnerable to cyclones to be so designed as to withstand the wind hazard as per BIS codes/National Building Codes. (iv) Comprehensive review and compliance of – Town and Country Planning Acts, Development Control Regulations – Planning and Building Standards Regulations Bureau of Indian Standards/Ministry of Urban Development State Urban Development Department/Urban Local Bodies, State Urban Development Department/Urban Local Bodies State Urban Development Department/Urban Local Bodies 49. (v) Put in place appropriate techno-financial regime. (vi) Capacity enhancement of Urban Local Bodies to enforce compliance of techno-legal regimes State Urban Development Department/Urban Local Bodies State Governments land-use planning and zoning regulations (vii) Legal framework for Land-use planning and zoning regulations to be reviewed. (viii) Zoning regulations to be enforced.

Ministry of Urban Development Department of Land Resources (MORD) Ministry of Environment and Forests (GoI) State Governments Plan schemes for vulnerability reduction and preparedness. State Governments. To formulate plan schemes and submit to Planning Commission State Governments.

III. Legal/Policy Framework

Disaster management to be listed in List-III – (Concurrent List) of Seventh Schedule to the Constitution: (i) Bill to be drafted. (ii) Bill to be brought before Parliament, Ministry of Home Affairs/ Ministry of Law (Legislative Department) Disaster Management Acts, Model Act to be circulated to the States. Ministry of Home Affairs, State Governments National Policy on Disaster Management, States to enunciate policy on Disaster Management. (i) Mainstreaming disaster management into planning and development process. (ii) Mandate safe construction. (iii) Coordinated action by all relevant departments as per policy – State Governments, State Disaster Management Codes Amendment of existing relief codes/scarcity codes/famine codes to incorporate mitigation, preparedness and planning measures at all levels from Community to State, Constitution of Emergency Support Teams/Disaster Management Teams/Committees /State Disaster Management Authorities, delegation of administrative and financial powers to disaster incident managers, etc., protocol to update the inventory of resources and plans, State Governments.

IV. Preparedness and Response

National Emergency Response Force/Specialist Response teams (a) Designation of units for conversion into Specialist Response Teams. (b) Designation of training centres. (c) Training of trainers. (d) Procurement of equipment (e) Training of teams. Ministry of Home Affairs Central Industrial Security Force/Indo-Tibetan Boarder Police/Border Security Force/Central Reserve Police Force Specialized Response Teams at State Level

(i) Designation of units for conversion into Specialist Response Teams.

(ii) Designation of training centres.

(iii) Training of trainers.

(iv) Procurement of equipment using CRF resources

(v) Training of teams.

State Department of Disaster Management/State Home Department, State Police Training College/ State Fire Training Institute.

V. National Network of Emergency Operation Centres [NNEOCs]

Setting up Emergency Operations Centre[EOC] at National level

(i) Multihazard resistant construction.

(ii) Communication system linkages.

(iii) Mobile EOCs for on-site disaster information management – Central Public Works Department

Department for Central Public Works Ministry of Home Affairs State level EOC

(i) Multihazard resistant construction.

(ii) Communication system linkages.

(iii) Mobile EOC for onsite disaster management information – State Governments District level EOC

(a) Multihazard resistant construction.

(b) Communication system linkages.

State Governments Putting Incident Command System in Place

(i) Designate nodal training centres.

(ii) Putting in place protocols/SOPs for Incident Command System.

Ministry of Home Affairs/Department of Personal and Training/Lal Bahadur Shastri National Academy of Administration/State Governments/Administrative Training Institutes Emergency Support Function Plan.

(i) Departments/agencies which perform emergency support functions to draw up ESF plans, constitute teams, Central Government Ministries/Departments State Governments and set apart resources in advance so that post-disaster response is India Disaster Resource Network. (i) A web-enabled GIS-based resource inventory listing out all the necessary resources for emergency response available at the district and State level throughout the country so that resources can be mobilized at short notice.

(ii) Set up servers, draw up, and install programmes, input data.

(iii) Half yearly updating.

Ministry of Home Affairs.

State Governments.

Communication linkages which will be functional even post-disaster.

(i) Draw up communication plan.

(ii) Obtain sanctions.

(iii) Put communication network in place.

Ministry of Home Affairs.

Directorate Coordination of Police Wireless.

State Governments.

Regional Response Centres.

(i) Identify location of regional response centres.

(ii) Identify caches of equipment required.

(iii) Obtain sanctions.

(iv) Put teams and caches of equipments in place.

Ministry of Home Affairs.

Border Security Force/Indo-Tibetan Border.

Police /Central Reserve.

Police Force/ Central Industrial Security Force.

Training in response to be made a part of training curriculum of CPMFs and State Police Forces.

(i) Draw up capsules.

(ii) Train trainers.

Ministry of Home Affairs.

State Governments.

State Disaster Management Plans.

(i) Plan to be drafted under the supervision of the Chief Secretary.

(ii) Plan will include mitigation, preparedness, and response elements.

(iii) The plan will be multidisciplinary to be drawn up in conjunction/consultation with all relevant departments concerned with mitigation, preparedness and response.

(iv) Plan to be updated once a year.

State Governments/State Disaster Management.

Authorities, District Disaster, Management Plans.

(i) To be drawn up under the supervision of District Magistrate/Collector and to include mitigation, preparedness, and response.

(ii) Emergency support functions by various departments to be included.

(iii) To be drawn up in consultation with all State Governments/State

Disaster Management Authorities and Relevant Departments.

(iv) District inventory of resources to be maintained.

Block Disaster Management Plans.

(i) To be drawn up under the supervision of District Magistrate/Collector and to include mitigation, preparedness and response.

(ii) Emergency support functions by various departments to be included.

(iii) To be drawn up in consultation with all relevant departments.

(iv) District inventory of resources to be maintained by State Governments/State

Disaster Management Authorities/Block Development Administration.

Community-based mitigation, preparedness, and response plans

(i) Enhance community capacity in multihazardprone States and districts to respond effectively to disasters – special attention to be given to empowering and capacity building of vulnerable communities and groups including women.

(ii) Set up and train village/panchayat (for rural areas) and wards/municipal council/corporations (for urban areas) disaster management committees and disaster management teams, e.g., identification of safe shelters and management – stockpiling of relief materials, etc., Early warning dissemination, first-aid and counselling assist in search and rescue.

(iii) Such plans to be made integral to annual development plan of local bodies.

(iv) Mitigation plans of the community and panchayats to receive priority under various rural development schemes administered by panchayats and urban local bodies.

State Governments/District Administration/Panchayati Raj Institution/Urban Local Bodies.

VI. Early Warning Systems

(i) State-of-the-art sensors to be set up.

(ii) Hazard monitoring, tracking, and modelling.

(i) IMD/CWC to carry-out a review of sensors available and draw up plans for strengthening the system.

(ii) Models to be updated to improve prediction accuracy. Indian Meteorological Department/ Central Water Commission/National Centre for Medium Range

Weather Forecasting Warning Protocols

(i) Warning protocols to be user-friendly.

(ii) Warning to be communicated as quickly as possible to the States/districts/community.

(iii) Protocols should be simple to understand.

(iv) Districts to set up protocols for communication of early warning to the community.

(v) Panchayats/local bodies to be used for early warning communication.

(vi) Communication linkages for early warning.

Ministry of Home Affairs/State Governments/Indian Meteorological Department/Central Water Commission/National Remote Sensing Agency/Information and Broadcasting/Doordarshan/All India Radio.

VII. Human Resource Development and Capacity Building

Training for services/cadres/agencies involved in mitigation, preparedness, or response.

(i) Training needs analysis/Human Resource Development Plan.

(ii) Drawing up of capsule courses for Ministry of Home Affairs-State Governments Training.

(iii) Training of trainers.

(iv) National Institute for Disaster Management to be strengthened.

(v) Setting up/strengthening training institutions in State faculties of disaster management in Administrative Training Institutes and Training of IAS/IPS.

State Administrative Service Officers/State Police

(i) Training curriculum for IAS/IPS and State. Administrative Service Officers/State Police Officers to include capsules in disaster management.

(ii) Training of Block/Village level staff.

(iii) Training of PRIs. Administrative Training Institutes/State Institutes of Rural Development and District Institutes of Education and Training to be used. Engineers/Architects Curriculum for undergraduate engineering and B.Arch. courses to be amended to include mitigation technologies in general and elements of earthquake engineering in particular State Governments All India Council for Technical Education

Indian Institute of Technologies Professional bodies-Health Professionals include crisis prevention, response and recovery, and trauma management in the MBBS curriculum.

Ministry of Health and Family Welfare Medical Council of India Youth organization NCC, NSS, Scouts and Guides to include disaster response, search and rescue in their orientation/training programmes.

Ministry of Youth and Sports, Ministry of Defence Masons /Mason training for safe construction, Ministry of Rural Development/Department of Urban Development/State Governments School curriculum to include disaster awareness.

Central and State Boards of Education National mass media campaign for awareness generation:

Design and develop a communication strategy for awareness campaign.

Use audio, visual, and print medium to implement awareness campaign. Development of resource materials on mitigation, preparedness, and response.

Non-government community-based organizations involved in awareness generation and community participation in disaster preparedness and mitigation planning.

(i) Facilitate network of non-government community-based organizations at national/State/district levels.

(ii) Coopted into the planning process and response mechanisms at all levels. Ministry of Home Affairs /National Institute for Disaster Management/Ministry of Home Affairs /National Institute for Disaster Management Corporate sectors involved in awareness generation and disaster preparedness and mitigation planning sensitization, training and coopting corporate sector and their nodal bodies in planning process and response mechanisms. Ministry of Home Affairs/ Federation of Indian Industries inter-State arrangements for sharing of resources during emergencies and lessons learnt.

(i) Arrangements for inter-State sharing of resources to be incorporated in State Ministry of Home Affairs/State Governments Disaster Management Plans.

(ii) Inter-State exposure visits to be facilitated for learning from the experiences of other States – Ministry of Home Affairs/State Governments.

VIII. Research and Knowledge Management

Institutionalize knowledge and lessons learnt in the process of working on the national road map.

(i) Assessment and evaluation of ongoing programmes and activities regular documentation of key lessons.

(ii) Establish India Disaster Resource Network as knowledge portal to pool and exchange information and knowledge among all concerned institutions and organization Ministry of Home Affairs State Governments/National Institute for Disaster Management Ministry of Home Affairs Develop national disasters database.

(a) Systematic inventorization of disasters.

(b) Trend analysis and reporting National Institute for Disaster Management promote research in national, State, and regional institutions in the areas of disaster risk reduction.

(1) Mitigation technologies for housing, roads and bridges, water supply and sewerage systems, and power utilities.

(2) Cost-effective equipments for specialized rapid response and preparedness in temporary and transition shelter in post-disaster situations Ministries/Departments of Central Government Search and rescue equipments provision of drinking water, emergency health and sanitation in post-disaster situations – post-trauma stress management and care.

(3) Promote participation of corporate sector in finding out technological solutions for disaster risk reduction.

8.5 ANNEXURE-II: DISASTER MANAGEMENT – THE DEVELOPMENT PERSPECTIVE

1. Five-Year Plan documents have, historically, not included consideration of issues relating to the management and mitigation of natural disasters. The traditional perception has been limited to the idea of "calamity relief", which is seen essentially as a non-plan item of expenditure. However, the impact of major disasters cannot be mitigated by the provision of immediate relief alone, which is the primary focus of calamity relief efforts. Disasters can have devastating effects on the economy; they cause huge human and economic losses, and can significantly set back development efforts of a region or a State. Two recent disasters, the Orissa Cyclone and the Gujarat Earthquake, are cases in point. With the kind of economic losses and developmental setbacks that the country has been suffering year-after-year, the development process needs to be sensitive towards disaster prevention and mitigation aspects. There is thus a need to look at disasters from a development perspective as well.

2. Further, although disaster management is not generally associated with plan financing, there are in fact a number of plan schemes in operation, such as for drought proofing, afforestation, drinking water, etc., which deal with the prevention and mitigation of the impact of natural disasters. External assistance for post-disaster reconstruction and streamlining of management structures also is a part of the plan. A specific, centrally sponsored scheme on disaster management also exists. The plan thus already has a defined role in dealing with the subject.

3. Recently, expert bodies have dwelt on the role of the Planning Commission and the use of plan funds in the context of disaster management. Suggestions have been made in this regard by the Eleventh Finance Commission, and also the High Powered Committee on Disaster Management. An approach on planning for safe development needs to be set out in the light of these suggestions.

4. This chapter reflects the considerations outlined above. It briefly outlines the global context and the Indian experience of disasters, sets out the institutional and financial arrangements for disaster management and the response towards these in the country, looks at directions for improvement, and concludes with a strategy to facilitate planning for safe national development in the Tenth Plan period.

The Global Context

5. There has been an increase in the number of natural disasters over the past years, and with it, increasing losses on account of urbanization and population growth, as a result of which the impact of natural disasters is now felt to a larger extent. According to the United Nations, in 2001 alone, natural disasters of medium to high range caused at least 25,000 deaths around the world, more than double the previous year, and economic losses of around US $ 36 billion. These figures would be much higher, if the consequences of the many smaller and unrecorded disasters that cause significant losses at the local community level were to be taken into account. Devastations in the aftermath of powerful earthquakes that struck Gujarat, El Salvador, and Peru; floods that ravaged many countries in Africa, Asia, and elsewhere; droughts that plagued Central Asia including Afghanistan, Africa, and Central America; the cyclone in Madagascar and Orissa; and floods in Bolivia are global events in recent memory. However, what is disturbing is the knowledge that these trends of destruction and devastation are on the rise instead of being kept in check.

6. Natural disasters are not bound by political boundaries and have no social or economic considerations. They are borderless as they affect both developing and developed countries. They are also merciless, and as such the vulnerable tend to suffer more at the impact of natural disasters. For example, the developing countries are much more seriously affected in terms of the loss of lives, hardship borne by population and the percentage of their GNP lost. Since 1991, two-thirds of the victims of natural disasters were from developing countries, while just 2 per cent were from highly developed nations. Those living in developing countries and especially those with limited resources tend to be more adversely affected. With the alarming rise in the natural disasters and vulnerability *per se,* the world community is strengthening its efforts to cope with it.

7. As a number of the most vulnerable regions are in India, natural disaster management has emerged as a high priority for the country. Going beyond the historical focus on relief and rehabilitation after the event, we now have to look ahead and plan for disaster preparedness and mitigation, in order that the periodic shocks to our development efforts are minimized.

The Indian Experience

Regional Vulnerabilities

8. Physical vulnerability relates to the physical location of people, their proximity to the hazard zone and standards of safety maintained to counter the effects. For instance, some people are vulnerable to flood only because they live in a flood-prone area. Physical vulnerability also relates to the technical capacity of buildings and structures to resist the forces acting upon them during a hazard event.

9. The extent to which a population is affected by a calamity does not purely lie in the physical components of vulnerability, but is contextual also to the prevailing social and economic conditions and it is consequential effect on human activities within a given society. Research in areas affected by earthquakes indicates that single parent families, women, handicapped people, children, and the aged are particularly vulnerable social groups. The geophysical setting with unplanned and inadequate developmental activity is a cause for increased losses during disasters. In the case of India, the contribution of over-population to high population density, which in turn results in escalating losses, deserves to be noted. This factor sometimes tends to be as important as physical vulnerability attributed to geography and infrastructure alone.

10. The continent of Asia is particularly vulnerable to disaster strikes. Between the years 1991 and 2000 Asia has accounted for 83 per cent of the population affected by disasters globally. While the number of people affected in the rest of the world were 1,11,159, in Asia the number was 5,54,439.Within Asia, 24 per cent of deaths due to disasters occur in India, on account of its size, population and vulnerability. Floods and high winds account for 60 per cent of all disasters in India. While substantial progress has been made in other sectors of human development, there is need to do more towards mitigating the effect of disasters.

11. Many parts of the Indian subcontinent are susceptible to different types of disasters owing to the unique topographic and climatic characteristics. About 54 per cent of the subcontinent's landmass is vulnerable to earthquakes while about 4 crore hectares is vulnerable to periodic floods. The decade 1990-2000, has been one of very high disaster losses within the country, losses in the Orissa Cyclone in 1999, and later, the Gujarat earthquake in 2001 alone amount to several thousand crore of rupees, while the total expenditure on relief and reconstruction in Gujarat alone has been to the tune of ₹ 11,500 crore.

12. Similarly, the country has suffered four major earthquakes in the span of last 50 years along with a series of moderate intensity earthquakes that have occurred at regular intervals. Since 1988, six earthquakes have struck different parts of the country. These caused considerable human and property losses.

13. Disasters lead to enormous economic losses that are both immediate as well as long-term in nature and demand additional revenues. Also, as an immediate fallout, disasters reduce revenues from the affected region due to lower levels of economic activity leading to loss of direct and

indirect taxes. In addition, unplanned budgetary allocation to disaster recovery can hamper development interventions and lead to unmet developmental targets.

14. Disasters may also reduce availability of new investment, further constricting the growth of the region. Besides, additional pressures may be imposed on finances of the government through investments in relief and rehabilitation work.

15. In the recent earthquake in Gujarat, more than 14,000 lives were lost, 10 lakh houses were damaged and the asset loss has been indicated to be worth ₹ 15,000 crore. It further emphasize the point that natural disasters cause major setbacks to development and it is the poorest and the weakest that are the most vulnerable to disasters. Given the high frequency with which one or the other part of the country suffers due to disasters, mitigating the impact of disasters must be an integral component of our development planning and be part of our poverty reduction strategy.

Institutional Arrangements

17. The country with its federal system of government has specific roles for the Central and State Governments. However, the subject of disaster management does not specifically find mention in any of the three lists in the 7th Schedule of the Indian Constitution, where subjects under the Central and State Governments as also subjects that come under both are specified. On the legal front, there is no enactment either of the Central or of any State Government to deal with the management of disasters of various types in a comprehensive manner.

18. The country has an integrated administrative machinery for management of disasters at the national, State, district and sub-district, levels. The basic responsibility of undertaking rescue, relief and rehabilitation measures in the event of natural disasters, as at present, is that of the State Governments concerned. The Central Government supplements the efforts of the States by providing financial and logistic support.

Central Level

19. The dimensions of response at the level of the Central Government are determined in accordance with the existing policy of financing relief expenditure and keeping in view the factors like:
    - (i) The gravity of a natural disaster.
    - (ii) The scale of the relief operation necessary.
    - (iii) The requirements of Central assistance for augmenting financial resources and logistic support at the disposal of the State Government.

20. The Contingency Action Plan (CAP) identifies initiatives required to be taken by various Central Ministries and Public Departments in the wake of natural calamities. It sets down the procedures and determines the focal points in the administrative machinery to facilitate launching of relief and rescue operations without delay.

21. The Ministry of Home Affairs is the nodal ministry for coordination of relief and response and overall natural disaster management, and the Department of Agriculture and Cooperation is the nodal ministry for drought management. Other ministries are assigned the responsibility of providing emergency support in case of disasters that fall in their purview.

Ministries Responsible for Various Categories of Disasters

The following decision making and standing bodies are responsible for disaster management at the Central level:

(a) Union Cabinet, headed by the Prime Minister.

(b) Empowered Group of Ministers, headed by the Deputy Prime Minister.

(c) National Crisis Management Committee (NCMC), under the chairmanship of the Cabinet Secretary.

(d) Crisis Management Group (CMG): under the chairmanship of the Central Relief Commissioner comprising senior officers from the various ministries and other concerned departments which reviews contingency plans, measures required for dealing with a natural disaster, and coordinates the activities of the Central Ministries and the State Governments in relation to disaster preparedness response and relief.

(e) Technical Organizations, such as the Indian Meteorological Department (cyclone/earthquake), Central Water Commission (floods), Building and Material Promotion Council (construction laws), Bureau of Indian Standards (norms), Defence Research and Development Organization (nuclear/biological), and Directorate General Civil Defence provide specific technical support to coordination of disaster response and management functions.

(f) The setting up of a National Disaster Management Authority (NDMA) is being contemplated by the Ministry of Home Affairs as the proposed apex structure within the government for the purpose.

Among other major organizational initiatives, it is proposed to:

(a) Establish a specialized and earmarked response team for dealing with nuclear/biological/chemical disasters.

(b) Establish search and rescue teams in each state.

(c) Strengthen communication systems in the North Eastern Region.

State Government

22. The responsibility to cope with natural disasters is essentially that of the State Government. The role of the Central Government is supportive in terms of supplementation of physical and financial resources. The Chief Secretary of the State heads a state level committee which is in overall charge of the relief operations in the State and the Relief Commissioners who are in charge of the relief and rehabilitation measures in the wake of natural disasters in their States function under the overall direction and control of the State level committee. In many States, Secretary, Department of Revenue, is also incharge of relief. State Governments usually have relief manuals and the districts have their contingency plan that is updated from time-to-time.

District and Local Level

23. The district administration is the focal point for implementation of all governmental plans and activities. The actual day-to-day function of administering relief is the responsibility of the Collector/ District Magistrate/Deputy Commissioner who exercises coordinating and supervising powers overall departments at the district level. Although it may not be a common phenomenon, there exists by and large in districts also a district level relief committee consisting of officials and non-officials.

24. The 73rd and 74th Constitutional Amendments recognize Panchayati Raj Institutions as 'Institutions of self- government'. The amendment has also laid down necessary guidelines for the structure of their composition, powers, functions, devolution of finances, regular holding of elections, and reservation of seats for weaker sections including women. These local bodies can be effective instruments in tackling disasters through early warning system, relief distribution, providing shelter to the victims, medical assistance, etc.

25. Other than the national, State, district, and local levels, there are various institutional stakeholders who are involved in disaster management at various levels in the country. These include the police and para-military forces, civil defence and homeguards, fire services, ex-servicemen, non-government organizations (NGOs), public and private sector enterprises, media and HAM operators, all of whom have important roles to play.

Armed Forces

26. The Indian armed forces are supposed to be called upon to intervene and take on specific tasks only when the situation is beyond the capability of civil administration. In practice, the armed forces are the core of the government's response capacity and tend to be the first responders of the Government of India in a major disaster. Due to their ability to organize action in adverse ground circumstances, speed of operational response and the resources and capabilities at their disposal, the armed forces have historically played a major role in emergency support functions such as communications, search and rescue operations, health and medical facilities, transportation, power, food and civil supplies, public works and engineering, especially in the immediate aftermath of disaster. Disaster management plans should incorporate the role expected of them so that the procedure for deploying them is smooth and quick.

External Linkages

27. The Government of India is a member of various international organizations in the field of disaster response and relief. While, as a policy, no requests for assistance or appeals are made to the international community in the event of a disaster, assistance offered *suo moto* is accepted. Linkages exist with the following organizations:

    (a) UN Office for Coordination of Humanitarian Affairs (UN OCHA), which has been made responsible by UN General Assembly mandate for all international disaster response.

    (b) United Nations Development Programme (UNDP), responsible for mitigation and prevention aspects of disaster management.

    (c) UN Disaster Assessment and Coordination (UNDAC) System, Streamlining institutional arrangements for disaster response.

28. Institutional arrangements for disaster response are the heart of disaster management systems. There is no dearth of personnel, both civilian and military, experienced in handling situations arising out of natural disasters. However, there certainty is a pressing need for improvement and strengthening of existing institutional arrangements and systems in this regard to make the initial response to a disaster more effective and professional. Most of the resources and expertise needed already exist with the government. What needs to be streamlined is how they should be integrated, trained, and deployed. Some of the areas where improvement is urgently needed are:

(a) Integrated planning for disasters, including the integration of relevant armed forces formations into disaster management planning at all levels from District to State and Central Government.

(b) Setting up of a modern, permanent national command centre or operations room, with redundant communications and data links to all State capitals. The national command centre or operations room needs to be manned on a 24-hour basis by professionals to cater for instant integrated response. There needs to be a properly equipped operations room at the State level as well.

(c) Establishment of a national standby, quick reaction team composed of experienced professionals, both military and civilian, drawn from Central and State Government staff to respond immediately by flying in a matter of hours an experienced response team to the locations when a disaster strikes. This team can be organized and run professionally on the same lines as the United Nations Disaster Assessment and Coordination (UNDAC) teams.

(d) Creation of urban search and rescue capacity at all levels, by establishing a fully equipped Search and Rescue unit, as part of the fire service in all State capitals, with trained staff and modern equipment such as thermal imagers, acoustic detection devices, etc. This is of immediate relevance since a major weakness exposed in the Gujarat earthquake was a lack of specialized urban search and rescue capability in India.

(e) Media policy geared to handling the growing phenomenon of real time television reporting, which generates enormous political pressures on a government to respond rapidly and efficiently. This needs attention since the effect is going to increase, not decrease in future.

(f) Closer interface with and better understanding of the international system for disaster response, and putting in place, systems for dealing with international assistance once it comes in, e.g., customs, immigration, foreign policy implications, etc. A greater appreciation is needed of the speed and automation of modern international response to a natural disaster. Closer interaction is required between of the Ministry of External Affairs and the relevant international agencies concerned with disaster response.

(g) Standard procedures for dealing with domestic humanitarian and relief assistance from non-government sources. Procedures and systems need to be set out to avoid confusion and ensure best utilization of the assistance being offered, just as in the case of systems for international assistance.

(h) Modern unified legislation for disaster management. In view of the current division of responsibilities between the State and Central Government into State, Central and concurrent lists, there is a need to create a body of legislation dealing with response to natural disasters and other emergencies, clearly delineating responsibilities and powers of each entity and specifying what powers or actions would need to be triggered on declaration of a disaster by the Government of India or a State Government. This legislation should also incorporate the current legislation dealing with chemical emergencies that has been created by the Ministry of Environment so that all emergencies are dealt with under one law. The legislation should include clear definitions of what constitutes a disaster at a national level.

Financial Arrangements

Financing of Relief Expenditures

29. The policy arrangements for meeting relief expenditure related to natural disasters are, by and large, based on the recommendations of successive Finance Commissions. The two main windows presently open for meeting such expenditures are the Calamity Relief Fund (CRF) and National Calamity Contingency Fund (NCCF). The Calamity Relief Fund is used for meeting the expenditure for providing immediate relief to the victims of cyclone, drought, earthquake, fire, flood, and hailstorm. Expenditure on restoration of damaged capital works should ordinarily be met from the normal budgetary heads, except when it is to be incurred as part of providing immediate relief, such as restoration of drinking water sources or provision of shelters, etc., or restoration of communication links for facilitating relief operations. The amount of annual contribution to the CRF of each State for each of the financial years 2000 to 2001 to 2004 to 2005 is as indicated by the Finance Commission. Of the total contribution indicated, the Government of India contributes 75 per cent of the total yearly allocation in the form of a non-plan grant, and the balance amount is contributed by the State Government concerned. A total of ₹ 11,007.59 crore was provided for the Calamity Relief Fund from 2000 to 2005.

30. Pursuant to the recommendations of the Eleventh Finance Commission, apart from the CRF, a National Calamity Contingency Fund (NCCF) Scheme came into force with effect from the financial year 2000 to 2001 and would be operative till the end of the financial year 2004 to 2005. NCCF is intended to cover natural calamities like cyclone, drought, earthquake, fire, flood, and hailstorm, which are considered to be of severe nature requiring expenditure by the State Government in excess of the balances available in its own Calamity Relief Fund. The assistance from NCCF is available only for immediate relief and rehabilitation. Any reconstruction of assets or restoration of damaged capital should be financed through reallocation of plan funds. There is need for defining the arrangements in this regard.

31. The initial corpus of the National Fund is ₹ 500 crore, provided by the Government of India. This fund is required to be recouped by levy of special surcharge for a limited period on Central taxes. An amount of about ₹ 2,300 crore has already been released to states from NCCF. A list of items and norms of expenditure for assistance chargeable to CRF/NCCF in the wake of natural calamities is prescribed in detail from time-to-time.

Financing of Disaster Management Through Five-Year Plans

32. Although not specifically addressed in Five-Year Plan documents in the past, the Government of India has a long history of using funds from the Plan for mitigating natural disasters. Funds are provided under plan schemes, i.e., various schemes of Government of India, such as for drinking water, employment generation, inputs for agriculture and flood control measures, etc. There are also facilities for rescheduling short-term loans taken for agriculture purposes upon certification by the district/State administration. Central Government's assets/infrastructure are to be repaired/rectified by the respective ministry/Department of Government of India. Besides this, at the occurrence of a calamity of great magnitude, funds flow from donors, both local and international, for relief and rehabilitation, and in few cases for long-term preparedness/preventive measures. Funds for the latter purposes are also available from multilateral funding agencies such as the World Bank. These form part of the State Plan.

33. There are also a number of important ongoing schemes that specifically help reduce disaster vulnerability. Some of these are: Integrated Wasteland Development Programme (IWDP), Drought Prone Area Programme (DPAP), Desert Development Programme (DDP), Flood Control Programmes, National Afforestation and Ecodevelopment Programme (NA and ED), Accelerated Rural Water Supply Programme (ARWSP), Crop Insurance, Sampurn Grameen Rozgar Yojana (SGRY), and Food for Work, etc.

Initiatives Proposed by Various Bodies Regarding Financing Under the Plan

34. References have recently been made to the role of the Plan in disaster management by the High Power Committee (HPC) on Disaster Management, as well as by the Eleventh Finance Commission. The HPC was constituted in 1999 and submitted its Report in October 2001. The HPC took an overview of all recent disasters (natural as well as man-made) in the country and identified common response and preparedness mechanisms on the basis of a series of consultations with a number of government, non-government, national, and international agencies and media organizations. An important recommendation of the Committee was that at least 10 per cent of plan funds at the national, State, and district levels be earmarked and apportioned for schemes which specifically address areas such as prevention, reduction, preparedness, and mitigation of disasters.

35. The Eleventh Finance Commission too paid detailed attention to the issue of disaster management and, in its chapter on calamity relief, came out with a number of recommendations, of which the following have a direct bearing on the plan:

(a) Expenditure on restoration of infrastructure and other capital assets, except those that are intrinsically connected with relief operations and connectivity with the affected area and population, should be met from the plan funds on priority basis.

(b) Medium-term and long-term measures be devised by the concerned ministries of the Government of India, the State Governments and the Planning Commission to reduce, and if possible, eliminate, the occurrences of these calamities by undertaking developmental works.

(c) The Planning Commission, in consultation with the State Governments and concerned ministries, should be able to identify works of a capital nature to prevent the recurrence of specific calamities. These works may be funded under the Plan.

Planning for Safe National Development

36. Development programmes that go into promoting development at the local level have been left to the general exercise of planning. Measures need also to be taken to integrate disaster mitigation efforts at the local level with the general exercise of planning, and a more supportive environment created for initiatives towards managing of disasters at all levels: national, State, district, and local. The future blueprint for disaster management in India rests on the premise that in today's society while hazards, both natural or otherwise, are inevitable, the disasters that follow need not be so and the society can be prepared to cope with them effectively whenever they occur. The need of the hour is to chalk out a multipronged strategy for total risk management, comprising prevention, preparedness, response, and recovery on the one hand, and initiate development efforts aimed towards risk reduction and mitigation, on the other Only then can we look forward to "sustainable development".

Disaster Prevention and Preparedness Measures Information and Research Network

37. Disaster prevention is intrinsically linked to preventive planning. Some of the important steps in this regard are:

   (a) Introduction of a comprehensive process of vulnerability analysis and objective risk assessment.

   (b) **Building a robust and sound information database:** A comprehensive database ofthe land use, demography, infrastructure developed at the national, State, and local levels along with current information on climate, weather and man-made structures is crucial in planning, warning, and assessment of disasters. In addition, resource inventories of governmental and non-governmental systems including personnel and equipment help in efficient mobilization and optimization of response measures.

   (c) **Creating state-of-the-art infrastructure:** The entire disaster mitigation game plan must necessarily be anchored to frontline research and development in a holistic mode. State-of-the-art technologies available worldwide need to be made available in India for upgradation of the disaster management system; at the same time, dedicated research activities should be encouraged, in all frontier areas related to disasters like biological, space applications, information technology, nuclear radiation, etc., for a continuous flow of high quality basic information for sound disaster management planning.

   (d) **Establishing linkages between all knowledge based institutions:** A National Disaster Knowledge Network, tuned to the felt needs of a multitude of users like disaster managers, decision makers, community, etc., must be developed as the network of networks to cover natural, man-made, and biological disasters in all their varied dimensions.

Capacity Building, Training and Education

38. Personnel involved in the exercise have to draw upon knowledge of best practices and resources available to them. Information and training on ways to better respond to and mitigate disasters to the responders go a long way in building the capacity and resilience of the country to

reduce and prevent disasters. Training is an integral part of capacity building as trained personnel respond much better to different disasters and appreciate the need for preventive measures. The directions in this regard are:

(a) The multisectoral and multihazard prevention-based approach to disaster management requires specific professional inputs. Professional training in disaster management should be built into the existing pedagogic research and education. Specialized courses for disaster management may be developed by universities and professional teaching institutions, and disaster management should be treated as a distinct academic and professional discipline, something that the American education system has done successfully. In addition to separate diploma/degree courses in disaster management, the subject needs to be discussed and taught as a specific component in professional and specialized courses like medicine, nursing, engineering, environmental sciences, architecture, and town and country planning.

(b) The focus towards preventive disaster management and development of a national ethos of prevention calls for an awareness generation at all levels. An appropriate component of disaster awareness at the school level will help increase awareness among children and, in many cases, parents and other family members through these children. Curriculum development with a focus towards dissemination of disaster-related information on a sustained basis, covering junior, middle, and high schools may be worked out by the different school boards in the country.

(c) Training facilities for government personnel involved in disaster management are conducted at the national level by the National Centre for Disaster Management (NCDM) at the Indian Institute of Public Administration, in New Delhi which functions as the nodal institution in the country for training, research and documentation of disasters. At the State level, disaster management cells operating within the State Administrative Training Institutes (ATIs) provide the necessary training. Presently, 24 ATIs have dedicated faculties. There is a need for strengthening specialized training, including training of personnel in disaster response.

(d) Capacity building should not be limited to professionals and personnel involved in disaster management but should also focus on building the knowledge, attitude, and skills of a community to cope with the effects of disasters. Identification and training of volunteers from the community towards first response measures as well as mitigation measures is an urgent imperative. A programme of periodic drills should be introduced in vulnerable areas to enable prompt and appropriate community response in the event of a disaster, which can help save valuable lives.

39. Capacity building for effective disaster management therefore needs to be grounded and linked to the community and local level responders on the one hand and also to the institutional mechanism of the State and the nation on the other.

Community Level Initiatives

40. The goal of any disaster management initiative is to build a disaster resistant/resilient community equipped with safer living and sustainable livelihoods to serve its own development purposes. The community is also the first responder in any disaster situation, thereby emphasizing the need for community level initiatives in managing disasters. To encourage such initiatives, the following are required:

(a) Creating awareness through disaster education and training and information dissemination are necessary steps for empowering the community to cope with disasters.

(b) Community-based approach followed by most NGOs and community based organizations (CBOs) should be incorporated in the disaster management system as an effective vehicle of community participation.

(c) Within a vulnerable community, there exist groups that are more vulnerable like women and children, aged and infirm and physically challenged people who need special care and attention especially during disaster situations. Efforts are required for identifying such vulnerable groups and providing special assistance in terms of evacuation, relief, aid, and medical attention to them in disaster situations.

41. Management of disasters should therefore be an interface between a community effort to mitigate and prevent disasters as also an effort from the government machinery to buttress and support popular initiatives.

Strengthening of Plan Activities

42. Given the pervasive nature of disasters and the widespread havoc caused by some of them, planned expenditure on disaster mitigation and prevention measures in addition to the CRF is required. The Central Sector Scheme of Natural Disaster Management Programmes has been implemented since 1993-1994 by the Department of Agriculture and Cooperation with the objective to focus on disaster preparedness with emphasis on mitigation and preparedness measures for enhanced capability to reduce the adverse impact of disasters. The major activities undertaken within this scheme include the setting up of the National Centre for Disaster Management (NCDM) at the Indian Institute of Public Administration, creation of 24 disaster management faculties in 23 states, research and consultancy services, documentation of major disaster events and forging regional cooperation. The Eighth Plan allocation of ₹ 6.30 crore for this scheme was increased to ₹ 16.32 crore in the Ninth Plan. Within this scheme, NCDM has conducted over 50 training programmes, training more than 1,000 people, while 24 disaster management centres with dedicated faculty have been established in the states. Over 4,000 people have been trained at the State level. In addition, some important publications and audio-visual training modules have been prepared and documentation of disaster events has been done.

43. Although limited in scope and outlays, the scheme has made an impact on the training and research activities in the country. Creation of faculties in disaster management in all 28 States is proposed to be taken up in the Tenth Plan in addition to community mobilization, human resource development, establishment of control rooms, and forging international cooperation in disaster management. There is also an urgent need for strengthening the disaster management pedagogy by creating disaster management faculties in universities, rural development institutes and other organizations of premier research.

44. Sustainability is the key word in the development process. Development activities that do not consider the disaster loss perspective fail to be sustainable. The compounded costs of disasters relating to loss of life, loss of assets, economic activities, and cost of reconstruction of not only assets but of lives can scarcely be borne by any community or nation. Therefore, all development schemes in vulnerable areas should include a disaster mitigation analysis, whereby

the feasibility of a project is assessed with respect to vulnerability of the area and the mitigation measures required for sustainability. Environmental protection, afforestation programmes, pollution control, construction of earthquake resistant structures, etc., should therefore have high priority within the plans.

45. The aim of a mitigation strategy is to reduce losses in the event of a future occurrence of a hazard. Structural mitigation may comprise construction of individual disaster resistant structures like retrofitted or earthquake-resistant buildings or creation of structures whose function is primarily disaster protection like flood control structures, dykes, levees, infiltration dams, etc.
46. Mitigation measures on individual structures can be achieved by design standards, building codes and performance specifications. Building codes, critical front-line defence for achieving stronger engineered structures, need to be drawn up in accordance with the vulnerability of the area and implemented through appropriate techno-legal measures.
47. Mitigation measures need to be considered in land use and site planning activities. Constructions in hazardous areas like flood plains or steep soft slopes are more vulnerable to disasters. Necessary mitigation measures need to be built into the design and costing of development projects.
48. Insurance is a potentially important mitigation measure in disaster-prone areas as it brings quality in the infrastructure and consciousness and a culture of safety by its insistence on following building codes, norms, guidelines, quality materials in construction, etc. Disaster insurance mostly works under the premise of 'higher the risk higher the premium, lesser the risk lesser the premium', thus creating awareness towards vulnerable areas and motivating people to settle in relatively safer areas.

The Path Ahead

49. For addressing natural calamities such as floods and drought, there already exist a number of plan schemes under which a lot is being done and can be done. State Governments need to make full use of the existing plan schemes and give priority to implementation of such schemes that will help in overcoming the conditions created by the calamity. In some cases this implies possible diversion of the funds from other schemes to those schemes the implementation of which will help meeting the situation. There may also be need in a crisis situation for certain re-appropriations/reallocations among the different departments.
50. The Planning Commission will aim at responding quickly to the needs of the Central Ministries/Departments/States in matters relating to the plan for meeting situations arising out of natural disasters, by enabling adjustment of schemes to meet the requirements as far as possible. A mechanism will be evolved to take expeditious decisions on proposals which involve transfer of funds from one scheme to another, or any other change which involves departure from the existing schemes/pattern of assistance, new schemes and relaxation in procedures, etc., in the case of natural disasters.
51. As the first responder in any disaster situation, however, each State needs to build a team, skilled personnel, make provision for specialized equipment, efficient communication network, and relevant, intelligent and easily accessible database. There is also a need to consider creation

of a plan scheme in each State basically to meet the minimum requirements for strengthening communications and emergency control rooms, thereby improving coordination and response to disasters. No new institutional structures need be created in such a scheme.

52. In particular, with regard to major disasters, it is also necessary for disaster mitigation components to be built into all development projects. In order to save larger outlays on reconstruction and rehabilitation subsequently, a mechanism would need to be worked out for allowing components that specifically help projects coming up in highly disaster-prone areas withstand the impact of natural disasters as part of approved project cost for projects financed under the plan.

53. The message for the Tenth Plan is that in order to move towards safer national development, development projects should be sensitive towards disaster mitigation. With the kind of economic losses and developmental setbacks that the country has been suffering year-after-year, it makes good economic sense to spend a little extra today in a planned way on steps and components that can help in prevention and mitigation of disasters, than be forced to spend many multiples more later on restoration and rehabilitation. The design of development projects and the process of development should take the aspect of disaster reduction and mitigation within its ambit; otherwise, the development ceases to be sustainable and eventually causes more hardship and loss to the nation.

8.6 ANNEXURE-III: GUIDELINES TO STATE GOVERNMENTS

(i) The State Department of Relief and Rehabilitation may be converted into Department of Disaster Management with the responsibility of looking at the whole cycle of disaster management-prevention, mitigation, preparedness, response, relief, and rehabilitation. Steps for prevention/mitigation will need to be taken across a number of departments. The Department of Disaster Management will coordinate the steps taken by the different departments of the government in these spheres.

(ii) Mitigation, preparedness, and response are multi-disciplinary activities involving a number of departments. In order to ensure the fullest involvement of the relevant departments, the State Government may consider setting up a State Disaster Management Authority under the Chairmanship of the Chief Secretary with the Secretaries of Departments of Water Resources, Health, Agriculture, Animal Husbandry, Roads, Communications, Rural Development, Public Works, Public Health Engineering, Finance, and Home as members. The Secretary of the Department of Disaster Management may be the member Secretary. This authority will ensure coordinated steps towards mitigation and preparedness as also coordinated response when a disaster strikes.

(iii) It has been noticed that while the local administration has the requisite skills and capabilities for carrying out search and rescue in recurrent types of disaster like flood, there is lack of capability for specialised search and rescue. Each State may consider setting up specialized search and rescue teams. The teams would need to be composite with one coy of the State Armed Police trained and equipped to carry-out specialized search and rescue; one mobile engineering unit with necessary equipment and one medical assistance team. These teams may be constituted and trained together so as to function as a unit under the overall charge of a designated officer. Guidance/advise required with reference to training and equipment will be provided by the Disaster Management Division of the Ministry of Home Affairs, Government of India.

(iv) It has been decided that fire services may be trained and equipped to function as all hazard response units as in other countries. This will necessitate some additional equipment and training to the fire units for carrying out search and rescue in all types of disasters. The Government of India will be initiating a separate project for this.

(v) The Ministry of Home Affairs had advised the State Governments that composite control rooms may be set up at the State level and at the district levels under the District Magistrates for coordinating law and order as well as disaster management and that allocations under the Modernization of Police Forces Schemes may be used for the this purpose. Steps may be taken to put such control room in place quickly with standby communication systems.

(vi) Disaster mitigation concerns/aspects may be made an essential term of reference for every plan project/development scheme in the areas vulnerable to disasters. In other words, every plan project will need to state as to how is addresses mitigation concerns. Plans/projects specifically addressing mitigation/prevention may be given a priority. The Secretary of Department of Disaster Management may be made a member for all bodies/teams constituted for scrutinizing/approving projects/plans.

(vii) Funds available under the ongoing schemes may be used for mitigation/preparedness. For example, funds under the rural development scheme can be used for construction of cycle shelters in areas prone to cyclones. Similarly, sites and designs of primary school buildings in flood-prone areas may be so selected so that they can serve as shelters in times of floods. The design requirements for primary school building and hospitals and other important public buildings in seismic zones V and IV would need to be in accordance with BIS norms for construction in these zones.

(viii) Every hazard-prone district may draw up specific hazard-related plans. These plans may be reviewed/updated in the months of April and May each year.

(ix) Every district located in area prone to hazard will need to maintain an online inventory of resources available in the government, public and private sector. This will enable easy and quick mobilization of resources in case of need. A Statewide online resources inventory would enable the mobilization of resources from neighbouring districts in cases of need.

(x) State in seismic zones V and IV may ensure that the BIS building codes for these zones have been adopted and are rigorously enforced by the municipal bodies. All construction in the government sector in these areas must conform to the BIS code.

(xi) The initial training curriculum of the field staff – VLWs, Karamcharis, Patwaris, Talhatis, Block Agriculture Officers, Block Animal Husbandry Officers other Block Supervisors, State Civil Service Officers, Constables, Subinspectors, Dy S. Ps, etc., in the States vulnerable to hazards may include capsules on basic do's and dont's in case of disasters; disaster mitigation and response, search and rescues techniques, etc. In-service training may be organized for staff already in service.

(xii) Special efforts may be put in for education and awareness. This should include awareness of basic design requirements for constructing private housing in seismic zones IV and V as well as in the belt vulnerable to cyclones.

(xiii) AICTE have been advised to include engineering aspects of disaster mitigation in the engineering courses at the undergraduate level. State Governments may take similar action with reference to engineering colleges under their universities.

(xiv) CBSE have been advised to include basic disaster related material in textbooks for classes 8th, 9th and 10th – the basic do's and dont's/precaution to be taken, etc. State Government may advise their Secondary Boards of Education to include similar in their textbooks.

8.7 MINISTRY OF HOME AFFAIRS (NDM DIVISION)

Disaster Management Existing Framework and New Initiatives

Existing Framework

1. In the federal set up of India, the basic responsibility for undertaking rescue, relief, and rehabilitation measures in the event of a disaster is that of the State Government concerned. The Central Government supplements the efforts of State Governments by providing financial and logistic support in case of major disasters. At the State level, response, relief and rehabilitation are handled by Departments of Relief and Rehabilitation. The State Crisis Management Committee is set up under the Chairmanship of Chief Secretary who is the highest executive functionary in the State. All the concerned departments and organizations of the State and Central Government Departments located in the State are represented in this Committee. This Committee reviews the action taken for response and relief and gives guidelines/directions as necessary.

2. A control room is established under the Relief Commissioner. The control room is in constant touch with the climate monitoring/forecasting agencies and monitors the action being taken by various agencies in performing their responsibilities.

3. The district level is the key level for disaster management and relief activities. The District Magistrate/Collector/Dy. Commissioner is the chief administrator in the district. He is the focal point in the preparation of district plans and in directing, supervising, and monitoring calamity relief. A District Level Coordination and Relief Committee is constituted and is headed by the Collector as Chairman with the participation of all other related government and non-governmental agencies and departments in addition to the elected representatives. The Collector is required to maintain close liaison with the State Government as well as the nearest units of Armed Forces/Central police organizations and other relevant Central Government organizations like Ministries of communications, water resources, drinking water, surface transport, who could supplement the efforts of the district administration in the rescue and relief operations. The District Magistrate/Collector and the Coordination Committee under him reviews preparedness measures prior to an impending hazard and coordinates response when the hazard strikes. As all the departments at the district level report to the Collector, there is an effective coordination mechanism ensuring holistic response.

4. Each State Government has relief manuals/codes which identify the role of each department in the State for managing the natural disasters. These are reviewed and updated periodically based on the experience of managing the disasters and the need of the State.

Funding Mechanisms

5. The policy and the funding mechanism for provision of relief assistance to those affected by natural calamities is clearly laid down. These are reviewed by the Finance Commission appointed by the Government of India every five years. The Finance Commission makes recommendation regarding the division of tax and non-tax revenues between the Central and the State Governments and also regarding policy for provision of relief assistance and the share of expenditure thereon. A Calamity Relief Fund (CRF) has been set up in each State as per the recommendations of the Eleventh Finance Commission. The size of the Calamity Relief Fund has been fixed by the Finance Commission after taking into account the expenditure on relief and rehabilitation over the past ten years.

   The Government of India contributes 75 per cent of the corpus of the Calamity Relief Fund in each State, 25 per cent is contributed by the State. The requirement of funds for response and relief is met from the CRF. Overall norms for relief assistance are laid down by a national committee with representatives of States as members. Different States can have state-specific norms to be recommended by State level committee under the Chief Secretary. Where the calamity is of such proportion that the funds available in the CRF will not be sufficient for provision of relief, the State seeks assistance from the National Calamity Contingency Fund (NCCF). When such requests are received, the requirements are assessed by a team from the Central Government and thereafter the assessed requirements are assessed by a Central team and thereafter the requirements are placed before an Inter-ministerial Group chaired by the Home Secretary. A High Level Committee chaired by the Home Minister with the Agriculture Minister, Finance Minister, and the Deputy Chairman – Planning Commission take decision regarding the release of assistance from the NCCF based on the report of the Central Team and the recommendations of the IMG thereon. In brief, the institutional arrangements for response and relief are well established and have proved to be robust and effective.

Role of Central Government

6. At the national level, the Ministry of Home Affairs is the nodal Ministry for all matters concerning disaster management except drought, which continues to be handled by the Ministry of Agriculture. The Central Relief Commissioner (CRC) in the Ministry of Home Affairs is the nodal officer for coordinating relief assistance for the natural and man-made disasters. The CRC receives information relating to forecasting/warning of a natural calamity from India Meteorological Department (IMD) or from Central Water Commission of Ministry of Water Resources on a continuing basis. These forecasts are also concurrently passed on to the State by the Agencies responsible for early warning. Whenever assistance is required by the States for handling a natural calamity, the assistance is coordinated by the Ministry of Home Affairs. Nodal Officers have been appointed in each Ministry/Department responsible for emergency support functions in the event of a disaster. The Central Relief Commissioner coordinates with the Nodal Officers to ensure that the requisite assistance is made available to the State.

Transfer of Subject

7. The subject of disaster management (except drought and epidemics) was transferred to the Ministry of Home Affairs from the Ministry of Agriculture in 2002. The change in the

Government of India (Allocation of Business) Rules, 1961 was made in February 2002. The actual transfer of work took place only in June 2002.

Change in Orientation

8. Prior to the transfer, the focus had been entirely on post-disaster relief and rehabilitation. Very little, if any, attention was paid to mitigation and preparedness. We have brought about a radical change in orientation – emphasizing mitigation, prevention, and preparedness. A strategic framework/road map has been drawn up with the approval of former Dy. Prime Minister and action is being taken as per the road map. A copy of the road map is at Annexure-I.

National Policy on Disaster Management

9. Despite the fact that we lose thousands of lives and property worth thousands of crore each year in disasters, we have not had a National Policy on Disaster Management. Where a number of ministries or where a broad segment of government is involved; it is useful to have a National Policy as it serves as a framework for action by all the relevant ministries/departments. A National Policy on Disaster Management has been drafted. In line with the changed focus, the policy proposes to integrate disaster mitigation into developmental planning.

Institutional Changes

10. The primary objective is to change the focus from relief and rehabilitation to mitigation and preparedness. MHA is working towards putting in place institutions which will reflect this holistic approach. The States have been advised (HS had written to all Chief Secretaries and the former Dy. Prime Minister has also written to all Chief Ministers in this regard) to convert their Departments of Relief and Rehabilitation into Department of Disaster Management. Ten States/UTs – Andhra Pradesh, Arunachal Pradesh, Bihar, Himachal Pradesh, Rajasthan, Tamil Nadu, Uttaranchal, Nagaland, Andaman and Nicobar Administration, and Lakshadweep have already acted on this.

11. The exercise of reducing vulnerabilities of mitigation or of preparedness or in fact of response is multidisciplinary. It involves a number of ministries/departments. Unfortunately, till date all departments have had the feeling that disaster management/response is the responsibility of the department of relief and rehabilitation alone. The States have, therefore, been advised to set up Disaster Management Authorities under the Chief Minister with the Ministers of Water Resources, Agriculture, Home, Health, PWD, Animal Husbandry, Urban Development and other Ministers who may be relevant as members. Eleven States and UTs – Tamil Nadu, Arunachal Pradesh, Uttaranchal, Orissa, Gujarat, Kerala, Nagaland, Delhi, Goa, A&N administration, and Chandigarh administration have notified the authority. The other States are in the process of setting up similar authorities.

12. At the National level, a National Emergency Management Agency is being set up. The proposal for setting up NEMA and building up specialized capabilities was considered by the Committee of Secretaries (COS) on April 21, 2004. Based on the recommendations of the COS, the Note for the Empowered Group of Ministers on Disaster Management is being revised for submission to Home Minister for approval.

Disaster Management Codes

13. In line with the changed approach, we are converting the relief codes into Disaster Management Codes by building into it the process necessary for drawing up disaster management and mitigation plans as well as elements of preparedness apart from response and relief. A Committee constituted under the Executive Director, National institute of Disaster Management is expected to submit the draft to the Ministry by June 30, 2004.

MITIGATION

Twelfth Finance Commission

14. The terms of Reference of the Twelfth Finance Commission were changed from what it was for the Eleventh Finance Commission so as to cover mitigation. A memorandum has been drawn up and sent to the Commission. In the memorandum, we have proposed a Disaster Mitigation Fund of ₹ 10,000 crore under which we will be assisting the States to take up mitigation projects.

Core Group on Earthquake Mitigation

15. A Core Group on Earthquake Mitigation has been set up having the most eminent authorities on earthquake engineering in the country as members. The States in seismic zones III, IV, and V have been advised to change their building bye-laws to incorporate the BIS codes for safe construction in the seismic zones. Some States have done this already. In order to help other States, a committee has been set up to draw up model building bye-laws and development control regulation for adoption by the States/UTs. The committee is expected to submit its report to the ministry by June 15, 2004.

16. Bureau of Indian Standards (BIS) is mandated to develop national codes and practices for design and construction of housing and all infrastructure projects. Structural safety of the built environment can be ensured only when these codes are observed in design and construction of all projects. These codes/documents need to be revised at regular intervals based on change in hazard zonation, building performance in past disasters and outcomes of research projects. It was observed that these codes are not revised periodically even though BIS is expected to do this once in every five years. A committee consisting of representatives of Ministry of Consumer Affairs, BIS and MHA is being constituted to review the development of codes relevant to earthquake risk mitigation and the protocol for revision by BIS. Availability to these codes in different parts of the country is also an issue as was observed in the studies post-Latur (1993) and Kachhh (2001) earthquakes. BIS has been advised to develop a plan of action to streamline revision of existing codes, development of new codes/documents/ commentaries and availability of codes all over the country including online access to codes related to earthquake risk reduction.

Training of Engineers/Architects/Masons in Seismically Safe Building Design and Construction

17. It has been observed that even where bye-laws have been amended to incorporate the BIS codes, these are not being implemented. The reason is that the engineers/architects practising in private sector are not trained in the relevant codes and neither are the engineers in the

regulatory bodies (the municipality/development authority). A project costing about ₹ 12.36 crore has been approved, wherein the municipal engineers of all cities in the seismic zones will be trained in the BIS codes as well as revised bye-laws, and certificate courses will be organized for engineers practising in the private sector. Eleven National Resource Institutes have been selected for imparting training to the Faculty Members of Civil Engineering Departments of State Resource Institutes.

State Governments are in the process of nominating the State Resource Institutes (Engineering Colleges) and the Faculty Members to be trained. A 6-week training module has been finalised for this purpose. The State Resource Institutes will train 10,000 engineers throughout the country in safe earthquake resistant constructions. They will also assist the State Governments in putting in place an appropriate techno-legal regime, in developing appropriate IEC materials, and in conducting the detailed evaluation of lifeline buildings and make recommendations for retro-fitting, where necessary. A copy of the approved programme for capacity building of engineers in earthquake risk management is at Annexure-II. A similar programme for training of 10,000 architects in conjunction with Indian Institute of Architects/Council of Architecture has been formulated and is under submission for approval.

18. Masons play an important role in construction of buildings and critical infrastructure. For most of the rural and many urban constructions, mason is the architect, engineer and builder. There is no formal system of training of masons in construction of multihazard resistant built environment. A programme to assist the States/UTs in training and certification of 30,000 masons in consultation with HUDCO and MORD is under formulation. The training module for masons to include multihazard resistant construction is under preparation by a committee constituted and revised curriculum will be a part of the vocational training programme of MHRD.

Awareness Campaign

19. This in itself will not be sufficient unless the people living in the seismic zones are also made aware of their vulnerability as well as the means of reducing that vulnerability. A nationwide media campaign is proposed. The Home Secretary had taken a meeting with the Secretary (I&B), DG, Doordarshan, and DG, DAVP to discuss this. In pursuance of this meeting, a Steering Committee was set up under the Chairmanship of Secretary (BM) to consider the matter in detail. The Prasar Bharti proposed to the Steering Committee that they may be given an opportunity to draw up the media plan. Prasar Bharti have made a presentation submitted a plan/proposal on the media campaign. The matter will be considered further by the Steering Committee in its next meeting scheduled to be held shortly.

Earthquake Engineering in Undergraduate Engineering Curricula

20. Uptil now, earthquake engineering was not a part of the undergraduate engineering curriculum which was the reason for the structural engineers not being aware of the elements necessary for earthquake resistant construction. A draft curriculum has been finalized for incorporation in the undergraduate engineering courses to be introduced from the current academic year. A similar curriculum has been finalized for architects, to be introduced in the Schools of Planning and Architecture.

Awareness Generation for Safe Construction in Rural Areas

21. For the rural areas, where people go for non-engineered construction, the strategy is of awareness generation by distribution of pamphlets bringing out essential features, which need to be incorporated into the construction so that it is safe; and of training the masons. Samples of pamphlets/posters which could be circulated have been compiled, and have been made available to States for adoption/translation into local languages.

Retrofitting of Lifeline Buildings

22. The above measures will take care of the future building stock. Insofar as existing building stock is concerned, these will need retrofitting. Since it is not possible to retrofit all the buildings, the focus is on lifeline buildings/buildings where people congregate – hospitals, schools, cinema halls, multistoried complexes, etc. The Home Secretary has written to the Chairman, Railway Board, Health Secretary, Secretary (Civil Aviation), Secretary (Power), and Secretary (Telecom) requesting them to have the railway stations, hospitals and airports/airport control towers, power stations and telecommunication installations located in the seismic zone, examined to see whether they need retrofitting, and, if so, to take action accordingly. They have also been requested to ensure that future construction in the seismic zones incorporate the features essential for safe construction as per the BIS code for that zone.

Earthquake Risk Mitigation Project

23. An Earthquake Mitigation Project has been drawn up, with an estimated cost of ₹ 1,039 crore. That project has been given in-principle clearance by the Planning Commission. The project is being submitted for in principle approval of Home Minister. Thereafter, the project will be appraised by the Committee on Non-plan Expenditure (CNE) before it is submitted for the approval of the Cabinet.

Urban Earthquake Vulnerability Reduction

24. Pending the clearance of the larger project, a project for earthquake mitigation in 38 identified cities which are in seismic zones III, IV, and V and which have a population of more than half a million as well as in other cities/areas covered under the GoI-UNDP project in 169 districts in 17 multihazard-prone States has been taken up. One hundred and eighteen orientation courses have been organized for engineers and architects on the BIS codes for seismically safe construction in 38 cities. Awareness generation programme has been started in these cities. These cities are also being assisted to change their building bye-laws. City disaster management plans are being developed under the project.

Cyclone Monitoring and Mitigation Group

25. A Cyclone Monitoring and Mitigation Group has been set up. This group is looking at protocols for cyclone warning and also the observation/monitoring platform which need to be strengthened. A project has been taken up with the United States for upgradation of models for cyclone track prediction.

Cyclone Risk Mitigation Project

26. A project for Cyclone Mitigation (estimated cost ₹ 1,050 crore) has been drawn up in consultation with the cyclone-prone States. This project envisages construction of cyclone shelters, coastal shelter belt plantation in areas which are prone to storm surges, strengthening of warning systems, training, and education, etc. This project has also been given in-principle clearance by the Planning Commission and the World Bank has agreed in principle to provide funding for the project. The project has been posed to the World Bank through Department of Economic Affairs. Counterpart funding will have to be provided in the plan budget.

GoI-UNDP Disaster Risk Management Project

27. One hundred and sixty-nine districts in seventeen multihazard-prone States have been taken up under the GoI-UNDP project. Under this project, the States are being assisted to draw up State, district and block disaster management plans; village disaster management plans are being developed in conjunction with the panchayati raj institutions and disaster management teams consisting of village volunteers are being trained in various preparedness and response functions such as search and rescue, first aid, relief coordination, shelter management, etc. Equipment needs for district and State Emergency Operation Centres have been identified by the State nodal agencies and equipment is being provided to these EOCs. Orientation training of masons, engineers, and architects in disaster resistant technology have been initiated in these districts and construction of model demonstration buildings will be started soon. A statement showing the achievements under the DRM programme from September 2002 to March 2004 is at Annexure-III.

Mainstreaming Mitigation in Rural Development Schemes

28. The Ministry of Home Affairs is working with the Ministry of Rural Development for changing the guidelines so that the houses constructed under IAY or school buildings/community buildings constructed under SGRY are earthquake/cyclone/flood resistant; as also that the schemes addressing mitigation are given priority under SGRY. Ministry of Rural Development are carrying out an exercise for this purpose. The matter is being closely followed up with that Ministry.

NE States and A&N Islands

29. A special focus is being given to North-Eastern States and the Andaman and Nicobar Islands. The North-Eastern Council has been made the nodal agency for the NE States. The NEC has been provided with a resource person/advisor in disaster management. A detailed presentation on the vulnerabilities of the NE region and the need for comprehensive disaster management plan was given to the Governor of Assam and Chairman, NEC. An action plan has been drawn up by NEC, which has been discussed in the Governing Body meeting of the NEC and a declaration namely "Shillong Declaration" has been adopted by all States in the NE region for integrating disaster management with development planning. One hundred and fourty officials and non-officials have been trained in disaster management to act as resource persons for the NE region.

30. For A&N Islands, a disaster management plan has been drawn up. This plan was discussed in a meeting of October 16, 2003 and cleared a Draft Disaster Management Regulations for A&N Islands have also been vetted.

Preparedness

Specialist Response Teams

31. Eight battalions of CPMFs are being converted into specialist response teams for responding to emergencies/disasters as well. Two training institutions – CISF/ NISA, Hyderabad and the ITBP/BTC, Bhanu (near Chandigarh) have been developed as nodal institutions for training the trainers as well as the teams. The training centres of CRPF(CTC-II at Coimbatore) and BSF Academy, Tekanpur have also been identified to impart such training to the teams from CRPF and BSF. Sixteen teams have already been trained at NISA, Hyderabad and BTC, Bhanu and training of more teams is continuing. Training of trainers of CRPF and BSF will be conducted at NISA, Hyderabad in June and September 2004, respectively.

National Emergency Response Force

32. It is proposed to constitute these eight battalions into a special force called the National Emergency Response Force (NERF). The elements which need financial sanction have already been included in the Note for the Empowered Group of Ministers on Disaster Management.

33. The States have also been advised to set up their own specialist teams for responding to disasters. They have been advised that we will provide assistance for training of trainers. Resources have been an important constraint for the States. We have, therefore, with the concurrence of the Finance Ministry, provided that 10 per cent of the annual inflows into the CRF can be used for the procurement of search and rescue equipment and communication equipment.

34. Apart from the eight battalions which are being developed into specialist units, it was decided that all the CPMFs should have the basic expertise in search and rescue so that they can be requisitioned for search and rescue by the States/district administration. A curriculum for this has been drawn up and integrated into the training curricula of the CPMFs.

Fire Services as Multihazard Response Units

35. In order to further strengthen our capacity for response, the fire services are proposed to be developed into multihazard response units (as is the practice in other countries). This will require additional equipment and training. A project for this (with an estimated cost of ₹ 2,457 crore) has been drawn up. The Planning Commission has given in-principle clearance to the project. The project is being submitted for in-principle approval of Home Minister. A note for the Committee on Non-plan Expenditure is being finalized.

Regional Response Centres

36. Regional response centres are being set up. Fourteen regional response centres have been identified – these are group centres or battalion headquarters where a cache of essential search and rescue equipment will be stored so that they can respond to any disaster in the neighbouring States immediately. Proposals for the cache of equipments are under consideration of Finance.

Emergency Operations Centres

37. The States are being assisted to set up control rooms/emergency operations centres at the State and district level. Assistance for this is being given under the GoI – UNDP project in the States covered by the project. Assistance under the Modernization of Police Scheme is also available for setting up EOCs.

38. The MHA Control Room has been strengthened with some additional equipment – SATPHONES and GPS and staff trained in their operation. A state of the art National EOC with superior structural features and communication facilities is proposed to be set up. A Committee of CPWD/BARC/DRDO has been constituted to finalize the design parameters. The project will be executed by CPWD and is scheduled to be completed by June 2006.

Communication System

39. The communication network between the national and the state EOCs and the site of the emergency/crises is currently based on the DOT network. It has been observed that in a calamity/hazard, communication is the first casualty. It is therefore decided to put in place multimode and multichannel communication systems so that enough redundancy is available. It has been decided that the POLNET will also be used for disaster management; and for this the POLNET communication facility will be extended to SDMs and Collectors as well as the Emergency Operation Centres. For emergency communications, discussions have also been held with the Department of Space (ISRO). They will be making available alternate satellite communication units to connect with State EOCs and mobile units which can be transported to the site of a disaster. A group had been set up for drawing up a communication plan for disaster management and the said group has submitted its report. This provides for a dedicated communication system for disaster management with built in redundancies. Phase I of the National Disaster Management Communication Plan to provide satellite based mobile voice/data/video communication between National EOC/State EOCs/mobile EOCs and remote disaster/emergency sites is under implementation and is expected to be completed by August 2004. Phase II of the communication plan to connect National/State/District EOCs with disaster/emergency sites is proposed to be completed by March 2006. The communication backbone to be used will include terrestrial link (DOT), POLNET, NICNET, ISDN, and SPACENET.

India Disaster Resource Network (IDRN)

40. One major step towards strengthening of our response system has been the launch of India Disaster Resource Network (IDRN). This is a web-based inventory of all specialist equipment required for emergency/disaster response. This will give at the touch of a button the location of specific equipment/specialist resources as well as the controlling authority for that resource so that it can be mobilized for response in the shortest possible time. This was launched on September 1, 2003. This inventory already has about 66,000 records/entries from 534 districts in 29 States/UTs.

Handling of Hazardous Materials

41. In the light of the experience of the Bhopal Gas Tragedy, the Ministry of Home Affairs has been interacting with Ministry of Environment and Forests and new guidelines have been sent to the states for industries handling hazardous materials. It has been prescribed that onsite and

offsite disaster response plans for the industries dealing with hazardous material be updated in consultation with district administration and that this may be rehearsed once every year. It has also been prescribed that these industries will carry-out awareness campaign for the population in the vicinity regarding the do's/dont's in case of any accident involving hazardous material.

Incident Command System

42. In order to professionalise the response, it is proposed to introduce the Incident Command System in the country. This system is in vogue in the United States and it provides for specialist Incident Command Teams with an Incident Commander and officers trained in different aspects of Incident Management – logistics, operations, planning, media management, etc. We are working with the US experts for training of officers in this system here. The LBSNAA, Mussoorrie has been designated as the mother training institution. Three programme for training of trainers has so far been held at LBSNAA. Fourty-two officers-trainers have been trained so far in basic and intermediate ICS course and 29 officers-trainers trained in planning module.

Human Resource Development

43. In order to further professionalize our response, it was decided to incorporate elements of disaster management in the training curriculum of All India Services (IAS, IPS, and Indian Forest Service). Curricula have been drawn up for this purpose and have been integrated into the training curriculum of these All India Services.

Disaster Awareness in School Education

44. It was felt that making disaster awareness a part of school curriculum would be an important step. Disaster awareness/do's and dont's have been made a part of classes – VIII and IX CBSE curricula. It is proposed to incorporate the elements of disaster awareness/do's and dont's in the curriculum of class X in the coming academic year. The State Governments have been advised to take similar steps *vis-à-vis* their school boards. We are working with the Council of Board of School Education (COBSE) to facilitate inclusion of disaster management in public education in all 39 School Boards in the country.

Hospital Preparedness for Emergencies

45. Hospital preparedness is crucial to any disaster response system. For the purpose, each hospital should have an emergency preparedness plan to deal with mass casualties and should be manned by trained health managers. The existing curriculum for medical doctors does not include emergency health management. Therefore, capacity building through in-service training of the current health managers and medical personnel in handling health emergencies is extremely essential. At the same time, the future health managers must acquire these skills systematically through the inclusion of health emergency management in the undergraduate and postgraduate medical curricula. In consultation with Medical Council of India (MCI), two committees have been constituted for preparation of curriculum for introduction of emergency health management in MBBS curriculum, and preparation of in-service training of hospital managers and professionals. Rajiv Gandhi University of Health Sciences, Karnataka have been identified as the lead national resource institution for the purpose.

46. While the Ministry of Health and Family Welfare has issued instructions to the states to evaluate the structural integrity of existing health institutions in high seismic zones and carry-out the necessary retrofitting activities, it is also important to address the integrity of non-structural elements like essential medical equipment as part of hospital preparedness for emergencies. Handling non-structural issues in hospitals would be both part of the envisaged sensitization and training of practising engineers and architects as well as hospital managers and administrators.

Transparency in Relief Operations

47. We are seeking to bring about transparency in relief operations. We have advised the State Governments that whenever relief material is distributed from CRF/NCCF, a list giving the details of the beneficiaries along with quantity/volume of relief distributed may be prepared ward-wise both for urban and rural areas and be made available to local representatives in panchayats and municipalities and should also be displayed there. The consolidated list should also be maintained at the block level/taluka level and made available to the general public on demand.

Civil Defence

48. A Committee was constituted to review the set up of Civil Defence. The Committee has given its recommendation based on which draft proposals are being formulated. CNE Notes for upgradation of National Civil Defence College and National Fire Service College are also under process. A Cabinet Note for strengthening of Civil Defence Organization is under preparation.

Status Report

49. A Status Report on Disaster Management in India was prepared in February 2004 for presentation and circulation in the World Congress on Natural Disaster Mitigation. The Report summarizes various initiatives taken by the Ministry. A copy of the Status Report (Red Book) is enclosed.

8.8 INFORMATION TECHNOLOGY AND NATURAL DISASTER MANAGEMENT IN INDIA

Abstract

It may be observed that advancement in Information Technology in the form of Internet, GIS, Remote Sensing, satellite communication, etc., can help a great deal in planning and implementation of hazards reduction measures. GIS can improve the quality and power of analysis of natural hazards assessments, guide development activities and assist planners in the selection of mitigation measures and in the implementation of emergency preparedness and response action. Remote sensing, on the other hand, as a tool can very effectively contribute towards identification of hazardous areas, monitor the planet for its changes on a real time basis, and give early warning to many impending disasters. Communication satellites have become vital for providing emergency communication and timely relief measures. Integration of space technology inputs into natural disaster monitoring and mitigation mechanisms is critical for hazard reduction. It is absolutely necessary to create awareness among the public as well as decision makers for allocating resources for appropriate investments in information technology. In this paper, an attempt has been made to highlight the role of information technology in management of natural disasters in India.

1. Introduction

It is a well known fact that natural disasters strikes countries, both developed and developing, causing enormous destruction and creating human sufferings and producing negative impacts on national economies. Due to diverse geo-climatic conditions prevalent in different parts of the globe, different types of natural disasters like floods, droughts, earthquakes, cyclones, landslides, volcanoes, etc., strikes according to the vulnerability of the area. India is considered as the world's most disaster-prone country. It has witnessed devastating natural disasters in recent past like droughts, floods, cyclones, earthquakes, landslides, etc.

2. Natural Disasters in India

India is a large country and prone to a number of natural hazards. Among all the natural disasters that country faces, river floods are the most frequent and often devastating. The shortfall in the rainfall cause droughts or drought-like situation in various parts of the country. The country has faced some severe earthquakes causing widespread damage to the life and property. India has a coastline of about 8,000 kms. which is prone to very severe cyclonic formations in the Arabian Sea and Bay of Bengal. Another major problem faced by the country is in the form of landslides and avalanches.

With an increase in the perception towards spreading a culture of prevention in the disaster management scenario, considerable emphasis is now being placed on research and development activities in the area of information technology for disaster preparedness and prevention. This has brought in a significant positive change even though the multitude and frequency of disasters in the country has increased.

3. Application of Information Technology in Disaster Management

Although it is not possible to completely avoid the natural disasters, but the sufferings can be minimized by creating proper awareness of the likely disasters and its impact by developing a suitable warning system, disaster preparedness and management of disasters through application of information technology tools. The changing trends have opened up a large number of scientific and technological resources and skills to reduce disaster risk. The IT tools are discussed below:

3.1 GIS and Remote Sensing: GIS provides a tool for effective and efficient storage and manipulation of remotely sensed data and other spatial and non-spatial data types for both scientific management and policy-oriented information. This can be used to facilitate measurement, mapping, monitoring, and modelling of variety of data types related to natural phenomenon. The specific GIS application in the field of risk assessment are: Hazard Mapping to show earthquake, landslides, floods or fire hazards. This map could be created for cities, districts, or even for the entire country and tropical cyclone threat maps are used by meteorological departments to improve the quality of the tropical storm warning services and quickly communicate the risk to the people likely to get affected by the cyclone. Remote sensing makes observation of any object from a distance without coming into actual contact.

measures. This enable the States to manage and provide for calamity relief on their own by drawing upon the resources available with a fund constituted for that purpose separately for each state. In addition to CRF, a National Fund for Calamity Relief (NFCR) has been created to deal with hazards of rare severity managed by a National Calamity Relief Committee (NCRC). The State Governments are required to submit memoranda for this purpose giving details of damage and destruction and the cost of relief and rehabilitation. On receipt of these memoranda, the Government of India decides on an individual basis whether a Central team is required to be deputed to assess the situation.

6. Administrative Structure of Disaster Management in India

The Department of Agriculture and Cooperation (DAC) in the Ministry of Agriculture, Government of India, is the nodal department for all matters concerning natural disasters relief at the Centre. The National Contingency Action Plan (CAP) facilitates launching of relief and rescue operations without delay. There are various committees at the national level for disaster management such as Cabinet Committee for effective implementation of relief measures in the wake of natural calamity; National Crisis Management Committee at the national level headed by the Cabinet Secretary who is in charge of various types of disasters and supporting ministries as members; Crisis Management Group reviews various measures required for dealing with a natural disaster, and coordinates activities of the Central ministries and the State Governments pertaining to disaster preparedness and relief and obtains information from nodal officers on measures relating to the above. Figure 8.1 shows the interaction pattern in the government.

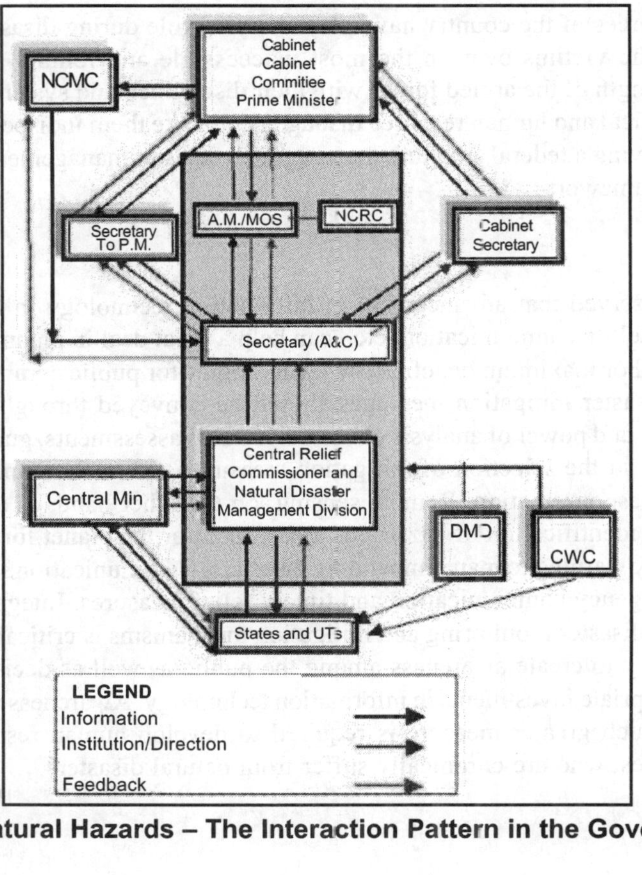

Figure 8.1: Natural Hazards – The Interaction Pattern in the Government

The State Governments are autonomous in organizing relief operations in the event of natural disaster and a long-term preparedness/rehabilitation measures. The State Governments efforts are supplemented by Central Government. There is a State Crisis Management Group (SCMC) under the Chairmanship of Chief Secretary/Relief Commissioner to take into consideration the infrastructure and guidance received, from time-to-time, from Government of India and formulate action plans for dealing with different natural disasters.There is a State Level Control Room set up whenever a disaster situation develops.

States are further divided into districts, each headed by the District Collector (also known as the District Magistrate or Deputy Commissioner), who is the focal point at the district level for directing, supervising, and monitoring relief measures for disaster and for preparation of district level plans. The Collector exercises coordinating and supervisory powers over functionaries of all the departments at the District level. The relief measures are reviewed by the District Relief Committee consisting of official and non-official members, including local legislators and members of parliament. In the wake of natural disasters, a control room is set up in the district for day-to-day monitoring of the rescue and relief operations on a continuing basis.

The Collector/Deputy Commissioner maintains close liaison with the Central Government authorities in the districts, namely, Army, Air Force an Navy, Ministry of Water Resources, etc., who supplement the effort of the District Administration in the rescue and relief operation.They also coordinates all voluntary efforts by mobilising the non-government organizations capable of working in such situations.

The armed forces of the country have played a vital role during disaster emergencies providing prompt relief to the victims even in the most inaccessible and remote areas of the country. The organizational strength of the armed forces with their disciplined and systematised approach, and with their skills in technical and human resource management make them indispensable for such emergency situations. India having a federal structure the integrated disaster management mechanism exists within the government framework.

7. Conclusions

It may be observed that advancement in information technology in the form of internet, GIS, remote sensing, satellite communication, etc., can help a great deal in planning and implementation of hazards reduction. For maximum benefit, new technologies for public communication should be made use and natural disaster mitigation messages should be conveyed through these measures. GIS can improve the quality and power of analysis of natural hazards assessments, guide development activities, and assist planners in the selection of mitigation measures and in the implementation of emergency preparedness and response action. Remote sensing, on the other hand, as a tool can very effectively contribute towards identification of hazardous areas, monitor the planet for its changes on a real time basis, and give early warning to many impending disasters. Communication satellites have become vital for providing emergency communication and timely relief measures. Integration of space technology inputs into natural disaster monitoring and mitigation mechanisms is critical for hazard reduction. It is absolutely necessary to create awareness among the public as well as decision makers for allocating resources for appropriate investments in information technology. Awareness and training in information technology in a much greater measure is required to develop human resources, particularly in the developing countries, who are chronically suffer from natural disasters.

The disasters usually occur in the well-defined areas, even though the community does not know the coping mechanism for the disaster. The disaster mitigation programmes must be extensively taken up covering various aspects at national level to minimize the disaster damages. There should be a greater emphasis on development of new technologies in disaster mitigation. The disaster preparedness and awareness is the only effective way of mitigating the impact of future disasters.

Forecasting and Warning of Disasters in India

India has elaborate, modernized cyclone detection and tracking systems, flood forecasting and warning systems covering major rivers and drought monitoring arrangements.

India has three crucial disaster warning systems:

1. The Indian Meteorological Department to look at drought, rainfall, cyclone, and crop position.
2. The Department of Space that undertakes satellite monitoring of drought and floods.
3. The Ministry of Water Resources which investigates riparian floods. The Meteorological Department has a coastal network of 10 cyclone detection radars, but the main instrument is the INSAT-IB.

Notwithstanding sophisticated warning systems for forecasting, the inadequacy of communication networks at local offices makes dissemination of warnings to the block level rather difficult.

Even if communication reaches block offices in time, absence of vehicles make it difficult for officials to disseminate information and organize evacuation in an emergency. This is particularly so in the case of far-flung, inaccessible villages, islets, or deltas.

Indian Meteorological Department (IMD)

The Director General of Meteorology is the Head of the India Meteorological Department, with headquarters at New Delhi. Four Additional Directors General are based in New Delhi and one in Pune (Maharashtra) and 20 Deputy Directors General, of which ten are located in New Delhi as the main functionaries of the IMD.

There are six Regional Meteorological Centres, each under a Deputy Director General with headquarters at Mumbai (Maharashtra), Chennai (Tamil Nadu), New Delhi, Kolkata (West Bengal), Nagpur (Maharashtra), and Guwahati (Assam).

Under the administrative control of the Deputy Director General are such operational units as Meteorological Centres at State capitals, forecasting offices, agrometeorological advisory service centres, flood meteorological offices, area cyclone warning centres, and cyclone warning centres.

In addition, separate divisions deal with specialized subjects such as:

- Agricultural meteorology
- Civil aviation
- Climatology
- Hydrometeorology

- ❖ Instrumentation
- ❖ Meteorological Telecommunication
- ❖ Regional Specialised Meteorological Centre
- ❖ Positional Astronomy
- ❖ Satellite Meteorology
- ❖ Seismology
- ❖ Training

The Council for Meteorology and Atmospheric Sciences (CMAS) under the chairmanship of the Secretary, Department of Science and Technology, is responsible for formulating and implementing the policies and programmes of the IMD.

Cyclones: IMD has Cyclone Warning Centres (ACWCS) and the necessary infrastructure to formulate and disseminate cyclone warnings. In addition, IMD has a satellite-based communication system called Cyclone Warning Dissemination System for direct cyclone warnings to the cyclone-prone coastal areas. A Cyclone Warning Division in New Delhi coordinates and supervises the entire cyclone warning programmes in the country.

Earthquakes: The IMD also operates a national network of 36 seismic stations for recording seismological observations, which have generated a substantive database over the years.

Rainfall: IMD monitors rainfall at the district level and makes long-range rainfall forecasts based on the parametric power regression model. These forecasts are utilised for drought mitigation planning.

Central Water Commission (CWC)

Flood forecasting is the most reliable, cost-effective, and non-structural measure for flood loss mitigation. The CWC runs a network of 157 flood forecasting stations located at various rivers in 12 States and one union territory.

These centres issue daily flood forecasts and warnings throughout the flood season from May to October. For achieving greater accuracy, the CWC has a procedure of carrying out a self-analysis and appraisal of the forecasting network at the end of the monsoon season.

The CWC also maintains consolidated national figures for losses incurred due to floods in various States, which assists in making allocations from the CRF.

8.9 DISASTER MANAGEMENT ACT, 2005

Disaster Management Act, 2005

An Act to provide for the effective management of disasters and for matters connected therewith or incidental thereto.

Be it enacted by Parliament in the 56th year of Republic of India as follows:

CHAPTER I: Preliminary

1. Short title, extent, and commencement.

   (a) This Act may be called the Disaster Management Act, 2005.

   (b) It extends to the whole of India.

   (c) It shall come into force on such date as the Central Government, may by its notification in the Official Gazette appoint; and different dates may be appointed for different provisions of this Act and for different States, and any reference to the commencement in any provision of this Act in relation to any State shall be construed as a reference to the commencement of that provision in that State.

2. Definitions: In this Act unless the context otherwise requires:

   (a) "Affected acre" means an area or part of the country affected by a disaster

   (b) "Capacity building" includes

      (i) Identification of existing resources and recourses to be acquired or created.

      (ii) Acquiring or creating resources identified under sub-clause (i).

      (iii) Organization and training of personnel and coordination of such training for effective management of disasters.

   (c) "Central Government" means the Ministry or Department of the Government of India having administrative control of disaster management.

   (d) "Disaster" means a catastrophe, mishap calamity, or grace occurrence in any area, arising from natural or man-made causes, or by accident or negligence which results in substantial loss of life or human suffering or damage to, and destruction of property or damage to, or degradation of, environment, and is of such a nature or magnitude as to be beyond the coping capacity of the community of the affected area.

   (e) "Disaster management" means a continuous and integrated process of planning, organizing, coordinating, and implementing measures which are necessary or expedient for:

      (i) Prevention of danger or threat of any disaster,

      (ii) Mitigation or reduction of risk of any disaster or its severity or consequences,

      (iii) Capacity building,

      (iv) Preparedness to deal with any disaster,

      (v) Prompt response to any threatening disaster situation or disaster,

      (vi) Assessing the severity of magnitude of effects of any disaster,

      (vii) Rehabilitation and reconstruction.

   (f) "District Authority" means the District Disaster Management Authority constituted under sub-section (1) of section 25,

   (g) "District Plan" means the plan for disaster management for the district prepared under section 31,

(h) "Local Authority" includes Panchayat Raj Institutions, Municipalities, a District Board, Cantonment Board, Town Planning Authority or Zilla Parishad or any other body or Authority, by whatever name, called, for the time being invested by law, for rendering essential services or, with the control and management of civic services within a specified local area,

(i) "Mitigation" means measures aimed at reducing the risk, impact, or effects of a disaster or threatening disaster situation,

(j) "National Authority" means the National Disaster Management Authority established under sub-section(1) of section 3,

(k) "National Executive Committee" means the Executive Committee of the National Authority constituted under sub-section (1) of section 8,

(l) "National Plan" means the plan for disaster management for the whole of the country prepared under section 11,

(m) "Preparedness" means the State of readiness to deal with a threatening disaster situation or disaster and the effects thereof,

(n) "Prescribed" means prescribed by the rules made under this Act,

(o) "Reconstruction" means construction or restoration of any property after a disaster,

(p) "Resources" includes manpower, services, materials, and provisions,

(q) "State Authority" means the State Disaster Management Authority established under sub-section (1) of section 14 and includes the Disaster Management Authority for the Union Territory constituted under that section.

(r) "State Executive Committee" means the Executive Committee of a State Authority constituted under sub-section (1) of section 20,

(s) "State Government" means the Department of Government of the State having administrative control of disaster management and includes Administrator of the Union Territory appointed by the President under Article 239 of the Constitution,

(t) "State Plan" means the plan for disaster management for the whole of the State prepared under section 23.

CHAPTER II: The National Disaster Management Authority

3. The Establishment of National Disaster Management Authority:

(a) With effect from such date as the Central Government, may by notification in the Official Gazette appoint in this behalf, there shall be established for the purpose of this Act, an Authority to be known as the National Disaster Management Authority.

(b) The National Authority shall consist of the Chairperson of such number of other members, not exceeding nine, as may be prescribed by the Central Government and, unless the rules otherwise provide, the National Authority shall consist of the following:

(i) The Prime Minister of India, who shall be the Chairperson of the National Authority, *ex-officio*,

(ii) Other members, not exceeding nine, to be nominated by the Chairperson of the National Authority.

(c) The Chairperson of the National Authority may designate one of the members nominated under clause (b) of sub-section (2) to be the Vice Chairperson of the National Authority.

(d) The term of office and conditions of service of members of the National Authority shall be such as may be prescribed.

4. Meetings of National Authority:

(a) The National Authority shall meet as and when necessary and at such time and place as the Chairperson of the National Authority may think fit.

(b) The Chairperson of the National Authority shall preside over the meetings of the National Authority.

(c) If for any reason the Chairperson of the National Authority is unable to attend any meeting of the National Authority, the Vice-chairperson of the National Authority shall preside over the meeting.

5. Appointment of officers and other employees of the National Authority:

The Central Government shall provide the National Authority with such officers, consultants and employees, as it considers necessary for carrying out the functions of the National Authority.

6. Powers and functions of the National Authority:

(a) Subject to the provisions of this Act, the National Authority shall have the responsibility for laying down the policies, plans, and guidelines for disaster management for ensuring timely and effective response to disaster.

(b) Without prejudice to generality of the provisions contained in sub-section(1) the National Authority may:

(i) Lay down policies on disaster management,;

(ii) Approve the National Plan,

(iii) Approve plans prepared by the Ministries or Departments of the Government of India in accordance with the National Plan,

(iv) Lay down guidelines to be followed by the State Authorities in drawing up the State Plan,

(v) Lay down guidelines to be followed by the different Ministries or Departments of the Government of India for the purpose of integrating the measures for prevention of disaster or the mitigation of its effects in their development plans and projects,

(vi) Coordinate the enforcement and implementation of the policy and plan for disaster management,

(vii) Recommend provision of funds for the purpose of mitigation,

(viii) Provide such support to other countries affected by major disasters as may be determined by the Central Government,

(ix) Take such other measures for the prevention of disaster, or the mitigation, or preparedness and capacity building for dealing with the threatening disaster situation or disaster as it may consider necessary,

(x) Lay down broad policies and guidelines for the functioning of the National Institute of Disaster Management.

(c) The Chairperson of the National Authority shall, in the case of emergency, have power to exercise all or any of the powers of the National Authority but exercise of such powers shall be subject to *ex-post facto* ratification by the National Authority.

7. Constitution of advisory committee by National Authority:

(a) The National Authority may constitute an advisory committee consisting of experts in the field of disaster management and having practical experience of disaster management at the national, State, or district level to make recommendations on different aspects of disaster management.

(b) The members of the advisory committee shall be paid such allowances as may be prescribed by the Central Government in consultation with the National Authority.

8. Constitution of National Executive Committee:

(a) The Central Government shall, immediately after issue of notification under sub-section (1) of section 3, constitute a National Executive Committee to assist the National Authority in the performance of its functions under this Act.

(b) The National Executive Committee shall consist of the following members, namely:

(i) The Secretary to the Government of India in charge of the Ministry or Department of the Central Government having administrative control of the disaster management, who shall be Chairperson, *ex-officio*,

(ii) The Secretaries to the Government of India in the Ministries or Departments having administrative control of the agriculture, atomic energy, defence, drinking water supply, environment and forests, finance (expenditure) health, power, rural development, science and technology, spare, telecommunication, urban development, water resources and the Chief of the Integrated Defence Staff of the Chiefs of Staff Committee, *ex-officio*.

(c) The Chairperson of the National Executive Committee may invite any other officer of the Central Government or a State Government for taking part in any meeting of the National Executive Committee and shall exercise such powers and perform such functions as may be prescribed by the Central Government in consultation with the National Authority.

(d) The procedure to be followed by the National Executive Committee in exercise of its powers and discharge of its functions shall be such as may be prescribed by the Central Government.

9. Constitution of sub-committees:

(a) The National Executive Committee may, as and when it considers necessary, constitute one or more sub-committees, for the efficient discharge of its functions.

(b) The National Executive Committee shall, from among its members, appoint the Chairperson of the sub-committee referred to in sub-section (1).

(c) Any person associated as an expert with any sub-committee may be paid such allowances as may be prescribed by the Central Government.

10. Powers and functions of National Executive Committee:

(a) The National Executive Committee shall assist the National Authority in the discharge of its functions and have the responsibility for implementing the policies and plans of the National Authority and ensure the compliance of directions issued by the Central Government for the purpose of disaster management in the country.

(b) Without prejudice to the generality of the provisions contained in sub-section (1) the National Executive Committee may:

(i) Act as the coordinating and monitoring body for disaster management,

(ii) Prepare the National Plan to be approved by the National Authority,

(iii) Coordinate and monitor the implementation of the National Policy,

(iv) Lay down guidelines for preparing disaster management plans by different Ministries or Departments of the Government of India and the State Authorities,

(v) Provide necessary technical assistance to the State Government and the State Authorities for preparing their disaster management plans in accordance with the guidelines laid down by the National Authority,

(vi) Monitor the implementation of the National Plan and the plans prepared by the Ministries or Department of the Government of India,

(vii) Monitor the implementation of the guidelines laid down by the National Authority for integrating of measures for prevention of disaster and mitigation by the Ministries or Departments in their development plans and projects,

(viii) Monitor, coordinate, and give directions regarding the mitigation and preparedness measures to be taken by different ministries or departments and agencies of the government,

(ix) Evaluate the preparedness at all governmental levels for the purpose of responding to any threatening disaster situation or disaster and give directions, where necessary, for enhancing such preparedness,

(x) Plan and coordinate specialized training programme for disaster management for different levels of officers, employees, and voluntary rescue workers,

(xi) Coordinate response in the event of any threatening disaster situation or disaster,

(xii) Lay down guidelines for, or give directions to, the concerned Ministries or Departments of the Government of India, the State Governments and the State authorities regarding measures to be taken by them in response to any threatening disaster situation or disaster,

(xiii) Require any department or agency of the government to make available to the National Authority or State Authority such men or material resources as are available with it for the purpose of emergency response, rescue, and relief,

(xiv) Advise, assist, and coordinate the activities of the Ministries or Departments of the Government of India, State Authorities, statutory bodies, other governmental or non-governmental organizations and others engaged in disaster management,

(xv) Provide necessary technical assistance or give advice to the State Authorities and district authorities for carrying out their functions under this Act,

(xvi) Promote general education and awareness in relation to disaster management,

(xvii) Perform such other functions as the National Authority may require it to perform.

11. National Plan

(a) There shall be drawn up a plan for disaster management for the whole of the country to be called the National Plan.

(b) The National Plan shall be prepared by the National Executive Committee having regard to the National Policy and in consultation with the State Governments and expert bodies or organizations in the field of disaster management to be approved by the National Authority.

(c) The National Plan shall include:

(i) Measures to be taken for the prevention of disasters, or the mitigation of their effects,

(ii) Measures to be taken for the integration of mitigation measures in the development plans,

(iii) Measures to be taken for the preparedness and capacity building to effectively respond to any threatening disaster situations or disaster,

(iv) Roles and responsibilities of different ministries or departments of the Government of India in respect of measures specified in clauses (a), (b), and (c).

(d) The National Plan shall be reviewed and updated annually.

(e) Appropriate provisions shall be made by the Central Government for financing the measures to be carried out under the National Plan.

(f) Copies of the National Plan referred to in sub-sections (2) and (4) shall be made available to the Ministries or Departments of the Government of India and such ministries or departments shall draws up their own plans in accordance with the National Plan.

12. Guidelines for minimum standards of relief:

The National Authority shall recommend guidelines for the minimum standards of relief to be provided to persons affected by disaster, which shall include:

(a) The minimum requirements to be provided in the relief camps in relation to shelter, food, drinking water, medical cover, and sanitation.

(b) The special provisions to be made for widows and orphans.

(c) *Ex-gratia* assistance on account of loss of life as also assistance on account of damage to houses and for restoration of means of livelihood.

(d) Such other relief as may be necessary.

13. Relief in loan repayment, etc:

The National Authority may, in cases of disaster of severe magnitude, recommend relief in repayment of loans or for grant of fresh loans to the persons affected by disaster on such concessional terms as may be appropriate.

CHAPTER III: State Disaster Management Authorities

14. Establishment of State Disaster Management Authority:

(a) Every State Government shall, as soon as may be after the issue of the notification under sub-section (1) of section 3, by notification in the Official Gazette, establish a State Disaster Management Authority for the State with such name as may be specified in the notification of the State Government.

(b) A State Authority shall consist of the Chairperson and such number of other members, not exceeding nine, as may be prescribed by the State Government and, unless the rules otherwise provide, the State Authority shall consist of the following members, namely:

(i) The Chief Minister of the State, who shall be Chairperson, *ex-officio*;

(ii) Other members, not exceeding eight, to be nominated by the Chairperson of the State Authority,

(iii) The Chairperson of the State Executive Committee, *ex-officio*.

(c) The Chairperson of the State Authority may designate one of the members nominated under clause (b) of sub-section (2) to be the Vice-chairperson of the State Authority

(d) The Chairperson of the State Executive Committee shall be the Chief Executive Officer of the State Authority, *ex-officio*. Provided that in the case of a Union Territory having Legislative Assembly, except the Union Territory of Delhi, the Chief Minister shall be the Chairperson of the Authority established under this section and in case of other Union Territories the Lieutenant Governor or the Administrator shall be the Chairperson of that Authority; Provided further that the Lieutenant Governor of the Union Territory of Delhi shall be the Chairperson and the Chief Minister thereof shall be the Vice-chairperson of the State Authority.

(e) The term of office and conditions of service of members of the State Authority shall be such as may be prescribed.

15. Meetings of the State Authority:

(a) The State Authority shall meet as and when necessary and at such time and place as the Chairperson of the State Authority may think fit.

(b) The Chairperson of the State Authority shall preside over the meetings of the State Authority.

(c) If for any reason, the Chairperson of the State Authority is unable to attend the meeting of the State Authority, the Vice-chairperson of the State Authority shall preside at the meeting.

16. Appointment of officers and other employees of the State Authority:

The State Government shall provide the State Authority with such officers, consultants, and employees as it considers necessary, for carrying out the functions of the State Authority.

17. Constitution of Advisory Committee by the State Authority:

(a) A State Authority may, as and when it considers necessary, constitute an advisory committee, consisting of experts in the field of disaster management and having practical experience of disaster management to make recommendations on different aspects of disaster management.

(b) The members of the advisory committee shall be paid such allowances as may be prescribed by the State Government.

18. Powers and functions of State Authority:

(a) Subject to the provisions of this Act, a State Authority shall have the responsibility for laying down policies and plans for disaster management in the State.

(b) Without prejudice to the generality of provisions contained in sub-section (1) the State Authority may;

(i) Lay down the State disaster management policy,

(ii) Approve the State Plan in accordance with the guidelines laid down by the National Authority,

(iii) Approve the disaster management plans prepared by the departments of the Government of the State,

(iv) Lay down guidelines to be followed by the departments of the government of the State for the purpose of integration of measures for prevention of disasters and mitigation in their development plans and projects and provide necessary technical assistance therefore,

(v) Coordinate the implementation of the State Plan,

(vi) Recommend provision of funds for mitigation and preparedness measures,

(vii) Review the development plans of the different departments of the State and ensure that prevention and mitigation measures are integrated therein,

(c) The Chairperson of the State Authority shall, in the case of emergency, have power to exercise all or any of the powers of the State Authority but the exercise of such powers shall be subject to *ex-post facto* ratification of the State Authority.

19. Guidelines for minimum standard of relief by State Authority:

The State Authority shall lay down detailed guidelines for providing standards of relief to persons affected by disaster in the stated; provided that such standards shall in no case be less than the minimum standards in the guidelines laid down by the National Authority in this regard.

20. Constitution of State Executive Committee:

(a) The State Government shall, immediately after issue of notification under sub-section (1) of section 14, constitute a State Executive Committee to assist the State Authority in the performance of its functions and to coordinate action in accordance with the guidelines laid down by the State Authority and ensure the compliance of directions issued by the State Government under this Act.

(b) The State Executive Committee shall consist of the following members, namely:

(i) The Chief Secretary to the State Government who shall be Chairperson, *ex-officio*.

(ii) Four Secretaries to the Government of the State of such departments as the State Government may think fit, *ex-officio*.

(c) The Chairperson of the State Executive Committee shall exercise such powers and perform such functions as may be prescribed by the State Government and such other powers and functions as may be delegated to him by the State Authority.

(d) The procedure to be followed by the State Executive Committee in exercise of its powers and discharge of its functions shall be such as may be prescribed by the State Government.

21. Constitution of sub-committees by the State Executive Committee:

(a) The State Executive Committee may, as and when it considers necessary, constitute one or more sub-committees, for efficient discharge of its functions.

(b) The State Executive Committee shall, from among its members, appoint the Chairperson of the sub-committee referred to in sub-section (1).

(c) Any person associated as an expert with any sub-committee may be paid such allowances as may be prescribed by the State Government.

22. Functions of State Executive Committee:

(a) The State Executive Committee shall have the responsibility for implementing the National Plan and State Plan and act as the coordinating and monitoring body for management of disaster in the State.

(b) Without prejudice to the generality of the provisions of sub-section (1), the State Executive Committee may,

(i) Coordinate and monitor the implementation of the National policy, the National Plan and the State Plan,

(ii) Examine the vulnerability of different parts of the State to different forms of disasters and specify measures to be taken for their prevention or mitigation,

(iii) Lay down guidelines for preparation of disaster management plans by the departments of the Government of the State and the District Authorities,

(iv) Monitor the implementation of disaster management plans prepared by the departments of the Government of the State and District Authorities,

(v) Monitor the implementation of the guidelines laid down by the State Authority for integrating of measures for prevention of disaster and mitigation by the departments in their development plans and projects,

(vi) Evaluate preparedness to all governmental or non-governmental levels to respond to any threatening disaster situation or disaster and give directions, where necessary, for enhancing such preparedness,

(vii) Coordinate response in the event of any threatening disaster situation or disaster,

(viii) Give directions to any Department of the Government of the State or any other Authority or body in the State regarding actions to be taken in response to any threatening disaster situation or disaster,

(ix) Promote general education, awareness, and community training in regard to the forms of disasters to which different parts of the State are vulnerable and the measures that may be taken by such community to prevent the disaster, mitigate and respond to such disaster,

(x) Advise, assist, and coordinate the activities of the Departments of the Government of the State, District Authorities, Statutory bodies and other governmental and non-governmental organizations engaged in disaster management,

(xi) Provided necessary technical assistance or give advice to district authorities and local authorities for carrying out their functions effectively,

(xii) Advise the State Government regarding all financial matters in relation to disaster management,

(xiii) Examine the construction in any local area, in the State and, if it is of the opinion that the standards laid for such construction for the prevention of disaster is not being or has not been followed, may direct the District Authority or the Local Authority, as the case may be, to take such action as may be necessary to secure compliance of such standards,

(xiv) Provide information to the National Authority relating to different aspects of disaster management,

(xv) Lay down, review, and update state level response plans and guidelines and ensure that the District level plans are prepared, reviewed, and updated,

(xvi) Ensure that communication systems are in order and the disaster management drills are carried out periodically,

(xvii) Perform such other functions as may be assigned to it by the State Authority or as it may consider necessary.

23. State Plan:

(a) There shall be a plan for disaster management for every State to be called the State Disaster Management Plan.

(b) The State Plan shall be prepared by the State Executive Committee having regard to the guidelines laid down by the National Authority and after such consultation with Local

Authorities, District authorities and the people's representatives as the State Executive Committee may deem fit.

(c) The State Plan prepared by the State Executive Committee under sub-section (2) shall be approved by the State Authority.

(d) The State Plan shall include:

(i) The vulnerability of different parts of the State to different forms of disasters,

(ii) The measures to be adopted for prevention and mitigation of disasters,

(iii) The manner in which the mitigation measures shall be integrated with the development plans and projects,

(iv) The capacity building and preparedness measures to be taken,

(v) The roles and responsibilities of each Department of the Government of the State in relation to the measures specified in clauses (b), (c), and (d) above,

(vi) The roles and responsibilities of different Departments of the Government of the State in responding to any threatening disaster situation or disaster.

(e) The State Plan shall be reviewed and updated annually.

(f) Appropriate provisions shall be made by the State Government for financing for the measures to be carried out under the State Plan.

(g) Copies of the State Plan referred to in sub-sections (2) and (5) shall be made available to the departments of the Government of the State and such departments shall draw up their own plans in accordance with the State Plan.

24. Powers and functions of State Executive Committee in the event of threatening disaster situation:

For the purpose of, assisting and protecting the community affected by disaster or providing relief to such community or, preventing or combating disruption or, dealing with the effects of any threatening disaster situation, the State Executive Committee may,

(a) Control and restrict, vehicular traffic to, from or within, the vulnerable or affected areas,

(b) Control and restrict the entry of any person into his movement within and departure from, a vulnerable or affected area,

(c) Remove debris, conduct search, and carry-out rescue operations,

(d) Provide shelter, food, drinking water, essential provisions, health care, and services in accordance with the standards laid down by the National Authority and State Authority,

(e) Give direction to the concerned departments of the Government of the State, any District Authority or other Authority, within the local limits of the State to take such measure or steps for rescue, evacuation or providing immediate relief saving lives or property, as may be necessary in its opinion,

(f) Require any department of the Government of the State or any other body or Authority or person in charge of any relevant resources to make available the resources for the purposes of emergency response, rescue, and relief,

(g) Require experts and consultants in the field of disaster to provide advice and assistance for rescue and relief,

(h) Procure exclusive or preferential use of amenities from any authority or person as and when required;

(i) Construct temporary bridges or other necessary structures and demolish unsafe structures which may be hazardous to public,

(j) Ensure that non-governmental organizations carry-out their activities in an equitable and non-discriminatory manner,

(k) Disseminate information to public to deal with any threatening disaster situation or disaster,

(l) Take such steps as the Central Government or the State Government may direct in this regard or take such other steps as are required or warranted by the form of any threatening disaster situation or disaster.

CHAPTER IV: District Disaster Management Authority

25. Constitution of District Disaster Management Authority:

(a) Every State Government shall as soon as may be after issue of notification under sub-section (1) of section 14, by notification in the Official Gazette, establish a District Disaster Management Authority for every District in the State with such name as may be specified in that notification.

(b) The District Authority shall consist of the Chairperson and such number of other members, not exceeding seven, as may be prescribed by the State Government and unless the rules otherwise provide, it shall consist of the following namely;

(i) The Collector or the District Magistrate or Deputy Commissioner, as the case may be, of the District who shall be chairperson, *ex-officio*,

(ii) The elected representative of the local Authority who shall be co-chairperson, ex-officio; provided that in the Tribal areas, as referred to in the Sixth Schedule to the constitution, the Chief Executive Member of the District Council of autonomous District, shall be the co-chairperson, *ex-officio*,

(iii) The Chief Executive officer of the District Authority, *ex-officio*,

(iv) The Superintendent of Police, *ex-officio*,

(v) The Chief Medical Officer of the District, *ex-officio*,

(vi) Not exceeding two other District level officers to be appointed by the State Government.

(c) In any District where Zilla Parishad exists, the Chairperson thereof shall be the co-chairperson of the District Authority.

(d) The State Government shall appoint an officer not below the rank of Additional Collector or Additional District Magistrate or Additional Deputy Commissioner, as the case may be, of the District to be the Chief Executive Officer of the District Authority to exercise such powers and perform such functions as may be prescribed by the State Government and such other powers and functions as may be delegated to him by the District Authority.

26. Powers of Chairperson of District Authority:

(a) The Chairperson of the District Authority shall in addition to presiding over the meetings of the District Authority, exercise and discharge such powers and functions of the District Authority as the District Authority may delegate to him.

(b) The Chairperson of the District Authority shall, in the case of an emergency have power to exercise all or any of the powers of the District Authority, but the exercise of such powers shall be subject to *ex-post facto* ratification of the District Authority.

(c) The District Authority or the Chairperson of the District Authority may, by general or special order, in writing, delegate such of its or his powers and functions under sub-section (1) or (2), as the case may be, to the Chief Executive Officer of the District Authority, subject to such conditions and limitations, if any as it or be deems fit.

27. Meetings:

The District Authority shall meet as and when necessary and at such time and place as the Chairperson may think fit.

28. Constitution of Advisory Committees and other Committees:

(a) The District Authority may, as and when it considers necessary, constitute one or more Advisory Committees and other committees for the efficient discharge of its functions.

(b) The District Authority shall, from among its members, appoint the Chairperson of the Committee referred to in sub-section (1).

(c) Any person associated as an expert with any committee or sub-committee constituted under sub-section (1) may be paid such allowances as may be prescribed by the State Government.

29. Appointment of officers and other employees of District Authority:

The State Government shall provide the District Authority with such officers, consultants, and other employees as it considers necessary for carrying out the functions of District Authority.

30. Powers and functions of District Authority:

(a) The District Authority shall act as the district planning, coordinating and implementing body for disaster management and take all measures for the purposes of disaster management in the district in accordance with the guidelines laid down by the National Authority and the State Authority.

(b) Without prejudice to the generality of the provisions of sub-section (1), the District Authority may,

(i) Prepare a disaster management plan including District response plan for the District,

(ii) Coordinate and monitor the implementation of the National Policy, State Policy, National Plan, State Plan, and District Plan,

(iii) Ensure that the areas in the District vulnerable to disaster are identified and measures for the prevention of disasters and the mitigation of its effects are undertaken by the departments of the Government at the District level as well as by the Local Authorities,

(iv) Ensure that the guidelines for prevention of disaster, mitigation of its effects preparedness and response measures as laid down by the National Authority and the State Authority are followed by all departments of the Government at the District level and the Local Authorities in the District.

(v) Give directions to different Authorities at the District level and Local Authorities to take such other measures for the prevention or mitigation of disasters as may be necessary,

(vi) Lay down guidelines for prevention of disaster management plans by the department of the Government at the District level and Local Authorities in the District,

(vii) Monitor the implementation of disaster management plans prepared by the Departments of the Government at the District level,

(viii) Lay down guidelines to be followed by the Departments of the Government at the District level for purposes of integration of measures for prevention of disasters and mitigation in their development plans and projects and provide necessary technical assistance therefore,

(ix) Monitor the implementation of measures referred to in clause (viii).

(x) Review the State of capabilities for responding to any disaster or threatening disaster situation in the District and give directions to the relevant departments or authorities at the District level for their upgradation as may be necessary,

(xi) Review the preparedness measures and give directions to the concerned departments at the District level or other concerned authorities where necessary for bringing the preparedness measures to the level required for responding effectively to any disaster or threatening disaster situation,

(xii) Organize and coordinate specialized raining programmes for different levels of officers, employees, and voluntary rescue workers in the District,

(xiii) Facilitate community training and awareness programmes for prevention of disaster or mitigation with the support of Local Authorities, Governments and non-governmental organizations,

(xiv) Set up, maintain, review, and upgrade the mechanism for early warnings and dissemination or proper information to public,

(xv) Prepare, review, and update District level response plan and guidelines,

(xvi) Coordinate response to any threatening disaster situation or disaster,

(xvii) Ensure that the Departments of the Government at the District level and the Local Authorities prepare their response plans in accordance with the District response plan,

(xviii) Lay down guidelines for, or give directions to, the concerned departments of the Government at the District level or any other Authorities within the local limits of the District to take measures to respond effectively to any threatening disaster situation or disaster,

(xix) Advise, assist and coordinate the activities of the Departments of the Government at the District level, statutory bodies and other governmental and non-governmental organizations in the District engaged in the disaster management,

(xx) Coordinate with, and give guidelines to, Local Authorities in the District to ensure that measures for the prevention or mitigation of threatening disaster situation or disaster in the District are carried out promptly and effectively,

(xxi) Provide necessary technical assistance or give advise to the Local Authorities in the District for carrying out their functions,

(xxii) Review development plans prepared by the Departments of the Government at the District level, statutory authorities or Local Authorities with a view to make necessary provisions therein for prevention of disaster or mitigation,

(xxiii) Examine the construction in any area in the District and, if it is of the opinion that the standards for the prevention of disaster or mitigation laid down for such construction is not being or has not been followed, may direct the concerned Authority to take such action as may be necessary to secure compliance of such standards,

(xxiv) Identify buildings and places which could, in the event of any threatening disaster situation or disaster, be used as relief centres or camps and make arrangements for water supply and sanitation in such buildings or places,

(xxv) Establish stockpiles of relief and rescue materials or ensure preparedness to make such materials provide information to the State Authority relating to different aspects of disaster management,

(xxvi) Available at a short notice,

(xxvii) Encourage the involvement of non-governmental organizations and voluntary social welfare institutions working at the grassroots level in the District for disaster management,

(xxviii) Ensure communication systems are in order, and disaster management drills are carried out periodically,

(xxix) Perform such other functions as the State Government or State Authority may assign to it or as it deems necessary for disaster management in the District.

31. District Plan:

(a) There shall be a plan for disaster management for every District of the State.

(b) The District plan shall be prepared by the District, after consultation with the Local Authorities and having regard to the National Plan and the State Plan, to be approved by the State Authority,

(c) The District Plan shall include

(a) The areas in the District vulnerable to different forms of disasters,

(b) The measures to be taken, for prevention and mitigation of disaster, by the Departments of the Government at the District level and Local Authorities in the District,

(c) The capacity building and preparedness measures required to be taken by the Departments of the Government at the District level and the Local Authorities in the District to respond to any threatening disaster situation or disaster,

(d) The response plans and procedures, in the event of a disaster, providing for: (i) allocation of responsibilities to the departments of the Government at the District level and Local Authorities in the District; (ii) prompt response to disaster and relief thereof; (iii) procurement of essential resources; (iv) establishment of communication links; (v) the dissemination of information to the public; (vi) such other matters as may be required by the State Authority.

(d) The District Plan shall be reviewed and updated annually.

(e) The copies of the District Plan referred to in sub-section (2) and (4) shall be made available to the Departments of the Government in the District.

(f) The District Authority shall send a copy of the District Plan to the State Authority which shall forward it to the State Government.

(g) The District Authority shall, review from time-to-time, the implementation of the Plan and issue such instructions to different departments of the Government in the District as it may deem necessary for the implementation thereof.

32. Plans by different Authorities at District level and their implementation:

Every office of the Government of India and of the State Government at the District level and the Local Authorities shall, subject to the supervision of the District Authority:

(a) Prepare a disaster management plan setting out the following namely:

(i) Provisions for prevention and mitigation measures as provided for in the District Plan and as is assigned to the department or agency concerned,

(ii) Provisions for taking measures relating to capacity-building and preparedness as laid down in the District Plan,

(iii) The response plans and procedures, in the event of any threatening disaster situation or disaster,

(b) Coordinate the preparation and the implementation of its plan with those of the other organizations At the district level including local authority, communities and other stakeholders,

(c) Regularly review and update the plan,

(d) Submit a copy of its disaster management plan and of any amendment thereto, to the District Authority.

33. Requisition by the District Authority:

The District Authority may by order require any officer or any Department at the district level or any local Authority to take such measures for the prevention or mitigation of disaster, or to effectively respond to it, as may be necessary, and such officer or department shall be bound to carry-out such order.

34. Powers and functions of District Authority in the event of any threatening disaster situation or disaster:

For the purpose of assisting, protecting, or providing relief to the community, in response to any threatening disaster situation or disaster, the District Authority may

(a) Give directions for the release and use of resources available with any Department of the Government and the local Authority in the district,

(b) Control and restrict vehicular traffic to, from and within the vulnerable or affected area;

(c) Control and restrict the entry of any person into, his movement within and departure from, a vulnerable or affected area,

(d) Remove debris, conduct search, and carry-out rescue operations,

(e) Provide shelter, food, drinking water and essential provisions, health care and services,

(f) Establish emergency communication systems in the affected areas,

(g) Make arrangements for the disposal of the unclaimed dead bodies,

(h) Recommend to any department of the Government of the State or any authority or body under that Government at the District level to take such measures as are necessary in its opinion,

(i) Require experts and consultants in the relevant fields to advise and assist as it may deem necessary,

(j) Procure exclusive or preferential use of amenities from any authority or person,

(k) Construct temporary bridges or other necessary structures and demolish structures which may be hazardous to public or aggravate the effects of the disaster,

(l) Ensure that the non-governmental organizations carry-out their activities in an equitable and non-discriminatory manner,

(m) Take such other steps as may be required or warranted to be taken in such a situation.

CHAPTER V: Measures by the Government for Disaster Management

35. Central Government to take measures:

(a) Subject to the provisions of this Act, the Central Government shall take all such measures as it deems necessary or expedient for the purpose of disaster management.

(b) In particular and without prejudice to the generality of the provisions of sub-section (1) the measures which the Central Government may take under that sub-section include measures with respect to all or any of the following matters, namely:

(i) Coordination of actions of the Ministries or Departments of the Government of India, State Governments, National Authority, State Authorities, governmental and non-governmental organizations in relation to disaster management,

(ii) Ensure the integration of measures for prevention of disasters and mitigation by Ministries or Departments of the Government of India into their development plans and projects,

(iii) Ensure appropriate allocation of funds for prevention of disaster, mitigation, capacity-building, and preparedness by the ministries or Departments of the Government of India.

(iv) Ensure that the Ministries or Departments of the Government of India take necessary measures for preparedness to promptly and effectively respond to any threatening disaster situation or disaster,

(v) Cooperation and assistance to State Governments, as requested by them or otherwise deemed appropriate by it,

(vi) Deployment of naval, military, and air forces, other armed forces of the union or any other civilian personnel as may be required for the purpose of this Act,

(vii) Coordination with the United Nations Agencies, International Organizations, and governments of foreign countries for the purposes of this Act,

(viii) Establish institutions for research, training, and developmental programmes in the field of disaster management,

(ix) Such other matters as it deems necessary or expedient for the purpose of securing effective implementation of the provisions of this Act.

(c) The Central Government may extend such support to other countries affected by major disaster as it may deem appropriate.

36. Responsibilities of Ministries or Departments of Government of India.

It shall be the responsibility of every Ministry or Department of the Government of India to:

(a) Take measures necessary for prevention of disasters, mitigation, preparedness, and capacity-building in accordance with the guidelines laid down by the National Authority.

(b) Integrate into its development plans and projects, the measures for prevention or mitigation of disasters in accordance with the guidelines laid down by the National Authority.

(c) Respond effectively and promptly to any threatening disaster situation or disaster in accordance with the guidelines of the National Authority or the directions of the National Executive Committee in this behalf,

(d) Review the enactments administered by it, its policies, rules and regulations, with a view to incorporate therein the provisions necessary for prevention of disasters, mitigation or preparedness,

(e) Allocate funds for measures for prevention of disaster, mitigation, capacity-building, and preparedness,

(f) Provide assistance to the National Authority and State Governments for:

(i) Drawing up mitigation, preparedness and response plans, capacity-building, data collection and identification and training of personnel in relation to disaster management,

(ii) Carrying out rescue and relief operations in the affected areas,

(iii) Assessing the damage from any disaster,

(iv) Carrying out rehabilitation and reconstruction.

(g) Make available its resources to the National Executive Committee or a State Executive Committee for the purpose of responding promptly and effectively to any threatening disaster situation or disaster, including measures for:

(i) Providing emergency communication in vulnerable or affected areas,

(ii) Transporting personnel and relief goods to and from the affected ares,

(iii) Providing evacuation, rescue, temporary shelter or other immediate relief,

(iv) Setting up temporary bridges, jetties and landing places,

(v) Providing, drinking water, essential provisions, health care, and services in an affected area,

(vi) Take such other actions as it may consider necessary for disaster management.

37. Disaster management plans of ministries or Departments of Government of India.

(a) Every ministry or Department of the Government of India shall:

(i) Prepare a disaster management plan specifying the following particulars namely,

- The measures to be taken by it for prevention and mitigation of disasters in accordance with the National Plan,
- The specifications regarding integration of mitigation measures in its development plans in accordance with the guidelines of the National Authority and the National Executive Committee,
- Its roles and responsibilities in relation to preparedness and capacity-building to deal with any threatening disaster situation or disaster,
- Its roles and responsibilities in regard to promptly and effectively responding to any threatening disaster situation or disaster,
- The present status of its preparedness to perform the roles and responsibilities specified in sub-clauses (iii) and (iv).
- The measures required to be taken in order to enable it to perform its responsibilities specified in sub-clauses (iii) and (iv).

(ii) Review and update annually the plan referred to in clause (a),

(iii) Forward a copy of the plan referred to in clause (a) or clause (b), as the case may be, to the Central Government which government shall forward a copy thereof to the National Authority for its approval.

(b) Every Ministry or Department of the Government of India shall:

(i) Make, while preparing disaster management plan under clause (a) of sub-section (1), provisions for financing the activities specified therein,

(ii) Furnish a status report regarding the implementation of the plan referred to in clause (a) of sub-section (1) to the National Authority, as and when required by it.

38. State Government to take measures.

(a) Subject to the provisions of this Act, each State Government shall take all measures specified in the guidelines laid down by the National Authority and such further measures as it deems necessary or expedient, for the purpose of disaster management.

(b) The measures which the State Government may take under sub-section (1) include measures with respect to all or any of the following matters, namely:

(i) Coordination of actions of different departments of the Government of the State, the State Authority, District Authorities, local authority, and other non-governmental organizations,

(ii) Cooperation and assistance in the disaster management to the National Authority and National Executive Committee, the State Authority and the State Executive Committee, the State Authority and the State Executive Committee and the District Authorities,

(iii) Cooperation with, and assistance to, Ministries or Departments of the Government of India in disaster management, as requested by them or otherwise deemed appropriate by it,

(iv) Allocation of funds for measures for prevention of disaster, mitigation, capacity-building, and preparedness by the departments of the Government of the State in accordance with the provisions of the State Plan and the District Plans,

(v) Ensure that the integration of measures for prevention of disaster or mitigation by the departments of the Government of the State in their development plans and projects,

(vi) Integrate in the State development plan, measures to reduce or mitigate the vulnerability of different parts of the State to different disasters,

(vii) Ensure the preparation of disaster management plans by different departments of the State in accordance with the guidelines laid down by the National Authority and the State Authority,

(viii) Establishment of adequate warning systems up to the level of vulnerable communities;

(ix) Ensure that different departments of the Government of the State and the District Authorities take appropriate preparedness measures,

(x) Ensure that in a threatening disaster situation or disaster, the resources of different departments of the Government of the State are made available to the National Executive Committee or the State Executive Committee or the District Authorities, as the case may be, for the purposes of effective response, rescue, and relief in any threatening disaster situation or disaster,

(k) Provide rehabilitation and reconstruction assistance to the victims of any disaster,

(l) Such other matters as it deems necessary or expedient for the purpose of securing effective implementation of provisions of this Act.

39. Responsibilities of Departments of the State Government:

It shall be the responsibility of every department of the Government of a State to:

(a) Take measures necessary for prevention of disaster, mitigation, preparedness and capacity-building in accordance with the guidelines laid down by the National Authority and the State Authority,

(b) Integrate into its development plans and projects, the measures for prevention of disaster and mitigation,

(c) Allocate funds for prevention of disaster, mitigation, capacity building, and preparedness;

(d) Respond effectively and promptly to any threatening disaster situation or disaster in accordance with the State Plan, and in accordance with the guidelines or directions of the National Executive Committee and the State Executive Committee,

(e) Review the enactments administered by it, its policies, rules and regulations with a view to incorporate therein the provisions necessary for prevention of disasters, mitigation, or preparedness,

(f) Provide assistance as required, by the National Executive Committee, the State Executive Committee and District Authorities, for:

(i) Drawing up mitigation, preparedness, and response plans, capacity-building, data collection and identification and training of personnel in relation to disaster management;

(ii) Assessing the damage from any disaster;

(iii) Carrying out rehabilitation and reconstruction;

(g) Make provision for resources in consultation with the State Authority for the implementation of the District Plan by its authorities at the district level;

(h) Make available its resources to the National Executive Committee or the District Authorities for the purpose of responding promptly and effectively to any disaster in the State, including measures for:

(i) Providing emergency communication with a vulnerable or affected area,

(ii) Transporting personnel and relief goods to and from the affected areas,

(iii) Providing evacuation, rescue, temporary shelter, or other immediate relief,

(iv) Carrying out evacuation of persons, or live-stock from an area of any threatening disaster situation or disaster,

(v) Setting up temporary bridges, jetties, and landing places,

(vi) Provide drinking water, essential provisions, health care and services in an affected area,

(i) Such other actions as may be necessary for disaster management.

40. Disaster management plan of the Departments of State:

(a) Every Department of the State Government, in conformity with the guidelines laid down by the State Authority, shall:

(i) Prepare a disaster management plan which shall lay down the following:

- The types of disasters to which different parts of the State are vulnerable.
- Integration of strategies for the prevention of disaster or the mitigation of its effects or both with the development plans and programmes by the department,
- The roles and responsibilities of the department of the State in the event of any threatening disaster situation or disaster and emergency support function it is required to perform,
- Present status of its preparedness to perform such roles or responsibilities or emergency support function under sub-clause (iii).
- The capacity-building and preparedness measures proposed to be put into effect in order to enable the ministries or departments of the Government of India to discharge their responsibilities under section 37,

(ii) Annually review and update the plan referred to in clause (a),

(iii) Furnish a copy of the plan referred to in clause (a) or clause (b), as the case may be, to the State Authority,

2. Every department of the State Government, while preparing the plan under sub-section (1), shall make provisions for financing the activities specified therein.

3. Every department of the state Government shall furnish an implementation status report to the state Executive Committee regarding the implementation of the disaster management plan referred to in sub-section (1).

CHAPTER VI: Local Authorities

41. Functions of the local authority:

(a) Subject to the directions of the District Authority, a local authority shall:

(i) Ensure that its officers and employees are trained for disaster management:

(ii) Ensure that resources relating to disaster management are so maintained as to be readily available for use in the event of any threatening disaster situation or disaster:

(iii) Ensure all construction projects under it or within its jurisdiction conform to the standards and specification laid down for prevention of disasters and mitigation by the National Authority, State Authority, and the District Authority,

(iv) Carry-out relief, rehabilitation, and reconstruction activities in the affected area in accordance with the State Plan and the District Plan.

(b) The local authority may take such other measures as may be necessary for the disaster management.

CHAPTER VII: National Institute of Disaster Management

42. (a) With effect from such date as the Central Government may, by notification in the official Gazette appoint in this behalf, there shall be constituted an institute to be called the National Institute of Disaster Management.

(b) The National Institute of Disaster Management shall consist of such number of members as may be prescribed by the Central Government.

(c) The term of office of, and vacancies among members of the National Institute of Disaster Management and manner of filling such vacancies shall be such as may be prescribed.

(d) There shall be governing body of the National Institute of Disaster Management which shall be constituted by the Central Government from amongst the members of the National Institute of Disaster Management in such manner as may be prescribed.

(e) The governing body of the National Institute of Disaster Management shall exercise such powers and discharge such functions as may be prescribed by regulations.

(f) The procedure to be followed in exercise of its powers and discharge of its functions by the governing body, and the term of office of, and the manner of filling vacancies among the members of the governing body shall be such as may be prescribed by the regulations.

(g) Until the regulations are made under this section, the Central Government may make such regulations; and any regulation so made may be altered or rescinded by the National Institute of Disaster Management in exercise of its powers.

(h) Subject to the provisions of this Act, the National Institute of Disaster Management shall function within the broad policies and guidelines laid down by the National Authority and be responsible for planning and promoting training and research in the area of disaster management, documentation, and development of national level information base relating to disaster management policies, prevention, and mechanisms.

(i) Without prejudice to the generality of the provisions contained in sub-section (8) the National Institute, for the discharge of its functions may – and mitigation measures.

(i) Develop training modules, undertake research and documentation in disaster management and organise training programmes,

(ii) Formulate and implement a comprehensive human resource development plan covering all aspects of disaster management,

(iii) Provide assistance in national level policy formulation,

(iv) Provide required assistance to the training and research institutes for development of training and research programmes for stakeholders including government functionaries and undertake training of faculty members of the State level training institutes,

(v) Provide assistance to the State Governments and State training institutes in the formulation of State level policies, strategies, disaster management framework and any other assistance as may be required by the State Governments or State training institutes for capacity-building of stakeholders, government including its functionaries, civil society members, corporate sector and peoples elected representatives,

(vi) Develop educational materials for disaster management including academic and professional courses,

(vii) Promote awareness among stakeholders including college or school teachers and students, technical personnel and others associated with multihazard mitigation, preparedness and response measures,

(viii) Undertake, organize, and facilitate study courses, conferences, lectures, seminars within and outside the country to promote the aforesaid objects,

(ix) Undertake and provide for publication of journals, research papers, and books and establish and maintain libraries in furtherance of the aforesaid objects,

(x) Do all such other lawful things as are conducive or incidental to the attainment of the above objects,

(xi) Undertake any other function as may be assigned to it by the Central Government.

43. Officers and other employees of the National Institute:

The Central Government shall provide the National Institute of Disaster Management with such officers, consultants and other employees, as it considers necessary, for carrying out its functions.

CHAPTER VIII:

44. National Disaster Response Force:

(a) There shall be constituted a National Disaster Response Force for the purpose of specialist response to a threatening disaster situation or disaster.

(b) Subject to the provision of this Act, the force shall be constituted in such manner and, the conditions of service of the members of the force, including disciplinary provisions therefore, be such as may be prescribed.

45. Control and direction, etc.:

The General superintendence, direction and control of the force shall be vested and exercised by the National Authority and the command and supervision of the force shall vest in an officer to be appointed by the Central Government as the Director General of the National Disaster Response Force.

CHAPTER IX: FINANCE, ACCOUNTS, AND AUDIT

46. National Disaster Response Fund:

(a) The Central Government may, by notification in the Official Gazette, constitute a fund to be called the National Disaster Response Fund for meeting any threatening disaster situation or disaster and there shall be credited thereto,

(i) An amount which the Central Government may, after due appropriation made by Parliament by law in this behalf provide,

(ii) Any grants that may be made by any person or institution for the purpose of disaster management.

(b) The National Disaster Response Fund shall be made available to the National Executive Committee to be applied towards meeting the expenses for emergency response, relief and rehabilitation in accordance with the guidelines laid down by the Central Government in consultation with the National Authority.

47. National Disaster Mitigation Fund.

(a) The Central Government may, by notification in the official gazette, constitute a fund to be called the National Disaster Mitigation Fund for projects exclusively for the purpose of mitigation and there shall be credited thereto such amount which the Central Government may, after due appropriation made by Parliament by law in this behalf, provide.

(b) The National Disaster Mitigation Fund shall be applied by the National Authority.

48. Establishment of funds by State Government

(a) The State Government shall, immediately after notifications issued for constituting the State Authority and the District Authorities, establish for the purposes of this Act the following funds, namely:

(i) The fund to be called the State Disaster Response fund.

(ii) The fund to be called the District Disaster Response fund.

(iii) The fund to be called the State Disaster Mitigation Fund.

(iv) The fund to be called the District Disaster Mitigation Fund.

(b) The State Government shall ensure that the funds established,

(i) Under clause (a) of sub-section (1) is available to the State Executive Committee.

(ii) Under sub-clause (c) sub-section (1) is available to the State Authority.

(iii) Under clauses (b) and (d) of sub-section (1) are available to the District Authority.

49. Allocation of Funds by Ministries and Departments

(a) Every Ministry or Departments of the Government of India shall make provisions, in its annual budge, for funds for the purposes of carrying out the activities and programmes set out in its disaster management plan.

(b) The provisions of sub-section (1) shall, *mutatis mutandis,* apply to departments of the Government of the State.

50. Emergency procurement and accounting:

Where by reason of any threatening disaster situation or disaster, the National Authority or the State Authority or the District Authority is satisfied that immediate procurement of provisions or materials or the immediate application of resources are necessary for rescue or relief,

(a) It may authorize the concerned department or authority to make the emergency procurement and in such case, the standard procedure requiring inviting of tenders shall be deemed to be waived,

(b) A certificate about utilization of provisions or materials by the controlling officer authorized by the National Authority, State Authority or District Authority, as the case may be, shall be deemed to be a valid document or voucher for the purpose of accounting of emergency, procurement of such provisions or materials.

CHAPTER X: Offences and Penalties

51. Punishment for obstruction, etc.:

Whoever, without reasonable cause – Obstructs any officer or employee of the Central Government or the State Government, or a person authorized by the National Authority or State Authority or District Authority in the discharge of his functions under this Act, or

Refuses to comply with any direction given by or on behalf of the Central Government or the State Government or the National Executive Committee or the State Executive Committee or the District Authority under this Act, shall on conviction be punishable with imprisonment for a term which may extend to one year or with fine, or with both, and if such obstruction or refusal to comply with directions results in loss of lives or imminent danger thereof, shall on conviction be punishable with imprisonment for a term which may extend to two years.

52. Punishment for false claim:

Whoever knowingly makes a claim which he knows or has reason to believe to be false for obtaining any relief, assistance, repair, reconstruction, or other benefits consequent to disaster from any office of the Central Government, the State Government, the National Authority, the State Authority or the District Authority, shall, on conviction be punishable with imprisonment for a term which may extend to two years, and also with fine.

53. Punishment for misappropriation of money or materials, etc.:

Whoever, being entrusted with any money or materials, or otherwise being in custody of, or dominion over, any money or goods, meant for providing relief in any threatening disaster situation or disaster, misappropriates or appropriates for his own use or disposes of such money or materials or any part thereof or wilfully compels any other person so to do, shall on conviction be punishable with imprisonment for a term which may extend to two years, and also with fine.

54. Punishment for false warning:

Whoever makes or circulates a false alarm or warning as to disaster or its severity or magnitude, leading to panic, shall on conviction, be punishable with imprisonment which may extend to one year or with fine.

55. Offences by the Departments of the Government:

Where an offence under this Act has been committed by any Department of the Government, the Head of the Department shall be deemed to be guilty of the offence and shall be liable to be proceeded against and punished accordingly unless he proves that the offence was committed without his knowledge or that he exercised all due diligence to prevent the commission of such offence.

Notwithstanding anything contained in sub-section (1), where an offence under this Act has been committed by a Department of the Government and it is proved that the offence has been committed with the consent or connivance of, or is attributable to any neglect on the part of, any officer, other than the head of the department, such officer shall be deemed to be guilty of that offence and shall be liable to be proceeded against and punished accordingly.

56. Failure of officer in duty or his connivance at the contravention of the provisions of this Act:

Any officer, on whom any duty has been imposed by or under this Act and who ceases or refuses to perform or withdraws himself from the duties of his office shall, unless he has obtained the express written permission of his official superior or has other lawful excuse for so doing, be punishable with imprisonment for a term which may extend to one year or with fine.

57. Penalty for contravention of any order regarding requisitioning:

If any person contravenes any order made under section 65, he shall be punishable with imprisonment for a term which may extend to one year or with fine or both.

58. Offence by Companies:

Where an offence under this Act has been committed by a company or body corporate, every person who at the time the offence was committed, was in charge of, and was responsible to, the company, for the conduct of the business of the company, as well as the company, shall be deemed to be guilty of the contravention and shall be liable to be proceeded against and punished accordingly; provided that nothing in this sub-section shall render any such person liable to any punishment provided in this Act, if he proves that the offence was committed without his knowledge or that he exercised due diligence to prevent the commission of such offence.

Notwithstanding anything contained in sub-section (1) where an offence under this Act has been committed by a company, and it is proved that the offence was committed with the consent or connivance of or is attributable to any neglect on the part of any director, manager, secretary, or other officer of the company, such director, manager, secretary or other officer shall also, be deemed to be guilty of that offence and shall be liable to be proceeded against and punished accordingly.

Explanation – for the purpose of this section:

"company" means any body corporate and includes a firm or other association of individuals,

"director" in relation to a firm, means a partner in the firm.

59. Previous sanction for prosecution:

No prosecution for offences punishable under sections 55 and 56 shall be instituted except with the previous sanction of the Central Government or the State Government, as the case may be, or of any officer authorized in this behalf, by general or special order, by such government.

60. Cognisance of offences:

No court shall take cognisance of any offence under this Act except on a complaint made by the National Authority, the State Authority, the Central Government, the State Government, the District Authority or any other authority or officer authorised in this behalf by that Authority or Government, as the case may be; or any person who has given notice of not less than 30 days in the manner prescribed ,of the alleged of offence and his intention to make a complaint to the National Authority, the State Authority, the Central Government, the State Government, the District Authority, or any other authority or officer authorised as aforesaid.

CHAPTER XI: Miscellaneous

61. Prohibition against discrimination:

While providing compensation and relief to the victims of disaster, there shall be no discrimination on the ground of sex, caste, community, descent or religion.

62. Power to issue direction by Central Government:

Notwithstanding anything contained in any other law for the time being in force, it shall be lawful for the Central Government to issue direction in writing to the Ministries or Departments of the Government of India, or the national Executive Committee or the State Government, State Authority, State Executive Committee, statutory bodies or any of its officers, or employees, as the case may be, to facilitate or assist in the disaster management and such Ministry or Department or Government or Authority, Executive Committee, statutory body, officer or employee shall be bound to comply with such direction.

63. Powers to be made available for rescue operations:

Any officer or authority of the Union or a State, when requested by the National Executive Committee, any State Executive Committee or District Authority or any person authorised by such Committee or Authority in this behalf, shall make available to that Committee or Authority or person, such officers and employees as requested for, to perform any of the functions in connection with the prevention of disaster or mitigation or rescue or relief work.

64. Making or amending rules, etc., in certain circumstances:

Subject to the provisions of this Act, if it appears to the National Executive Committee, State Executive Committee or the District Authority, as the case may be, that provisions of any rule, regulation, notification, guidelines, instruction, order, scheme or bye-laws, as the case may be, are required to be made or amended for the purpose of prevention of disaster or the mitigation thereof, it may require the amendment of such rules, regulation, notification, guidelines, instruction, order, scheme or bye-laws, as the case may be, for that purpose and the appropriate department or authority shall take necessary action to comply with the requirements.

65. Power of requisition of resources, provisions, vehicles, etc., for rescue operations, etc.:

(a) If it appears to the National Executive Committee, State Executive Committee or District Authority or any officer as may be authorized by it in this behalf that:

(i) Any resources with any authority or person are needed for the purpose of prompt response,

(ii) Any premises are needed or likely to be needed for the purpose of rescue operations,

(iii) Any vehicle is needed or is likely to be needed for the purpose of transport of resources from disaster affected areas or transport of resources to the affected area or transport in connection with rescue rehabilitation, or reconstruction, such authority may, by order in writing, requisition such resources or premises or such vehicle, as the case may be, and may make such further orders as may appear to it to be necessary or expedient in connection with the requisitioning.

(b) Whenever an resources, premises or vehicle is requisitioned under sub-section (1), the period of such requisition shall not extend beyond the period for which such resources, premises or vehicle is required for any purpose of the purposes mentioned in that sub-section.

(c) In this section. –

"resources" includes men and material resources;

"services "includes facilities;

"premises" means any land, building or part of a building and includes a hit, shed or other structure or any part thereof;

"vehicle" means any vehicle used or capable of being used for the purpose of transport, whether propelled by mechanical power or otherwise.

66. Payment of compensation:

Whenever any Committee, Authority or officer referred to in sub-section:

(a) of section 65, in pursuance of that section requisitions any premises, there shall be paid to the persons interested compensation the amount of which shall be determined by taking into consideration the following, namely:

The rent payable in respect of the premises, or if no rent is so payable, the rent payable for similar premises in the locality,

If as consequence of the requisition of the premises the person interested is compelled to change his residence or place of business, the reasonable expenses (if any) incidental to such change:

Provided that where any person interested being aggrieved by the amount of compensation so determined makes an application within the 30 days to the Central Government or the State Government, as the case may be, for referring the matter to an arbitrator, the amount of compensation to be paid shall be such as the arbitrator appointed in this behalf by the Central Government or the State Government, as the case may be determine:

Provided further that where there is any dispute as to the title to receive the compensation or as to the apportionment of the amount of compensation, it shall be referred by the Central Government or the State Government, as the case may be, to an arbitrator appointed in this behalf by the Central Government or the State Government as the case may be, for determination and shall be determined in accordance with the decision of such arbitrator.

Explanation. In this sub-section, the expression 'person interested' means the person who was in actual possession of the premises requisitioned under section 65 immediately before the requisition, or where no person was in such actual possession, the owner of such premises.

(b) Whenever any Committee, Authority or officer, referred to in sub-section (1) of section 65 in pursuance of that section requisitions any vehicle, there shall be paid to the owner thereof compensation the amount of which shall be determined by the Central Government or the State Government, as the case may be, on the basis of the fares or rates prevailing in the locality for the hire of such vehicles.

Provided that where the owner of such vehicle being aggrieved by the amount of compensation so determined makes an application within the prescribed time to the Central Government or the State Government, as the case may be, for referring the matter to an arbitrator, the amount of compensation to be paid shall be such as the arbitrator appointed in this behalf by the Central Government or the State Government, as the case may be, may determine.

Provided further that where immediately before the requisitioning the vehicle or vessel was by virtue of a hire purchase agreement in the possession of a person other than the owner, the amount determined under this sub-section as the total compensation payable in respect of the requisition shall be apportioned between the person and the owner in such manner as they may agree upon, and in default of agreement, in such manner as an arbitrator appointed by the Central Government or the State Government, as the case may be, in this behalf may decide.

67. Direction to medical or communication of warnings, etc.:

The National Authority, testate Authority, or a District Authority may recommend to the government to give direction to any authority or person in control of any audio or audio-visual media or such other means of communication as may be available to carry any warning or advisories regarding any threatening disaster situation or disaster, and the said means of communication and media as designated shall comply with such direction.

68. Authentication of orders or decisions:

Every order or decision of the National Authority or the National Executive Committee, the State Authority, or the State Executive Committee or the District Authority, shall be authenticated by such officers of the National Authority or the National Executive Committee or the State Executive Committee, or the District Authority, as may be authorised by it in this behalf.

69. Delegation of powers:

The National Executive Committee, State Executive Committee, as the case may be, by general or special order in writing, may delegate to the Chairperson or any other member or to any officer, subject to such conditions and limitations, if any, as maybe specified in the order, such of its powers and functions under this Act as it may deem necessary.

70. Annual Report:

(a) The National Authority shall prepare once every year, in such form and at such time as may be prescribed, an annual report giving a true and full account of its activities during the previous year and copies thereof shall be forwarded to the Central Government and that Government shall cause the same to be laid before both Houses of Parliament within one month of its receipt.

(b) The State authority shall prepare once in every year, in such form and at such time as may be prescribed, an annual report giving a true and full account of its activities during the previous year and copies thereof shall be forwarded to the State Government and that government shall cause the same to be laid before each houses of the State Legislature where it consists of two houses, or where such Legislature consists of one House, before that House.

71. Bar of jurisdiction of Court:

No Court (except the Supreme Court or a High Court) shall have jurisdiction to entertain any suit or proceeding in respect of anything done, action taken, orders made, direction, instruction or guidelines issued by the Central Government, National Authority, State Government, State Authority or District Authority in pursuance of any power conferred by, or in relation to its functions by this Act.

72. Act to have overriding effect:

The provisions of this act, shall have effect, notwithstanding anything inconsistent therewith contained in any other law for the time being in force or in any instrument having effect by virtue of any law other than this Act.

73. Action taken in good faith:

No suit or prosecution or other proceeding shall lie in any court against the Central Government or the National Authority or the State Government or the State Authority or the District Authority or Local Authority or any officer or employee of the Central Government or the National Authority or the Sate Government or the State Authority or the District Authority or Local Authority or any person working for on behalf of such government or authority in respect of any work done or purported to have been done or intended to be done in good faith by such Authority or Government or such officer or employee or such person under the provisions of this Act or the rules or regulations made thereunder.

74. Immunity from legal process:

Officers and employees of the Central Government, National Authority, National Executive Committee, State Government, State Authority, State Executive Committee or District Authority shall be immune from legal process in regard to any warning in respect of any impending disaster communicated or disseminated by them in their official capacity or any action taken or direction issued by them in pursuance of such communication or dissemination.

75. Power of Central Government to make rules:

(a) The Central Government may, by notification in the Official Gazette, make rules for carrying out the purposes of this Act.

(b) In particular, and without prejudice to the generality of the foregoing power, such rules may provide for all or any of the following matters, namely:

(i) The composition and number of the members of the National Authority under sub-section (2), and the term of office and conditions of service of members of the National Authority under sub-section (4) of section 3.

(ii) The allowances to be paid to the members of the Advisory Committee under sub-section (2) of section 7.

(iii) The powers and functions of the Chairperson of the National Executive Committee under sub-section (3) of section 8 and the procedure to be followed by the National Executive Committee in exercise of its powers and discharge of its functions under sub-section (4) of section 8.

(iv) Allowances to be paid to the persons associated with the sub-committee constituted by the National Executive Committee under sub-section (3) of section 9.

(v) The number of members of the National Institute of Disaster Management under sub-section (2), the term of the office and vacancies among members and the manner of filling such vacancies under sub-section (3) and the manner of constituting the Governing Body of the National Institute of Disaster Management under sub-section (4) of section 42.

(vi) The manner of constitution of the force, the conditions of service of the members of the force, including disciplinary provisions under sub-section (2) of section 44.

(vii) The manner in which notice of the offence and of the intention to make a complaint to the National Authority, the State Authority, the Central Government, the State Government, or the other authority or officer under clause (b) of section 60.

(viii) The form in which and the time within which annual report is to be prepared under section 70.

(ix) Any other matter which is to be, or may be prescribed or in respect of which provision is to be made by rules.

76. Power to make regulations:

(a) The National Institute of Disaster Management, with the previous approval oft he Central Government may, by notification in the Official Gazette, make regulations consistent with this Act and the Rules made thereunder to carry-out the purposes of this Act.

(b) In particular, and without prejudice to the generality of the foregoing power, such regulations may provide for all or any of the following matters, namely.

(i) Powers and functions to be exercised and discharged by the governing body.

(ii) Procedure to be followed by the governing body in exercise of the powers and discharge of its functions.

(iii) Any other matter for which under this Act provision may be made by the regulations.

77. Rules and regulations to be laid before Parliament:

Every rule made by the Central Government and every regulation made by the National Institute of Disaster Management under this Act shall be laid, as soon as may be after it is made, before each House of Parliament, while it is in session, for a total period of thirty days which may be comprised of one session or in two or more successive sessions, and if, before the expiry of the session immediately following the session or the successive sessions aforesaid, both Houses agree in making any modification in the rule or regulation or both Houses agree that the rule or regulation should not be made, the rule or regulation shall thereafter have effect only in such modified form or be of no effect, as the case may be, so, however, that any such modification or annulment shall be without prejudice to the validity of anything previously done under that rule or regulation.

78. Power of State Government to make rules:

(a) The State Government may, by notification in the Official Gazette, make rules to carry-out the provisions of this Act.

(b) In particular, and without prejudice to the generality of the foregoing power, such rules may provide for all or any of the following matters, namely.

(i) The composition and the number of the members of the State Authority under sub-section (2), and the term of office and conditions of service of the members of the State Authority under sub-section (5) of section 14.

(ii) The allowances to be paid to the members of the advisory committee under sub-section (2) of section 17,

(iii) The powers and functions of the Chairperson of the State Executive Committee under sub-section (3), and the procedure to be followed by the State Executive Committee in exercise of its powers and discharge of its functions under sub-section (4) of section 20,

(iv) Allowances to be paid to the persons associated with the sub-committee constituted by the State Executive Committee under sub-section (3) of section 21,

(v) The composition and the number of members of the District Authority under sub-section (2) and the powers and functions to be exercised and discharged by the Chief Executive Officer of the District authority under sub-section (3) of section 25,

(vi) Allowances payable to the persons associated with any committee constituted by the District Authority as experts under sub-section (3) of section 28,

(vii) Any other matter which is to be or may be, prescribed, or in respect of which provision is to be made by the rules.

(c) Every rule made by the State Government under this Act shall be laid, as soon as may be after it is made, before each House of the State Legislature where it consists of two Houses, or where such Legislature consists of one House before that House.

79. Power to remove difficulties:

(a) If any difficulty arise in giving effect to the provisions of this Act, Central Government or the State Government, as the case maybe, by notification in the Official Gazette, make order not inconsistent with the provisions of this Act as may appear to it to be necessary or expedient for the removal of the difficulty.

(b) Every order made under this section shall be laid, as soon as may be after it is made, before each House of Parliament or the Legislature, as the case may be.

Case Study – 1: Bhopal Disaster

Bhopal memorial for those killed and disabled by the 1984 toxic gas release

The **Bhopal disaster** is the world's worst industrial catastrophe. It occurred on the night of December 2-3, 1984 at the Union Carbide India Limited (UCIL) pesticide plant in Bhopal, Madhya Pradesh, India. A leak of methyl isocyanate gas and other chemicals from the plant resulted in the exposure of hundreds of thousands of people. Estimates vary on the death toll. The official immediate death toll was 2,259 and the government of Madhya Pradesh has confirmed a total of 3,787 deaths related to the gas release. Others estimate that 3,000 died within weeks and that another 8,000 have since died from gas-related diseases. A government affidavit in 2006 stated the leak caused 5,58,125 injuries including 38,478 temporary partial and approximately 3,900 severely and permanently disabling injuries.

UCIL was the Indian subsidiary of Union Carbide Corporation (UCC). Indian Government controlled banks and the Indian public held 49.1 per cent ownership share. In 1994, the Supreme Court of India allowed UCC to sell its 50.9 per cent share. The Bhopal plant was sold to McLeod Russel (India) Ltd. UCC was purchased by Dow Chemical Company in 2001.

Civil and criminal cases are pending in the United States District Court, Manhattan and the District Court of Bhopal, India, involving UCC, UCIL employees, and Warren Anderson , UCC-CEO at the time of the disaster. In June 2010, seven ex-employees, including the former UCIL chairman, were convicted in Bhopal of causing death by negligence and sentenced to two years imprisonment and a fine of about $2,000 each, the maximum punishment allowed by law. An eighth former employee was also convicted but died before judgment was passed.

On February 28, 2011 the Supreme Court of India issued notice to the Union Carbide Corporation, Dow Chemicals and others on the Centre's extraordinary petition seeking an additional compensation of ₹ 7,844 crore for the victims of 1984 Bhopal gas tragedy. Through its curative petition, the Central Government has requested Supreme Court to take a relook at the entire evidence and enhance the compensation amount. The bench also decided to hear CBI's curative petition asking the court to restore the stringent charges of culpable homicide not amounting to murder against the accused in the criminal case.

Summary of Background and Causes

The UCIL factory was built in 1969 to produce the pesticide Sevin (UCCs brand name for carbaryl) using methyl isocyanate (MIC) as an intermediate. A MIC production plant was added in 1979.

During the night of December 2-3, 1984, water entered a tank containing 42 tons of MIC. The resulting exothermic reaction increased the temperature inside the tank to over 200°C (392°F) and raised the pressure. The tank vented releasing toxic gases into the atmosphere. The gases were blown by northwesterly winds over Bhopal.

Theories differ as to how the water entered the tank. At the time, workers were cleaning out a clogged pipe with water about 400 feet from the tank. The operators assumed that owing to bad maintenance and leaking valves, it was possible for the water to leak into the tank. However, this water entry route could not be reproduced. UCC also maintains that this route was not possible, but instead alleges water was introduced directly into the tank as an act of sabotage by a disgruntled worker via a connection to a missing pressure gauge on the top of the tank. Early the next morning, a UCIL manager asked the instrument engineer to replace the gauge. UCILs investigation team found no evidence of the necessary connection; however, the investigation was totally controlled by the government denying UCC investigators access to the tank or interviews with the operators. The 1985 reports give a picture of what led to the disaster and how it developed, although they differ in details.

Factors leading to the magnitude of the gas leak include:

- Storing MIC in large tanks and filling beyond recommended levels.
- Poor maintenance after the plant ceased MIC production at the end of 1984.
- Failure of several safety systems (due to poor maintenance).
- Safety systems being switched off to save money – including the MIC tank refrigeration system which could have mitigated the disaster severity.

The problem was made worse by the mushrooming of slums in the vicinity of the plant, non-existent catastrophe plans, and shortcomings in health care and socio-economic rehabilitation.

Public Information

Much speculation arose in the aftermath. The closing of the plant to outsiders (including UCC) by the Indian Government and the failure to make data public contributed to the confusion. The Council of Scientific and Industrial Research (CSIR) were forbidden to publish their data on health effects until after 1994. The initial investigation was conducted entirely by CSIR and the Central Bureau of Investigation.

Plant Production Process

Methylamine (1) reacts with phosgene (2) producing methyl isocyanate (3) which reacts with 1-naphthol (4) to yield carbaryl (5).

UCC produced carbaryl using MIC as an intermediate. After the Bhopal plant was built, other manufacturers including Bayer produced carbaryl without MIC, though at a greater manufacturing cost. However, Bayer also uses the UCC process at the chemical plant once owned by UCC at Institute, West Virginia, USA.

Contributing Factors

Other factors identified by the inquiry included: use of a more dangerous pesticide manufacturing method, large-scale MIC storage, plant location close to a densely populated area, undersized safety devices, and the dependence on manual operations.

Plant management deficiencies were also identified – lack of skilled operators, reduction of safety management, insufficient maintenance, and inadequate emergency action plans.

The chemical process, or "route", used in the Bhopal plant reacted methylamine with phosgene to form MIC (methyl isocyanate), which was then reacted with napthol to form the final product, carbaryl. This route differed from MIC-free routes used elsewhere, in which the same raw materials are combined in a different manufacturing order, with phosgene first reacted with the naphthol to form a chloroformate ester, which is then reacted with methyl amine. In the early 1980s, the demand for pesticides had fallen, but production continued, leading to build-up of stores of unused MIC.

Work Conditions

Attempts to reduce expenses affected the factory's employees and their conditions. Kurzman argues that "cuts ... meant less stringent quality control and thus looser safety rules. A pipe leaked? Don't replace it, employees said they were told ... MIC workers needed more training? They could do with less. Promotions were halted, seriously affecting employee morale and driving some of the most skilled ... elsewhere". Workers were forced to use English manuals, even though only a few had a grasp of the language.

By 1984, only six of the original twelve operators were still working with MIC and the number of supervisory personnel was also cut in half. No maintenance supervisor was placed on the night shift and instrument readings were taken every two hours, rather than the previous and required one-hour readings. Workers made complaints about the cuts through their union but were ignored. One employee was fired after going on a 15-day hunger strike. 70 per cen of the plant's employees were fined before the disaster for refusing to deviate from the proper safety regulations under pressure from management.

In addition, some observers, such as those writing in the Trade Environmental Database (TED) Case Studies as part of the Mandala Project from American University, have pointed to "serious communication problems and management gaps between Union Carbide and its Indian operation", characterized by "the parent companies [sic] hands-off approach to its overseas operation" and "cross-cultural barriers". The personnel management policy led to an exodus of skilled personnel to better and safer jobs.

Equipment and Safety Regulations

Union Carbide MIC Plant

It emerged in 1998, during civil action suits in India, that the plant was not prepared for problems. No action plans had been established to cope with incidents of this magnitude. This included not informing local authorities of the quantities or dangers of chemicals used and manufactured at Bhopal.

- The MIC tank alarms had not worked for four years.
- There was only one manual back-up system, compared to a four-stage system used in the US.
- The flare tower and the vent gas scrubber had been out of service for five months before the disaster. The gas scrubber therefore did not treat escaping gases with sodium hydroxide (caustic soda), which might have brought the concentration down to a safe level. The maximum pressure the scrubber could handle, provided it had been operating, was only a quarter of the pressure during the leak. The flare tower could only hold a quarter of the gas that leaked in 1984.
- To reduce energy costs, the refrigeration system was idle. The MIC was kept at 20^{0}C, not the 4.5^0 advised by the manual.
- The steam boiler, intended to clean the pipes, was out of action for unknown reasons.
- Slip-blind plates that would have prevented water from pipes being cleaned from leaking into the MIC tanks through faulty valves were not installed. Their installation had been omitted from the cleaning check list.
- The water pressure was too weak to spray the escaping gases from the stack. They could not spray high enough to reduce the concentration of escaping gas.
- According to the operators the MIC tank pressure gauge had been malfunctioning for roughly a week. Other tanks were used rather than repairing the gauge. The build-up in temperature and pressure is believed to have affected the magnitude of the gas release. UCC investigation studies have disputed this hypothesis.
- Carbon steel valves were used at the factory, even though they corrode when exposed to acid.
- UCC admitted in their own investigation report that most of the safety systems were not functioning on the night of December 3, 1984.
- The design of the MIC plant, following government guidelines, was "Indianized" by UCIL engineers to maximize the use of indigenous materials and products. Mumbai-based Humphreys and Glasgow Consultants Pvt. Ltd., were the main consultants, Larsen & Toubro fabricated the MIC storage tanks, and Taylor of India Ltd., provided the instrumentation.

Previous Warnings and Incidents

A series of prior warnings and MIC-related accidents had occurred:

- In 1976, the two trade unions reacted because of pollution within the plant.
- In 1981, a worker was splashed with phosgene. In panic he ripped off his mask, thus inhaling a large amount of phosgene gas; he died 72 hours later.
- In January 1982, there was a phosgene leak, when 24 workers were exposed and had to be admitted to hospital. None of the workers had been ordered to wear protective masks.
- In February 1982, an MIC leak affected 18 workers.
- In August 1982, a chemical engineer came into contact with liquid MIC, resulting in burns over 30 per cent of his body.

- In October 1982, there was a leak of MIC, methylcarbaryl chloride, chloroform and hydrochloric acid. In attempting to stop the leak, the MIC supervisor suffered intensive chemical burns and two other workers were severely exposed to the gases.
- During 1983 and 1984, leaks of the following substances regularly took place in the MIC plant: MIC, chlorine, monomethylamine, phosgene, and carbon tetrachloride, sometimes in combination.
- Reports issued months before the incident by UCC engineers warned of the possibility of an accident almost identical to that which occurred in Bhopal. The reports never reached UCC's senior management.
- UCC was warned by American experts who visited the plant after 1981 of the potential of a "runaway reaction" in the MIC storage tank. Local Indian authorities warned the company of problems on several occasions from 1979 onwards.

The Leakage

In November 1984, most of the safety systems were not functioning. Many valves and lines were in poor condition. Tank 610 contained 42 tons of MIC, much more than safety rules allowed. During the nights of December 2-3, a large amount of water entered tank 610. A runaway reaction started, which was accelerated by contaminants, high temperatures and other factors. The reaction generated a major increase in the temperature inside the tank to over 200°C (400°F). This forced the emergency venting of pressure from the MIC holding tank, releasing a large volume of toxic gases. The reaction was sped up by the presence of iron from corroding non-stainless steel pipelines. It is known that workers cleaned pipelines with water. They were not told by the supervisor to add a slip-blind water isolation plate. Because of this, and the bad maintenance, the workers consider it possible for water to have accidentally entered the MIC tank. UCC maintains that a "disgruntled worker" deliberately connected a hose to a pressure gauge.

Timeline, Summary

At the plant

- 21:00 Water cleaning of pipes starts.
- 22:00 Water enters tank reaction starts.
- 22:30 Gases are emitted from the vent gas scrubber tower.
- 00:30 The large siren sounds and is turned off.
- 00:50 The siren is heard within the plant area. The workers escape.

Outside

- 22:30 First sensations due to the gases are felt-suffocation, cough, burning eyes and vomiting.
- 1:00 Police are alerted. Residents of the area evacuate. Union Carbide director denies any leak.
- 2:00 The first people reached Hamidia Hospital. Symptoms include visual impairment and blindness, respiratory difficulties, frothing at the mouth, and vomiting.

- ❖ 2:10 The alarm is heard outside the plant.
- ❖ 4:00 The gases are brought under control.
- ❖ 7:00 A police loudspeaker broadcasts: "Everything is normal".

Health Effects

Short-term Health Effects

Reversible reaction of glutathione (top) with methyl isocyanate (MIC, middle) allows the MIC to be transported into the body.

The leakage caused many short-term health effects in the surrounding areas. Apart from MIC, the gas cloud may have contained phosgene, hydrogen cyanide, carbon monoxide, hydrogen chloride, oxides of nitrogen, monomethyl amine (MMA), and carbon dioxide, either produced in the storage tank or in the atmosphere.

The gas cloud was composed mainly of materials denser than the surrounding air, stayed close to the ground and spread outwards through the surrounding community. The initial effects of exposure were coughing, vomiting, severe eye irritation, and a feeling of suffocation. People awakened by these symptoms fled away from the plant. Those who ran inhaled more than those who had a vehicle to ride. Owing to their height, children and other people of shorter stature inhaled higher concentrations. Many people were trampled trying to escape.

Thousands of people had succumbed by the morning hours. There were mass funerals and mass cremations as well as disposal of bodies in the Narmada river. 1,70,000 people were treated at hospitals and temporary dispensaries. 2,000 buffalo, goats, and other animals were collected and buried. Within a few days, leaves on trees yellowed and fell off. Supplies, including food, became scarce owing to suppliers, safety fears. Fishing was prohibited as well, which caused further supply shortages.

A total of 36 wards were marked by the authorities as being "gas affected", affecting a population of 5,20,000. Of these, 2,00,000 were below 15 years of age, and 3,000 were pregnant women. In 1991, 3,928 deaths had been certified. Independent organizations recorded 8,000 dead in the first day. Other estimations vary between 10,000 and 30,000. Another 1,00,000 to 2,00,000 people are estimated to have permanent injuries of different degrees.

The acute symptoms were burning in the respiratory tract and eyes, blepharospasm, breathlessness, stomach pains and vomiting. The causes of deaths were choking, reflexogenic circulatory collapse and pulmonary oedema. Findings during autopsies revealed changes not only in the lungs but also cerebral oedema, tubular necrosis of the kidneys, fatty degeneration of the liver and necrotising enteritis. The stillbirth rate increased by up to 300 per cent and neonatal mortality rate by 200 per cent.

Hydrogen Cyanide Debate

Whether hydrogen cyanide was present in the gas mixture is still a controversy. Exposed to high temperatures, MIC breaks down to hydrogen cyanide (HCN). According to Kulling and Lorin, at + 200°C, 3 per cent of the gas is HCN. However, according to another scientific publication, MIC when heated in the gas phase starts to break down to hydrogen cyanide (HCN) and other products above 400°C. Concentrations of 300 ppm can lead to immediate collapse.

Laboratory replication studies by CSIR and UCC scientists failed to detect any HCN or HCN-derived side products. Chemically, HCN is known to be very reactive with MIC. HCN is also known to react with hydrochloric acid, ammonia, and methylamine (also produced in tank 610 during the vigorous reaction with water and chloroform) and also with itself under acidic conditions to form trimers of HCN called triazenes. None of the HCN-derived side products were detected in the tank residue.

The non-toxic antidote sodium thiosulfate (Na2S2O3) in intravenous injections increases the rate of conversion from cyanide to non-toxic thiocyanate. Treatment was suggested early, but because of confusion within the medical establishments, it was not used on large-scale until June 1985.

Long-term Health Effects

Victims of Bhopal disaster asking for Warren Anderson's extradition from the USA.

It is estimated 1,00,000 to 2,00,000 people have permanent injuries. Reported symptoms are eye problems, respiratory difficulties, immune and neurological disorders, cardiac failure secondary to lung injury, female reproductive difficulties and birth defects among children born to affected women. The Indian Government and UCC deny permanent injuries were caused by MIC or the other gases.

Aftermath of the Leakage

- Medical staff were unprepared for the thousands of casualties.
- Doctors and hospitals were not informed of proper treatment methods for MIC gas inhalation. They were told to simply give cough medicine and eye drops to their patients.
- The gases immediately caused visible damage to the trees. Within a few days, all the leaves fell off.
- 2,000 bloated animal carcasses had to be disposed of.

- "Operation Faith": On December 16, the tanks 611 and 619 were emptied of the remaining MIC. This led to a second mass evacuation from Bhopal.
- Complaints of a lack of information or misinformation were widespread. The Bhopal plant medical doctor did not have proper information about the properties of the gases. An Indian Government spokesman said that "Carbide is more interested in getting information from us than in helping our relief work".
- As of 2008, UCC had not released information about the possible composition of the cloud.
- Formal statements were issued that air, water, vegetation and foodstuffs were safe within the city. At the same time, people were informed that poultry was unaffected, but were warned not to consume fish.

Compensation from Union Carbide

- The Government of India passed the Bhopal Gas Leak Disaster Act that gave the government rights to represent all victims in or outside India.
- UCC offered US $350 million, the insurance sum. The Government of India claimed US$ 3.3 billion from UCC. In 1989, a settlement was reached under which UCC agreed to pay US$470 million (the insurance sum, plus interest) in a full and final settlement of its civil and criminal liability.
- " When UCC wanted to sell its shares in UCIL, it was directed by the Supreme Court to finance a 500-bed hospital for the medical care of the survivors. Bhopal Memorial Hospital and Research Centre (BMHRC) was inaugurated in 1998. It was obliged to give free care for survivors for eight years.

Economic Rehabilitation

- After the accident, no one under the age of 18 was registered. The number of children exposed to the gases was at least 2,00,000.
- Immediate relief was decided two days after the tragedy
- Relief measures commenced in 1985 when food was distributed for a short period and ration cards were distributed.
- Widow pension of the rate of ₹ 200/per month (later ₹ 750) was provided.
- One-time *ex-gratia* payment of ₹ 1,500 to families with monthly income ₹ 500 or less was decided.
- Each claimant was to be categorized by a doctor. In court, the claimants were expected to prove "beyond reasonable doubt" that death or injury in each case was attributable to exposure. In 1992, 44 per cent of the claimants still had to be medically examined.
- From 1990 interim relief of ₹ 200 was paid to everyone in the family who was born before the disaster
- The final compensation (including interim relief) for personal injury was for the majority ₹ 25,000 (US$ 830). For death claim, the average sum paid out was ₹ 62,000 (US$ 2,058).

- Effects of interim relief were more children sent to school, more money spent on treatment, more money spent on food, improvement of housing conditions.
- The management of registration and distribution of relief showed many shortcomings.
- In 2007, 10,29,517 cases were registered and decided. Number of awarded cases were 5,74,304 and number of rejected cases 4,55,213. Total compensation awarded was ₹ 1,546.47 crore.

Occupational Rehabilitation

- 33 of the 50 planned work-sheds for gas victims started. All except one was closed down by 1992.
- 1986, the MP government invested in the Special Industrial Area Bhopal. 152 of the planned 200 work-sheds were built. In 2000, 16 were partially functioning.
- It is estimated that 50,000 persons need alternative jobs, and that less than 100 gas victims have found regular employment under the government's scheme.

Habitation Rehabilitation

- 2,486 flats in two- and four-story buildings were constructed in the "Widows colony" outside Bhopal. The water did not reach the upper floors. It was not possible to keep cattle. Infrastructure like buses, schools, etc., were missing for at least a decade.

Health Care

- In the immediate aftermath of the disaster, the health care system became tremendously overloaded. Within weeks, the State Government established a number of hospitals, clinics and mobile units in the gas-affected area.
- Radical health groups set up JSK (the People's Health Centre) that was working a few years from 1985.
- Since the leak, a very large number of private practitioners have opened in Bhopal. In the severely affected areas, nearly 70 per cent do not appear to be professionally qualified.
- The Government of India has focused primarily on increasing the hospital-based services for gas victims. Several hospitals have been built after the disaster. In 1994, there were approximately 1.25 beds per 1,000, compared to the recommendation from the World Bank of 1.0 beds per 1,000 in developing countries.
- The Bhopal Memorial Hospital and Research Centre (BMHRC) is a 350-bedded super speciality hospital. Heart surgery and hemodialysis are done. Major specialities missing are gynaecology, obstetrics and paediatrics. Eight mini-units (outreach health centres) were started. Free health care for gas victims should be offered until 2006. The management has faced problems with strikes, and the quality of the health care is disputed.

Environmental Rehabilitation

- When the factory was closed in 1985-1986, pipes, drums and tanks were cleaned and sold. The MIC and the Sevin plants are still there, as are storages of different residues. Isolation material is falling down and spreading.
- The area around the plant was used as a dumping area for hazardous chemicals. In 1982 tubewells in the vicinity of the UCC factory had to be abandoned. UCC's laboratory tests in 1989 revealed that soil and water samples collected from near the factory and inside the plant were toxic to fish. Several other studies have shown polluted soil and groundwater in the area.
- Reported polluting compounds include naphthol, naphthalene, Sevin, tarry residue, mercury, toxic organochlorines, volatile organochlorine compounds, chromium, copper, nickel, lead, hexachloroethane, hexachlorobutadiene, and the pesticide HCH.
- In order to provide safe drinking water to the population around the UCC factory, there is a scheme for improvement of water supply.
- In December 2008, the Madhya Pradesh High Court decided that the toxic waste should be incinerated at Ankleshwar in Gujarat.

Union Carbide's Defense

Now owned by Dow Chemical Company, Union Carbide denies allegations against it on its website dedicated to the tragedy. The corporation believes that the accident was the result of sabotage, stating that safety systems were in place and operative. It also stresses that it did all it could to alleviate human suffering following the disaster.

Investigation into Possible Sabotage

Theories differ as to how the water entered the tank. At the time, workers were cleaning out pipes with water. The workers maintain that entry of water through the plant's piping system during the washing of lines was possible because a slip-blind was not used, the downstream bleeder lines were partially clogged, many valves were leaking, and the tank was not pressurized. The water, which was not draining properly through the bleeder valves, may have built up in the pipe, rising high enough to pour back down through another series of lines in the MIC storage tank. Once water had accumulated to a height of 6 m. (20 feet), it could drain by gravity flow back into the system. Alternatively, the water may have been routed through another standby "jumper line" that had only recently been connected to the system. Indian scientists suggested that additional water might have been introduced as a "back-flow" from the defectively designed vent-gas scrubber. However, none of these postulated routes of entry could be duplicated when tested by the Central Bureau of Investigators (CBI) and UCIL engineers. The company cites an investigation conducted by the engineering consulting firm Arthur D. Little, which concluded that a single employee secretly and deliberately introduced a large amount of water into the MIC tank by removing a meter and connecting a water hose directly to the tank through the metering port. Carbide claims such a large amount of water could not have found its way into the tank by accident, and safety systems were not designed to deal with intentional sabotage. Documents cited in the Arthur D. Little Report state that the Central Bureau of Investigation (CBI) along with UCIL engineers tried to simulate the water-washing hypothesis as a route of the entry of water into the tank. This all-important test failed to support this as a route of water entry. UCC claims the plant staff falsified numerous records to distance themselves from the incident, and that the Indian Government impeded its investigation and declined to prosecute the employee responsible, presumably because that would weaken its allegations of negligence by Union Carbide.

Safety and Equipment Issues

The corporation denies the claim that the valves on the tank were malfunctioning, claiming that "documented evidence gathered after the incident showed that the valve close to the plant's water-washing operation was closed and leak-tight. Furthermore, process safety systems-in place and operational – would have prevented water from entering the tank by accident". Carbide states that the safety concerns identified in 1982 were all allayed before 1984 and "none of them had anything to do with the incident".

The company admits that "the safety systems in place could not have prevented a chemical reaction of this magnitude from causing a leak". According to Carbide, "in designing the plant's safety systems, a chemical reaction of this magnitude was not factored in" because "the tank's gas storage system was designed to automatically prevent such a large amount of water from being inadvertently introduced into the system" and "process safety systems-in place and operational – would have prevented water from entering the tank by accident". Instead, they claim that "employee sabotage – not faulty design or operation – was the cause of the tragedy".

Response

The company stresses the "immediate action" taken after the disaster and their continued commitment to helping the victims. On December 4, the day following the leak, Union Carbide sent material aid and several international medical experts to assist the medical facilities in Bhopal.

Union Carbide states on its website that it put $2 million into the Indian Prime Minister's immediate disaster relief fund on December 11, 1984. The corporation established the Employees' Bhopal Relief Fund in February 1985, which raised more than $5 million for immediate relief.

According to Union Carbide, in August 1987, they made an additional $4.6 million in humanitarian interim relief available.

Union Carbide states that it also undertook several steps to provide continuing aid to the victims of the Bhopal disaster after the court ruling, including:

- The sale of its 50.9 per cent interest in UCIL in April 1992 and establishment of a charitable trust to contribute to the building of a local hospital. The sale was finalized in November 1994. The hospital was begun in October 1995 and was opened in 2001. The company provided a fund with around $90 million from sale of its UCIL stock. In 1991, the trust had amounted approximately $100 million. The hospital caters for the treatment of heart, lung and eye problems.
- Providing "a $2.2 million grant to Arizona State University to establish a vocational-technical centre in Bhopal, which was constructed and opened, but was later closed and levelled by the government".
- Donating $5 million to the Indian Red Cross.
- Developing the Responsible Care system with other members of the chemical industry as a

response to the Bhopal crisis, which is designed "to help prevent such an event in the future by improving community awareness, emergency preparedness and process safety standards".

❖ Long-term fallout.

Legal action against Union Carbide has dominated the aftermath of the disaster. However, other issues have also continued to develop. These include the problems of ongoing contamination, criticisms of the clean-up operation undertaken by Union Carbide, and a 2004 hoax.

Legal Action Against Union Carbide

Legal proceedings involving UCC, the United States and Indian Governments, local Bhopal authorities, and the disaster victims started immediately after the catastrophe.

Legal Proceedings Leading to the Settlement

On December 14, 1984, the Chairman and CEO of Union Carbide, Warren Anderson, addressed the US Congress, stressing the company's "commitment to safety" and promising to ensure that a similar accident "cannot happen again". However, the Indian Government passed the Bhopal Gas Leak Act in March 1985, allowing the Government of India to act as the legal representative for victims of the disaster, leading to the beginning of legal wrangling.

In 1985, Henry Waxman, a Californian Democrat, called for a US government inquiry into the Bhopal disaster, which resulted in US legislation regarding the accidental release of toxic chemicals in the United States.

March 1986 saw Union Carbide propose a settlement figure, endorsed by plaintiffs' US attorneys, of $350 million that would, according to the company, "generate a fund for Bhopal victims of between $500-600 million over 20 years". In May, litigation was transferred from the US to Indian courts by US District Court Judge. Following an appeal of this decision, the US Court of Appeals affirmed the transfer, judging, in January 1987, that UCIL was a "separate entity, owned, managed and operated exclusively by Indian citizens in India". The judge in the US granted UCC's forum request, thus moving the case to India. This meant that, under US federal law, the company had to submit to Indian jurisdiction.

Litigation continued in India during 1988. The Government of India claimed US$ 350 million from UCC. The Indian Supreme Court told both sides to come to an agreement and "start with a clean slate" in November 1988. Eventually, in an out-of-court settlement reached in 1989, Union Carbide agreed to pay US$ 470 million for damages caused in the Bhopal disaster, 15 per cent of the original $3 billion claimed in the law suit. By the end of October 2003, according to the Bhopal Gas Tragedy Relief and Rehabilitation Department, compensation had been awarded to 554,895 people for injuries received and 15,310 survivors of those killed. The average amount to families of the dead was $2,200.

Throughout 1990, the Indian Supreme Court heard appeals against the settlement from "activist petitions". In October 1991, the Supreme Court upheld the original $470 million, dismissing any other outstanding petitions that challenged the original decision. The Court ordered the Indian Government "to purchase, out of settlement fund, a group medical insurance policy to cover 1,00,000 persons who may later develop symptoms" and cover any shortfall in the settlement fund. It also requested UCC and its subsidiary "voluntarily" fund a hospital in Bhopal, at an estimated $17 million, to specifically treat victims of the Bhopal disaster. The company agreed to this.

Charges against Warren Anderson and Others

UCC Chairman and CEO Warren Anderson was arrested and released on bail by the Madhya Pradesh Police in Bhopal on December 7, 1984. The arrest, which took place at the airport, ensured Anderson would meet no harm by the Bhopal community. Anderson was taken to UCC's house after which he was released six hours later on $2,100 bail and flown out on a government plane. In 1987, the Indian Government summoned Anderson, eight other executives and two company affiliates with homicide charges to appear in Indian court. Union Carbide balked, saying the company is not under Indian jurisdiction.

In 1991, local Bhopal authorities charged Anderson, who had retired in 1986, with manslaughter, a crime that carries a maximum penalty of ten years in prison. He was declared a fugitive from justice by the Chief Judicial Magistrate of Bhopal on February 1, 1992, for failing to appear at the court hearings in a culpable homicide case in which he was named the chief defendant. Orders were passed to the Government of India to press for an extradition from the United States.

The US Supreme Court refused to hear an appeal of the decision of the lower federal courts in October 1993, meaning that victims of the Bhopal disaster could not seek damages in a US Court.

In 2004, the Indian Supreme Court ordered the Indian Government to release any remaining settlement funds to victims. In September 2006, the Welfare Commission for Bhopal Gas Victims announced that all original compensation claims and revised petitions had been "cleared".

In 2006, the Second Circuit Court of Appeals in New York City upheld the dismissal of remaining claims in the case of Bano v. Union Carbide Corporation. This move blocked plaintiffs' motions for class certification and claims for property damages and remediation. In the view of UCC, "the ruling reaffirms UCC's long-held positions and finally puts to rest – both procedurally and substantively – the issues raised in the class action complaint first filed against Union Carbide in 1999 by Haseena Bi and several organizations representing the residents of Bhopal". The U.S. Supreme Court refused to hear an appeal of the decision of the lower federal courts in October 1993, meaning that victims of the Bhopal disaster could not seek damages in a US Court.

In 2004, the Indian Supreme Court ordered the Indian Government to release any remaining settlement funds to victims. In September 2006, the Welfare Commission for Bhopal Gas Victims announced that all original compensation claims and revised petitions had been "cleared".

In 2006, the Second Circuit Court of Appeals in New York City upheld the dismissal of remaining claims in the case of Bano v. Union Carbide Corporation. This move blocked plaintiffs' motions for class certification and claims for property damages and remediation. In the view of UCC, "the ruling reaffirms UCC's long-held positions and finally puts to rest – both procedurally and substantively – the issues raised in the class action complaint first filed against Union Carbide in 1999.

In June 2010, seven former employees of the Union Carbide subsidiary, all Indian nationals and many in their 70s, were convicted of causing death by negligence and each sentenced to two years imprisonment and fined ₹ 1 lakh (US$2,124). All were released on bail shortly after the verdict. The names of those convicted are: Keshub Mahindra, former non-executive chairman of Union Carbide India Limited; V.P. Gokhale, managing director; Kishore Kamdar, vice-president; J. Mukund, works manager; S.P. Chowdhury, production manager; K.V. Shetty, plant superintendent; and S.I. Qureshi, production assistant. Federal class action litigation, Sahu v. Union Carbide *et. al.*, is presently pending on appeal before the Second Circuit Court of Appeals in New York. The litigation seeks damages for personal injury, medical monitoring and injunctive relief in the form of cleanup of the drinking water supplies for residential areas near the Bhopal plant. A related complaint seeking similar relief for property damage claimants is stayed pending the outcome of the Sahu appeal before the federal district court in the Southern District of New York.

Ongoing Contamination

Chemicals abandoned at the plant continue to leak and pollute the groundwater. Whether the chemicals pose a health hazard is disputed.

Contamination at the site and surrounding areas was not caused by the gas leakage. The area around the plant was used as a dumping ground for hazardous chemicals. By 1982 tubewells in the vicinity of the UCC factory had to be abandoned. In 1991, the municipal authorities declared water from over 100 tubewells to be unfit for drinking.

UCC's laboratory tests in 1989 revealed that soil and water samples collected from near the factory were toxic to fish. Twenty-one areas inside the plant were reported to be highly polluted. In 1994 it was reported that 21 per cent of the factory premises were seriously contaminated with chemicals.

Studies made by Greenpeace and others from soil, groundwater, wellwater and vegetables from the residential areas around UCIL and from the UCIL factory area show contamination, with a range of toxic heavy metals and chemical compounds.

Substances found, according to the reports, are naphthol, naphthalene, Sevin, tarry residues, alpha naphthol, mercury, or ganochlorines, chromium, copper, nickel, lead, hexachlorethane, hexachlorobutadiene, pesticide HCH (BHC), volatile organic compounds and halo-organics. Many of these contaminants were also found in breast milk.

In 2002, an inquiry found a number of toxins, including mercury, lead, 1,3,5 trichlorobenzene, dichloromethane and chloroform, in nursing women's breast milk. Well water and groundwater tests conducted in the surrounding areas in 1999 showed mercury levels to be at "20,000 and 6 million times" higher than expected levels; heavy metals and organochlorines were present in the soil. Chemicals that have been linked to various forms of cancer were also discovered, as well as trichloroethylene, known to impair foetal development, at 50 times above safety limits specified by the United State Environmental Protection Agency (EPA).

In an investigation broadcast on BBC Radio 5 on November 14, 2004, it was reported that the site is still contaminated with 'thousands' of metric tons of toxic chemicals, including benzene hexachloride and mercury, held in open containers or loose on the ground. A sample of drinking water from a well near the site had levels of contamination 500 times higher than the maximum limits recommended by the World Health Organization.

In 2009, a day before the 25th anniversary of the disaster, Centre for Science and Environment (CSE), a Delhi-based pollution monitoring lab, released latest tests from a study showing that groundwater in areas even three kms from the factory up to 38.6 times more pesticides than Indian standards.

The BBC took a water sample from a frequently used hand pump, located just north of the plant. The sample, tested in UK, was found to contain 1,000 times the World Health Organization's recommended maximum amount of carbon tetrachloride, a carcinogenic toxin. This shows that the groundwater has been contaminated due to toxins leaking from the factory site.

Criticisms of Clean-up Operations

Environmentalists have warned that the contamination may lead to decades of slow poisoning, and diseases affecting the nervous system, liver and kidneys in humans. According to activists, there are studies showing that the rates of cancer and other ailments are high in the region. Activists have demanded that Dow clean up this toxic waste, and have pressed the Government of India to demand more money from Dow.

UCC states that "after the incident, UCIL began clean-up work at the site under the direction of Indian Central and State Government authorities", which was continued after 1994 by the successor to UCIL, Eveready Industries, until 1998, when it was placed under the authority of the Madhya Pradesh Government. Critics of the clean-up undertaken by Carbide, such as the International Campaign for Justice in Bhopal, claim that "several internal studies" by the corporation, which evidenced "severe contamination", were not made public; the Indian authorities were also refused access. They believe that Union Carbide "continued directing operations" in Bhopal until "at least 1995" through Hayaran, the U.S.-trained site manager, even after the sale of its UCIL stock. The successor, Eveready Industries, abruptly relinquished the site lease to one department of the State Government while being supervised by another department on an extensive clean-up programme. The Madhya Pradesh authorities have announced that they will "pursue both Dow and Eveready" to conduct the clean-up as joint tortfeasors.

The successor, Eveready Industries India, Limited (EIIL), ended its 99-year lease in 1998 and turned over control of the site to the State Government of Madhya Pradesh. Currently, the Madhya Pradesh Government is trying to force Dow and EIIL to finance clean-up operations.

On March 7, 2009, Indian scientists of the Indian Council of Medical Research (ICMR) have decided to investigate the long-term health effects of the disaster. Studies will also be conducted to see if the toxic gases caused genetic disorders, low birth weight, growth and development disorders, congenital malformation and biological markers of MIC/toxic gas exposure.

Case Study – 2: Gujarat Earthquake

2001 Bhuj Earthquake: Preliminary Report from IIT Kanpur

A Powerful Earthquake of magnitude 6.9 on Richter Scale rocked the Western Indian State of Gujarat on the 26th January, 2001. It caused extensive damage to life and property. This earthquake was so devastating in its scale and suffering that the likes of it had not been experienced in past 50 years. Leaving thousands seriously injured, bruised, and handicapped; both physically, psychologically, and economically.

The epicentre of the quake was located at 23.6 north Latitude and 69.8 east Longitude, about 20 km North-east of Bhuj Town of the Kutch district in Western Gujarat. At a depth of only 23 kms below surface this quake generated intense shaking which was felt in 70 per cent region of India and far beyond in neighbouring Pakistan and Nepal too. This was followed by intense after shocks that became a continued source of anxiety for the populace. The Seismicity of the affected Area of Kutch is a known fact with a high incidence of earthquakes in recent times and in historical past. It falls in Seismic Zone V.

The only such zone outside the Himalayan Seismic Belt. In last 200 years important damaging earthquakes occurred in 1819, 1844, 1845, 1856, 1869, and 1956 in the same vicinity as 2001 earthquake. Twenty-one of the total 25 districts of the State was affected in this quake. Around 18 towns, 182 talukas and 7,904 villages in the affected districts have seen large-scale devastation. The affected areas even spread up to 300 kms from the epicentre. In the Kutch district, four major urban areas – Bhuj, Anjar, Bachau, and Rapar suffered near total destruction. The rural areas in the region are also very badly affected with over 450 villages almost totally destroyed.

In addition, widespread damages also occurred in Rajkot, Jamnagar, Surendranagar, Patan, and Ahmedabad districts. Other Urban areas such as Gandhidham, Morvi, Rajkot, and Jamnagar have also suffered damage to major structures, infrastructure and industrial facilities. Ahmedabad the capital was also severely affected.

Gujarat earthquake is very significant from the point of view of earthquake disaster mitigation in India. The problems observed in this disaster are no different from other major recent earthquakes in the world. The issues in the recovery and reconstruction phase are: the proper understanding risk among different stakeholders, training and confidence-building among the professionals and masons with appropriate development planning strategies. This quake has provided numerous examples of geo-technical and structural failures. The traditional wisdom of design and construction practises of engineered buildings prevalent in this country came under criticism for the first time. It has triggered comprehensive understanding on what needs to be done in this regard.

22 High Powered Committee Report on National Disaster Management, Ministry of Agriculture, New Delhi, 2001.

A common site of destruction of the villages in the meizoseismal area. Rubble of collapsed buildings being cleared at Anjaar. Narrow lanes caused significant casualties and made rescue and relief very difficult. Kudos to the rescue/relief workers for their daring efforts!! Virtually nothing could be recovered from most RC frame buildings that collapsed. Clearing of debris from collapse of numerous multistorey RC frame buildings was an even bigger challenge to relief distribution after the earthquake. Temporary shelters in the town of Morbi.

Chamoli (Himalaya, India) Earthquake of March 29, 1999

The Chamoli earthquake of 29 March, 1999 in northern India is yet another important event from the viewpoint of Himalayan seismotectonics and seismic resistance of non-engineered constructions. The earthquake occurred in a part of the Central Himalaya, which is highly prone to earthquakes and has been placed in the highest seismic zone (zone V) of India. There has been a bitter controversy during the recent years regarding the seismic safety of a 260-m-high rock-fill dam under construction at Tehri, about 80 kms west of the epicentre. Fortunately, there are no major cities in the meizoseismal region and the population density is the second lowest in the state. The earthquake caused death of about 100 persons and injured hundreds more.

Maximum MSK intensity was up to VIII at a few locations. The quake was felt at far-off places such as Kanpur (440 kms south-east from the epicentre), Shimla (220 kms north-west), and Delhi (280 kms south-west). Maximum death and damage occurred in the district of Chamoli where about 63 persons died and over 200 injured; about 2,595 houses collapsed and about 10,861 houses were partially damaged. In all, about 1,256 villages were affected. A few buildings at the faraway mega-city of Delhi sustained non-structural damages. No instances of liquefaction were reported. Longitudinal cracks in the ground were seen in some locations in the affected area.

Emergency Response

Fortunately, the number of fatalities in the earthquake was relatively less at about 100 as compared to about 800 in the 1991 Uttarkashi earthquake. Interestingly, at the time of earthquake a popular movie was being screened by a TV channel and many people who were awake could easily escape. The area has major Hindu shrines and draws huge tourist traffic during May to October; the timing of this earthquake was fortunately during the lean tourist season. Hence, the task of search and rescue operations was easier and was carried out by the local people. Army and para military personnel were also called-into help in relief operations the very next day. Some cash compensation, food rations, and cloth tents were provided by the State Government. By March the winter is over, and hence, cloth tents were sufficient for temporary shelters.

Food and other supplies had to be air-dropped to numerous villages which were normally inaccessible by motorable roads or cut-off due to landslides. Due to poor accessibility, relief operations were quite challenging and caused dissatisfaction in remote villages which could not be attended to on time.

The headquarters for Chamoli district is at Gopeshwar, 10 kms by road from Chamoli. Since Gopeshwar did not experience major damages, the entire administrative machinery could function effectively. However, frequent visits by senior politicians and administrators from the State and Central Governments may have significantly diverted attention of the district officials. Damage assessment for individual houses was initiated by the revenue officials immediately after the earthquake. This was also a difficult task due to the inaccessibility of many villages leading to some complaints about the fairness in damage assessment.

Significant aftershock activity, which included a few events of M >5, created a lot of fear among the people and they hesitated to sleep indoors even when their dwellings had little or no damage. Speculations about an impending large earthquake added to the fear and panic. Massive forest fires, which are common during this time of the year, drove some wild animals towards the villages adding to the insecurity. Impending monsoons in the next two months remained a major concern; slope failures and additional damage to partially damaged houses were feared.

Non-structural damage to some buildings in far-off Delhi clearly underlines the potential for a major disaster there. Considering the political and social significance of such an eventuality, efforts should be directed towards effective earthquake disaster mitigation and management in the Indian capital.

The September 29, 1993, M6.4 Killari, Maharashtra Earthquake in Central India

Most of the world seismicity is concentrated along the plate boundaries. However, a significant number of earthquakes, including some large and damaging ones, do occur within the plates. Our understanding of intracratonic seismogenesis and the hazard it entails is poor, in part because data are scarce.

The 1993 Killari earthquake in central peninsular India is the latest intracratonic event to be responsible for a large disaster. The positive side of this tragedy is that it will provide new insights into geologic, engineering and cultural factors that control the distribution and degree of damage, which will aid in turn the development of a more effective hazard reduction programme for peninsular India and similar intrapolate environments.

This report summarizes our observations during a ten-day investigation of the mesoseismal area of the 1993 Killari earthquake. Several aspects of the earthquake were investigated, ranging from the surface rupture and related deformation to the pattern of damage to engineered and traditional structures. Finally, the rescue and reconstruction efforts following the earthquake brought out important issues that are generally relevant to earthquake hazard reduction in traditional rural settings; these are also briefly discussed.

Emergency Response

The affected area does not suffer from floods and was considered Aseismic. The only natural disaster known in the area is drought. Hence, the earthquake took the people and administration by surprise. It took the administration 2 to 4 days to effectively organize rescue and relief operations. What then followed appeared to be well-organized and effective. Civilian as well as military authorities cooperated in the effort.

Since the reconnaissance team did not visit the affected areas of Karnataka, the discussion here is based on the response in the districts of Latur and Osmanabad only.

Of all the villages devastated by the quake, only the village of Killari had a wireless connection with the district police headquarters at Latur. Within minutes, the information about the devastation in Killari was conveyed to Latur and from there to the State headquarters at Bombay. Immediately, about 20 policemen stationed at Ausa (28 km) were rushed to Killari, followed by district level administrators (District Collector, Superintendent of Police, etc). About 50 policemen were also dispatched from

Latur (42 kms). Immediate search and rescue was conducted by the survivors and the limited police rescue teams. As the day progressed, information about equally severe devastation from nearby villages started reaching Killari. By early next morning (October 1), the Indian army took over the task of search and rescue. By the afternoon of the day of the earthquake, many curious onlookers had arrived in the area. This led to traffic jams and hampered the task of search and rescue. Beginning October 2, entry to the affected area was controlled to allow entrance only to government personnel and members of volunteer organizations.

The task of search and rescue became extremely difficult due to the heavy rains, which immediately followed the earthquake and the enormous quantities of the rubble. In places 2-3 m of rubble has to be removed to extricate the bodies. The narrow village streets were choked by fallen rubble, which further hampered rescue operations. Mass cremations that were held on the first two days after the earthquake were done without adequate record keeping. This led to confusion about the actual number of deaths. At one time, the newspapers were reporting up to 30,000 dead. Later it was discovered that about 9,000 fatalities actually occurred.

Recovery Medical Aid: The number of injured in Maharashtra was about 15,500. About 50 mobile teams of doctors were pressed into service; at least doctor was made available at each of the affected villages. The 125 beds civil hospital at Latur had to convert the nearby Rajasthan School into a hospital ward to care for about 300 indoor patients. On the other hand, the rural medical college and hospital at Ambe Jogai, which is only 60 kms from Latur, had a 510-bed capacity but only had 86 patients maximum at any given time. On the whole, in a few days, there were more government and private doctors available than could be used.

Food, Water, and Provisions: Cooked food was provided in the affected villages during the first fortnight by large number of voluntary agencies and the army. After 15 days, the community kitchens were closed. Enough rations and other provisions to last a month were provided to the people, requiring them to cook their own food.

Temporary Shelter: Immediate shelter was provided by erecting temporary galvanized iron sheet houses. Each shelter consisted of 5 units of about 15 m^2 areas each; each affected family was offered one such unit. Common toilets and hand operated borewells were provided. Some families chose to take tents and tin sheets instead and made their own shelters.

Resettlement and Housing: A large number of villages which were totally destroyed are being relocated to places not far away. Most of the sites for relocation have been identified. Every affected family will be provided a housing unit with a covered area of 20, 40, or 60 m^2 (depending on the needs of the family) and an open area of 15 to 45 m^2 for animal shelters and future extensions. The government will bear the cost of only 20 m^2 of the housing per family. For houses with a larger constructed area, the remaining cost will be treated as a long-term low-interest loan payable on terms similar to those for World Bank loans.

Transportation: The primary mode of transport in the area is bus. The affected area has no rail network. The nearest railway stations are at Latur and Sholapur. The nearest airports are at Hyderabad and Aurangabad. Since there was no damage to roads or bridges, the bus services were not adversely affected, even though the lanes inside the villages were blocked with the rubble of collapsed houses. Most of the villages have been temporarily shifted to new locations to the main roads.

Communications: An excellent communication network was set up after the earthquake. Initially, a number of HAM sets were called in. Later, solar-powered satellite communication towers were installed in most of the bigger villages. The district collectors were provided with a hotline to the chief secretary at Bombay. This enabled the State to take immediate action on the requests from the local administrations for men and materials.

Economic Activity: The economy of the area is primarily farm based with very few industries. The only major industry in the region was a sugar factory at Killari Pati, which had closed quite sometime prior to the earthquake. It suffered no apparent damage and was being used as a relief distribution centre.

A large chicken farm about 15kms north of the epicentral area reported that egg production fell substantially after the quake. Production was still down about 7 per cent three weeks later. (No fluctuations in egg laying preceded the quake.)

Although it is harvesting season for the Kharif crop and the sowing season the rabi crop, the farmers have been unable to resume regular farming activity. This is due to incessant rains, unexpected at this time of year, and the non-availability of farm labourers, who do not seem concerned about daily wages due to the availability of free relief provisions. There are reports that the government may have to help in harvesting by bringing in labour from outside the area.

Case Study – 3: Chernobyl

What Happened?

At 1:24 a.m. on April 26, 1986, there was an explosion at the Soviet nuclear power plant at Chernobyl. One of the reactors overheated, igniting a pocket of hydrogen gas. The explosion blew the top off the containment building, and exposed the molten reactor to the air. Thirty-one power plant workers were killed in the initial explosion, and radioactive dust and debris spewed into the air.

It took several days to put out the fire. Helicopters dropped sand and chemicals on the reactor rubble, finally extinguishing the blaze. Then the Soviets hastily buried the reactor in a sarcophagus of concrete. Estimates of deaths among the clean-up workers vary widely. Four thousand clean-up workers may have died in the following weeks from the radiation.

The countries now known as Belarus and Ukraine were hit the hardest by the radioactive fallout. Winds quickly blew the toxic cloud from Eastern Europe into Sweden and Norway. Within a week, radioactive levels had jumped over all of Europe, Asia, and Canada. It is estimated that 70,000 Ukrainians have been disabled, and five million people were exposed to radiation. Estimates of total deaths due to radioactive contamination range from 15,000 to 45,000 or more.

To give you an idea of the amount of radioactive material that escaped, the atomic bomb dropped on Hiroshima had a radioactive mass of four-and-a-half tons. The exposed radioactive mass at Chernobyl was fifty tonns.

In the months and years following, birth defects were common for animals and humans. Even the leaves on the trees became deformed.

Today, in Belarus and Ukraine, thyroid cancer and leukemia are still higher than normal. The towns of Pripyat and Chernobyl in the Ukraine are ghost towns. They will be uninhabitable due to radioactive contamination for several hundred years. The worst of the contaminated area is called "The Zone", and it is fenced off. Plants, meat, milk, and water in the area are still unsafe. Despite the contamination, millions of people live in and near The Zone, too poor to move to safer surroundings.

Further, human genetic mutations created by the radiation exposure have been found in children who have only recently been born. This suggests that there may be another whole generation of Chernobyl victims.

Recent reports say that there are some indications that the concrete sarcophagus at Chernobyl is breaking down.

How a Nuclear Power Plant Works

The reactor at Chernobyl was composed of almost 200 tons of uranium. This giant block of uranium-generated heat and radiation. Water ran through the hot reactor, turning to steam. The steam ran the turbines, thereby generating electricity. The hotter the reactor, the more electricity would be generated.

Left to itself, the reactor would become too reactive – it would become hotter and hotter and more and more radioactive. If the reactor had nothing to cool it down, it would quickly meltdown – a process where the reactor gets so hot that it melts – melting through the floor. So, engineers needed a way to control the temperature of the reactor, to keep it from the catastrophic meltdown. Further, the engineers needed to be able to regulate the temperature of the reactor – so that it ran hotter when more electricity was needed, and could run colder when less electricity was desired.

The method they used to regulate the temperature of the reactor was to insert heat-absorbing rods, called control rods. These control rods absorb heat and radiation. The rods hang above the reactor, and can be lowered into the reactor, which will cool the reactor. When more electricity is needed, the rods can be removed from the reactor, which will allow the reactor to heat up. The reactor has hollow tubes, and the control rods are lowered into these reactor tubes, or raised up out of the reactor tubes. At the Chernobyl-type reactors, there are 211 control rods. The more control rods that are inserted, the colder the reactor runs. The more control rods that are removed, the hotter the reactor becomes.

How a Nuclear Power Plant Works

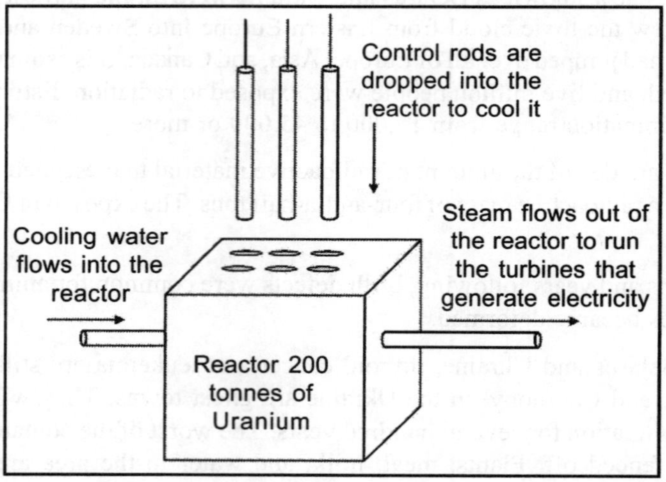

Soviet safety procedures demanded that at least 28 rods were inserted into the Chernobyl reactor at all times. This was a way to make sure that the reactor would not overheat.

Water was another method to moderate the temperature of the reactor. When more water ran through the reactor, the reactor cooled faster. When less water ran through the reactor, the reactor stayed hot.

Chernobyl Background

The list of senior engineers at Chernobyl was as follows: Viktor Bryukhanov, the plant director, was a pure physicist, with no nuclear experience.

Anatoly Dyatlov, the deputy chief engineer, served as the day-to-day supervisor. He had worked with reactor cores but had never before worked in a nuclear power plant. When he accepted the job as deputy chief engineer, he exclaimed, "you don't have to be a genius to figure out a nuclear reactor".

The engineers were Aleksandr Akimov, serving his first position in this role; Niko Fomin, an electrical engineer with little nuclear experience; Gennady Metlenko, an electrical engineer; and Leonid Toptunov, a 26-year-old reactor control engineer. The engineers were heavy in their experience of electric technology, but had less experience with the uniqueness of neutron physics.

The confidence of these engineers was exaggerated. They believed they had decades of problem-free nuclear work, so they believed that nuclear power was very safe. The engineers believed that they could figure out any problem. In reality, there had been many problems in the Soviet nuclear power industry. The Soviet state tried to keep problems a secret because problems are bad PR.

The Soviets had a number of nuclear accidents (this is a partial list of Soviet accidents before Chernobyl). In 1957 in Chelyabinsk, there was a substantial release of radioactivity caused by a spontaneous reaction in spent fuel; in 1966 in Melekess the nuclear power plant experienced a spontaneous surge in power, releasing radiation; In 1974, there was an explosion at the nuclear power plant in Leningrad; later in 1974, at the same nuclear power plant, three people were killed and radiation was released into the environment; in 1977, there was a partial meltdown of nuclear fuel at Byeloyarsk; in 1978 at Byeloyarsk, the reactor went out of control after a roof panel fell onto it; in 1982 at Chernobyl, radioactivity was released into the environment; in 1982, there was a fire at Armyanskaya; and in 1985, 14 people were killed when a relief valve burst in Balakovo.

Had the engineers at Chernobyl had the information of the previous nuclear accidents, perhaps they would have known to be more careful. It is often from mistakes that we learn, and the engineers at Chernobyl had no opportunity to learn.

As a footnote, don't think that the problems were just those mistake-laden Soviets. Here is a partial list of American accidents before Chernobyl: in 1951, the Detroit reactor overheated, and air was contaminated with radioactive gasses; in 1959, there was a partial meltdown in Santa Susanna, California; in 1961, three people were killed in an explosion at the nuclear power plant at Idaho Falls, Idaho; in 1966, there was a partial meltdown at a reactor near Detroit; in 1971, 53,000 gallons of radioactive water were released into the Mississippi River from the Monticello plant in Minnesota; in 1979, there was population evacuation and a discharge of radioactive gas and water in a partial meltdown at Three Mile Island; in 1979, there was a discharge of radiation in Irving Tennessee; in 1982, there was a release of radioactive gas into the environment in Rochester, New York; in 1982, there was a leak of radioactive gasses into the atmosphere at Ontario, New York; in 1985, there was a leak of radioactive water near New York City; and in 1986, one person was killed in an explosion of a tank of radioactive gas in Webbers Falls, Oklahoma.

The engineers at Chernobyl didn't know about these nuclear accidents. These were secrets that the Soviets kept from the nuclear engineers. Consequently, no one was able to learn from the mistakes of the past. The nuclear plant staff believed that their experience with nuclear power was pretty much error-free, so they developed an overconfidence about their working style.

So, according to Gregori Medvedev (the Soviet investigator of Chernobyl), their practice became lazy and their safety practices slipshod. Further, the heavy bureaucracy and hierarchy of the Soviet system created an atmosphere where every decision had to be approved at a variety of higher levels. Consequently, the hierarchical system had quelled the operators' creativity and motivation for problem-solving.

April 25, 1:00 p.m.

The engineers at Chernobyl had volunteered to do a safety test proposed by the Soviet government. In the event of a reactor shutdown, a back-up system of diesel generators would crank up, taking over the electricity generation. However, the diesel engines took a few minutes to start producing electricity. The reactor had a turbine that was meant to generate electricity for a minute or two until the diesel generators would start operating. The experiment at Chernobyl was meant to see exactly how long that turbine would generate the electricity.

The experiment required that the reactor be operating at 50 per cent of capacity. On April 25th, 1986, at 1:00 p.m., the engineers began to reduce the operating power of the reactor, by inserting the control rods into the reactor. This had the effect, you may recall, of cooling off the reactor – making it less reactive.

They also shutdown the emergency cooling system. They were afraid that the cooling system might kick in during the test, thereby interfering with the experiment. They had no authorization to deactivate the cooling system, but they went ahead and deactivated it.

The experiment called for running the reactor at 50 per cent capacity, thereby generating only half the electricity. At 2:00 p.m., a dispatcher at Kiev called and asked them to delay the test because of the higher-than-expected energy usage. They delayed the test, but did not reactivate the emergency cooling system.

April 25, 11:00 p.m.

At 11:00 p.m., they began the test again. Toptunov, the senior reactor control engineer, began to manually lower the reactor to 50 per cent of its capacity so that they could begin the turbine safety experiment.

Lowering the power generation of a nuclear reactor is a tricky thing. It is not like lowering the thermostat in a house. When you lower the thermostat in the house from 72⁰ to 68⁰, the temperature in the house will drop to 68⁰ and stay there. But in a nuclear reactor, the dropping of the temperature is not only the result of lowering the reactivity, but is also be cause of lowering the reactivity. In other words, the coldness of the reactor will make the reactor colder. This is called the self-damping effect. Conversely, when the reactor heats up, the heat of the reactor will make itself hotter (the self-amplifying effect).

So, when the control rods are dropped into the reactor, the reactivity goes down. And the water running through the reactor also lessens reactivity. But the lower reactivity also makes the reactor itself less reactive. So, the Chernobyl reactor damped itself, even as the water and the control rods damped its reactivity.

It is typically hard for people to think in terms of exponential reduction or exponential increase. We naturally think of a linear (straight-line) reduction or a linear increase. We have trouble with self-damping and self-amplifying effects, because they are non-linear by definition.

So, the engineers oversteered the process, and hit the 50 per cent mark, but they were unable to keep it there. By 12:30 a.m., the power generation had dropped to 1 per cent of capacity.

Chernobyl-type reactors are not meant to drop that low in their capacity. There are two problems with the nuclear reactor running at 1 per cent of capacity. When reactivity drops that low, the reactor runs unevenly and unstably, like a bad diesel engine. Small pockets of reactivity can begin that can spread hot reactivity through the reactor. Secondly, the low running of the reactor creates unwanted gasses and byproducts (xenon and iodine) that poison the reactor. Because of this, they were strictly forbidden to run the reactor below 20 per cent of capacity.

In the Chernobyl control room, Dyatlov (the chief engineer in charge of the experiment), upon hearing the reactor was at 1 per cent, flew into a rage. When the reactor capacity is very low, it will not be able to conduct safety experiment. With the reactor at 1 per cent capacity, Dyatlov had two options:

1. One option was to let the reactor go cold, which would have ended the experiment, and then they would have to wait for two days for the poisonous byproducts to dissipate before starting the reactor again. With this option, Dyatlov would no doubt have been reprimanded, and possibly lost his job.
2. The other option was to immediately increase the power. Safety rules prohibited increasing the power if the reactor had fallen from 80 per cent capacity. In this case, the power had fallen from 50 per cent capacity – so they were not technically governed by the safety protocols.

Dyatlov Ordered the Engineers to Raise Power

Today, we know the horrible outcome of this Chernobyl chronology. It is easy for us to sit back in our armchairs, with the added benefit of hindsight, and say Dyatlov made the wrong choice. Of course, he could have followed the spirit of the protocols and shut the reactor down. However, Dyatlov did not have the benefit of hindsight. He was faced with the choice of the surety of reprimand and the harming of his career vs. the possibility of safety problems. And, we know from engineers and technical operators everywhere, safety protocols are routinely breached when faced with this kind of choice. Experts tend to believe that they are experts, and that the safety rules are for amateurs.

Further, safety rules are not designed so that people are killed instantly when the safety standard is broken. On a 55-mile per hour limit on a highway, cars do not suddenly burst into flames at 56 miles per hour. Infact, there is an advantage to going 56 miles an hour as opposed to 55 (you get to your destination faster). In the same way, engineers frequently view safety rules as troublesome, and there is an advantage to have the freedom to disregard them.

Infact, we experience this psychologic everyday, usually without thinking about it. When you come toward an intersection, and the light turns yellow, you reach a point where you either have to go through on a yellow light, or come to a stop. Many people go through on the yellow, even though there is a greater risk. So, in a split second, we decide between the surety of sitting at a red light or the possibility, albeit slight, of a safety problem to go through the yellow light. There is a clear advantage to take the risk (as long as you aren't in an accident). While the stakes were higher at Chernobyl, the same psychologic applies.

At this point in the Chernobyl process, there were 28 control rods in the reactor – the minimum required. Increasing power would mean that even more control rods would have to be removed from the reactor. This would be a breach of protocol – the minimum number of rods was 28. Dyatlov gave the order to remove more control rods.

Toptunov, the reactor control engineer, refused to remove any more rods. He believed it would be unsafe to increase the power. With the reactor operating at 1 per cent, and the minimum number of control rods in the reactor, he believed it would be unsafe to remove more rods. He was abiding by a strict interpretation of the safety protocols of 28 rods.

But Dyatlov continued to rage, swearing at the engineers and demanding they increase power. Dyatlov threatened to fire Toptunov immediately if he didn't increase the power.

The 26-year-old Toptunov was faced with a choice. He believed he had two options:

1. He could refuse to increase power – but then Dyatlov would fire him immediately, and his career would be over.
2. His other choice was to increase power, recognizing that something bad might happen.

Toptunov looked around. All the other engineers – including his supervisors – were willing to increase power. Toptunov knew he was young and didn't have much experience with reactors. Perhaps this kind of protocol breach was normal. Toptunov was faced with that choice of the surety of his career ending vs. the possibility of safety problems. Toptunov decided to agree and increase the power.

Tragically, it would be the last decision Toptunov would ever made.

April 26, 1:00 a.m.

By 1:00 a.m., the power of the reactor was stable at 7 per cent of capacity. Only 18 control rods were in the reactor (safety protocols demanded that no less than 28 control rods should always be in the reactor).

At 1:07 a.m., the engineers wanted to make sure the reactor wouldn't overheat, so they turned on more water to ensure proper cooling (they were now pumping five times the normal rate of water through the reactor). The extra water cooled the reactor, and the power dropped again. The engineers responded by withdrawing even more control rods. Now, only three control rods were inserted in the reactor.

The reactor stabilized again. The engineers, satisfied with the amount of steam they were getting (they needed steam for their experiment) shut-off the pumps for the extra water. They shut-off the water, apparently only considering the effect that the water would have on the experiment – and did not consider the effect that the water was having on the reactor. At this point, with only three control rods in the reactor, the water was only thing keeping the reactor cool. Without the extra cool water, the reactor began to get hot. Power increased slowly at first. As the reactor got hotter, the reactor itself made the reactor hotter – the self-amplifying effect. The heat and reactivity of the reactor increased exponentially.

The engineers were trying to watch multiple variables simultaneously. The water, the steam, the control rods, and the current temperature of the reactor all were intertwined to affect the reactivity of the reactor. People can easily think in cause and effect terms. Had their only been one variable that controlled the reactivity, the results would probably have been different. However, people have difficulty thinking through the process when there are a multitude of variables, all interacting in different ways.

People are not processors of unlimited information. There is a limited amount of information with which a person can work. With the safety of hindsight, we can sit back and make a judgment saying, "they didn't think through all their information." However, this kind of linear judgement does not tell us why they didn't see what is obvious to our hindsight.

At 1:22 a.m. (90 seconds before the explosion), the engineers were still relaxed and confident. Dyatlov, infact, was seeing his turbine safety experiment coming to a successful conclusion. In what turned out to be a tragic irony, he encouraged his engineers by suggesting, "in two or three minutes it will all be over".

Thirty seconds before the explosion, the engineers realized the reactor was heating up too fast. With only three control rods in the reactor, and then shutting off the water, the reactor was superheating. In a panic, they desperately tried to drop control rods into the reactor, but the heat of the reactor had already melted the tubes into which the control rods slid.

The floor of the building began to shake, and loud banging started to echo through the control room. The coolant water began to boil violently, causing the pipes to burst. The super-heating reactor was creating hydrogen and oxygen gases. This explosive mixture of gasses accumulated above the reactor. The heat of the reactor was building fast, and the temperature of the flammable gasses was rising.

April 26, 1:24 a.m.

Finally, the gases detonated, destroying the reactor and the protective containment building. The control room was far enough away from the containment building to escape destruction, but the explosion shook the entire plant. Debris caved in around the control room members, and Dyatlov, Akimov, Toptunov, and the others were knocked to the floor. Dust and chalk filled the air. While they knew there had been an explosion, they hoped and prayed the explosion had not come from the reactor. Toptunov and Akimov ran over the broken glass and ceiling debris to the open door, and ran across the compound towards the containment building. There, they saw the horrifying, unspeakable sight. There was rubble where the reactor had been. They saw flames shooting up 40-feet high, burning oil squirting from pipes onto the ground, black ash falling to the ground, and a bright purple light emanating from the rubble.

Within a few minutes, fire fighters had arrived. The firefighters, most with no protective equipment, heroically worked to extinguish the fire, hoping to prevent further damage to the three other reactors at the plant. Most of the firefighters died from the radiation exposure.

Bryukhanov (the plant director), who was not at the plant at the time, had been contacted and told about an explosion. In the chaos, those informing Bryukhanov of the explosion still did not know the total amount of devastation. Bryukhavov, still desperately hoping that the reactor was intact, called Moscow to inform them that while there had been an explosion, the reactor had not sustained any damage.

Again, with the benefit of hindsight, we can say that Bryukhanov should have acted quicker. It's true that many lives could have been saved if he had acted differently. However, his actions are not uncommon in these kinds of situations. A common reaction is called "horizontal flight", where people retreat from the worst-case scenario, convincing themselves to believe the best-case scenario. Bryukhanov had convinced himself that the reactor was not in danger. And after all, someone from the plant had called and given an ambiguous message. Surely they would have known if the reactor had been destroyed.

April 26, 4:00 a.m.

At 4:00 a.m, the command from Moscow came back: keep the reactor cool. The authorities in Moscow had no idea that the damage was so catastrophic.

Akimov, Dyatlov, and Toptunov, their skin brown from the radiation, and their bodies wrenched from internal damage, had already been taken away to the medical centre.

At 10:00 a.m., Bryukhanov, the plant director, was informed that the reactor had been destroyed. Bryukhanov rejected the information, preferring to believe that the reactor was still intact. He informed Moscow that the reactor was intact and radiation was within normal limits.

Later that day, experts from around the Soviet Union came to Chernobyl, and found the horrifying truth. The reactor had indeed been destroyed, and fifty tons of radioactive fuel had instantly evaporated. The wind blew the radioactive plume in a northwesterly direction. Belarus and Finland were going to be in the path of the radioactive cloud.

The Days Afterward

The secretive Soviet state was slow to act. Soviet bureaucracy debated whether to evacuate nearby cities, and how much land should be evacuated. They were slow in their response, slow to evacuate, and slow to inform the world of the disaster. It took over 36 hours before authorities began to evacuate nearby residents. Two days later, the nightly news (the fourth story) reported that one of the reactors was 'damaged'.

Within a few days, radiation detectors were going off all over the world. The Soviets continued to try to hide the issue from the world and their own residents.

Several months later, Bryukhanov was arrested, still believing that he did everything right. Dyatlov survived the radiation sickness, and was arrested in December of that year. He believed he was a scapegoat for the accident. Akimov died a few weeks after the disaster, but till the very end continued to say, "I did everything right. I don't know how it happened".

The Radiation Cloud on April 27, 1986

from http://www.worldprocessor.com/53.htm

Problem-solving Errors

Wooden-Headedness, Barbara Tuchman, in her book, March of Folly (1984), describes a characteristic she calls "wooden-headedness". In the book, she chronicles people in history that made monumental errors and continued to make the errors after there was evidence that the policy was folly. Wooden-headedness is the "I've made up my mind, don't confuse me with the facts" mentality.

Wooden-headedness is not an ignorance of the facts, but a refusal to see the facts. It's a tunnel vision, a preoccupation with one course of action even when there is evidence that the course of action is either not working, or even backfiring. Wooden-headedness begins with the assumption that "I'm correct". The wooden-header believes that all their assumptions are correct, their view of reality is untarnished, and their strategies are perfect. They continue to pursue the course of action without ever re-evaluating their assumptions or rethinking their strategy.

Wooden-headedness and overconfidence often go hand-in-hand. Part of the overconfidence at Chernobyl came from no one speaking up about the dangerous path they were pursuing (only Toptunov spoke up against the process, but he quickly caved under Dyatlov's pressure to reheat the reactor). Part of the overconfidence came from the lack of independent thinking caused by the out-of-control hierarchical Soviet bureaucracy – the engineers didn't feel a need to question the path they were going down. Part of the overconfidence came from a lack of knowledge about past nuclear accidents.

Preoccupation and Overfocus

The engineers at Chernobyl were grossly preoccupied with their safety experiment. They were so obsessed with completing the experiment that they lost sight of the larger picture of nuclear safety.

Dyatlov was so obsessed with finishing the experiment that he refired the reactor when it had dropped to 1 per cent of capacity. He was so obsessed with finishing the experiment that he threatened to fire Toptunov – who had refused to reheat the already unstable reactor. Even after the disaster, Dyatlov (and many others) still believed everything they did was right – and showed no capacity to rethink their assumptions.

Preoccupation is a common problem among leaders. People can become so overfocused on one aspect of the whole picture, that they don't give new incoming information the importance it deserves. Psychologists call this a "loss of situation awareness", although the term does not explain why they became situationally unaware. Dorner (1996) found that when a decision maker gets preoccupied with a detail, they will frequently ignore incoming information that tells them that their detail has become irrelevant.

Horizontal Flight

Horizontal flight is the tendency to retreat into an idea or strategy that is safe when everything around the person is going to hell.

Bryukhanov showed horizontal flight by his absolute refusal to believe that the reactor had exploded, even when he was being told by his own staff. Dyatlov showed horizontal flight by believing that he could do anything to the reactor and still be safe. The Soviet bureaucracy showed horizontal flight in their failure to act quickly.

Again, this is a common response to difficult problems. At the end of World War II, Joseph Goebbels was designing new medals for the soldiers – only a few days before the end of the Third Reich. When situations become intolerable, we frequently move into areas where we have control – whether or not it makes sense.

Conclusion

While there were a few design errors that contributed to the disaster, the Chernobyl case study illustrates that people's problem-solving errors can be catastrophic. The grim chronology of Chernobyl outlines the unfolding of a logic of human error. It illustrates the development of human error – how it is not a decision, but a process. Human error, ubiquitous in all its forms and modes, unfolds with a peculiar logic that is all its own.

Bibliography, References, and Further Reading

1. Chernobyl children show DNA changes [Electronic Version]. (2001, May 8). BBC. Available at http://news.bbc.co.uk/hi/english/sci/tech/newsid_1319000/1319386.stm
2. Chernousenko, V.M. (1991). Chernobyl: Insight from the inside. New York: Springer-Verlag.
3. Dorner, M. (1996). The logic of failure: Recognizing and avoiding error in complex situations. Cambridge, MA: Perseus Books.
4. Medvedev, G. (1991). The truth about Chernobyl. New York: Basic Books.
5. Mozes, A. (December 10, 2001). Chernobyl's young have high rate of thyroid cancer [Electronic Version]. Reuters. Available at http://dailynews.yahoo.com/h/nm/20011210/hl/cancer_22.html
6. Shcherbak, Y.M. (1996). Ten years of the Chernobyl era [Electronic Version]. Scientific American. Available at http://www.sciam.com/0496issue/0496shcherbak.html
7. The Chernobyl accident: What happened [Electronic Version]. (2000, June 5). BBC. Available at http://news.bbc.co.uk/hi/english/world/europe/newsid_778000/778477.stm
8. The Chernobyl cancer world record [Electronic Version]. (2001, October 23). BBC. Available at http://news.bbc.co.uk/hi/english/health/newsid_1615000/1615299.stm
9. United Nations Environment Programme. (1987). State of the environment report, 1987, major environmental reports. Report of the executive director. April 6, 1987, Na. 87-0156-8939.

Case Study – 4: Disaster Vulnerability of Coastal States

A SHORT CASE STUDY OF ORISSA, INDIA BY DIPANKAR C. PATNAIK AND DR. N. SIVAGNANAM

Abstract

The State of Orissa is one of the most disaster-prone States in the Indian Union. Orissa's six coastal districts are often subjected to tropical storm systems like cyclones as well as storm induced flooding and surges. With the burgeoning population, the threat of the coastal vulnerability risk has increased manifold. Severe flooding caused by storm surges during the 1999 supercyclone caused massive damage to life and property. Although it is not possible to completely wish away the risk posed by such disasters yet much of the damage could be prevented by efficient preparedness plans at different levels of civil society. The need for better access to vital information through a scientific disaster preparedness and response system is long-felt. The need of the hour is effective risk mapping and assessment.

The paper assesses the vulnerability of the Coastal States of India with special case study of Orissa. Through the study of historical data, the vulnerability of the coast is established. The socio-economic fabric of the State of the Orissa along with the physiographic conditions is also studied. It focuses on the study of changing seasonal trends understood through cultural semantics. It also tries to address the problem of Cyclone Hazard Risk Management in the coastal areas in relation to the Indian Disaster management Framework.

Indian Coastal Scenario

India has more than 9,000 kms long stretch of coastline including island territories. The coast touches 60 districts spread over 10 maritime States while having a very complex landforms and coastal processes. The east coast is different from west coast in many respects. In west, there are no deltas but headlands, bays and lagoons are common. The length of the eastern coast is approx. 2,200 kms and the western coast is approx. 2,500 kms. By and large, the east coast is known for flat terrain dotted with beaches, coastal sand bars – dunes, backwaters, deltas, saltpans, mangroves, and mud flats. The western coast has narrow rolling plains, few sandy beaches and plenty of natural inlets coupled with rocky outcrops. It is marked by the significant absence of the deltas. The northern coast of Saurashtra, Gujarat and Maharashtra is tide dominated, whereas the southern coast of Karnataka and Kerala is wave dominated. The west coast is rocky cliffy and provides broad continental shelf while the east coast is covered with sediment providing comparatively narrow shelf. Important sand spits on the east coast of India include Manamel Kudi sand spit in Palk Bay, Sriharikota Island, Kakinada or Godavari point spit or Hope Island, Sacramento Shoal, False point sand spit, Chilika spit, and Palmiras Shoals (mouth of Dhamra River). Formation of Shoals, banks, and sand spits are common on the deltaic coast on the east as against west where rivers generally form estuaries. These variations between the coasts attract different kinds of natural hazards and disasters. However, the coastal problems in India are site specific and range from silting of creeks to periodic coastal disasters like cyclones and floods. The complexity is due to varied wave and tidal regimes, coastal configuration and fluctuating sea levels.

The Coastal State of Orissa

Orissa, an ancient land of spectacular beauty lies on the eastern side of India between 81°24' and 87° 29' E longitudes and 17°48' and 22°34' N latitudes. It extends over an area of 1,55,842 sq. kms. Jharkhand and West Bengal surround it on the North, Chhattisgarh on the west, Andhra Pradesh on the south and Bay of Bengal on the east. A total of 105 towns and 51,124 villages make it the eleventh most populous State in the country. Orissa, on the eastern sea board of India, enjoys a tropical monsoon type of climate like most other parts of the country. Its annual average rainfall is about 200 cm. Orissa, on the eastern coast of India, is not only attains rains from the south-west monsoon branch from the Bay of Bengal like the west coast, but also from the annual cyclones from the Bay of Bengal which influence it and bring copious rain with two seasonal peaks, July-August and October-November. Maldistribution poses a serious problem in the case of forest resources of Orissa. The main occupation of over 80 per cent of the people of Orissa is agriculture. Forests cover about 43 per cent of the area of the state. Because of its mineral wealth and strategic location it attracts foreign investment in steel, aluminium, power, refineries, and infrastructure. Orissa is also emerging as a player in the outsourcing IT (Information Technology) and IT services industry. Apart from irrigation, floods, droughts, low yield per hectare and division and fragmentation of holidays are the most important agricultural problem of the State. In addition, the bountiful forest resources and agricultural products provide ample scope for the development of forest-based and agro-based industries. The total population of Orissa was 36,706,920 as per the provisional results of the Census of India 2001. The population of the State rose by 15.94 per cent from 1991-2001. The sex ratio (i.e., the number of females per thousand males) of population was recorded as 972. Total literacy has risen from 49.09 per cent in 1991 to 63.61 per cent in the 2001 Census.

Table 1: Orissa – Population Statistics

Population Decadal Growth 1991-2001		
Persons	Males	Females
36,706,920	18,612,340	18,094,580

Coastal Activities

Orissa has a rich heritage in terms of coastal activities. The earliest known mariners in India hailed from Orissa and the voyages of the sailors have been illustrious with victorious campaigns in lands as far as Ceylon (Sri Lanka), Bali, and Sumatra (present day Indonesia).There are about 1,263 mechanized boats and 3,500 country craft operating from fishing centres like Chandipur, Chudamani, Salugaon, Kalupadgha, Pathara and Najari, where fishing jetties have been constructed at Gopalpur, Dhamara, and Astarang all weather fishing ports have been built. While at Paradeep a large deep sea fishing port has come up.

Disasters in India

India is one of the most disaster-prone countries in the world due to its geo-climatic conditions. Today more than ever before, India is vulnerable to these natural disasters. Floods, droughts, cyclones, earthquakes and landslides have been recurrent phenomena. About 60 per cent of the landmass is prone to earthquakes of various intensities; over 40 million hectares is prone to floods; about 8 per cent of the total area is prone to cyclones and 68 per cent of the area is susceptible to drought. In the decade 1990-2000, an average of about 4,344 people lost their lives and about 30 million people were affected by disasters every year. The loss in terms of private, community and public assets has been astronomical. This is partly because of the rising population as well largely to the climatic changes in the world which have influenced and increased the frequency of many disasters.

Cyclones are the one of the most catastrophic disasters to affect the Indian Coastal Community. Over the last century alone more than a lakh people have perished in the subcontinent due to the fury of the cyclones. At the global level, there has been considerable concern over natural disasters. Even as substantial scientific and material progress is made, the loss of lives and property due to disasters has not decreased. In fact, the human toll and economic losses have mounted. It was in this background that the United Nations General Assembly, in 1989, declared the decade 1990-2000 as the International Decade for Natural Disaster Reduction with the objective to reduce loss of lives and property and restrict socio-economic damage through concerted international action, especially in developing countries.

Cyclones

Tropical cyclones are intense low pressure systems which develop over warm sea. They are capable of causing immense damage due to strong winds, heavy rains and storm surges. The frequency of the TC in the Bay of Bengal is 4 to 5 times more than in the Arabian Sea. The extensive coastal belt of India is very vulnerable to the deadly storms known as tropical cyclones. About 4 to 6 such storms originate in the Bay of Bengal and the Arabian Sea every year. Tropical cyclones, which are characterized by torrential rain, gales and storm surges, cause heavy loss of human lives and destruction of property.

They also result in extensive damage to standing crops and loss of cattle. Flood and drought are common to many States in India, but only a few states are subject to cyclones and tornado. Orissa is one of the few. Cyclone has in recent years become a regular feature like flood and drought. The cyclonic storms during the monsoon which originate in the Bay of Bengal often cross the east coast between Paradeep and Chandbali and make a north-west ward journey proceeding over Kendujhar towards Sambalpur and then decrease in intensity. There are two cyclonic peaks in their occurrence, one during May-July and the other during October-November. As far as the periodicity of the occurrence of the storms is concerned, the maximum number of cyclones occurred during south-west monsoon period (154) followed by the post-monsoon period of the north-east monsoon (70) and pre-monsoon period (57). Cyclones in India generally strike the east coast; some of the Arabian Sea Cyclones strike the west coast of India as well mainly the Gujarat and North Maharashtra coast. Out of the storms that develop in the Bay of Bengal, over 58 per cent approach or cross the east coast in October and November. India has a very long coastline of 8,041 kms, large parts of which are vulnerable to cyclone. On an average, one or four cyclones or deep depressions hit eastern coast of India. The economic and human loss is also a periodic factor in these areas. The east coast of India experiences regular cyclones in the months of September-October and occasionally during March-April.

Orissa Coast

The 482 kms long stretch of Orissa coast is an important sector on the east coast of India with respect to physical distinctiveness, biota and marine resources. Nearly two-thirds of total population lives in coastal regions and major towns are located in this zone only. The Orissa coast extends from south of Digha in the north to Girisola in the south. The entire coastal strip varies in width from 40 to 50 kms comprising the districts of Baleshwar, Bhadrak, Kendrapada, Jagatsinghpur, Khurda, Puri, and Ganjam. The main agricultural products of the region include paddy, black gram, coconuts, betel leaves, cashew nuts, etc. Fish catch and prawn culture are dominating the scene. Poverty and underdevelopment is the striking feature. Overall accessibility to villages is poor and the situation worsens in the monsoon months. The narrow, level coastal strip, including the Mahanadi River delta, is exceedingly fertile. Rainfall is heavy and regular, and two crops of rice (by far the most important cereal) are grown annually.

Orissa has 30 districts out of which nine are coastal districts. There are 30 rivers of medium and minor category.The coastal lowland receives about 152 cm rain a year because it comes directly under the influence of tropical depression originating in the Bay of Bengal. Orissa coast accounts for 8 per cent of the coastline of India. The entire fish catch of Orissa is from within a distance of 10-15 kms from the coast.

Hazard Type - Time of Occurrence - Potential Impact

Cyclone May, September, October, and November – Loss of life, livestock, crop and infrastructure

Drought April to June crop loss, water scarcity

Flood June to September loss of life, crop infrastructure and animals

Fire accidents summer and winter human loss and house damage

Natural Disaster Threats to Orissa Coast

Orissa is facing environmental degradation worse than any other states in the country. About 85 per cent of the coastal zone of Orissa is under very fragile condition due to deforestation and conversion of forest patches to agricultural purposes. Coastal erosion has increased due to cyclonic storms that hit Orissa in 1943, 1950, 1965, 1970, 1982, 1984, 1988, 1989, 1991, 1993, 1995, and 1999. Surging waves, strong winds and torrential rains are associated with the cyclones. The coastal floods affected areas lying below 3 and 5 m surface heights during low and medium magnitude cyclones. Even villages above the 10 m mark were not spared by the magnitude of the supercyclone of 1999. Coastal Orissa as per the records available, experienced 23 larger cyclones during the 20th century and most of the severe cyclones hit the coast in the pre-monsoon months, i.e., May-June and retreating monsoon months, i.e., October-November. During storms, the high tide line over the raised water level goes right up to the base of the dune cliff. Surging tidal waves break the barriers of earthen embankments and sand dunes and flood the human habitations in low lands. Loose and unconsolidated materials of the sand dunes thus usually get eroded in a single storm. River bank erosion in similar way is also pronounced by high energy current flow and wave dash. High wind speed caused by cyclone increases wave dash and changes the current pattern of rivers.

Thus, unconsolidated materials produced by fresh silt accumulation over the river banks are easily eroded by wave dash and changing current pattern of the cyclones. Coastline is severely damaged due to natural calamities and population pressures. The vegetation which is mainly responsible to check the erosion has been under serious threat. At places it has been removed for fuel-wood requirement and at many places it is completely denuded in the name of developmental activities such as construction of resorts, hotels, tourist bungalows, guest houses, etc. As a fallout, the coastal villages experience severe cyclonic winds and the damage is phenomenal. The super cyclone of 1999 leading to colossal losses to men, material and the environment is the best example. The saline water of the sea that entered the interior villages unchecked not only spoiled the cultivated lands but also the drinking water sources.

The Changing Seasonal Regime — Traditional Knowledge and Modern Semantics

The older generation of people remember six distinct seasons grishma (summer), barsa (rains), sarata (autumn), hemanta (dew), sisira (winter), and basanta (spring). Traditionally the arrival of these seasons was seen through the signs in one's immediate environment, the onset of the monsoons and the climate phenomena were studied and predicted using means like the traditional Panjika (a traditional weather book).

The people of Orissa have always relied on ancient knowledge systems to predict the weather and plan their agriculture and other activities. Traditional weather forecasting methods have been preserved in strong oral proverbs, which, for generations, farmers considered essential knowledge for their farming.

Below is an example of a proverb from western Orissa:

Shrabana masara adya chouthi.

Chari digu jebe megha na uthi.

Dakhina digaru bahile baa.

Chasi bhai hala nangala dhari bidesh ja.

(At the dawn of the rainy season, if clouds do not form from each of the four directions, and if the wind is from the south then the farmers must pack up and migrate in search of bread and butter.)

Likewise, there are several indicators to predict the rains:

Dahuk gagale barsa hesi.

Dhamna gachke chadhle barsa hesi.

Chanti anda buhile barsa hesi.

(When the bronze-winged jacana bird calls (a short harsh grunt), when the hybrid cobra or local snake climbs a tree, and when red ants start transporting eggs, rain comes.)

Source: Richard Mahapatra 2006

However, it has changed now, with only two seasons: Rains and summer, with winter only spread in a short phase between the two. Intense heat has forced the people to discard the traditionally auspicious months of March-May due to the peak summer regimes. It rains during September and October, causing crop losses and floods. Over the last decade, most of the big floods occurred during

September and October. Scanty rainfall during the crucial months of June and July has triggered massive conflicts: for the past five years various police stations across the State have recorded close to 34,000 cases pertaining to conflicts over water. Of these, 50 per cent occur between June and August.

Natural Disaster Management Framework in India

The need for a paradigm shift in the thinking of and action on natural disasters has been long felt. The supercyclone in Orissa in October 1999 underscored the need to adopt a multidimensional endeavour involving diverse scientific, engineering, financial and social processes; the need to adopt multidisciplinary and multisectoral approach and incorporation of risk reduction in the developmental plans and strategies. Globally, the latest disaster management plans focus on the integration of the disaster management process and the development mechanism. This would ensure a multidisciplinary and multisectoral approach towards the issue of natural disasters. Further, it has been understood that the mitigation is cost-effective than post-disaster management.

Conclusion

Thus it is observed that the State of Orissa needs to attain an effective disaster management network at the earliest. Accelerated erosion, progressive siltation, and overall degradation of coastal belts are a common sight throughout India. There is an urgent need for their protection as the coastal resources are of immense value for present and future populations. The threat of the natural disasters can only be curtailed through a hybrid approach where a confluence of technology and social acceptance is evolved and practiced.

Bibliography

1. Elsner, J.B., and B. Kocher, 2000, Global tropical cyclone activity: A link to the North Atlantic Oscillation. Geophys. Res. Lett., 27, pp. 129-132.

2. Islam, M. M. and Sado, K. 2002, Development of priority map flood counter measures by remote sensing data with geographic information system, Journal of Hydrologic Engineering, 7 (5), pp. 346-355.

3. Landsea, C.W. 2000, Climate variability of tropical cyclones: Past, Present, and Future. In Storms, R.A. Pielke, Sr., and R.A. Pielke, Jr., Eds., Routledge, pp. 220-241.

4. Nott, J., and M. Hayne, 2001, High frequency of 'supercyclones' along the Great Barrier Reef over the past 5,000 years. Nature, 413, pp. 508-512.

5. Pielke, Jr., R.A., and Pielke, Sr., R.A., 1997, Hurricanes: Their Nature and Impacts on Society. John Wiley and Sons, p. 279.

Case Study – 5: Landslide Studies in India

Y.P. SHARDA*

LHIM and EPE Division, Geological Survey of India, New Delhi.

Status of Natural Hazards

India is vulnerable to different natural hazards due to its proximity to geodynamically active locales and unique climatic pattern. Both these factors in different combinations lead to the occurrence of disasters resulting from natural hazards like floods, earthquakes, drought, cyclones, and landslides in different parts of the country at frequent intervals. It is estimated that about 60 per cent of landmass of the country is vulnerable to earthquakes of different magnitudes; about 8 per cent of total area is susceptible to cyclone hazard; about 68 per cent of the area is drought prone; 12 per cent of area is susceptible to floods and approximately 15 per cent of total area of the country is susceptible to landslides. The disaster situation in the country is further compounded by increased vulnerabilities related to rapidly growing population, unplanned urbanization and fast-paced industrialization, rapid development in high risk areas, environmental degradation and climate change. It is observed that impact of natural disasters is felt more severely by people who are socio-economically weak because their habitats are located in vulnerable areas and not designed to withstand the impact of natural disasters. Therefore, the processes of poverty eradication and disaster management are intricately linked.

The severity of natural disasters in the country is indicated by the estimate of the Ministry of Home Affairs which states that in the decade 1990-2000, annually, an average of about 4,344 people lost their lives and about 30 million people were affected by disasters. In recent years, a rising trend in both natural as well as man-made disasters is evident. Statistics indicates that during 1994-1998, approximately 120 million were affected by the natural disasters and economic losses resulting from same during the period were estimated to be ₹ 2,86,780 million. These figures climbed to 560 million and ₹ 4,74,640 million during 1998-2003.

Recent Developments in Disaster Management in India

Until recently, the disaster management was post-disaster rehabilitation and relief centric. Drought and floods were considered as major disasters. Three major disasters during recent times, include the Malpa Landslide of August 1998, Supercyclone of Orissa in 1999, and Bhuj earthquake in 2001. These events led to a sea change in the Disaster Management scenario in the country. During August 1999, a High Power Committee (HPC) reviewed the disaster management in the country. After Bhuj earthquake of January 26, 2001, the disaster management process moved forward quickly and there was paradigm shift from post-disaster relief centric to pro-active approach that integrates disaster mitigation into developmental planning.

Y.P. SHARDA*

LHIM and EPE Division, Geological Survey of India, New Delhi Committee was set up after Bhuj earthquake of 2001 for making recommendations on the preparation of Disaster Management plans and for suggesting effective mitigation mechanisms. The 10th Five-Year Plan also had, for the first time, a chapter on Disaster Management and the terms of reference of 12th Finance Commission were changed and it was remandated to look into the requirements of disaster mitigation and prevention, apart from the routine attention paid by it to the matters related to relief and rehabilitation. The year 2004 can be considered as watershed as far as disaster management in India is concerned. This year marked a paradigm shift from erstwhile response-centric syndrome to a proactive prevention, mitigation and preparedness-driven approach in case of disaster management and all the related activities. The main philosophy was that investment in prevention, mitigation and preparedness will not only conserve the developmental gains but also minimize losses to lives, livelihood, and property.

Landslides

Landslides are one of the natural hazards that affect at least 15 per cent of land area of our country exceeding 0.49 million km^2. Landslides of different types occur frequently in geodynamically active domains in Himalaya, Northeastern India as also in stable domains in Western Ghats and Nilgiri Hills of southern India. Landslides have had disastrous consequences and in 2005, over 500 lives were lost due to landslides.

Recurring impact of these is felt in 21 States and Mahe Enclave of Union Territory of Pudducherry to a variable extent. Keeping the frequent recurrence, landslides were identified as a significant natural hazard. As a part of management of this significant natural hazard, National Core Group for Landslide Hazard Mitigation was formed the terms of reference of the Core Group comprising key national ministries and institutions, was set up to draw a strategy for monitoring the impact of landslides, devising landslide hazard mitigation, monitoring the activities related to landslide hazard mitigation including landslide hazard zonation, evolving an Early Warning System and protocols for landslide hazard/ risk reduction. The Geological Survey of India was declared Nodal Agency for landslide hazard mitigation studies. The responsibilities of this Nodal Agency included: (1) coordinating and undertaking geological studies for landslide hazard mitigation, (2) carrying out landslide hazard zonation on different spatial scales, (3) monitoring landslides and snow avalanches, (4) studying the factors responsible for sliding, (5) suggesting precautionary and preventive measures, (6) developing a quick response mechanism to investigate the incidences on emergency basis, (7) evolving an early warning system, (8) developing an inventory/ databases on landslide hazard, (9) develop awareness strategy and awareness programmes hazard, and (10) coordinate the landslide studies in the country to ensure that LHZ is carried out as per the prescribed parameters. The Core Group also entrusted further responsibilities to the Nodal Agency in the form of an action plan that included finalization of uniform methodologies for LHZ on macro-scales and meso-scales, LHZ of vulnerable areas on macro scales, identify critical slopes and prioritize areas for detailed studies. State Governments were to suggest routes for this exercise and GSI to carry-out mapping. Other agencies identified to collaborate in this effort are NRSA, Survey of India (SOI), India Meteorological Department (IMD), and Central Water Commission (CWC).

After Indian Ocean Tsunami of December 2004, the Government of India enacted the Disaster Management Act on December 23, 2005. One of the provisions of this Act included creation of National Disaster Management Authority (NDMA) headed by the Prime Minister, to spearhead and implement a holistic and integrated approach to disaster management in the country. The DM Act, 2005 lays down institutional and coordination mechanism at all levels and provides for establishment of Disaster Mitigation and Disaster Response Fund at national, State, and district levels.

With establishment of NDMA, some more responsibilities, in addition to existing ones, were entrusted to GSI as Nodal Agency. These include assisting NDMA in drawing up the policies, plans, and guidelines in case of landslide hazard and advise NDMA in technical matters. GSI being Nodal Agency for Landslide Hazard Mitigation has been made part of Disaster Management Support Network and control room equipped with latest communication systems and having continuous connectivity with other primary nodes and disaster management control rooms of the States vulnerable to disasters was established at GSI, New Delhi with a view to exchange disaster-related data and information on real-time basis.

Status of Landslide Studies

The landslide studies in the country can be categorized as pre- and post-disaster studies. The pre-disaster studies include landslide hazard zonation mapping on different scales to identify the areas/locales susceptible to landslide hazard. The landslide hazard zonation maps thus developed provide an assessment of the safety of existing habitations and infrastructural elements, and help plan further developmental activities in mountainous regions. The post-disaster studies include development of inventory data bases of existing landslides, assessment of landslide incidences occurring in different parts of the country as a part of quick response to landslide occurrence, detailed studies of selected landslides, and studies of landslides with an effort to stabilize them. The stabilization efforts include treatment measures after establishing the causes responsible for destabilizing the slopes using geological and geotechnical investigations. Institutions like the Geological Survey of India (GSI), Central Building Research Institute (CBRI), Central Road Research Institute (CRRI), National Remote Sensing Agency (NRSA), Wadia Institute of Himalayan Geology (WIHG), Defence Terrain Analysis Laboratory (DTRL), Govind Ballabh Pant Institute of Himalayan Environment, and IIT-Roorkee besides many other academic institutions and individuals are engaged in both pre- and post-disaster landslide studies in the country. Besides these, Border Roads Organization (BRO) is the organization that faces the fury of landslides every year.

Pre-disaster Studies

The pre-disaster studies include landslide hazard zonation mapping in different parts of the country and assessment of slope stability aspects at the sites of different infrastructural facilities. The landslide hazard zonation on macro (1:50,000 or 1:25,000 scales) and meso (1:10,000 or 1: 5,000) scales has been taken up by Geological Survey of India. The methodology standardized by the Bureau of Indian Standards (BIS) through IS-14496 (Part 2): 1998 has been followed to carry-out landslide hazard zonation mapping in different parts of the country. After covering some areas following these BIS guidelines, it was felt that certain parameters need modification and these are under review. Efforts are being made to use GIS as data and map integration tools. Landslide zonation mapping in parts of Ravi Basin, Himachal Pradesh; Yamuna Basin, Uttarakhand; Imphal Town, Manipur; Kohima City, Nagaland; and Kolasib and Cachar districts, Mizoram and Manipur, were continued. Landslide hazard zonation on macro-scales include Guwahati Urban Area; Coonoor Area, Nilgiri district, Tamilnadu; Thodupuzha Area, Idukki district, Kerala; along NH-39 between Kohima and Imphal, Nagaland and Manipur; between Imphal and Nungba along NH-53, Manipur; Lunglei area, Mizoram. Landslide Hazard Zonation of parts of Darjeeling district of West Bengal covered an area of 1,527 sq. kms was carried out employing facet and related slope morphometry parameters derived from Digital Elevation Model (DEM) using different remote sensing (ERDAS IMAGINE 8.7 and LPS Suite) routines and GIS (ARC/INFO and ILWIS 3.3) techniques. Another 600 sq. kms area out of targeted 1070sq. kms was covered through landslide hazard zonation mapping in Sikkim with the help of DEM and SRTM Dem. The other efforts in this field include LHZ mapping in Chamoli and Almora districts in Ramganga basin; around Ranikhet in Uttarakhand; around Shimla in Himachal Pradesh; part of Mumbai-Goa Highway and area around Malshej Ghat area in Maharashtra. With this the landslide hazard zonation mapping has been completed covering about 49,000 sq. kms in different States and 4,700 line kilometres along National and State Highways.

Scientists from Central Road Research Institute (CRRI) analysed the landslide hazard potential in Patalganga Valley, Garhwal region of Western Himalaya (Kumar *et.al.,* 2005). In addition to above LHZ mapping on meso-scales (1:10,000 or 5,000 scales) has been taken up by GSI in some States. These include area around Lunglei Town, Mizoram; Kurisumala, Kottayam district, Kerala; and area around Vaishnodevi Shrine, Jammu and Kashmir. The R&D studies in this field include review and appraisal of existing methodologies by some workers (Sarkar and Kanungo 2005 a and b; Jaiswal, 2006; Sharma, 2006) and introduction of alternate approaches by others. Sarkar and Kanungo (2004) suggested an integrated approach for landslide susceptibility mapping using remote sensing and 100 Glimpses of Geoscience Research in India GIS on the basis of studies carried out in Darjeeling Himalaya. Kanungo *et.al.,* (2006 a) suggested GIS-based landslide hazard zonation using Neuro-fuzzy weighing. Kanungo *et.al.*, (2006 b), advocated Fuzzy Gama Operator for integration of thematic maps. Kanungo *et. al.* (2006 c) again carried out a comparative study of conventional, ANN black box, fuzzy and combined neural and fuzzy weighing procedures for landslide susceptibility zonation in Darjeeling Himalaya. Deva and Srivastava (2006) suggested a grid-based approach for classifying the terrain into five categories using three factors that include lithology, ruggedness number and land use/land cover. Pachauri (2007) based on the LHZ mapping carried out in Chamoli area of Uttarakhand concluded that facet-based LHZ is very effective tool for landslide mapping in high relief areas in Himalayas and is cost-effective.

Champatiray *et. al.* (2007) also suggested a fuzzy-based method for landslide hazard zonation in active seismic zone of Himalaya. Landslide Risk Zonation Studies, though not very common in India, have been attempted by some workers as R&D efforts. Pachauri *et.al.,* (2006) attempted risk zonation of an area in Garhwal Himalayas and concluded that rock fall velocity modelling can be useful in landslide risk zonation of an area. Kanungo *et. al.* (2006d) developed and implemented a linguistic rule based fuzzy approach to prepare Landslide Risk Assessment (LRA) map of Darjeeling Himalayas. In this methodology the LRA has been considered a function of landslide potential (LP) and resource damage potential (RDP). The LP and RDP have been characterized by LSZ and resource maps.

Awareness generation has been identified as a significant component of disaster management process and GSI has conducted one-day interactive workshops as a part of Contact Programme in many landslide affected States. This programme will continue in future till all the target groups are covered. In addition, National Institute of Disaster Management (NIDM) has also been engaged in conducting training programmes in different disaster-prone States.

Post-disaster Studies

The post-disaster studies were governed by the emerging disaster management scenario. These include: (1) development and updating of inventory data bases (of existing landslide incidences) on a continuing basis, (2) quick response to landslide incidences, (3) preliminary assessment and detailed studies of existing disastrous or potentially disastrous landslides posing danger to habitations, and (4) infrastructural elements and other civil projects.

Development of inventory databases of existing and new landslide incidences in different parts of the country, are considered an essential input for assessing the status of hazard in an area. A landslide information reporting proforma was developed for reporting the occurrence of landslides to the DMS control room at GSI, New Delhi. The format for storing the data bases is in-stage of finalization. In addition, the reports, technical notes, newspapers are being scanned for information on existing and new landslide events, to continuously update the inventory. In addition, different regions of GSI are preparing the inventories of the landslides. The quick response to occurrence of landslide every year has also helped immensely in updating the inventory, GSI published inventory of landslides of Northwest Himalaya in 2005 (Gupta, 2005). Landslide studies include reconnoitery studies followed by detailed analysis, preliminary monitoring of a few landslides and efforts to stabilize the disastrous landslides.

The preliminary/reconnoitery studies of specific slides were carried out to assess the magnitude of problem, suggest remedial measures and identify the slides that require detailed studies. The work carried included study of 34 incidences in Himachal Pradesh, 65 incidences in Uttarakhand, 20 landslide in Jammu & Kashmir, 111 in West Bengal, 4 incidences around Guwahati in Assam, four in Meghalaya, 5 in Nagaland, 3 incidences in Manipur, six landslides that occurred in August 2006 in Andhra Pradesh, 19 landslide incidences in Kerala, 31 slides in Tamil Nadu, 54 in Karnataka, 5 in Goa, 24 in Maharashtra, 2 incidences in Orissa, 3 incidences in Madhya Pradesh. In addition, the vulnerability of habitations in Jammu & Kashmir due of co-seismic landslides that occurred due to October 8, 2005 Kashmir earthquake was assessed and distress and slope failures induced by February 14, 2006 Sikkim earthquake were also studied by GSI.

The detailed studies of certain landslides were carried out by CRRI and CBRI. Some of these are Paglajhora landslide in Darjeeling district, West Bengal, B2, Elaichi and Serwani landslides in Sikkim, Sonapur landslide in Meghalaya, Kallala, Nitukottapara, Munnar landslides in Kerala, Kallar, Barliar Check post in Tamil Nadu, Mao slide along Dimapur-Imphal National Highway in Nagaland Bhilar landslide in Maharashtra and Surabi landslide in Uttarakhand.

Monitoring of the landslides by GSI included, Kallala landslide in Kerala, 9th Mile landslide in Sikkim, Bhilar landslide in Maharashtra, Surabi landslide in Uttarakhand and Hospital slide in Nilgiri district, Tamil Nadu.

The landslides have been analysed in details. CBRI examined Phata landslide, Uttaranchal (Ghosh *et.al.,* 2006). CRRI studies examined rock fall in Mumbai-Pune Expressway, evaluation of failure potential of Narayanbagar landslide, District Chamoli, Uttaranchal. A detailed study of debris and earth flow on National Highway-39, near Kohima, Nagaland (Kumar *et. al.,* 2008) and geological and geotechnical investigations of Patalganga landslide adjacent to NH-58, in Garhwal Himalaya, Uttaranchal (Kumar *et. al.,* 2006), were also carried out. Attempts have also been made to stabilize the landslides. Multidisciplinary and multiinstitutional studies on Varunavat landslide of September 24, 2003, on a hill overlooking the Uttarakashi town. Field and laboratory tests, physical/numerical modelling experiments enable evolution of practical and cost-effective treatment measures. The team included CRRI, CBRI, NIRM, WIHG, IIT-Roorkee, and GSI.

Some of the treatment measures included grading of steep overburden covered slopes with provision of horizontal berms and covering these with bio-degradable geo-textiles (mainly coir), provision of a wide berm at the interface of overburden with bedrock, strengthening of distressed and landslide studies in India 101 weathered rock mass through shaft piling, consolidation grouting, rock bolting and cable anchoring, erecting geogrid structure, providing effective drainage, and strengthening the toe of the hill by providing a well-designed retaining wall. In addition, the CRRI designed the corrective measures for critical slopes in Kol Dam Project, Himachal Pradesh.

Case Study – 6: Stampede at Sabarimala Tragedy

Pulmedu Uppupara after the stampede A Malikappuram Amma search for his son and relatives at the Kumali Hospital where the dead bodies lied. Victims of Pulmedu Stampede Pulmedu is an auspicious site of utmost emotional importance in the sacred Sabarimala Poonkavanam. One among the eighteen hills that form the Poonkavanam, Pulmedu is only seven kilometres away from Sabarimala. About three-fourths of the total pilgrims to the hill shrine trek to Sabarimala by this forest route. The Maharaja of Trvanacore, the Raja of Pandalam and the Raja of Poonjar had chosen the Pulmedu route to visit Sabarimala from very old days. The route has attained a place in the hearts of Sabarimala pilgrims for reasons of faith and also history.

In the tragedy that occurred at Pulmedu on the Makaravilakku day, on January 14, 2011 at around 8 p.m., 102 Ayyappa devotees died in an unprecedented rush and the resultant melee. More than fifty were injured. The condition of many of those injured is critical. The hills at Pulmedu are the tallest. With no trees around, the entire Poonkavanam area including Sabarimala temple, Ponnambalamedu, Pamba River, Saramkuthi, Malikappuram is clearly visible from this vantage position. It is therefore only natural that the devotees throng to Pulmedu. The holy kite – Krishnaparundu – circling the sky while Thiruvabharanam, the ornaments of the Lord are brought in procession to Sabarimala, ascending the eighteen steps, Pathinettam padi with Thiruvabharanam and the subsequent Deeparadhana were all viewed in total devotion amid chanting of Saranamanthram on the day of Makaravilakku. Within a few minutes the celestial light appeared at Ponnambalamedu, the Moolasthanam of Sree Ayyappa.

The entire atmosphere reverberated with the shouts of 'Swamiye Saranam Ayyappa' by three lakh odd devotees assembled at Pulmedu. With their hearts sobbing and minds fully satisfied by the darshan of Makarajyothi and Makaravilakku, the Ayyappa devotees started their return journey from the hilltop. As the rush thickened several devotees on the return journey fell down one after another. Those who fell down were run over by the thousands in the rush. The tragedy took the toll of 102 lives. Neither there was power supply nor water supply. Also no safety measures or arrangements for relief work. All these added to the misery and the fury.

Most of those who lost their lives belonged to economically and socially weaker sections. Their families have been orphaned. Most of those dead were the main pillars of their families, leaving behind penniless wives and children, girls to be married off and houses with construction unfinished. Those left behind do not know to go ahead in the days to come. Many students have been forced to discontinue studies. Some families are on the verge of being evicted for having failed to pay rent. The 102 unfortunate Ayyappa devotees who lost their lives are our own brothers. Even while struggling for breath in the stampede, they were holding close to their chests, the Irumudikkettu they were carrying, chanting Saranamanthra, their concern was that the Irumudikkettu should be intact, receiving every hit for themselves. They have, therefore, turned immortal.

Let us pay our homage to the great souls. Let us share the grief of their families. Let us pray for them.

Case Study – 7: Three Mile Island Accident

The Three Mile Island accident was a partial core meltdown in Unit 2 (a pressurized water reactor manufactured by Babcock & Wilcox) of the Three Mile Island Nuclear Generating Station in Dauphin County, Pennsylvania near Harrisburg, United States in 1979.

The power plant was owned and operated by General Public Utilities and Metropolitan Edison (Met Ed). It was the most significant accident in the history of the USA commercial nuclear power generating industry, resulting in the release of up to 481 PBq (13 million curies) of radioactive gases, and less than 740 GBq (20 curies) of Iodine-131.

The accident began at 4 a.m. on Wednesday, March 28, 1979, with failures in the non-nuclear secondary system, followed by a stuck-open Pilot-Operated Relief Valve (PORV) in the primary system, which allowed large amounts of nuclear reactor coolant to escape. The mechanical failures were compounded by the initial failure of plant operators to recognize the situation as a loss-of-coolant accident due to inadequate training and human factors, such as human-computer interaction design oversights relating to ambiguous control room indicators in the power plant's user interface. In particular, a hidden indicator light led to an operator manually overriding the automatic emergency cooling system of the reactor because the operator mistakenly believed that there was too much coolant water present in the reactor and causing the steam pressure release. The scope and complexity of the accident became clear over the course of five days, as employees of Met Ed, Pennsylvania state officials, and members of the U.S. Nuclear Regulatory Commission (NRC) tried to understand the problem, communicate the situation to the press and local community, decide whether the accident required an emergency evacuation, and ultimately end the crisis. The NRC's authorization of the release of 40,000 gallons of radioactive waste water directly in the Susquehanna River led to a loss of credibility with the press and community.

In the end, the reactor was brought under control, although full details of the accident were not discovered until much later, following extensive investigations by both a presidential commission and the NRC. The Kemeny Commission Report concluded that "there will either be no case of cancer or the number of cases will be so small that it will never be possible to detect them. The same conclusion applies to the other possible health effects". Several epidemiological studies in the years since the accident have supported the conclusion that radiation released from the accident had no perceptible effect on cancer incidence in residents near the plant, though these findings are contested by one team of researchers.

Public reaction to the event was probably influenced by the China Syndrome, a movie which had recently been released and which depicts an accident at a nuclear reactor. Communications from officials during the initial phases of the accident were felt to be confusing. The accident crystallized anti-nuclear safety concerns among activists and the general public, resulted in new regulations for the nuclear industry, and has been cited as a contributor to the decline of new reactor construction that was already underway in the 1970s.

"The incident was rated a five on the seven-point International Nuclear Event Scale: Accident With Wider Consequences".

In the nighttime hours preceding the incident, the TMI-2 reactor was running at 97per cent of full power, while the companion TMI-1 reactor was shutdown for refuelling. The chain of events leading to the partial core meltdown began at 4 a.m. EST on March 28, 1979, in TMI-2's secondary loop, one of the three main water/steam loops in a pressurized water reactor.

Workers were cleaning a blockage in one of the eight condensate polishers (sophisticated filters cleaning the secondary loop water), when, for reasons still unknown, the pumps to the polishers stopped running. When a polisher bypass valve did not trip, the polisher water stopped flowing to the secondary's main feed water pumps, which also shutdown. When the steam generators stopped receiving water, this triggered the turbine to shutdown and the reactor to perform an emergency shutdown (SCRAM): control rods were inserted into the core to control the rate of fission. All this happened in eight seconds. But the reactor continued to generate decay heat, and because steam was no longer being used by the turbine, the steam generators no longer removed that heat from the reactor's primary water loop.

Once the secondary feed water pumps stopped, three auxiliary pumps activated automatically. However, because the valves had been closed for routine maintenance, the system was unable to pump any water. The closure of these valves was a violation of a key NRC rule, according to which the reactor must be shutdown if all auxiliary feed pumps are closed for maintenance. This failure was later singled out by NRC officials as a key one, without which the course of events would have been very different.

Due to the loss of heat removal from the primary loop and the failure of the auxiliary system to activate, the primary loop pressure began to increase, triggering the pilot-operated relief valve (PORV) at the top of the pressurizer (a pressure active-regulator tank) to open automatically. The relief valve should have closed again when the excess pressure had been released, and electric power to the solenoid of the pilot was automatically cut, but the relief valve stuck open due to a mechanical fault. The open valve permitted coolant water to escape from the primary system, and was the principal mechanical cause of the true coolant-loss meltdown crisis that followed.

Human Factors – Confusion Over Valve Status

Critical human factors and user interface engineering problems were revealed in the investigation of the reactor control system's user interface. An indicator lamp in the control room was designed to light when electric power was applied to the solenoid that operated the pilot valve of the PORV. Operators misinterpreted the unlighted indicator to mean that the main relief valve was closed. In reality, the lamp only indicated that power had been removed from the solenoid. Because this indicator was not designed to unambiguously indicate the actual position of the main relief valve, the operators did not correctly diagnose the problem for several hours.

The design of the PORV indicator light was fundamentally flawed, because it implied that the PORV was shut when it went dark. When everything was operating correctly this was true, and the operators became habituated to rely on it. However, when things went wrong and the main relief valve stuck open, the unlighted lamp was actually misleading the operators by implying that the valve was shut. This caused the operators considerable confusion, because the pressure, temperature and levels in the primary circuit, so far as they could observe them via their instruments, were not behaving as they would have done if the PORV was shut – which they were convinced it was. This confusion contributed to the severity of the accident because the operators were unable to break out of a cycle of assumptions that conflicted with what their instruments were telling them. It was not until a fresh shift came in who did not have the mindset of the first set of operators that the problem was correctly diagnosed. But by then, major damage had occurred.

The operators had not been trained to understand the ambiguous nature of the PORV indicator and look for alternative confirmation that the main relief valve was closed. There was a temperature indicator downstream of the PORV in the tail pipe between the PORV and the pressurizer that could have told them the valve was stuck open, by showing that the temperature in the tail pipe remained higher than it should have had the PORV shut. But, this temperature indicator was not part of the "safety grade" suite of indicators designed to be used after an incident, and the operators had not been trained to use it. Its location on the back of the desk also meant that it was effectively out of sight of the operators.

Consequences of Stuck Valve

As the pressure in the primary system continued to decrease, reactor coolant continued to flow, but it was boiling inside the core. First, small bubbles of steam formed and immediately collapsed, known as nucleate boiling. As the system pressure decreased further, steam pockets began to form in the reactor coolant. This departure from nucleate boiling caused steam voids in coolant channels, blocking the flow of liquid coolant and greatly increasing the fuel plate temperature. The steam voids also took up more volume than liquid water, causing the pressurizer water level to rise even though coolant was being lost through the open PORV. Because of the lack of a dedicated instrument to measure the level of water in the core, operators judged the level of water in the core solely by the level in the pressurizer. Since it was high, they assumed that the core was properly covered with coolant, unaware that because of steam forming in the reactor vessel, the indicator provided false readings. This was a key contributor to the initial failure to recognize the accident as a loss-of-coolant accident, and led operators to turn off the emergency core cooling pumps, which had automatically started after the PORV stuck and core coolant loss began, due to fears the system was being overfilled.

With the PORV still open, the quench tank that collected the discharge from the PORV overfilled, causing the containment building sump to fill and sound an alarm at 4:11 a.m., This alarm, along with higher than normal temperatures on the PORV discharge line and unusually high containment building temperatures and pressures, were clear indications that there was an ongoing loss-of-coolant accident, but these indications were initially ignored by operators. At 4:15 a.m., the quench tank relief diaphragm ruptured, and radioactive coolant began to leak out into the general containment building. This radioactive coolant was pumped from the containment building sump to an auxiliary building, outside the main containment, until the sump pumps were stopped at 4:39 a.m.

After almost 80 minutes of slow temperature rise, the primary loop's four main pumps began to cavitate as a steam bubble/water mixture, rather than water, passed through them. The pumps were shutdown, and it was believed that natural circulation would continue the water movement. Steam in the system prevented flow through the core, and as the water stopped circulating it was converted to steam in increasing amounts. About 130 minutes after the first malfunction, the top of the reactor core was exposed and the intense heat caused a reaction to occur between the steam forming in the reactor core and the Zircaloy nuclear fuel rod cladding, yielding zirconium dioxide, hydrogen, and additional heat. This fiery reaction burned off the nuclear fuel rod cladding, the hot plume of reacting steam and zirconium damaged the fuel pellets which released more radioactivity to the reactor coolant and produced hydrogen gas that is believed to have caused a small explosion in the containment building later that afternoon.

At 6 a.m., there was a shift change in the control room. A new arrival noticed that the temperature in the PORV tail pipe and the holding tanks was excessive and used a backup valve – called a block valve – to shut-off the coolant venting via the PORV, but around 32,000 US gal (1,20,000 L) of coolant had already leaked from the primary loop. It was not until 165 minutes after the start of the problem that radiation alarms activated as contaminated water reached detectors; by that time, the radiation levels in the primary coolant water were around 300 times expected levels, and the plant was seriously contaminated.

Emergency Declared

At 6:56 a.m., a plant supervisor declared a site emergency, and less than half an hour later station manager Gary Miller announced a general emergency, defined as having the "potential for serious radiological consequences" to the general public. Metropolitan Edison notified the Pennsylvania Emergency Management Agency (PEMA), which in turn contacted State and local agencies, governor Richard L. Thornburgh and lieutenant governor William Scranton III, to whom Thornburgh assigned responsibility for collecting and reporting on information about the accident. The uncertainty of operators at the plant was reflected in fragmentary, ambiguous, or contradictory statements made by Met Ed to government agencies and to the press, particularly about the possibility and severity of off-site radiation releases. Scranton held a press conference in which he was reassuring, yet confusing, about this possibility, stating that though there had been a "small release of radiation no increase in normal radiation levels" had been detected. These were contradicted by another official, and by statements from Met Ed, who both claimed that no radiation had been released. Infact, readings from instruments at the plant and off-site detectors had detected radiation releases, albeit at levels that were unlikely to threaten public health as long as they were temporary, and providing that containment of the then highly contaminated reactor was maintained.

Angry that Met Ed had not informed them before conducting a steam venting from the plant and convinced that the company was downplaying the severity of the accident, state officials turned to the NRC. After receiving word of the accident from Met Ed, the NRC had activated its emergency response headquarters in Bethesda, Maryland and sent staff members to Three Mile Island. NRC chairman Joseph Hendrie and commissioner Victor Gilinsky initially viewed the accident, in the words of NRC historian Samuel Walker, as a "cause for concern but not alarm". Gilinsky briefed reporters and members of Congress on the situation and informed White House staff, and at 10 a.m. met with two other commissioners. However, the NRC faced the same problems in obtaining accurate information as the State, and was further hampered by being organizationally ill-prepared to deal with emergencies, as it lacked a clear command structure and the authority to tell the utility what to do, or to order an evacuation of the local area.

In a 2009 article, Gilinsky wrote that it took five weeks to learn that "the reactor operators had measured fuel temperatures near the melting point". He further wrote: "We didn't learn for years – until the reactor vessel was physically opened — that by the time the plant operator called the NRC at about 8 a.m., roughly one-half of the uranium fuel had already melted".

It was still not clear to the control room staff that the primary loop water levels were low and that over half the core was exposed. A group of workers took manual readings from the thermocouples and obtained a sample of primary loop water. Seven hours into the emergency, new water was pumped into the primary loop and the backup relief valve was opened to reduce pressure so that the loop could be filled with water. After 16 hours, the primary loop pumps were turned on once again, and the core temperature began to fall. A large part of the core had melted, and the system was still dangerously radioactive.

On the third day following the accident, a hydrogen bubble was discovered in the dome of the pressure vessel, and became the focus of concern. A hydrogen explosion might not only breach the pressure vessel, but, depending on its magnitude, might compromise the integrity of the containment vessel leading to large-scale release of radiation. However, it was determined that there was no oxygen present in the pressure vessel, a prerequisite for hydrogen to burn or explode. Immediate steps were taken to reduce the hydrogen bubble, and by the following day it was significantly smaller. Over the next week, steam and hydrogen were removed from the reactor using a catalytic recombiner and, controversially, by venting straight to the atmosphere.

Radioactive Material Release

Once the first line of containment is breached during a reactor plant accident, there is a possibility that the fuel or the fission products held inside can be released into the environment. Although the zirconium fuel cladding has been breached in other nuclear reactors without generating a release to the environment, at TMI-2 operators permitted fission products to leave the other containment barriers. This occurred when the cladding was damaged while the PORV was still stuck open. Fission products were released into the reactor coolant. Since the PORV was stuck open and the loss of coolant accident was still in progress, primary coolant with fission products and/or fuel was released, and ultimately ended up in the auxiliary building. This auxiliary building was outside the containment boundary. This was evidenced by the radiation alarms that eventually sounded. However, since very little of the fission products released were solids at room temperature, very little radiological contamination was reported in the environment. No significant level of radiation was attributed to the TMI-2 accident outside of the TMI-2 facility. Noble gases such as xenon 131 (a byproduct of the decay of radioactive iodine) made up the bulk of the release of radioactive materials from TMI-2, with the next most abundant element being iodine.

Within hours of the accident the United States Environmental Protection Agency (EPA) began daily sampling of the environment at the three stations closest to the plant. By April 1, continuous monitoring at 11 stations was established and was expanded to 31 stations two days later. An inter-agency analysis concluded that the accident did not raise radioactivity far enough above background levels to cause even one additional cancer death among the people in the area. The EPA found no contamination in water, soil, sediment, or plant samples.

Researchers at nearby Dickinson College, which had radiation monitoring equipment sensitive enough to detect Chinese atmospheric atomic weapons testing, collected soil samples from the area for the ensuing two weeks and detected no elevated levels of radioactivity, except after rainfalls (likely due to natural radon plate out, not the accident). Also, white-tailed deer tongues harvested over 50 miles (80 kms) from the reactor subsequent to the accident were found to have significantly higher levels of Cs-137 than in deer in the counties immediately surrounding the power plant. Even then, the elevated levels were still below those seen in deer in other parts of the country during the height of atmospheric weapons testing. Had there been elevated releases of radioactivity, increased levels of Iodine-131 and Cesium-137 would have been expected to be detected in cattle and goat's milk samples. Yet elevated levels were not found.

A later scientific study noted that the official emission figures were consistent with available dosimeter data, though others have noted the incompleteness of this data, particularly for releases early on.

According to the official figures, as compiled by the 1979 Kemeny Commission from Metropolitan Edison and NRC data, a maximum of 480 petabecquerels (13 million curies) of radioactive noble gases (primarily xenon) were released by the event. However, these noble gases were considered relatively harmless, and only 481-629 GBq (13-17 curies) of thyroid cancer-causing iodine-131 were released. Total releases according to these figures were a relatively small proportion of the estimated 37 EBq (10 billion curies) in the reactor. It was later found that about half the core had melted, and the cladding around 90 per cent of the fuel rods had failed, with five feet of the core gone, and around 20 tons of uranium flowing to the bottom head of the pressure vessel, forming a mass of corium. The reactor vessel, the second level of containment after the cladding, maintained integrity and contained the damaged fuel with nearly all of the radioactive isotopes in the core.

Anti-nuclear political groups disputed the Kemeny Commission's findings, claiming that independent measurements provided evidence of radiation levels up to five times higher than normal in locations hundreds of miles downwind from TMI. According to Randall Thompson, a health physics technician employed to monitor radioactive emissions at TMI after the accident, radiation releases were hundreds if not thousands of times higher. Some other insiders, including Arnie Gundersen, a former nuclear industry executive who is now an expert witness in nuclear safety issues, make the same claim; Gundersen offers evidence, based on pressure monitoring data, for a hydrogen explosion shortly before 2 p.m. on March 28, 1979, which would have provided the means for a high dose of radiation to occur. Gundersen cites affidavits from four reactor operators according to which the plant manager was aware of a dramatic pressure spike, after which the internal pressure dropped to outside pressure. Gundersen also notes that the control room shook and doors were blown off hinges. However, official NRC reports refer merely to a "hydrogen burn". The Kemeny Commission referred to "a burn or an explosion that caused pressure to increase by 28 pounds per square inch in the containment building". The *Washington Post* reported that "At about 2 p.m., with pressure almost down to the point where the huge cooling pumps could be brought into play, a small hydrogen explosion jolted the reactor".

Aftermath

Voluntary Evacuation

Twenty-eight hours after the accident began William Scranton III, the lieutenant governor appeared at a news briefing to say that Metropolitan Edison, the plant's owner, had assured the state that "everything is under control". Later that day, Scranton changed his statement, saying that the situation was "more complex than the company first led us to believe". There were conflicting statements about radiation releases. Schools were closed and residents were urged to stay indoors. Farmers were told to keep their animals under cover and on stored feed.

Governor Dick Thornburgh, on the advice of NRC Chairman Joseph Hendrie, advised the evacuation "of pregnant women and pre-school age children within a five-mile radius of the Three Mile Island facility". The evacuation zone was extended to a 20 mile radius on Friday March 30. Within days, 1,40,000 people had left the area. More than half of the 6,63,500 population within the 20 mile radius remained in that area. According to a survey conducted in April 1979, 98 per cent of the evacuees had returned to their homes within 3 weeks.

Post-TMI surveys have shown that less than 50 per cent of the American public were satisfied with the way the accident was handled by Pennsylvania State Officials and the NRC, and people surveyed were even less pleased with the utility (General Public Utilities) and the plant designer.

Investigations

Several state and federal government agencies mounted investigations into the crisis, the most prominent of which was the President's Commission on the Accident at Three Mile Island, created by Jimmy Carter in April 1979. The commission consisted of a panel of twelve people, specifically chosen for their lack of strong pro- or anti-nuclear views, and headed by chairman John G. Kemeny, president of Dartmouth College. It was instructed to produce a final report within six months, and after public hearings, depositions, and document collection, released a completed study on October 31, 1979. The investigation strongly criticized Babcock and Wilcox, Met Ed, GPU, and the NRC for lapses in quality assurance and maintenance, inadequate operator training, lack of communication of important safety information, poor management, and complacency, but avoided drawing conclusions about the future of the nuclear industry. The heaviest criticism from the Kemeny Commission concluded that "fundamental changes were necessary in the organization, procedures, practices 'and above all – in the attitudes' of the NRC and the nuclear industry". Kemeny said that the actions taken by the operators were "inappropriate" but that the workers "were operating under procedures that they were required to follow, and our review and study of those indicates that the procedures were inadequate" and that the control room "was greatly inadequate for managing an accident".

The Kemeny Commission noted that Babcock and Wilcox's PORV valve had previously failed on 11 occasions, nine of them in the open position, allowing coolant to escape. More disturbing, however, was the fact that the initial causal sequence of events at TMI had been duplicated 18 months earlier at another Babcock and Wilcox reactor, owned by Davis-Besse. The only difference was that the operators at Davis-Besse identified the valve failure after 20 minutes, where at TMI it took 80 minutes; and the Davis-Besse facility was operating at 9 per cent power, against TMI's 97 per cent. Although Babcock engineers recognised the problem, the company failed to clearly notify its customers of the valve issue.

Upon his return to Dartmouth, Kemeny addressed Dartmouth College students. When asked what caused the meltdown, he replied that the proximate cause would probably never be known. The Government Affairs Vice-president confirmed that the Metropolitan Edison Company, which operated the company, had shortly before received a warning from the Nuclear Regulatory Commission (NRC) that Babcock and Wilcox reactor valves were vulnerable to failure under certain conditions. He said he had sent it on to the Vice-president of Engineering, who confirmed that he had read it. Shortly after that, the two men met at the watercooler where the Government Affairs VP asked the Engineering VP a question. The Government Affairs VP remembered the question as "Is there a problem here?" The Engineering VP thought the question was "Have you solved the problem?" Both VPs agreed that the answer was "no". One walked away believing that the problem was solved. The other believed that he had informed his bosses that there was a problem. The issue was never resolved. Kemeny told the students that he believed it never would be. The proximate cause of the meltdown remains unknown and no proof of negligence was ever uncovered.

The Pennsylvania House of Representatives conducted its own investigation, which focused on the need to improve evacuation procedures.

In 1985, a television camera was used to see the interior of the damaged reactor. In 1986, core samples and samples of debris were obtained from the corium layers on the bottom of the reactor vessel and analyzed.

Global history of the use of nuclear power. The Three Mile Island accident is one of the factors cited for the decline of new reactor construction.

According to the IAEA, the Three Mile Island accident was a significant turning point in the global development of nuclear power. From 1963 to 1979, the number of reactors under construction globally increased every year except 1971 and 1978. However, following the event, the number of reactors under construction in the US declined every year from 1980 to 1998. Many similar Babcock and Wilcox reactors on order were cancelled – in total, 51 American nuclear reactors were cancelled from 1980 to 1984.

The 1979 TMI accident did not, however, initiate the demise of the US nuclear power industry. As a result of post-oil-shock analysis and conclusions of overcapacity, 40 planned nuclear power plants had already been cancelled between 1973 and 1979. No US nuclear power plant had been authorized to begin construction since the year before TMI. Nonetheless, at the time of the TMI incident, 129 nuclear power plants had been approved; of those, only 53 (which were not already operating) were completed. Federal requirements became more stringent, local opposition became more strident, and construction times were significantly lengthened to correct safety issues and design deficiencies.

Globally, the cessation of increase in nuclear power plant construction came with the more catastrophic Chernobyl disaster in 1986.

Cleanup

Three Mile Island Unit 2 was too badly damaged and contaminated to resume operations; the reactor was gradually deactivated and permanently closed. TMI-2 had been online only thirteen months but now had a ruined reactor vessel and a containment building that was unsafe to walk in. Cleanup started in August 1979 and officially ended in December 1993, with a total cleanup cost of about $1 billion. Initially, efforts focused on the cleanup and decontamination of the site, especially the defuelling of the damaged reactor. Starting in 1985, almost 100 short tons (91 t) of radioactive fuel were removed from the site.

The first major phase of the cleanup was completed in 1990, when workers finished shipping 150 tons of radioactive wreckage to Idaho for storage at the Department of Energy's National Engineering Laboratory. However, the contaminated cooling water that leaked into the containment building had seeped into the building's concrete, leaving the radioactive residue impractical to remove. In 1988, the Nuclear Regulatory Commission announced that, although it was possible to further decontaminate the Unit 2 site, the remaining radioactivity had been sufficiently contained as to pose no threat to public health and safety. Accordingly, further cleanup efforts were deferred to allow for decay of the radiation levels and to take advantage of the potential economic benefits of retiring both Unit 1 and Unit 2 together.

Health Effects and Epidemiology

In the aftermath of the accident, investigations focused on the amount of radiation released by the accident. According to the American Nuclear Society, using the official radiation emission figures. "The average radiation dose to people living within ten miles of the plant was eight millirem, and no more than 100 millirem to any single individual. Eight millirem is about equal to a chest X-ray, and 100 millirem is about a third of the average background level of radiation received by US residents in a year."

Based on these emission figures, early scientific publications on the health effects of the fallout estimated one or two additional cancer deaths in the 10 mi (16 km) area around TMI. Disease rates in areas further than 10 miles from the plant were never examined. Local activism in the 1980s, based on anecdotal reports of negative health effects, led to scientific studies being commissioned. A variety of studies have been unable to conclude that the accident had substantial health effects.

The Radiation and Public Health Project cited calculations by Joseph Mangano, who has authored 19 medical journal articles and a book on Low Level Radiation and Immune Disease, that reported a spike in infant mortality in the downwind communities two years after the accident. Anecdotal evidence also records effects on the region's wildlife. For example, according to one anti-nuclear activist, Harvey Wasserman, the fallout caused "a plague of death and disease among the area's wild animals and farm livestock", including a sharp fall in the reproductive rate of the region's horses and cows, reflected in statistics from Pennsylvania's Department of Agriculture, though the Department denies a link with TMI.

Activism and Legal Action

Anti-nuclear protest at Harrisburg in 1979, following the Three Mile Island Accident.

The TMI accident enhanced the credibility of anti-nuclear groups, who had predicted an accident, and triggered protests around the world.

Members of the American public, concerned about the release of radioactive gas from the TMI accident, staged numerous anti-nuclear demonstrations across the country in the following months. The largest demonstration was held in New York City in September 1979 and involved 2,00,000 people, with speeches given by Jane Fonda and Ralph Nader. The New York rally was held in conjunction with a series of nightly "No Nukes" concerts given at Madison Square Garden from September 19 to 23 by Musicians United for Safe Energy. In the previous May, an estimated 65,000 people, including California Governor Jerry Brown, attended a march and rally against nuclear power in Washington D.C.

In 1981, citizens' groups succeeded in a class action suit against TMI, winning $25m in an out-of-court settlement. Part of this money was used to found the TMI Public Health Fund. In 1983, a federal grand jury indicted Metropolitan Edison on criminal charges for the falsification of safety test results prior to the accident. Under a plea-bargaining agreement, Met Ed., pleaded guilty to one count of falsifying records and no contest to six other charges, four of which were dropped, and agreed to pay a $45,000 fine and set up a $1 million account to help with emergency planning in the area surrounding the plant.

According to Eric Epstein, chair of Three Mile Island Alert, the TMI plant operator and its insurers paid at least $82 million in publicly documented compensation to residents for "loss of business revenue, evacuation expenses and health claims". Also according to Harvey Wasserman, hundreds of out-of-court settlements have been reached with alleged victims of the fallout, with a total of $15m paid out to parents of children born with birth defects. However, a class action law suit alleging that the accident caused detrimental health effects was rejected by Harrisburg US District Court Judge Sylvia Rambo. The appeal of the decision in front of US Third Circuit Court of Appeals also failed.

Lessons Learned

Three Mile Island has been of interest to human factors engineers as an example of how groups of people react to and make decisions under stress. There is now a general consensus that the accident was exacerbated by human error because operators were overwhelmed with information, much of it irrelevant, misleading, or incorrect. As a result of the TMI-2 incident, nuclear reactor operator training has been improved. Before the incident, training focused on diagnosing underlying problems; afterward, it focused on reacting to an emergency by going through a standardized check list aimed to ensure that the core is receiving enough coolant under sufficient pressure.

In addition to the improved operating training, improvements in quality assurance, engineering, operational surveillance, and emergency planning have been instituted. Improvements in control room habitability, "sight lines" to instruments, ambiguous indications, and even the placement of "trouble" tags were made; some trouble tags were covering important instrument indications during the accident. Improved surveillance of critical systems, structures, and components required for cooling the plant and mitigating the escape of radionuclides during an emergency were also implemented. In addition, each nuclear site needed to have an approved emergency plan to direct the evacuation of the public within a ten mile Emergency Planning Zone (EPZ), and to facilitate rapid notification and evacuation. This plan is periodically rehearsed with federal and local authorities to ensure that all groups work together quickly and efficiently.

In 1979, as Pennsylvania secretary of health Gordon K. MacLeod, MD criticized the state's preparedness, in the event of a nuclear accident. MacLeod criticized the state for not having potassium iodide — which protects the thyroid gland in the event of exposure to radioactive iodine — in stock, as well as for not having physicians on Pennsylvania's equivalent to the Nuclear Regulatory Commission.

The Three Mile Island accident inspired Charles Perrow's Normal Accident Theory, in which an accident occurs, resulting from an unanticipated interaction of multiple failures in a complex system. TMI was an example of this type of accident because it was "unexpected, incomprehensible, uncontrollable and unavoidable". But Perrow's conclusion that the accident was unavoidable is belied by the fact that a TMI control room operator wrote a memo warning of "a very serious accident" if the condensate system problems were not properly addressed. He stated that "the resultant damage could be very significant". Additionally, James Cresswell, an NRC inspector, warned for two years that a design flaw with U-shaped tubes could prevent coolant circulation and cause an accident like that which would occur at TMI. His warnings were ignored until the NRC met with him six days before the accident at TMI.

The China Syndrome

The accident at the plant occurred twelve days after the release of the movie *The China Syndrome*. It featured Jane Fonda as a news anchor at a California television station. In the film, a major nuclear plant crisis takes place while Fonda's character and her cameraman (Michael Douglas) are at the plant producing a series on nuclear power. She proceeds to raise awareness of how unsafe the plant is. Coincidentally, there is a scene in which Fonda's character speaks with a nuclear safety expert, who says that a meltdown could render an area "the size of Pennsylvania permanently uninhabitable". Also, the fictional near-accident in the movie stems from plant operators overestimating the amount of water within the core.

After the release of the film, Fonda began lobbying against nuclear power – the only actor in the film to do so. In an attempt to counter her efforts, the nuclear physicist Edward Teller, "father of the hydrogen bomb" and long-time government science adviser, personally lobbied in favour of nuclear power.

Current Status

Viewed from the west, Three Mile Island currently uses only one nuclear generating station, TMI-1, which is on the left. TMI-2, to the right, has not been used since the accident. Note that this is a pre-accident photo taken when TMI-2 was in operation.

Unit 1 had its license temporarily suspended following the incident at Unit 2. Although the citizens of the three counties surrounding the site voted by a margin of 3:1 to permanently retire Unit 1, it was permitted to resume operations in 1985. General Public Utilities Corporation, the plant's owner, formed General Public Utilities Nuclear Corporation (GPUN) as a new subsidiary to own and operate the company's nuclear facilities, including Three Mile Island. The plant had previously been operated by Metropolitan Edison Company (Met-Ed), one of GPU's regional utility operating companies. In 1996, General Public Utilities shortened its name to GPU Inc. Three Mile Island Unit 1 was sold to AmerGen Energy Corporation, a joint venture between Philadelphia Electric Company (PECO), and British Energy, in 1998. In 2000, PECO merged with Unicom Corporation to form Exelon Corporation, which acquired British Energy's share of AmerGen in 2003. Today, AmerGen LLC is a fully owned subsidiary of Exelon Generation and owns TMI Unit 1, Oyster Creek Nuclear Generating Station, and Clinton Power Station. These three units, in addition to Exelon's other nuclear units, are operated by Exelon Nuclear Inc., an Exelon subsidiary.

General Public Utilities was legally obliged to continue to maintain and monitor the site, and therefore retained ownership of Unit 2 when Unit 1 was sold to AmerGen in 1998. GPU Inc. was acquired by FirstEnergy Corporation in 2001, and subsequently dissolved. FirstEnergy then contracted out the maintenance and administration of Unit 2 to AmerGen. Unit 2 has been administered by Exelon Nuclear since 2003, when Exelon Nuclear's parent company, Exelon, bought out the remaining shares of AmerGen, inheriting FirstEnergy's maintenance contract. Unit 2 continues to be licensed and regulated by the Nuclear Regulatory Commission in a condition known as Post Defuelling Monitored Storage (PDMS).

Today, the TMI-2 reactor is permanently shutdown with the reactor coolant system drained, the radioactive water decontaminated and evaporated, radioactive waste shipped off-site, reactor fuel and core debris shipped off-site to a Department of Energy facility, and the remainder of the site being monitored. The owner says it will keep the facility in long-term, monitored storage until the operating license for the TMI-1 plant expires at which time both plants will be decommissioned. In 2009, the NRC granted a license extension which means the TMI-1 reactor may operate until April 19, 2034.

References

1. A b Minutes to Meltdown: Three Mile Island – National Geographic
2. Kemeny, p. 12.
3. Walker, pp. 234-237.
4. Stephen J. Dubner and Steven D. Levitt (September 16, 2007). "The Jane Fonda Effect". The *New York Times*. http://www.nytimes.com/2007/09/16/magazine/16wwln-freakonomics-t.html?_r=1. Retrieved December 29, 2008.

Annexure – I

NATURAL DISASTER MITIGATION STRATEGIES

Earthquake Mitigation

Before the Disaster	During the Disaster	After the Disaster
◆ Check for hazards in the home. ◆ Identify safe places in each room. ◆ Locate safe places outdoors. ◆ Ensure all family members know how to respond after an earthquake. ◆ Teach children when and how to call 9-1-1. ◆ Have disaster supplies on. ◆ Develop an emergency communications plan in case of separation during the earthquake. ◆ Ask an out-of-state relative or friend to serve as the family contact.	◆ **If indoors:** Take cover under a piece of heavy furniture or against an inside wall and stay inside. ◆ **If outdoors:** Move into the open, away from buildings, streetlights, and utility wires and remain there until shaking stops. ◆ **If in a moving vehicle:** Stop quickly, stay in vehicle, move to a clear area away from buildings, trees, overpasses, or utility wires.	◆ Be prepared for after shocks. ◆ Help injured or trapped persons and give first aid where appropriate. ◆ Listen to a battery-operated radio for emergency information. ◆ Stay out of damaged buildings and return home only when authorities say it is safe.

EXTREME HEAT MITIGATION

Before the Disaster	During the Disaster	After the Disaster
• Install window air-conditioners. • Install temporary reflectors to reflect heat outside. • Consider keeping storm windows up year round. • Check air-conditioning ducts for proper insulation. • Reduce, eliminate, or reschedule strenuous activities.	• Protect windows that receive sun by hanging draperies or shades. • Conserve electricity. • Stay indoors as much as possible; eat well-balanced light meals and drink water regularly. • Limit intake of alcoholic beverages. • Dress in loose fitting clothes. • Allow body to get acclimated to the heat within the first few days of a heat wave, avoid sunshine and use sunscreen if needed. • Avoid extreme temperature changes.	• *First Aid for conditions* after a drought/extreme heat: • *Sunburn* (skin redness and pain, possible swelling, blisters, fever, headaches) – shower using soap to remove oils that may block pores. If blistering occurs, apply dry, sterile dressings and get medical attention. • *Heat Cramps* (painful spasms in leg and abdominal muscles) – Place firm pressure on cramping muscles or gentle massage to relieve spasm. Give sips of water, however if nausea occurs, discontinue. • *Heat Exhaustion* (heavy sweating, weakness, skin cold, pale, and clammy, weak pulse, fainting and vomiting may occur) – lay victim down in a cool place, loosen clothing and apply cool, wet cloths. Give sips of water, however if nausea occurs, discontinue. Seek medical attention if vomiting occurs. • *Heat/Sun Stroke* [high body temperature (+106?), hot and dry skin, rapid pulse, possible unconsciousness, no perspiration] – Call 9-1-1 immediately to get victim to a hospital immediately. Delay can be fatal.

FLOOD MITIGATION

Before the Disaster	During the Disaster	After the Disaster
• Learn warning signs and community alert systems. • Stockpile emergency building materials. • Install check valves in sewer traps to prevent flood waters from backing up in sewer drains. • Plan and practice an evacuation route. • Have disaster supplies on hand • Develop an emergency communication plan in case of separation. • Ask an out-of-state relative to serve as the "family contact". • Teach family members how and when to turn off the gas, electricity, and water and teach children how and when to call 9-1-1. • Ask your insurance agent about flood insurance.	• During a flood watch: If indoors: • Turn on battery-operated radio to get latest emergency information. • Get pre-assembled emergency supplies. • If told to leave, do so immediately. *If outdoors:* • Climb to high ground and stay there. • Avoid walking through any floodwaters. • If in a car, turn around and go another way; if your car stalls, abandon it immediately and climb to higher ground. *During an evacuation:* • If advised to evacuate, do so immediately to avoid flooded roads, being sure to follow recommended evacuation routes and listen to radio for evacuation instructions.	• Don't return home until authorities express express it is safe to do so. • Help neighbours whom may need assistance. • Use extreme caution when entering buildings. • Inspect foundations for cracks or other damage and examine walls, floors, doors, and windows to make sure that the building is not in danger of collapsing. • Watchout for animals, especially poisonous snakes, that may have come into your home with flood waters. • Watch for loose plaster and ceilings that could fall. • Take pictures of damage for insurance claims. • Look for fire hazards. • Throw away all food (including canned) that has come in contact with flood waters. • Pump out flooded basements gradually (~ 1/3 amount of water per day) to avoid structural damage. • Service damaged septic tanks, cesspools, pits, and leaching systems ASAP-damaged sewage systems are health hazards.

HURRICANE MITIGATION

Before the Disaster	During the Disaster	After the Disaster
◆ Plan an evacuation route and learn safe routes inland. ◆ Have disaster supplies on hand. ◆ Develop an emergency communication plan in case of separation. ◆ Ask an out-of-state relative to serve as the "family contact". ◆ Teach family members when and how to turn off gas and electricity. ◆ Trim back dead or weak branches from trees. ◆ Check into flood insurance. ◆ Teach children when and how to call 9-1-1. ◆ Make arrangements for family pets because some emergency shelters may not allow pets.	*Hurricane Watch (conditions within 24-36 hours):* ◆ Listen to battery-operated radio for progress reports; check emergency supplies. ◆ Fuel car. ◆ Bring in outdoor objects. ◆ Secure buildings by closing and boarding up windows. ◆ Remove outside antennas. ◆ Turn refrigerator and freezer to coldest settings. ◆ Store drinking water in clean bathtubs, jugs, and bottles. ◆ Moor boat securely or move to a designated safe place; anchor trailer to ground. ◆ Review evacuation plan. *Hurricane Warning (conditions expected in 24 hours or less):* ◆ Listen to radio for instructions. ◆ Tie down mobile home and evacuate immediately. ◆ Store valuables in waterproof container. ◆ Avoid elevators. *If at home:* ◆ Stay inside, away from anything glass. ◆ Keep a supply of batteries and flashlights ◆ Avoid open flames as a source of light. ◆ If power is lost, turn off major appliances to reduce power "surge". ◆ If evacuation is necessary: leave ASAP, avoiding flooded roads and washed-out bridges. ◆ Secure home by unplugging appliances and turning off electricity and the main water valve. ◆ If time permits, elevate furniture to protect it from flooding. ◆ Bring pre-assembled emergency supplies and warm clothing. ◆ Take blankets and sleeping bags to a shelter and leave immediately.	◆ Stay tuned to radio for information, returning home only when authorities advise it is safe to do so. ◆ Help injured or trapped persons and give first aid where appropriate. ◆ Avoid loose or dangling power lines and report them to the power company or fire department. ◆ Beware of snakes, insects, and animals driven to higher ground by flood water. ◆ Open windows and doors to ventilate and dry your home. ◆ Check refrigerated foods for spoilage. ◆ Take pictures of the damage for insurance claims. ◆ Drive only if necessary and avoid flooded roads and washed-out bridges. ◆ Use telephones only for emergency calls.

LANDSLIDES AND MUDFLOW MITIGATION

Before the Disaster	During the Disaster	After the Disaster
◆ Get a ground assessment of your property ◆ Minimize home hazards (plant ground cover on slopes, build retaining walls, and in mudflow areas, build channels or deflection walls to direct flow around buildings) *Recognize landslide warning signs:* ◆ Doors/windows stick or jam for the first time, new cracks appear in plaster or foundations, outside walks, walls, or stairs pull away from buildings, underground utility lines break, bulging ground appears at base of a slope, ground slopes downward in one direction and may begin shifting in that direction under your feet; faint rumbling sound that increases in volume as landslide nears ◆ Make evacuation plans, planning at least two routes allowing for blocked and closed roads ◆ Develop an emergency communication plan and ask an out-of-state relative or friend to serve as the family contact ◆ Purchase flood insurance.	*If indoors:* ◆ Stay inside and get cover under a sturdy piece of furniture. *If outdoors:* ◆ Try to get out of path of mudflow ◆ Run to nearest high ground in a direction away from path ◆ If rocks and other debris are approaching, run for nearest shelter such as a group of trees or a building ◆ If escape is not possible, curl into a tight ball and protect your head. *Be cautious of sinkholes:* ◆ Sinkholes occur when ground water dissolves a vulnerable land surface such as limestone, causing the land surface to collapse from lack of support.	*Stay away from slide area* ◆ Check for injured and trapped persons and give first aid where needed ◆ Listen to battery-operated radios for emergency information ◆ Remember flooding may occur after a mudflow or landslide ◆ Check for damaged utility lines and report damage to the utility company ◆ Check the building foundation, chimney, and surrounding land for damage ◆ Replant damaged ground as soon as possible since erosion caused by loss of ground cover can lead to flash flooding.

TORNADO MITIGATION

Before the Disaster	During the Disaster	After the Disaster
• Conduct tornado drills into each season • Designate an area in the home as a shelter • Have disaster supplies on hand • Develop an emergency communication plan in case of separation • Ask an out-of-state relative to serve as the "family contact" • Know the difference between a tornado watch (issued when tornadoes are possible in your area) and a warning (tornadoes have been sighted by radar) • Take shelter in a building with a strong foundation • If shelter is not available, lie in ditch or low-lying area a safe distance away from the mobile home *Learn danger signs:* • An approaching cloud of debris can mark the location even if a funnel is not visible, before a tornado hits, the wind may die down and the air may become still, and generally occur near the edge of a thunderstorm; you can often see clear skies following a tornado	*If at home:* • Go to the storm cellar or lowest part of the building. • If there is no basement, go to an inner hallway/room without windows, • Go to the centre of the room, staying away from the corners because they attract debris. • Get under a piece of sturdy furniture and hold on to it. • Use arms to protect head and neck. • If in a mobile home, get out and find shelter. *If at work or school:* • Go to the lowest level in the building, avoiding wide-span roofs (auditoriums, cafeterias). • Get under a sturdy piece of furniture and hold on. • Use arms to protect head and neck. *If outdoors:* • Try to get inside; if that is impossible, lie in a ditch or low-lying area or crouch near a strong building; be aware of flooding potential. • Use arms to protect head and neck. *If in a car:* • Never try to outdrive the tornado. • Get out of the car immediately and try to find shelter in a building. • If shelter is impossible, lie in a ditch or low-lying area away from the vehicle.	• Help injured or trapped persons, give first aid when appropriate, and do not try to move injured persons unless they are in danger of further injury • Turn on radio/television to get latest emergency information • Stay out of damaged buildings and return home only when authorities say it is safe • Use telephone only for emergency calls • Clean up spilled medicines, bleaches, gasoline, or other flammable liquids immediately • Leave the building if you smell gas or chemical fumes • Take pictures of the damage for insurance claims • Remember to help neighbours who may need assistance.

TSUNAMI MITIGATION

Before the Disaster	During the Disaster	After the Disaster
• Find out if your house is in danger and know the height of your street above sea level • Be familiar with warning signs (earthquakes, ground rumbling, or rapid rise and fall of coastal waters) • Ensure all family members know how to respond • Make evacuation plans with more than one route and pick an elevated inland location • Teach children how and when to call 9-1-1 • Have disaster supplies on hand (flashlight, extra batteries, portable battery-operated radio, first aid kit, emergency food and water, non-electric can opener, cash and credit cards, and sturdy shoes) • Develop an emergency communications plan in case of separation during the earthquake. Ask an out-of-state relative or friend to serve as the family contact.	• Listen to radio for emergency and evacuation information • Climb to higher ground as soon as warning of a tsunami is released • Stay away from the beach – if you can see the wave, you are too close to escape it • Do not assume that one wave means the danger is over – the next wave may be larger than the first • Stay out of the area and do not return until authorities say it is safe to do so.	• Stay tuned to radio for emergency information • Help injured or trapped persons and give first aid where appropriate • Do not move seriously injured persons unless they are in immediate danger of further injury • Stay out of damaged buildings • Enter home with caution, checking for electrical shorts and live wires • Do not use appliances or lights until properly checked by an electrician • Open windows and doors to help dry the building • Shovel mud while it is still moist to give walls and floors an opportunity to dry • Check food supplies, throwing out all fresh food that may be contaminated and have tap water tested by local health department.

VOLCANO MITIGATION

Before the Disaster	During the Disaster	After the Disaster
◆ Learn about community warning systems and of disasters that can come from volcanoes (earthquakes, flooding, landslides, mudflows, thunderstorms, tsunamis) ◆ Make evacuation plans to higher ground with a backup route ◆ Get a pair of goggles and a throw-away breathing mask for each member of the household teach children how and when to call 9-1-1 ◆ Have disaster supplies on hand (flashlight, extra batteries, portable battery-operated radio, first aid kit, emergency food and water, non-electric can opener, cash and credit cards, and sturdy shoes) ◆ Develop an emergency communications plan in case of separation during the earthquake. Ask an out-of-state relative or friend to serve as the family contact.	◆ Follow evacuation order issued by authorities ◆ Avoid areas downwind of the volcano *If indoors:* ◆ Close all windows, doors, and dampers ◆ Put all machinery inside a garage or bam ◆ Bring animals and livestock into closed shelters *If outdoors:* ◆ Seek shelter immediately ◆ If caught in a rockfall, roll into a ball to protect head ◆ Avoid low-lying areas where poisonous gases can collect and floods can be dangerous ◆ If caught near a stream beware of mudflows. ◆ Wear long-sleeved shirts and pants ◆ Use goggles to protect eyes and a dust-mask or damp cloth over face to help breathing ◆ Keep car engines turned off ◆ Stay out of the area. ◆ Mudflows can occur when rain falls through ash-carrying clouds or when rivers are dammed during an eruption and are most dangerous close to stream channels; if on a bridge and notice a mudflow upstream, DO NOT cross the bridge – the mudflow can destroy a bridge quickly.	◆ Listen to radio for emergency information ◆ Stay away from ashfall *When outside:* ◆ Cover mouth and nose to protect from inhaling ash and wear goggles to protect eyes ◆ Keep skin covered to avoid irritation or burns ◆ Avoid contact with any amount of ash if you have a respiratory ailment ◆ Avoid driving in heavy ashfall (it may clog engines and stall vehicles) ◆ Clear roofs of ashfall (could cause buildings to collapse) ◆ Help neighbours who may require special assistance.

WILDFIRE MITIGATION

Before the Disaster	During the Disaster	After the Disaster
◆ Learn and teach safe fire practices ◆ Build fires away from nearby trees or bushes, always have a way to extinguish a fire, never leave a fire unattended ◆ Obtain local building codes and weed abatement ordinances for buildings near wooded areas ◆ Use fire-resistant materials when building, renovating, or retrofitting structures ◆ Create a safety zone to separate home from combustible plants and vegetables ◆ Install electrical lines underground, if possible ◆ Prune all branches around residence to a height of 8-10 feet ◆ Keep trees adjacent to buildings free of dead or dying wood and moss ◆ Remove all dead limbs, needles, and debris from rain gutters ◆ Store combustible/flammable materials in approved safety containers and keep away from home ◆ Keep chimney clean ◆ Avoid open burning, especially during dry season. Install smoke detectors on every level of your home ◆ Make evacuation plans from home and neighbourhood and have backup plans ◆ Avoid using wooden shakes and shingles for roofing ◆ Use only thick, tempered safety glass in large windows and doors ◆ Have disaster supplies on hand (flashlights, extra batteries, portable radios, first aid kits, emergency food and water, non-electric can opener, essential medicines, cash and credit cards, and sturdy shoes) ◆ Develop an emergency communication plan in case of separation ◆ Ask an out-of-state relative to serve as the "family contact"	If trapped in a wildfire, you CANNOT outrun it: ◆ Crouch in a pond or river and cover head and upper body with wet clothing ◆ If a body of water is unavailable, look for shelter in a cleared area or among a bed of rocks and lie flat and cover body with wet clothing or soil. ◆ Listen to radio for emergency information ◆ Remove combustible items (outdoor furniture, umbrellas, tarp coverings, and firewood) from around the home ◆ Take down flammable drapes and curtains and close all venetian blinds or non-combustible window coverings ◆ Close all doors and windows inside home to prevent draft ◆ Close gas valves and turn off pilot light ◆ Turn on a light in each room for visibility in heavy smoke ◆ Place valuables that will not be damaged by water, in a pool or pond ◆ If hoses and adequate water are available, leave sprinklers on roofs and anything that might be damaged by fire ◆ Be ready to evacuate all family members and pets when fire nears or when instructed to do so by local officials.	◆ Be cautious when re-entering a burned wildland area – hot spots can flare up without warning ◆ Check the roof immediately and extinguish any sparks or embers and the attic for hidden burning sparks ◆ Recheck for smoke and sparks throughout the home for several hours afterward ◆ Breathe the air close to the ground through a wet cloth to avoid scorching lungs or inhaling smoke.

Annexure – II

Do's:

You and Your Family

- Educate your children, wife, and other family members in respect of natural and man-made disasters and other crises. In case of your being unaware, take help of Civil Defence and Home Guard organisation and other NGOs. Develop habit in you and your children to spare one per cent of you busy time to think about individual security and security interests.
- Keep the phone numbers of the local police station, police control rooms, fire stations, schools, colleges, TV station, All India Radio, ambulance services, and chemists for emergency use.
- Guide children to remain at schools in emergency.
- Prepare an emergency kit of items and essentials in the house including essential documents and valuables.
- Store food and water for survival in case you had a pre-warning.
- Any suspicious incidents observed be reported to police on 103. Callers do not have to give their identity on the phone. Information of immediate use be conveyed to control rooms to help early relief.
- Carry your identity card, residential telephone number or address or personal card with you. Have your blood group and any medical allergies recorded with you.
- Check information in case of disasters and crises from ward, civil defence/homeguard, and BMC, TV, and All India Radio Control room.
- Learn to fight such emergencies untidily.
- Support authorities and NGOs.
- Identify scooters, cars, and vehicles parked in society and identify vehicles which are unknown and parked for long.
- Organize societies and muhalla committees to educate people.

Dont's:

- ❖ Do not encourage rumours.
- ❖ Do not blame any community for any crises.
- ❖ Do not encourage communal hatred in such situations.

Do's:

Your Place of Work

- ❖ Your mode of travel by car, bus, train, and taxi be known to your people.
- ❖ High rises buildings must check their electric and water supplies and organize periodic mockup drills for firefighting and escape routes.
- ❖ Drills for bomb blast, threats be organised and practised.
- ❖ Air/helicopter evacuation be examined and organized from selected rooftops of high rises.
- ❖ Firefighting equipment be kept serviceable and periodic check is effected.
- ❖ Office societies be organized and prepared to coordinate such emergencies of fire brigade, medical help, and other assistance. Such people be nominated and they should guide relief.
- ❖ Everyone must know use of fire extinguisher in emergency.
- ❖ Security guards are trained to coordinate in such crises.

Do's:

In Transit

- ❖ Be concerned and develop habit of surveillance when out of our house. Check your seat in cinema hall, train, bus, and air. Have you observed a bird, she jumped around and looks in all directions before selecting a spot on a tree for her security. Do we learn anything from this bird instinct?
- ❖ Look for the objects, baggage, at bus stand, railway stations, compartments, airport, which is unclaimed.
- ❖ Unknown vehicles parked at airports, railway stations, and bus stands have to be kept under surveillance by common citizens, and this alertness may help authorities.
- ❖ Bus, trains, and airlines passengers who notice any suspicious behaviour of copassengers, be brought to the notice of officials,
- ❖ Every passenger should identify a friend or relations residence in case of requirement of staying away in emergency. The family should know about such a plan.

Dont's:

- ❖ Do not touch any suspicious object. Report to concerned people.
- ❖ Do not crowd the object.
- ❖ Passengers should not accept parcels from unknown persons in hurry while boarding train or bus.

Do's and Dont's:

In Chemical, Nuclear, and Biological Warfare

- ❖ **Chemical Weapons:** Citizens can identify such attacks by observing people who start coughing, vomiting, or seizing.

Do's:

- ❖ Evacuate the area immediately and dial disaster management control room for help.
- ❖ If indoors, exit the building rapidly as possible.
- ❖ Once outside, if you believe that you may have been exposed to toxic substance, discard you inhibition to remove you clothes, remove your clothes immediately, which may save your life.
- ❖ Taking out your clothes can remove 80 per cent of the contamination hazards.
- ❖ Look for a nearby water tap or fountain, pool or other source of water so that you can quickly and thoroughly rinse any skin part that may have been exposed.
- ❖ Fire brigades on arrival in area may spray water on everyone affected and decontaminated.
- ❖ Remain calm.
- ❖ Medical attention shall be needed and first aid to be given to seriously affected people.
- ❖ Evacuate most seriously exposed individuals.
- ❖ If you happen to be in open and outdoor, you may observe birds and small animals falling to the ground due to poisonous gas. You must immediately move indoors and create a physical barrier between you and toxic cloud. A building protection is preferred, however, getting in side your car will also help you.
- ❖ Shut all doors and windows of the house and put-off fans and air-conditioners.
- ❖ Try to plug flow of air or wind to your rooms.
- ❖ Stay indoors.
- ❖ Listens radio, TV, News, and Announcements.
- ❖ Authority will notify you when it is safe to come out.
- ❖ Have a bath immediately on entry to the house and keep your cloth in a plastic bag, it will help remove any contamination that might have occurred before you were able to get indoors. It may be done in period of less than a minute or one minute.
- ❖ You may like to keep gas, mask handy.

- **Biological Weapons:** Biological weapons have been described as "the poor mans atom bomb". These viruses could be spread through water and food. Some of the suggested points for use of common people are.

Do's:

- On hearing report of that, biological agents have been released, stay indoors.
- Shut all windows and doors and turn-off fans and air-conditioners.
- A gas mask can provide an excellent respiratory protection.
- Put a physical barrier between you and agent dissemination.
- Reach for medical help.
- Boil your drinking water.
- Ascertain and check your vegetable and food items.

Nuclear Warfare:

Do's:

- To protect from heat and flash, any light material or foliage cover will give reasonable protection to human body.
- Gamma radiation protection requires a shallow or trench which is 4 to 5 feet deep people remaining at the bottom of such shelter will be safe.
- For blast and earth shock, strong shelters have to be planned in societies and have to be strong enough and these not to protrude above ground level.
- Being in shelter/trenches can prevent radioactive fallout. The requirement of protection is similar to hear and flash. A chemical protective mask may be useful.

The suggested DO's and DONT's for Prevention/Protection against NUCLEAR, BIOLOGICAL And CHEMICAL weapons as under:

A. NUCLEAR WAR

DO's:

Before the Attack:

- Construct/identify basements in your residence where the whole family can stay in for a fortnight.
- In case no basement available, then in the open space in front of your house, construct bunkers as in conventional war (as some protection is better than no protection)
- Stock the shelter with non-perishable foods and water to be replaced regularly before getting unhygienic.
- Construct the toilet facilities in the basement/shelter.

- ❖ Store ample candles and battery lights.
- ❖ Remove stocks flammables, if any.
- ❖ Keep battery operated miniature transistor /TV sets in the basement.
- ❖ Familiarize with instructions/operational procedures being broadcasted/telecasted at stipulated by CD authorities.
- ❖ Paste blackpaper on window/door glass panels.
- ❖ Familiarize with community shelters in your locality in consultation with CD/Revenue/police authorities.

During Attack:

- ❖ In open, immediately drop to ground and remain in lying position.
- ❖ Protect eyes and exposed skin areas by covering eyes and face with hand.
- ❖ Protect ears by fingers or thumbs after covering eyes with palms to prevent ear drum rupture.
- ❖ Stay down after the initial shock wave. Wait for the winds to die down and debris to stop falling.
- ❖ If blast wave does not arrive within 5 seconds of the flash, you were far enough from the ground zero and initial, radiation exposure will not exceed 150 reds.
- ❖ Drive out of the way of any windows or doors to avoid injury due to glass/window splinters.
- ❖ If in vehicle, on detection of flash, drive from the vehicle to a face down, in prone position. Drive in the direction of the flash to avoid the vehicle over turning on you due to blast.

After Attack:

- ❖ Stay down under cover until debris stop falling.
- ❖ Stay calm. Burn, injuries dazzle and concern over production exposure may combine to create panic.
- ❖ Blast wind will generally end in one to two minutes after burns, cuts band bruises are not different than conventional injuries. Dazzle is temporary and vision should return in few seconds.
- ❖ If survived the blast, the chances of being exposed to lethal dose of radiation is relatively small unless located in an early fallout area.
- ❖ Expect some initial disorientation as the blast wave may blow down and carry away many prominent and familiar features. Beware of weakened structures and trees from collapsing.
- ❖ Putout fires before they spread.
- ❖ Improve over cover. Cover the openings of shelters to prevent the entry of fallout particles.
- ❖ When coming from contaminated area, follow simple decontamination procedure like removal of clothing outdoors and having a bath before entering safe areas.

Dont's:

- Do not consume open food/drinks/water/beverages, etc., lying under the open sky.
- Do not move out of shelters/basements unless instructed by authorities
- Do not stir up dust or brush against things main moving in fallout areas.
- Do not smoke, eat, or drink in exposed area.
- Do not kneel, lie, or sit on the ground.
- Do not walk barefooted or in open slippers.
- Do not move out of your shelter without proper protection to breathing passages at least during the first 24 hours after the blast.
- Do not use flour from gunny bags, foods wrapped in paper, water from open pools/lakes.
- Do not dust your ventilators indiscriminately.
- Do not permit contaminated persons in basements/shelters unless decontaminated.

B. BIOLOGICAL WARFARE:

Do's:

- Follow permanent implementation of body hygiene measures such as trimming of fingernails regularly and washing hands with soap and water before eating or drinking.
- Follow active immunization as available.
- Wash all new vegetables in detergents before cooking or eating.
- Report any case of sickness in the family/neighbourhood to health authorities.
- Help authorities in destruction of infected stocks of food, crops, livestock, etc.
- Keep your premises clean.
- Spray/use insecticides to keep vectors away.
- Store ample food and water under cover and replace the same regularly before getting spoiled.
- Use mosquito nets/repellents at night.

Dont's:

- Do not allow waste particularly food waste material to accumulate in or around your premises.
- Do not allow open pools/collection of water in surrounding area.
- Do not panic and stay calm.
- Do not consume stale food material.

C. CHEMICAL WARFARE:

Do's:

- ❖ Keep calm and do not panic.
- ❖ Listen to the radio and follow official instructions. Inform your neighbours especially the elderly and handicapped and assist them.
- ❖ Stay inside if at home or shelter in a building and close all doors and windows. Seal all exterior openings and turn-off the ventilation, air-conditioning and heating.
- ❖ Protect your mouth and nose, if in the open, with a wet cloth or a protective mask.
- ❖ Take shelter in the nearest building and remain inside until otherwise instructed by the authorities.
- ❖ Do not telephone as this overloads the system.
- ❖ Follow the orders of the civil, defence, fire services, police or other intervening services.
- ❖ Eat only food stored inside a building such as tinned food and preserved one. Drink only from bottles or cartons. Follow the instructions on the use of tap water.
- ❖ If you are in a car, turn-off the ventilation and close the windows. Listen to the radio and take shelter in the nearest building. Follow the instructions of the authorities.

Dont's:

- ❖ Do not consume open food/drinks/water beverages, etc., lying under the open sky.
- ❖ Do not move out of shelters/basement unless instructed by authorities.
- ❖ Do not stir up dust or brush against things when moving in contaminated areas.
- ❖ Do not smoke, eat, or drink in exposed areas.
- ❖ Do not kneel, lie, or sit on the ground.
- ❖ Do not walk barefooted or in open slippers.
- ❖ Do not move out of your shelter without proper protection to breathing passages.
- ❖ Do not permit contaminated persons in basements/shelter unless decontaminated for the chemical vapours.
- ❖ **Warning of Air Raid:** Warning of an imminent raid enables the public to be prepared for an air attack and to take air shelter. Aircraft will be spotted with the help of radars in time when they are miles away from the target. The control centre will immediately pass on the warning to other concerned and siren will be sounded.

  Do's for general public after siren will be sounded, before Air raid.

Do's

(a) Taking cover in the open

I. On hearing the warning or the sound of enemy bombers, lie flat on the ground with your face downward, keep your chest slightly above the ground and rest on your elbows. Plug your ears with cotton wool and if this is not available, plug them with the corners of your dhoti, sari, or turban, etc. Place a rolled-up handkerchief or a corner of your dhoti, etc., between your teeth to keep the mouth open and not to be affected by the earth shock which may cut you tongue.

II. The splinters and debris fly outward and upward and therefore lie flat on the ground. You are safer there.

(b) When very near a building

I. Walls, archways, and doorways are good protection. Go and stand near them. Do not lean directly against a wall.

(c) Inside a building

I. It is better to be near an inside than an outside wall.

II. Avoid being in the direct line of a door or windows.

III. Remember the extreme danger of flying glass. The safest part of the house will be away from the windows, etc., and to be in the angle of a wall.

(d) When in a train

I. Turn-off the lights and crawl under the seats. Do not lookout of the windows.

(e) When in a tram or bus

I. Stop it. Leave it. Go out and act as if you were in the open.

(f) When in your own motor car

I. Stop your car on the left hand, closest to the edge of the road.

II. Leave the car unlocked. Keep the switch key in its place so that if you are a casualty, the car can be driven by others.

III. Keep the window open.

IV. Get out of the car and act as if you were out in the open.

(g) When at a cinema

I. Remain seated and keep calm. You are safer there than anywhere else.

(h) When in a bullock cart or tonga, etc.

I. Unyoke the animals and tie them to the nearest tree or strong pole where they will not obstruct traffic. Go out and act as if in the open.

Dont's

(a) Taking cover in the open

I. On hearing the warning or the sound of enemy bombers do not run to cover if there is no time.

II. Never look up during an air raid.

AFTER AN AIR RAID

❖ **Water:** Use water in the cisterns and tank if your supply is cut-off. Economize in the use of water, as it will be needed for firefighting.

❖ **Electricity:** If mains or meterboards are damaged, report it to the warden. If the electric installation in your house is damaged, send for an electrician.

❖ **Sewers:** If the waste disposal system is damaged, use disinfectants freely and burn or bury your rubbish. If your house is slightly damaged, try to repair it. In case it is destroyed go to the house of a friend or to a relief centre. Ask the police or warden where these are.

❖ **Attend to the injured:** In case of slight injury, go to the first aid post for treatment. In case of severe injury await the help of a first aid party. Keep the patient warm, reassure him, enable him to breathe easily by removing any dust or grit from his nose and mouth. Control bleeding, relieve pain, support fractured limbs by improvized splints and give artificial respiration.

❖ **Fighting Fires:**

(a) Look round the area for fires. With the help of sand, water, and stirrup pumps tackle the fires in their initial stages. If it gets out of control, call your neighbour and inform the warden. If you are lucky, see if you can help others. While dealing with an incendiary bomb, protect your eyes and make sure not to direct a jet of water on the bomb.

(b) If the room is on fire, close all doors and windows. It will help prevent spreading of fire. While entering it, crawl along the floor and keep as close to the floor as possible. Keep close to the wall.

(c) If someone's clothes catch fire, wrap him up in a rug or blanket and roll him on the ground.

(d) If you are caught within a house on fire, escape through the windows by using a rope or bedsheets after having tied one end to some strong point beside the house. Call for help from an opening if unable to escape through the window.

(e) Do not go alone into a building on fire if you can do sc in the company of another.

(f) Exercise great care while removing debris from the neighbourhood of a casualty. Do not pull timber out of the wreckage because it may cause further collapse. Do not crawl over the debris unless absolutely unavoidable. Do not touch loose electric wiring. Protect the casualty from falling debris by providing tarpaulin or other cover.

RESCUE IN AN AIR RAID

DO's

(a) Keep calm.

(b) Make proper reconnaissance before starting rescue work.

(c) Keep as near as possible to the wall when on damaged stairs.

(d) Exercise great care while removing debris from the vicinity of the casualty.

(e) Protect the casualty from falling debris and dust with the help of iron sheets, tarpaulins, etc.

(f) Free the nose and mouth of the casualty from dust and grit to case his breathing.

(g) Reassure the patient and get him taken home to bed, if the injury is not severe.

(h) Loosen all clothing and keep the patient lying down and warm.

(i) Give artificial respiration, if needed, control bleeding, if any, as far as possible, and relieve pain of the casualty by supporting fractures by improvised splints.

(j) Contact immediately the nearest First Aid Post for proper medical attendance for the casualty.

Dont's

(a) Do not get panicky.

(b) Do not pull timber out of the wreckage indiscriminately or you may cause further collapse.

(c) Do not touch loose electric wiring.

(d) Do not crawl over the debris or disturb part of the damaged structure unless you are compelled to do so by circumstances.

MUMBAI MUNICIPAL CORPORATION

A Guide to Prepare Community for Surviving Earthquake in Urban Areas

Before the Earthquake

It is essential that we are prepared for a earthquake. Seismic experts do not rule out the possibility of an earthquake anywhere in Maharashtra including Mumbai. We do not know when this will happen.

When an earthquake occurs, your first warning may be a shaking sensation if you are in a building. It may also be followed with a sudden noise or roar. You may find yourself completely topsy-turvy. It may be a scary situation! It may last a few seconds or go on for a few minutes. Breaking glass, and things falling around could hurt you. Be prepared for aftershocks.

We can't prevent an earthquake. But we can:

- ❖ Be prepared by injury.
- ❖ Be prepared to minimize damage to your home.
- ❖ Be prepared to manage our survival afterwards for at least 72 hours without help.

Your family preparedness for such a situation is a must. You must prepare and practice what to do during and after an earthquake.

- ❖ Plan your needs in such a situation. Write down and exercise your safety plan.
- ❖ Known the safe and dangerous places in your home.

Safe: Under heavy tables or desks, inside corridor, corners of rooms or archways.

Dangerous: Near window or mirrors, under any objects that can fall, the kitchen – where the stove, refrigerator or contents of cupboards may move violently, doorways, because the shaking may slam the door on you. Practice taking cover.

- ❖ Train members of your family to use fire extinguisher.
- ❖ Plan and practice evacuation.
- ❖ Talk to your children about the earthquake: what to do if they are at home, at school, if the quake separates your family.
- ❖ Arrange an alternative family place if your present area is out of bound. Each family member should carry the contact phone number and address.
- ❖ Remind your family to relay on emergency authorities for guidance. Broadcast reports on radio and television will have instructions.
- ❖ Make sure each member of your family knows how to shut-off the utilities – gas, electricity and water. (Do not shut-off the gas unless there is a leak or a fire. If the gas is turned off, don't turn it on again – that must be done by a qualified technician.)
- ❖ Your plan should include a list of where emergency supplies and equipment are stored.
- ❖ Share your emergency plan with neighbours.

During the Earthquake

Preparations for an earthquake include knowing what to do while it is happening. By learning and practicing what you should try to do, you will be more able to remain calm enough to protect yourself and help others. Know what to do, wherever you are. In summary, you should take cover and stay there.

- ❖ If you're inside your home, stay there. Get out of the kitchen safer places are inside hall, in corners, in archways. Take cover under a heavy table, desk or any solid furniture that you can get under and hold onto. Protect your head and face. Doors may slam on you figures if you are in a doorway. Avoid areas near windows.
- ❖ If you are in a yard outside your home, stay there and get clear of buildings and wires that could fall on you.
- ❖ Don't go outside where you may be hit by falling debris – pavements next to tall buildings are particularly dangerous.
- ❖ Avoid lifts – if you are in a lift when an earthquake happens, press all floors buttons and get out when you can. High-rise residents will hear fire alarms go off and electricity may fail.

- ❖ If you are in a vehicle, pull over to the sight (leave the road clear) away from bridges, over-bridges and buildings. Stay in your vehicle.
- ❖ If you are in a crowed public place, take cover and watch that you don't get trampled. In shopping centres, take cover in the nearest store and keep away form windows, neon signs, and display shelves of heavy objects.
- ❖ Remain in protected place until the shacking stops. Anticipate after shocks – they may occur after the first quake.
- ❖ Try to remain calm and help others.

After the Earthquake

Preparation of an earthquake also include knowing what to do and not do, after the shaking stops – when there is a danger from aftershocks, fire, falling building materials, debris, etc. Remain calm. You may have to take charge of others. Take care of life threatening situations first. Remember, you may be on your own for 72 hours or more.

- ❖ Check your home for structural damage and other hazards.
- ❖ Check yourself and others nearby for injuries – administer first aid quickly and carefully.
- ❖ If you are evacuating, locate and take your pack of emergency supplies with you.
- ❖ Use a torch to check utilities and not shut them off unless damaged. Leaking gas will smell. Do not light matches or turn on light switches – until you are sure there are no gas leaks or flammable liquids.
- ❖ Wear sturdy shoes, if there's debris, particularly broken glass.
- ❖ Check your neighbours after looking your own family. Your first help after and earthquake usually will come from family and friends.
- ❖ Confine frightened pets.
- ❖ Do not flush toilets if you suspects nearby sewer lines are broken.
- ❖ Carefully cleanup any spilled hazardous material.
- ❖ Secure your home against intruders.
- ❖ Turn on your battery-power radio (or car radio) and listen for broadcast emergency instructions.
- ❖ Do not use your telephone, expect it an extreme emergency.
- ❖ Do not use your vehicle, expect in an extreme emergency.
- ❖ Stay at least ten metres from downed power lines.
- ❖ Avoid sea line because of the threat of large waves.

Handing over of building after construction

Developers shall handover at least the following documents:

1. Property register card with CTS plan.
2. Set of approved/completion plans.
3. Occupation permission/building completion certificate.
4. Drainage completion certificate along with completion plan of house drainage system.
5. Structural plans as executed at site with detail of design and the stability certificate issued by the structural engineer.
6. Plan of electrical layout.
7. Plan of pumping layout.
8. Layout of firefighting installations.
9. Architect's certificate for carpet area/built-up area of each flat.
10. NA permission issued by the collector.
11. Exemption order issued by C.A. (UL C&R) Act, 1976.
12. List of important agencies involved, their names, address, telephone numbers, etc., *viz.*:
    (a) Architect
    (b) Structural Engineer
    (c) Site supervisor
    (d) Licensed plumber/plumbing contractor
    (e) Electrical contractor
    (f) Contractor for civil work
    (g) Developer

Maintenance of buildings: A building, however sound it may be, needs regular maintenance to keep it in healthy condition. However, awareness in this respect is lacking in the occupants, which is evident from the condition of buildings in Mumbai. Occupants who spend liberally for decoration of their premises do not show the same spirit as and when they are asked to contribute towards repairs and maintenance of their buildings. It is important to carry-out timely maintenance works to prevent deterioration of the buildings.

Do's:

1. Get the building inspected by a qualified engineer after ten years of its occupation and at an interval of five years thereafter for structural assessment and carry-out the works suggested by him.
2. Attend to all the leakages promptly.

3. Keep all the sanitary pipes, water pipes, and its fittings in good condition by replacing the broken parts promptly.
4. Check terrace waterproofing before every monsoon and attend to the repairs. Renewal of waterproofing layer, whenever necessary, shall be undertaken to prevent leakage from terrace.
5. Any cracks, plaster peeling off, exposed reinforcement, etc., shall be immediately brought to notice of structural engineer.
6. Render two coats of waterproof cement paint for external face of the building at regular intervals.
   (a) Cement paint every three years (b) Acrylic paint every five years
7. Preventive maintenance of lifts shall be done by giving service contracts to the lift companies. Arrange operation of lifts by liftman.
8. Keep the water pump in working condition. Yearly contract for maintenance is advisable.
9. Firefighting installation shall be maintained through qualified agencies.
10. Keep the terrace clean especially during monsoon.

Dont's:

1. Do not allow any unauthorised additions/alterations thereby loading the existing structure.
2. Do not allow any internal changes without consulting the structural engineer and without obtaining prior approval of MCGM wherever necessary.
3. Do not allow extension of toilets or lavatories over other rooms.
4. Do not permit internal works such as replacement of flooring, repairs of internal plastering, repairs to RCC members, renovation of toilets or kitchen, etc., without consulting the professionals in the field.
5. Do not allow gardening in any manner unless specifically designed.
6. Change of internal loading shall not be allowed.
7. Subsequent addition of lofts shall not be permitted.

Additions, alterations, and repairs of building

There are certain "Do's and Dont's" for proper maintenance of buildings. Every user of the building is responsible for proper maintenance of the building and therefore he should be aware of these Do's and Dont's.

Do's:

1. The Society or Association of every building should have copies of approved plans, structural plans, services plan (plumbing/drainage/electrical/AC ducting, etc.)
2. The Society should maintain copies of as built drawings, soil investigation reports, material test results, concrete test results as well as result of any other tests including that on the building component.

3. The Society should also have record of any subsequent modifications as per actual site conditions from time-to-time.
4. The Society should formulate the policy for any kind of additions, alterations, and repairs to be carried out by members.
5. The Society should ensure that any additions or authorizations are permitted only after scrutiny and approval of the structural consultant.
6. The Society members desirous to carrying out any additions, alterations should take prior NOC from Society by applying for the same with plan and Structural Stability Certificate from Structural Engineer and not Interior Designers.
7. The Society should verify the same from their Structural Consultant/Architect prior to giving the required NOC. The Society should consider the views of all the affected members before giving the NOC.
8. The Society should grant NOC to the member for proposed additions and alterations subject to permission from Municipal Corporation.
9. The Society should ask the member certain amount as Security Deposit towards fulfilment of Terms and Conditions of NOC and to safeguard the property of other members and Society.
10. The Security Deposit should be released only after NOC from adjoining members on same floor as well as just below and just above floors and NOC from Society's Structural Consultant/ Architect.
11. The leakages from bathroom, WC, kitchen and drainage, plumbing systems and from terraces should be attended immediately. Generally, societies take action on external leakages and internal leakages being the responsibility of members concerned, normally remain unattended. Every Society should formulate the policy for immediate repairs of internal leakages to save the building from further damage. Growth of plants in drainage pipes should be removed periodically.
12. The building should be painted with good quality cement paint, externally at every four to five years.
13. In case of cracks to RCC remember the building should be repaired/restructured under the guidance and supervision of Structural Engineer.
14. Structural Audit of buildings is essential at the interval of around every ten years. The recommendations should be compulsorily implemented by Society on priority basis.

Dont's:

1. Tampering of structural members, i.e., columns, beams and slabs and walls, load bearing walls, should not be allowed under any circumstances. Even chiselling or cutting into structural members for laying electric conduits or drainage pipes should not be allowed.
2. RCC slabs should not be loaded beyond for which it is designed. Shifting of walls resulting in loading directly on slab without proper beam below should not be allowed.

3. Shifting of toilets or creating new toilets on normal RCC slab should not be allowed.

4. Balconies should not be allowed to be converted into bathrooms and kitchens. Even additional weight by way of planters storage with box type grills should not be allowed on any cantilevered portion of building such as balcony or chajja.

5. Change of the user from residential to commercial or godown should not be allowed because generally the slab of residential premises is not designed to take additional load of commercial or godown premises.

6. Additional water storage tanks should not be allowed resting on terrace slabs directly or without proper consultation from Structural Consultant.

References

1. Sing, *Disaster Management.* APH Publisher, New Delhi.
2. Saravana Kumar, *Disaster Management.* Himalaya Publishing House, New Delhi.
3. Goel, *Encyclopedia of Disaster Management.* Deep and Deep, New Delhi.
4. Sahni, *Disaster Mitigation; Experiences and reflections.* PHI learning, New Delhi.
5. Shaw, *Disaster Management.* Orient Longman, New Delhi.
6. Sundar, *Disaster Management.* Sarup & Sons, New Delhi.
7. G.K. Ghosh, *Disaster Management.* APH Publications, New Delhi.
8. Singh, *Disaster Management: Future.* APH Publications, New Delhi.
9. Ayaz Ahmed, *Disaster Management.* Anmol Publications, New Delhi.
10. Gaur, *Disaster Management.* Authors Press, New Delhi.
11. Carter Nick, *Disaster Management.* Asian Development Bank, Manila.
12. World Disaster report. Fed., of Red Cross and Red Crescent Societies.
13. Environmental Hazard – Assessing risk and reducing disaster. Keith, London.
14. Disaster prevention for sustainable development – Economic and Policy Issues. Mohan Munasinghe and Caroloine Clarke, WB, Washington.
15. Natural Disaster Reduction. Ministry of Agriculture GoI.
16. Geneva Mandate on Disaster Reduction. Int. Decade for Natural Disaster Reduction Programme Forum.
17. Sarma and Vinod K., *Disaster Management.* Indian Institute of Public Admn, New Delhi.
18. Sing, Prakesh Mandel *et.al.,* Disaster Response in India. Centre for Excellence for Disaster Management.
19. P. C. Sinha, *Encyclopedia of Disaster Management.* Anmol Publications, New Delhi.
20. Frederick J. Cuny, *Disaster and Development*
21. Review of National Hazards Management Activities, Org. of American States Depts. of Regional Development.
22. S.P. Gupta, *Hazard and Vulnerability Analysis.* Asian Institute of Technology.
23. Andrew Maskrey, *Disaster Mitigation – Community based approach.* Oxfam Dev. Guidelines

24. D. Alexander, *National Disasters*. Terra, London.

25. Haddow George D and Jane a Bullock, Introduction to Emergency Management. Butterworth-Heinemann, Amsterdam.

26. B.P. *et.al.,* Winser, Natural Hazards – People's vulnerability.

27. D. Alexander, Natural Disaster. UCL Press, London.

28. Albala Bertrand J M, Political Economy of large natural disasters with ref. to developing Countries. Clarendon Press Oxford.

29. E. Allen, Recovery after Disaster – Achieving sustainable development, Mitigation and Equity. Belhaven, London.

30. Genovese *et.al.,* Disaster Preparedness. New York.

31. Hurricane Evacuation Behaviour. *Int. Journal of Mass Emergencies*.

32. Burton *et.al*., The Environmental Hazard. Guilford Press, London.

33. N. Carter, Disaster Managers Handbook. Asian Development Bank, Manila.

34. B. Smith *et.al*., Mitigation and Adaptation Strategies.

35. A.W. Coburn, Vulnerability and Risk assessment. UNDP Disaster Management Programme.

36. Disaster Risk Management. Inter-American, Development Bank, WDC.

37. Bhatta *et.al*., Natural Calamities in Orissa. Commonwealth Publishers, New Delhi.

38. H.P. Gupta, Lattur Earthquake. Indian Institute of Pub. Admn.

39. Alexander, Principles of Emergency Planning and Management. Terra Publishing.

40. Bohem, Disaster Prevention and Disaster Preparedness. University of California.

41. Regional Policy Dialogue on National System for Comprehensive Disaster Management. Iner-American Development Bank WDC.

42. M. J. Howard *et.al*., Infectious Disease Emergencies in Disaster.

43. Race and Disaster Warning Response. Battelle Human Affairs Research Centre, Seattle WA.

44. O. Morgan, Infectious Disease Risk from Dead Bodies following disaster.

45. P.C. Sinha, Disaster Relief: Rehabilitation and Emergency Humanitarian Assistance. SBS Publishers.

46. Bhargava and Gopal, *Environmental Challenges and Ecological Disaster – a Global Perspective*.

47. A.S. Arya, Disaster Mitigation – Keynote paper.

48. Natural Disaster Reduction – South Asia Regional Report. Ministry of Agri. GoI.

49. *Disaster Management*. Thaha Publications.

50. Internet – Various sites.